Islam and Disability

This book explores the position of Islamic theology and jurisprudence towards people with disabilities. It investigates how early and modern Muslim scholars tried to reconcile the existence of disability with the concept of a merciful God, and also looks at how people with disabilities might live a dignified and productive life within an Islamic context.

In his analysis of Islamic theology, Ghaly pays attention to how theologians, philosophers and Sufis reflected on the purposes behind the existence of this phenomenon, and how to reconcile the existence of disability with specific divine attributes and an All-Merciful God. Simultaneously exploring the perspective of Muslim jurists, the book focuses on how people with disabilities can lead a dignified life in the financial and non-financial sense, in an extensive analysis of topics such as the human dignity of people with disabilities and the role of Greek physiognomy, their employability, medical treatment, social life with the main focus on marriage-related issues, financial life and means of living.

Investigating the topic of disability from early and modern Islamic perspectives, the author provides an analysis of Muslim discussions on various bioethical questions. As such, this book will be of great relevance to current heated debates on the human rights of people with disabilities, as well as providing a valuable resource for courses on multicultural bioethics, Islamic theology, Islamic law and medical anthropology.

Mohammed Ghaly is currently an Assistant Professor of Islamic studies at Leiden University, The Netherlands. He did Islamic Studies in English at al-Azhar University in Cairo, Egypt and received his bachelor with cum laude in 1999. In 2002, he received his M.A. degree in Islamic studies also with cum laude from Leiden University. In 2008, he defended his PhD dissertation at the same university on 'Islam and Disability: Perspectives in Islamic Theology and Jurisprudence'. Ghaly is currently embarking upon a post-doctoral research project on Islamic bioethics. The main focus of this project is the interplay of international Islamic religio-scientific institutions based in the Muslim world and Muslims living as religious minorities in the West.

Routledge Islamic Studies Series

This broad-ranging series includes books on Islamic issues from all parts of the globe and is not simply confined to the Middle East.

Historians, State and Politics in Twentieth Century Egypt
Contesting the nation
Anthony Gorman

The New Politics of Islam
Pan-Islamic foreign policy in a world of states
Naveed Shahzad Sheikh

The Alevis in Turkey
The emergence of a secular Islamic tradition
David Shankland

Medieval Islamic Economic Thought
Filling the great gap in European economics
S.M. Ghazanfar

The West and Islam
Western liberal democracy versus the system of shura
Mishal Fahm al-Sulami

The Regency of Tunis and the Ottoman Porte, 1777–1814
Army and government of a North-African eyâlet at the end of the eighteenth century
Asma Moalla

Islamic Insurance
A modern approach to Islamic banking
Aly Khorshid

The Small Players of the Great Game
The settlement of Iran's eastern borderlands and the creation of Afghanistan
Pirouz Mojtahed-Zadeh

Interest in Islamic Economics
Understanding riba
Abdulkader Thomas

Islam in Nordic and Baltic Countries
Göran Larsson

Islam and Disability
Perspectives in theology and jurisprudence
Mohammed Ghaly

Islam and Disability

Perspectives in theology and jurisprudence

Mohammed Ghaly

Routledge
Taylor & Francis Group
LONDON AND NEW YORK

First published 2010
by Routledge
2 Park Square, Milton Park, Abingdon, Oxon OX14 4RN

Simultaneously published in the USA and Canada
by Routledge
270 Madison Avenue, New York, NY 10016

Routledge is an imprint of the Taylor & Francis Group, an informa business

Typeset in Times New Roman
by Keystroke, Tettenhall, Wolverhampton
Printed and bound in Great Britain
by CPI Antony Rowe, Chippenham, Wiltshire

British Library Cataloguing in Publication Data
A catalogue record for this book is available
from the British Library

Library of Congress Cataloging-in-Publication Data
Ghaly, Mohammed.
Islam and disability : perspectives in theology and jurisprudence /
Mohammed Ghaly.
p. cm.–(Routledge Islamic studies series; 11)
Includes bibliographical references and index.
1. People with disabilities–Religious aspects–Islam. 2. Islam
and justice. I. Title.
HV1552.G43 2010
297.2′7–dc22

2009021757

ISBN 10: 0-415-54757-1 (hbk)
ISBN 10: 0-203-86508-1 (ebk)

ISBN 13: 978-0-415-54757-4 (hbk)
ISBN 13: 978-0-203-86508-8 (ebk)

To my wife, Karima,
to our cute twins, Khadija and Maryam,
to our new baby, Mustapha,
to my mother, Fawziyya,
to the memory of my father, Mustapha,
with all love and gratitude

Contents

Foreword

The present book is the edited version of the author's PhD thesis for Leiden University (2008), which I had the privilege of supervising as Leiden's Professor of Islamic Studies. It scrutinizes Islamic theological and legal thought in relation to disability and people living with disabilities. Such a work was urgently needed. For a long time, substantial religious studies on disability and people with disabilities have been written from the perspectives of Judaism and Christianity only. Studies on Islam and disability remained very limited in scope; it was even believed that classical Islam possessed no special terminology to denote the phenomenon of disability and people with disabilities, and had certainly not developed specific normative perspectives and approaches towards them.

Dr Ghaly deciphered the codes of this terminological enigma and succeeded in finding the hidden door giving access, for the first time, to a real treasure house of Islamic sources, which shed the fullest and the clearest light on the issues at hand. In this masterpiece he approaches his subject from classical angles within the Islamic sciences. First of all, he looks at it from the perspectives of speculative and practical theology. On the level of Islamic jurisprudence, he discusses the possible influence of Greek physiognomy on Islamic legal thought concerning people with disabilities; he analyses the views of the jurists concerning the dignity, employability, medical treatment (both physical and spiritual) and financial aid and economic position (in family and society). The result is a treatment of the subject which is both comprehensive and innovative.

After studying this book, readers might be left puzzled by the exceptional wealth of concepts and ideas on disability and related phenomena contained in the Islamic tradition, as compared to both the Jewish and Christian traditions. How should this conspicuous difference be explained? My provisional answer to that comparative question would be, first of all, that the Koran is rich in concepts concerning the origins of good and evil, human suffering and divine justice. In fact, it already contained the nucleus of the themes which were to play a central role in the evolving Islamic theological discussions and the wider Islamic religious thought concerning disability and the disabled. In the second place, there is *the pragmatic and empirical nature of Islamic law*, recognizing, on the basis of the Koran and tradition, people with disabilities as special categories for which both ritual and social rules must be interpreted in order to accommodate their special position.

Last but not least, there is *the unparalleled level of development of philosophy and the natural sciences, including medicine*, in classical Islamic civilization. All these factors combine to explain the secret of this outstanding study. This book is essential not only for specialists dealing with disabilities in the fields of medicine and social psychology, but for students of Islamic civilization in general.

Professor Dr P.S. van Koningsveld
Professor Emeritus of Islamic Studies
Leiden University, the Netherlands
27 April 2009

Preface

This book is a revised version of my PhD thesis which was conducted at Leiden University, The Netherlands, and funded by the Prince Salman Center for Disability Research, Riyadh, the Kingdom of Saudi Arabia.

My interest in this topic dates back to the beginning of this century, when in 2001 I started writing my MA thesis on the financial rights of people with disabilities. The main focus of this thesis was on both normative opinions in Islamic jurisprudence and the then current situation of Muslims living in the Netherlands. While working on this MA thesis, I realized that understanding the reality of Muslims living with disabilities, wherever they live, not to mention making any effort to improve this reality, cannot happen without understanding the religious tradition to which these people belong. Thus, the main aim of this study is to delve into this tradition and try to understand the diverse perspectives therein.

As for the motives of writing on this topic, I have been mainly moved by ethical concerns, namely, paying attention to this group of people who have been enduring an unprivileged position not only in the financial and social sense but also within the field of academic studies. I remember how difficult it was for me in the beginning to find modern studies relevant to this topic or to trace the relevant information in the classical sources. As time went on, I became aware of the richness of the discussions in the Islamic tradition on the phenomenon of disability and people living with disabilities. I hope this book will be an honest reflection of this reality.

In this study, I did my best to present the Islamic tradition exactly as formulated by the early and the modern Muslim scholars themselves. That is why the reader will not find a separate chapter on disability as presented in the Qur'ān or the Sunna. Relevant sayings from these two sources are everywhere in this study but alongside the interpretations given by Muslim scholars. By presenting this comprehensive overview of the ideas within the Islamic tradition on disability, I believe the reality of Muslims with disabilities will be much easier to understand and to place in its proper context. For instance, I have written a number of articles and participated in different seminars and conferences where I made use of information available in this study in order to understand and analyse the reality of

Muslims with disabilities living in the Netherlands.[1] This experience proved to be very appealing and helpful to the Dutch organizations which provide care for people with disabilities.

I am glad I chose this topic, which opened my eyes to a new world of knowledge and ideas. I hope the reader will enjoy reading this book as much as I enjoyed writing it.

Acknowledgements

The great pleasure of completing this work has not made me forget the great help generously offered by many. I am extremely grateful to my colleagues at Leiden University, notably Professor Dr P.S. van Koningsveld who supervised my PhD dissertation most capably and was kind enough to agree to write the foreword to this book. He showed admirable patience and professionalism during my PhD research, especially with my occasional stubbornness. My gratitude goes also to the staff of the Prince Salman Center for Disability Research (PSCDR), which funded my PhD research.

Besides Leiden University and the PSCDR, many people provided me with advice and support including Islamologists, Muslim scholars, specialists in the field of disability studies and officials from international organizations, especially those affiliated to the United Nations Organization (UNO). I hereby express my gratitude to them all and my apologies for having no space to mention each of them by name. My wholehearted gratitude also goes to the three anonymous reviewers who reviewed the first draft of this book and provided me with very useful comments.

Previous versions of parts of this book appeared in the following articles: 'Writings on Disability in Islam: The 16th Century Polemic on Ibn Fahd's *al-Nukat al-Ziraf*', *Arab Studies Journal*, vol. XIII no. 2/vol. XIV no. 1, Fall 2005/Spring 2006, pp. 9–38; 'Physical and Spiritual Treatment of Disability in Islam: Perspectives of Early and Modern Jurists', *Journal of Religion, Disability and Health*, vol. XII. no. 2, 2008, pp. 105–143; 'Physiognomy: A Forgotten Chapter of Disability in Islam: The Discussions of Muslim Jurists', *Bibliotheca Orientalis*, vol. 66, issue 3–4. I hereby thank these journals which have already published parts of this research and then granted me permission to include them in this book.

The final note is reserved for my family. The support given by my wife Karima Joundi is too generous to be repaid. My cute twins, Maryam and Khadija, and recently our young man in the family, Mustapha, have been very fine additions to my life. They have been a source of great motivation and inspiration to my work. Finally, a note of gratitude is due to my mother whose constant support, kindness and tenderness can never be properly expressed, let alone rewarded.

Mohammed Ghaly
April, 2008
Leiden, The Netherlands

Abbreviations

ASJ	*Arab Studies Journal*
BSOAS	*Bulletin of the School of Oriental and African Studies*
DI	*Disability and Society*
ECFR	*European Council for Fatwa and Research*
EI	*Encyclopaedia of Islam*, CD-ROM Edition v. 1.0, Koninklijke Brill NV, Leiden, The Netherlands, 2003
EQ	*Encyclopaedia of the Qur'ān*
HI	*Hamdard Islamicus*
IC	*Islamic Culture*
ICIDH	*International Classification of Impairments, Disability and Handicaps*
IFA	*Islamic Fiqh Academy*
IIFA	*International Islamic Fiqh Academy*
ILO	*International Labour Organization*
ILS	*Islamic Law and Society*
IOMS	*Islamic Organization for Medical Sciences*
IQ	*Islamic Quarterly*
IS	*Islamic Studies*
JAOS	*Journal of the American Oriental Society*
JESHO	*Journal of the Economic and Social History of the Orient*
JIS	*Journal of Islamic Studies*
JRAS	*Journal of the Royal Asiatic Society*
JRDH	*Journal of Religion, Disability & Health*
MMLAD	*Majallat Majma' al-Lugha al-'Arabiyya bi Dimashq*
MW	*Muslim World*
SI	*Studia Islamica*
SRECFR	*Scientific Review of the European Council for Fatwa and Research*
UNDP	*United Nations Development Programme*
WHO	*World Health Organization*

1 Introduction

1.1 United Nations Organization: global interest in people with disabilities

According to recent reports of the United Nations Organization, people with disabilities are the world's largest minority. They number 650 million people, representing about 10 per cent of the world's population. According to the World Health Organization (WHO), this figure is increasing through population growth, medical advances and the ageing process. In countries with life expectancies over 70 years, individuals spend on average about eight years, or 11.5 per cent of their life span, living with disabilities. The UN Development Programme (UNDP) stated that 80 per cent of persons with disabilities live in developing countries.[1] The UN Special Rapporteur declared in 2000, 'In all countries, in all types of living conditions, the consequences of disability interfere in the lives of disabled persons to a degree which is not at all acceptable.'[2] These facts have been among the decisive motivations behind an increasing international interest in improving the conditions of people with disabilities.

As the main body representing all countries of the world, the United Nations Organization's activities reflect this international interest. On 20 December 1971, the UN General Assembly proclaimed the Declaration on the Rights of Mentally Retarded Persons. It called for national and international action to ensure that this declaration will be used as a common basis and frame of reference for the protection of the rights of those people.[3] This was followed by the Declaration on the Rights of Disabled Persons, proclaimed by the UN General Assembly on 9 December 1975.[4] About a year later, on 16 December 1976, the UN General Assembly adopted Resolution 31/123 by which it proclaimed 1981 as the International Year of Disabled Persons.[5] The period 1983–1992 was declared by the UN as the decade of people with disabilities.[6] On 20 December 1993, the Standard Rules on the Equalization of Opportunities for Persons with Disabilities were adopted by the United Nations General Assembly in its Resolution 48/96.[7] One of the latest developments in this regard is the Convention on the Rights of Persons with Disabilities adopted on 13 December 2006 by the United Nations. The Optional Protocol of this convention was opened for signature by all states at the United Nations Headquarters in New York on 30 March 2007.[8]

This increasing concern with disability-related issues and the rights of people with disabilities has also evoked interest in the cultural position of religion *vis-à-vis* the phenomenon of disability. Many of the UN documents on people with disabilities made reference to this dimension, especially the Standard Rules on the Equalization of Opportunities for Persons with Disabilities, the twelfth of which concentrated on religion.[9] In this framework, there exists an increasing interest in studying the relation between disability and religion in general. Islam was no exception in this respect.[10]

1.2 Islam

As member states of the UN, Islamic countries were involved in many of the activities promoting interest in people with disabilities, such as the UN Standard Rules on the Equalization of Opportunities for Persons with Disabilities[11] and the Convention on the Rights of People with Disabilities.[12] Islamic countries' interest in this important issue was also crystallized in a large number of conferences, some of which were organized in cooperation with the UN or WHO. For instance, the year 1981 witnessed the Kuwait Regional Conference on the Disabled held in April, which issued the 'Arab Declaration on Work with the Disabled'.[13]

Some of these conferences focused on the importance of studying the viewpoint of Islam on disability-related issues. For instance, the tenth Juristic Medical Symposium entitled 'Al-Mushāwara al-buldāniyya ḥawl tashrīʿāt al-ṣiḥḥa al-nafsiyya bimā fī dhālik al-sharīʿa al-islāmiyya' (Regional Conference on Legislations of Psychological Health in Different Religious Codes of Law including the Islamic Jurisprudence) was held in Kuwait from 29 September to 2 October 1997. This symposium was organized by the Islamic Organization for Medical Sciences in cooperation with the World Health Organization East Mediterranean Regional Office (WHO EMRO). Eleven papers submitted to this symposium tackled the topic of disability from an Islamic perspective.[14] A parallel conference was held from 23 to 26 October 2000 in Riyadh, Saudi Arabia. This was organized by the Disabled Children's Association and the Prince Salman Center for Disability Research. More than 200 papers were submitted to the conference. It adopted important resolutions, one of which was on the encouragement of research into perspectives within Islam on people with disabilities.[15] The last example in this context is the international conference entitled 'Rehabilitation of the Disabled and Care for the Elderly in the Islamic World: Strategies for the 21st Century'. This conference was held by the Islamic World Council on Disability and Rehabilitation on 10–12 February 2001 in Khartoum, Republic of Sudan.[16] Among the topics discussed there were the rights of disabled persons from the viewpoint of Islamic Sharīʿa such as medical treatment, rehabilitation, work, training, exemption from tax and customs duty, equality, participation, social integration and equal opportunities.[17]

Undoubtedly all these activities helped to evoke considerable interest among modern scholars of Islam as well. For example, two Saudi scholars, ʿAbd Allāh b. Jibrīn (b. 1352/1933)[18] and ʿAbd al-Muḥsin b. Nāṣir Āl ʿAbīkān (head of the advisory body for legal aspects which participated in drafting the legal code of disability in the Kingdom of Saudi Arabia),[19] called for more research into the status of people with disabilities in Islam. Other scholars called for the development of a special branch of Islamic jurisprudence focusing exclusively on people with disabilities, and entitled *Fiqh al-iʿāqa wa al-muʿawwaqīn* – 'Fiqh of disability and people with disabilities'. This term – as far as I am aware – was coined by the Shīʿite scholar Muḥammad Shams al-Dīn in a paper presented to the tenth Juristic Medical Symposium held by the Islamic Organization for Medical Sciences (IOMS) and WHO in 1997 in Kuwait. This call was met with approval by, for instance, the well-known contemporary scholar, Yūsuf al-Qaraḍāwī.[20]

Recently, a number of modern studies have been conducted to fill in the current gap on Islam and disability.[21] However, this project is still in its initial phase.[22] Besides detailing the results of these previous studies, this book constitates, to my knowledge, the first comprehensive study of the position of people with disabilities within both Islamic theology and Islamic jurisprudence as reflected in the perspectives of both early and modern Muslim scholars.

1.3 Methodological approach, research questions and focus

Bearing in mind that none of the main Islamic sources consulted in this study provided a comprehensive survey of the status of people with disabilities in Islam, the main objective here is to piece together the disparate and sporadic information on disability in these sources and to mould them into a coherent and systematic form. In this sense, the approach adopted in this study can be characterized as 'systematic and constructive'. Another characteristic of my approach is its adherence to the human rights tendency which is currently prevalent in global discussions and studies on disabilities. The reader searching for information on the rights of people with disabilities, such as rights to medical treatment, employment, financial care, marital life, etc., will find relevant information in this study.

Islamic sources present Islam as a religion composed of a number of rulings that its adherents are asked to abide by. These rulings are divided into those related to beliefs (*iʿtiqādiyya*) and those related to practical actions (*ʿamaliyya*).[23] The former were the subject of Islamic theology (*ʿaqīda*) whereas the latter were the subject of Islamic jurisprudence (*fiqh*). Thus portraying an overall view of persons with disabilities in Islam necessitates studying the relevant discussions in these two Islamic sciences. Surveying the broad spectrum of perspectives and discussions on people with disabilities expressed in these two main Islamic sciences will therefore be the main focus of this study.

Based on what has been stated here, the main question in this study will be: what is the status of people with disabilities in Islam as viewed by Islamic theology and Islamic jurisprudence? Following this introductory chapter which presents an overall picture, the other seven chapters examine the status of people with disabilities in Islamic theology and Islamic jurisprudence.

Discussions in Islamic theology concerning people with disabilities will be treated in two chapters. Chapter 2 treats one main question: why does disability exist since Allah is the Omnipotent, All-Just and All-Merciful? Theological discussions relevant to this question fall under the broad theme of 'speculative theology'. This chapter deals with the theological clarifications and justifications put forward by Muslim scholars in response to the existence of disabilities. Chapter 3 treats the question: what should be done, in spiritual terms, if someone is already living with a disability? Discussions on this question fall under the broad heading of 'Practical theology'. They investigate mainly Muslim theologians' views on how to keep a spiritual balance in life despite the existence of disabilities and other misfortunes.

Chapters 4–8, dedicated to Islamic jurisprudence, focus on what are now called the rights of people with disabilities. The main question can be formulated as: what is the social and financial position of people with disabilities as recorded in the juristic sources of Islam? Chapter 4, 'Human dignity of people with disabilities', studies whether disabilities injure, harm or diminish the dignity guaranteed in Islam for human beings in general. Chapter 5, 'The ethics of writing on people with disabilities', again focuses on a human rights issue, namely, to what extent an author writing about this group should take account of the sensitivity of the topic. The remaining three chapters focus more on the financial position of people with disabilities. The topics discussed in these chapters, such as employment or medical treatment are classified as financial because they normally involve earning or paying money. Since work is the main source of financial revenue, juristic discussions on the employability of people with disabilities form the main topic of Chapter 6. Because disability is usually perceived, rightly or wrongly, as the main obstacle to finding a suitable job, the possibilities of medical treatment for people with disabilities is investigated from a juristic perspective in Chapter 7. Chapter 8 discusses the overall theme of financial security for people with disabilities who cannot independently cover their own financial needs. In other words, how can a person with a disability enjoy financial security if he/she cannot work and the disability cannot be treated?

Now, an explanatory note on these two domains and the main focus in each domain is in order.

1.3.1 Islamic theology

'Theology' comes from a Greek word composed of *theos* (God) and *logos* (discourse). This western term was used to denote the study of religious beliefs.[24] The Islamic science of studying these beliefs had more than one name, the most famous of which was *'ilm al-kalām*.[25] However, there are other names for this science such as *al-fiqh al-akbar*,[26] *'ilm uṣūl al-dīn*,[27] *'ilm al-'aqā'id*,[28] *'ilm al-tawḥīd*,[29] *'ilm al-tawḥīd wa al-ṣifāt*[30] and *'ilm al-naẓar wa al-istidlāl*.[31]

The subject matter of this science is the religious beliefs (*'aqā'id*) of Muslims. It is concerned with firmly establishing these beliefs by adducing proofs and banishing doubts.[32] The main theme of this science was, first, the *ilāhiyyāt* or *naẓariyyāt* (speculative theology), which was mainly concerned with the existence of God, the Creation and the necessity of the Prophethood from a philosophical perspective. The second part was the *sam'iyyāt* (traditional theology), containing a systematic elaboration of the doctrine based on the data of the revelation. The *nubuwwāt* (matters pertaining to Prophethood) were usually classified under the category of *sam'iyyāt* but, according to some authors, represented a distinct category constituting a link between *ilāhiyyāt* or *naẓariyyāt* and *sam'iyyāt*.[33]

Discussions on disability-related issues are to be located, mainly, in the first theme, the *ilāhiyyāt*, because it dealt with (1) the existence of God (*wujūd Allāh*) and His attributes and (2) the actions of God (*af'āluh ta'ālā*).[34] One of the main topics of *ilāhiyyāt* in which these two items were discussed was *al-qaḍā' wa al-qadar* (fate and predestination).[35] *Al-Qaḍā' wa al-qadar* in Islamic theology focused on two main points. The primary focus was the issue of man's freedom to act and God's predestination. This point falls beyond the scope of this study.[36] The second point was the adversities, afflictions and misfortunes befalling creatures as an essential part of God's predetermined course of events, and this point constitutes the focus of this book. Muslim theologians did not speak about disabilities as a distinct topic: one can hardly find any chapter specifically on people with disabilities. Abū al-Ḥasan al-Ash'arī's (d. 324/935–6) chapter entitled *Mas'ala fī īlām al-aṭfāl*, 'Question concerning the torture of the infants', in his book *Al-Ibāna* (Illumination) could be an exception. In it, al-Ash'arī discussed children with leprosy, whose hands and feet fall off.[37] Disabilities were usually included in discussions on broader themes like *muṣība*[38] (affliction or calamity), *sayyi'a*[39] (misfortune or evil), *sharr*[40] (evil) and the like. These are Qur'anic terms whose interpretation by the Companions of the Prophet (*saḥāba*), their Successors (*tābi'ūn*) and scholars of Qur'anic exegesis (*tafsīr*) shows that different sorts of disabilities were included in their meaning.[41]

One of the key terms which permeated the theological discussions in Islamic sources on disability was *ta'līl*, whose most used English equivalent is 'theodicy'. For a better understanding of the subsequent theological discussions, a note on this Arabic term and its English equivalent is in order.

The term *ta'līl* denoted 'causation' or 'search for causes' and referred to the logical relationship between cause and effect.[42] This term was used by Muslim jurists and theologians in two different contexts. In the juridical usage, *ta'līl* and its derivative *'illa* (effective cause) did not exactly refer to a causal relationship between two phenomena. It meant rather the *ratio* of the law, its value and its purpose.[43] Apart from Abū Ḥāmid al-Ghazālī (d. 1111) who discussed the issue of *ta'līl* extensively in his book *Shifā' al-ghalīl* (Quenching the Thirst), more than one Muslim jurist wrote books with the title *ta'līl* dedicated to investigating the values and purposes of the law.[44]

The theological usage of *ta'līl* was more concerned with God's actions. In other words, *ta'līl* in this sense indicated the quest for the divine and wise purposes (*ḥikam*) for God's actions.[45] The meaning of *ta'līl* was not restricted to developing arguments to clarify or justify pain, suffering, evil and the like. *Ta'līl* was a generic term indicating that God's actions can be rationalized, whether they are deemed good or bad from the human perspective. Ending up in Paradise or Hell in the Hereafter and the question of whether this was dependent on one's good or bad deeds in this life or on God's foreordained judgment are among the issues discussed within the broad spectrum of *ta'līl*.[46] In relation to the main focus of this study, our discussions will be restricted to those attempts to develop rational arguments in order to clarify or justify the existence of disabilities and other forms of suffering. This restricted sense of *ta'līl* is close to the term 'theodicy' coined by Gottfried Leibniz (d. 1716) from the Greek *theos* (God) and *dikē* (justice).[47]

To recapitulate, disability as viewed in Islamic theology is a very under-researched, if not completely unstudied, topic, despite its crucial importance.[48] To my mind, relevant discussions available in theological sources of Islam fall also within the human rights approach. To a believing person living with disabilities, answering the ontological and theological questions about the existence of disability in life and how to deal with it according to the norms of one's religion is by no means less important or less urgent than answering the financial and medical needs.

*1.3.2 Islamic jurisprudence (*fiqh*)*

Fiqh means 'understanding', 'knowledge', 'intelligence', and thus can be applied to any branch of knowledge (as in *fiqh al-lugha*, the science of lexicography). In the technical sense it is knowledge of the practical religious rulings from their detailed proofs.[49] 'Jurisprudence' is the most common English equivalent for the Arabic term *fiqh*. However, 'jurisprudence' does not convey the full meaning of *fiqh*. For instance, *fiqh* covers all issues in life, whether those between humans and God (*'ibādāt*) or those between humans only (*mu'āmalāt*). 'Jurisprudence', on the other hand, is restricted to inter-human issues and has nothing to do with what happens between man and God.[50]

The subject matter of this science comprised the practical rulings derived from the detailed proofs of the Sharī'a, such as the Qur'anic verses and the prophetic traditions. These rulings were always discussed by Muslim jurists under two main headings: *'ibādāt* (liturgical and religious observances) and *mu'āmalāt* (social dealings) which included more or less the rest.[51] A number of jurists added the heading of *'uqūbāt* (punishments) or *munākaḥāt* (marriage affairs).[52] Rulings pertaining to people with disabilities were disseminated throughout these chapters. It was exceptional in juristic sources for a specific chapter to be allotted to people with disabilities.

A note on internal developments within this science is also in order. Four main Sunni schools, in addition to two other schools in the Shī'ī tradition, have gained predominance in Islamic jurisprudence and remain influential to this day. The Ḥanafī school was the official school of law during the Ottoman Empire and still remains prevalent in countries such as Turkey and Pakistan and among Muslims in India. The Mālikī school is still dominant in many Islamic countries, especially Morocco, Algeria, Tunisia, Libya and some parts of Egypt. The Shāfi'ī school today prevails in countries such as Egypt, Iraq, Malaysia and Indonesia. The Ḥanbalī school is prevalent in the Gulf countries, especially the Kingdom of Saudi Arabia, where it is the official school to be followed by judges.[53]

Other schools of law appeared in Islamic history and might still play a role in juristic discussions at the present time, but they are far less influential than the previously mentioned four schools. The Ẓāhirī school serves as a clear example in this regard. This school reached its final shape at the hand of the Andalusian scholar Ibn Ḥazm (d. 1063). This school has no body of adherents or geographical centres in the Islamic world at present. However, the works of Ibn Ḥazm have remained important sources for modern specialists in Islamic jurisprudence.[54]

The Shī'ī tradition of Islam also developed its own schools of law. The Ja'farī school is the school of law within Twelver Shī'ism. The great majority of Shī'īs now follow this school, such as those living in Iran, Lebanon, Bahrain, etc. The Ja'farī school is often quoted in Sunni juristic sources, for example the juristic encyclopedia prepared in Egypt by a group of Muslim Sunni scholars.[55]

At present, writings of early authorities in the aforementioned schools of law still play a crucial role and represent a starting point for modern Muslim scholars. However, strict affiliation to one of these schools, especially in Sunni circles, is not as strong as it was in the past. Additionally, new issues which did not exist in earlier times, especially those relevant to bioethical questions, have forced modern scholars to introduce fresh and independent reasoning, known in jurists' parlance as *ijtihād*. Keeping in mind the complexity of these novel issues, new juristic councils were established where different well-known modern religious scholars united their efforts and also cooperated with specialists in other fields such as the medical, biological and sometimes human sciences. This is known in legal terms as collective reasoning (*ijtihād jamā'ī*).[56]

Consequently, legal advice (fatwas) given by such councils usually enjoys wide acceptance among the Muslim public. However, those who issue such fatwas are still far from being a final court of appeal and thus can still be challenged or rejected by individual competent Muslim scholars. Geographically, some of these councils are based in the Muslim world whereas others are in the West and thus focus mainly on issues relevant to Muslims in the West. As for the councils based in Muslim countries, the Islamic Fiqh Academy (IFA), the International Islamic Fiqh Academy (IIFA) and the Islamic Organization for Medical Sciences are usually perceived as the most authoritative. The IFA, affiliated to the Muslim World League, was established in 1977 and is based in Mecca, Saudi Arabia.[57] The IIFA, affiliated to the Organization of the Islamic Conference, was established in 1981 and is based in Jeddah, Saudi Arabia. The IOMS was established in 1984 and based in Kuwait.[58] Of the councils based in western countries, the European Council for Fatwa and Research (ECFR) is of crucial importance at present. The ECFR was established in 1997 in Dublin, Ireland. This council is one of the main theorists and advocates of the modern trend within Islamic jurisprudence which keeps in mind the particular position of Muslims as religious minorities living in a non-Muslim context, and is known as Islamic Jurisprudence for Muslim Minorities (*Fiqh al-Aqalliyyāt*).[59]

Speaking about allotting an independent chapter to the juristic rulings on hermaphrodites, Vardit Rispler-Chaim (Haifa University) said, 'the blind and the lame, the deaf and the dumb, whose disabilities are detected in higher percentages in both infants and adults, and are evident, have never been allotted separate chapters and are only sporadically discussed in the fiqh.' This statement should not be taken without reservation, especially concerning the blind. For instance, the contemporary Kuwaiti scholar 'Abd Allāh Muḥammad 'Abd Allāh said that the Shāfi'ī jurist, Abū Yaḥyā Zakariyyā al-Anṣārī (d. 926/1520), was the first to write a chapter entitled 'Bāb aḥkām al-a'mā' (A Chapter on the Rulings of the Blind) in his book *Taḥrīr tanqīḥ al-lubāb*.[60] However, al-Anṣārī was not the first in this respect but was following a tradition established by earlier Shāfi'ī jurists such as Abū Ḥāmid al-Ghazālī (d. 1111) in his book in *Al-Rawnaq* (Glamour),[61] al-Nawawī (d. 676/1277) in *Al-Majmū' sharḥ al-muhadhdhab*,[62] and al-Suyūṭī (d. 911/1505) in *Al-Ashbāh wa al-naẓā'ir* (The Similars and Parallels).[63] The same tradition can also be traced among Ḥanafī jurists such as Ibn Nujaym (d. 970/1563) in *Al-Ashbāh wa al-naẓā'ir* (The Similars and Parallels) and the commentary on this book by Aḥmad b. Muḥammad al-Ḥamawī (d. 1098/1687) in *Ghamz 'uyūn al-baṣā'ir fī sharḥ al-ashbāḥ wa al-naẓā'ir* (Winking the Fountains of Insights in Explaining the Similars and Parallels).[64]

To recapitulate, the disability-related issues in this science should be studied not only through the subject matter but through the terms used for denoting disabilities. In a bid to systematize such rulings and put them in a context understandable to the current reality, the main focus of this study was the main practical means by which people living with disabilities can still lead, in the social and the financial sense, an honourable life.

Bearing in mind that these practical means are always expressed in modern times under the broad term 'rights', attention will first be given to the equivalent term in Arabic, *ḥaqq*, in order to avoid any possible confusion or misunderstanding about the use of this modern term in a juristic sense.

Linguistically, *ḥaqq* means either 'truth', i.e. 'what corresponds to facts', and its opposite is *bāṭil* (untrue); or it means 'established fact' (*al-thābit*) and therefore 'reality'.[65] In the technical sense, *ḥaqq* had two main definitions based on these two linguistic denotations. In the theological context, derived directly from the first linguistic denotation, it referred to the judgement identical to truth (correct judgement) and was thus used to indicate the contentions, beliefs, religions and sects in the sense that they include the *ḥaqq*.[66] In the juristic context, based on the second linguistic denotation, *ḥaqq* referred to what has been decided for someone by the Islamic Sharī'a for his/her interest.[67] However, there may be a propensity in the classical Islamic sources towards obligations rather than rights. Thus the right to life, for instance, is expressed in the Islamic system as the duty to save life.[68] A closer examination, however, reveals that a mere propensity in the style of communication does not have a negative effect upon the substance and the validity of rights in the Sharī'a. The ruling conveyed the notion of right (when viewed from the vantage point of a right holder) or the notion of obligation (when viewed from the position of the party responsible for putting this right into practice). Hence, all that has been done by the modern studies is that they have just reversed the focal point, i.e. by using 'rights' instead of 'obligations', but the main content and purport remained the same in both cases.[69]

Furthermore, the term *ḥaqq* in Islam always involved a sense of nobility and also sometimes sacredness. The Qur'anic use of this term indicates that it sometimes referred to God (Qur'ān 6:62, 20:114, 22:06) and other times to the holy scripture of Muslims, the Qur'ān (Qur'ān 4:170, 5:48, 10:94). All this clothed the term with a specific aura in the Islamic context.[70]

As for the divisions of *ḥuqūq* (rights), they were divided on more than one level. Here we choose the divisions relevant to our concern, i.e. people with disabilities. In terms of the recipient of *ḥuqūq*, Muslim jurists distinguished between two main spheres of *ḥuqūq*, namely, *ḥuqūq Allāh* (lit. claims or rights of God or public rights) and *ḥuqūq al-'ibād* or *ḥuqūq al-ādamiyyīn* (claims or rights of men or human beings). The first sphere stood for the rights of the Islamic community at large. These rights were attributed to God only in order to glorify their value and stress the exhaustiveness of their benefits lest they be accorded to a specific person. The second sphere covered claims of private individuals in their dealings with each other.[71] In terms of their content, *ḥuqūq* were divided into financial (*māliyya*) and non-financial rights (*ghayr māliyya*).[72] In terms of enforceability, *ḥuqūq* were divided into religious (*dīnī*) and juridical (*qaḍā'ī*). The former, although validated by the Sharī'a, cannot be proven or enforced by a court. Most of the rights of God (i.e. *'ibādāt*, *kaffārāt*, etc.) fell into this category. Rights without a particular party as the right holder such as a religious endowment (*waqf*) for the poor and the indigent also fell into this category.[73] Juridical rights, on the other hand, are susceptible to proof at the behest of the right holder, and the Sharī'a court had the power to adjudicate on them. One of the examples of this right was the wife's right to maintenance by her husband.[74]

Although the term *ḥaqq*, pl. *ḥuqūq*, was not restricted to people with disabilities per se, it was always connected with them, especially in the modern literature. Expressions like *ḥuqūq al-mu'awwaqīn* (rights of people with disabilities) have become key expressions in modern literature on people with disabilities in Islam.[75]

1.4 Terminology used

Approaching Islamic sources to search for relevant material on 'disability' is practically impossible without understanding the terminology used.

Information available in Islamic sources indicates that using precise and non-offensive terminology was a point given consideration in the Islamic tradition. It was told, for instance, that some of the Companions of the Prophet used the term *majnūn* (lit. means insane) to label a person with mental disability in a context that could indicate contempt. Thereupon, the Prophet, in a bid to rephrase the term, is reported to have said, 'This [man] is *muṣāb* [lit. smitten]. *Junūn* [insanity] comes only as a result of disobeying God – The Almighty.'[76] In modern times, changes in terminology reflect a different understandings of disability as a phenomenon.[77]

1.4.1 English usage

The development of the English terminology used to describe people with disabilities can best be illustrated by the international classifications produced by the WHO. The International Classification of Impairments, Disabilities and Handicaps (ICIDH) was first published for trial purposes in 1980. This classification adopted three main terms, impairment, disability and handicap. Impairment was used to mean 'any loss or abnormality of psychological or anatomical structure or function'. Disability was interpreted as 'any restriction or lack (resulting from an impairment) of ability to perform an activity in the manner or within the range considered normal for a human being'. Finally, handicap was defined as 'a disadvantage for a given individual, resulting from an impairment or disability, that limits or prevents the fulfilment of a role that is normal, depending on age, sex, social and cultural factors, for that individual'.[78] Commenting on these definitions, Deborah Kaplan, Director of the World Institute on Disability, said that handicap is therefore a distortion of the relationship between disabled persons and their environment. It occurs when they encounter cultural, physical or social barriers which prevent their access to the various social systems that are available to other citizens.[79]

A new classification was introduced by the International Classification of Functioning, Disability and Health (ICF). This new classification came after systematic field trials and international consultation over years and was finally endorsed for international use by the fifty-fourth World Health Assembly on 22 May 2001 (Resolution WHA54.21).[80] New terms were used in this classification with specific meanings that differed from everyday usage and were intended to convey the potential for positive experiences.[81]

In the 2001 version of ICF, 'disability' was defined as an umbrella term for impairments, activity limitations and participation restrictions. It denoted the negative aspects of the interaction between an individual (with a health condition) and that individual's contextual factors (environmental and personal factors).[82] Again the main elements of this definition were further defined as follows.

Impairment is 'a loss or abnormality in body structure or physiological function (including mental functions)'. Abnormality here is used strictly to refer to a significant variation from established statistical norms (i.e. as a deviation from a population within measured standard norms) and should be used only in this sense.

Activity limitations[83] are

> difficulties that an individual may have in executing activities. An activity limitation may range from slight to a severe deviation in terms of quantity or quality in executing the activity in a manner to the extent that is expected of people without the health condition.

Participation restrictions[84] are 'problems an individual may experience in involvement in life situations. The presence of a participation restriction was determined by comparing an individual's participation to that which is expected of an individual without disability in that culture or society.'[85]

Despite all these collective efforts made by the WHO, there is still no consensus among specialists on what is either preferable or objectionable terminology.[86] For instance, expressions such as 'cripple' and 'gimp' have gone out of favour within the disabled community because of their negative connotations of passivity and the implication that impairment is a person's primary identifiable attribute. Nonetheless, some people with disabilities continue to use 'cripple' as a rhetorical device.[87] Also, euphemisms for persons with disabilities such as 'differently abled', 'physically challenged' and 'handicapable' have been rejected by some people on the grounds that they are verbal garbage describing everyone and no one.[88]

Rispler-Chaim was right when she pointed out that quarrels around the right term or the definition of 'what is disability?' or 'who are people with disabilities?' are not only semantic in nature. Political, economic and cultural dimensions can also play crucial roles. For instance, being classified as a person with a disability in many societies and countries today would entail social and legal benefits and economic assistance from the state, either as direct financial support or as discounted services offered to this category of people. What is and is not viewed as disability, Rispler-Chaim added, depends on cultural criteria.[89] The same holds true for terminology: the terms seen as offending in a specific time or specific place can be welcomed in other times or other places. Thus relativism remains the dominant factor in all terms and definitions used in this field.

1.4.2 Arabic usage

The most common Arabic equivalents currently used for disability are *i'āqa*,[90] *'awaq* and *ta'wīq*. The passive participles of these verbal nouns, meaning a person with disability, are respectively *mu'āq*, *ma'ūq* and *mu'awwaq*. There are also various euphemisms used in the modern literature to refer to people with disabilities such as *al-fi'āt al-khāṣṣa* (special groups), *dhawū al-iḥtiyājāt al-khāṣṣa* (people with special needs), *al-afrād ghayr al-'ādiyyīn* (abnormal individuals), etc.[91]

The terminology used in the aforementioned ICF international classifications issued by the WHO has also been rendered into Arabic. For instance, *'ajz* was used as an equivalent for 'disability',[92] *i'āqa* for 'handicap',[93] *i'tilāl* for 'impairment', *al-waẓā'if wa al-bunā al-jismiyya* for 'body functions and structure',[94] *al-anshiṭa* for 'activities', *al-taḥaddud fī al-anshiṭa* for 'activity limitations',[95] *al-musāhama* for 'participation'[96] and *al-taqalluṣ fī al-musāhama* for 'participation restrictions'.[97]

However, these terms cannot be traced in early Islamic literature. Even if we came across one of the derivatives of such terms, the significance would not be the same as that of the modern term.[98] To give just one example, the stem *'-w-q* – of which the derivatives *ta'wīq* and *'awaq* are the most common in this regard – is recorded in the classical Arabic lexicons but with other meanings.[99] For instance, *'ā'iq* (plural *'awā'iq*) is 'that [thing] driving away from what is good' (*khayr*), as in *'awā'iq al-dahr* (impediments of time).[100] In this sense the plural form of the active participle *mu'awwiq*, i.e. *mu'awwiqūn*, was used in the Qur'ān (33:18) to denote those who drive people away from practising Jihad.[101]

As for terminology used in classical Islamic sources, Rispler-Chaim remarked:

> I could not identify any single general term that would combine all people with disabilities as a group. . . . It is only in contemporary literature that we find sometimes generalized terms, such as *aṣḥab al-'ahat* or *dhawu al-'ahat* ('owners' or bearers of impairments, defects), *mu'awwaqun* or *mu'aqun* (literally those held back by difficulty and limitations on their mental or physical functions) and *'ajaza* or *'ajizun*, pl. of *'ajiz* (weak person, unable to do things like the old).[102]

According to Rispler-Chaim, the only exception was the word *marīḍ* (sick or ill person), which can be a general term used to denote a wide range of disabilities.[103]

A trawl through early Islamic sources in general and those on Islamic jurisprudence in particular shows that the above observation is imprecise. First of all, the term *aṣḥāb al-'āhāt* or *dhawū al-'āhāt* is found not only in contemporary literature. For instance, *dhawū al-'āhāt* was a common term in early Arabic literature to refer to people with different disabilities. However, it is important to recognize that the application of this term goes beyond that of 'people with disabilities', as we understand today. For instance, it may commonly include the bald, those who are very short or very tall, those whose pregnancies were abnormally long or short and so forth.[104] In the juristic literature, *'āha* was defined as a legal term originally used for describing the defects striking plants and animals, and later also used to denote chronic defects and disabilities that afflict humans.[105] Furthermore, in the sixteenth century when Ibn Fahd (d. 1547) wrote his book on people with disabilities, he called them *dhawū al-'āhāt,* as in the title of his book, *Al-Nukat al-ẓirāf fī al-maw'iẓa bi dhawī al-'āhāt min al-ashrāf* (Cute Anecdotes of Seeking Admonition from the Luminaries of People with Disabilities).

At any rate this was not the only term used in classical literature to refer to people with disabilities in general. I give just a few examples, *'aḍb*[106] is a verbal noun denoting *shalal* (paralysis), *khabal* (insanity) and *'araj* (lameness). The passive participle, *al-ma'ḍūb*, denoted a weak person who cannot hold fast riding on a camel.[107] *Al-Ḍa'īf*, (pl. *al-ḍu'afā'*) literally means the weak. This term occurred in the Qur'ān (2:282) and was interpreted as referring to people with different sorts of mental and physical disabilities such as lunacy, dumbness, speech disorders[108] or the loss of a limb, and thus was synonymous with *mukhdaj* (clarified below).[109] *Ahl al-balā'* (people of affliction) was used, especially in sources on theological issues,[110] to signify people with physical or mental disabilities.[111] In this sense, this term was used in a number of prophetic traditions such as the tradition speaking about the state of *ahl al-balā'* and *ahl al-'āfiya* (people of wellness) on the Day of Judgment.[112]

Aṣḥāb al-a'dhār (people with excuses) was used, especially in sources on Islamic jurisprudence, to refer to those people whose disabilities had been recognized as valid reasons for exemption from specific religious obligations.[113] *Muṣāb* literally means 'smitten'. It was sometimes used independently to denote a person with a mental disability.[114] However, it was often used with the preposition *bi* denoting ‘smitten with’ or ‘by’. For instance, *muṣāb bi baṣarih* or *bi iḥdā ‘aynayh* means ‘smitten with disorders of the eyes, and so on.[115] *Nughāsh*, which can also be pronounced *nughāshiyy* or *naghghāsh*, means ‘dwarf’ or ‘someone with a physical or mental disability’.[116]

Besides these terms denoting disabilities in general, other terms were used for physical rather than mental disabilities and likewise mental rather than physical ones. As for terms used to denote physical disabilities in particular, we can mention the following examples. *Al-fālij* (hemiplegia) is defined as a disease affecting one side of the body, and maybe both, and causing paralysis.[117] *Khidāj* literally denotes incompleteness and the passive participle, *mukhadj,* denotes a baby born before term and also a person whose body is incomplete, i.e. defective, in missing a limb or one of the senses.[118] For instance, *mukhadj al-yad* means ‘the one without a hand’.[119] *Mūdan* and *mathdūn* have synonymous denotations.[120] *Nāqiṣ al-khalq* literally means ‘someone whose physical appearance is incomplete’. The term was commonly used in Islamic literature to refer to people with a physical deficiency or defect.[121] *Qi‘ād* originally denoted a disease affecting a camel’s hips and making it fall over. The passive participle, *muq‘ad*, denoted one afflicted with an illness in the body so that he/she cannot walk.[122] Terms like *a‘raj* and *aksaḥ* have synonymous denotations.[123] Finally, *zamāna* denoted a long illness and comprised almost every defect such as blindness, lameness, amputated limbs and the like which hinder a person from earning his livelihood by his own work. The person afflicted with *zamāna* was called *zamin* and *zamīn*.[124]

As for terms denoting mental disabilities in particular, Abū al-Qāsim Ibn Ḥabīb (d. 406/1015) counted more than thirty such terms, for example *majnūn*, *aḥmaq*, *ma‘tūh* (denoting especially one who is born with mental illness), *akhraq*, etc.[125]

Terms denoting specific disabilities such as blindness (*‘amā*), deafness (*ṣamam*), dumbness (*kharas*) and so forth have not been discussed here because there is no significant difference between the Arabic terms and their English equivalents. Just one point is in order to avoid possible confusions. References to specific sorts of disabilities such as blindness, deafness, dumbness and the like occur frequently in the Qur’ān (e.g. 2:18 and 171, 6:39, 11:24, 13:19, 17:72, 47:23) in negative contexts. Neglecting available commentaries on the Qur’ān and depending solely on internet sites containing a directory of the Qur’ān text with a web search facility, the contemporary researcher Majid Turmusani made use of such verses to claim that the Qur’ān adopted a negative attitude towards people with disabilities.[126] Rispler-Chaim consulted two Qur’ān translations and two early commentaries which suggested that these verses refer to such disabilities in the metaphorical rather than the literal sense. However, she concluded that it remained uncertain in her view whether these verses referred to real disabilities or metaphorical ones.[127] Checking the context of these verses and consulting a large number of early and modern Qur’ān commentaries would show that Turmusani’s claim was baseless and Rispler-Chaim’s doubts were unnecessary. The main theme of such verses, as indicated by the Islamic sources, was a number of stubborn people who repeatedly refused to listen to the divine message conveyed by His prophets. Due to this misbehaviour, they were punished by being deprived of God's mercy because their eyesight, hearing and other senses did not lead them to grasp the Divine message. In the end they were like the deaf who cannot hear and the blind who cannot see and thus there was no longer any hope that their situation would get better and that they would give an ear to the prophets' admonitions. At any rate, the Qur'anic verses did not mean that those people could not, in the literal sense, see or hear any more.[128] This metaphorical usage of disabilities was also very common among the Arabs and is not specific to the Qur'an.[129] Qur'anic references to people with disabilities, in the literal sense, made them liable to legal exemptions rather than reproach or blame (e.g. 24:61, 48:17, 80:1–11). It is to be noted that the Sufi literature and some modern studies such as that by the Syrian scholar, Sa'dī Abū Jayb made the Qur'anic distinction between disabilities in the metaphorical sense and those in the literal sense as the basis for their viewpoint that the *real* disability which degrades one's position is the one afflicting one's heart and soul rather than one's body.

A final note on the terminology used in this study is in order. Expressions such as 'persons with disabilities' are the most frequently used in this study because they are acceptable to most people with disabilities.[130] Moreover, such terminology underscores the conviction that an individual's disability is just one of many personal characteristics, rather than being the identifying feature of that person's self.[131] In recent civil rights legislation, including the Americans with Disabilities Act of 1990, the expression 'persons with disabilities' was employed most regularly. In the literature of the disability rights movement, this designation is also the main one.[132] However, the reader will come across other terms, such as 'affliction' and 'suffering', which would seem contrary to the civil rights focus of the aforementioned term. The use of these terms which might be offensive is necessary to give a faithful image of the literature consulted in this study. For instance, when Muslim theologians used the term *ahl al-balâ'* (people with afflictions) to denote people with disabilities, the term did not imply, in its historical context, contempt for this group. However, I am aware that using such terms nowadays might be very offensive. So I hope the reader will forgive me for the incidental use of such terms in this study for the sake of being faithful to the texts I am quoting. The transliterated classical Arabic terms are sometimes used besides the modern English terms where doing otherwise could harm the clarity of the text.

Part I

Islamic theology

2 Speculative theology

2.1 Introductory remarks

The existence of disabilities and other forms of suffering has always raised questions such as: how does one understand or justify the presence of nasty and painful things in the light of the fact that God the Compassionate, the Merciful, is the Supreme Power and that He has control over this universe?[1] Providing an answer to this question has occupied the minds of people throughout human history. Some explanations were at the expense of God, denying His existence or ascribing evil to one god and goodness to another, etc. However, for thinkers who adopted the theistic position and believed in a revealed faith, there were strict guidelines to be followed in any resolution of the tension between the affirmation of God's existence and the reality of the existent evil in what He created.[2]

In the Islamic tradition, the first person to raise the aforementioned question was the father of humanity, Adam. In a prophetic tradition, it is related that God showed Adam his offspring, and he found remarkable discrepancies among them: rich and poor, strong and weak, etc. In another tradition, Adam saw among his offspring people with leprosy (*baraṣ*), elephantiasis (*judhām*), blindness and the like. Adam asked his Lord, 'Why did you do so with my offspring?' Another form of the question was 'Would not you better have made them equal?' God answered, 'I did so in order to be thanked', and in another version, 'so that My gift will be thanked for.'[3] The simplistic presentation given in this tradition did not put an end to this complicated issue. The question posed by Adam continued to be posed in Islamic tradition.

For a good understanding of the theological discussions on this issue, a note on the image of God, His attributes and names in the Islamic tradition is indispensable. The main entry to God's character in Islam is through His names and attributes.[4] Studying these names and attributes has always been a central point of concern for Muslim scholars. For instance, a chapter in theology manuals[5] and ḥadīth collections is usually devoted to the divine names and attributes,[6] and a vast genre of literature has developed on God's attributes and names.[7] According to some scholars, this genre has established an independent science known as *'Ilm al-asmā' wa al-ṣifāt* (science of [Divine] names and attributes).[8]

The central point of agreement was the perfect and flawless character of God, implying that no defect or deficiency can be attributed to Him, or to His mercy, wisdom, justice or omnipotence. This agreement among scholars can be explained by the following points.

First, His names are described in the Qur'ān as *Al-Ḥusnā*, indicating that these names denote the fairest, most beautiful and perfect attributes.[9] Second, there are a number of God's names whose meaning clearly and directly indicates this perfect character. The best-known name in this regard is *Al-Quddūs* (The Holy) which indicates the absence of all blemishes, and also that neither imagination nor sight can penetrate the mystery of God.[10] Finally, the Qur'ān harshly warns those who practise *ilḥād* concerning these names: 'call on Him by His Names and keep away from those that pervert them. They shall be punished for their misdeeds' (7:180). Linguistically, *ilḥād* means 'deviating from the right path'. Used in this context, it refers to those who deny any of these names or their connotations. In short, the perfect character of God as depicted by these names was, for Muslim scholars, a red line that should not be crossed.[11]

In this vein, the overarching concern, when investigating the issues of pain and suffering, continued to be that these issues can only be confronted with acknowledgement that no human catastrophe can call into question the omnipotence and all-embracing will of God, or His justice, mercy and solicitude for the welfare of mankind.[12] These remained the red lines, crossing which amounted to transgression.

Two main groups did transgress. The first group included those who were declared heretics and infidels. The main representatives of this group were Jahm b. Ṣafwān (executed 128/745),[13] to whom the Jahmiyya[14] is ascribed, the poet Abū al-'Alā' al-Ma'arrī (d. 1057), the philosopher Abū 'Īsā al-Warrāq (d. *c*. 247/861)[15] and his pupil Ibn al-Rāwandī (who died at the middle or end of the fourth/tenth century).[16] The joint thesis of this group concerning the justification of evil and pain was interpreted by Muslim scholars as casting doubt on the perfect and flawless character of God.[17]

Jahm b. Ṣafwān was outspoken in his denial that God is merciful. To him, this denial was a way of glorifying God and distinguishing Him from His creatures and also a way of understanding suffering in life. It is related that he used to gather his followers around lepers who were writhing in pain and would say mockingly, 'The most merciful of the merciful [i.e. God] does such things!' To him these evils showed that mercy had no place, only might and power void of mercy or wisdom.[18] Such ideas cost Jahm b. Ṣafwān many charges and ultimately his life. The Ash'arī heresiographer 'Abd al-Qāhir al-Baghdādī (d. 429/1037) says about him,

> We condemn him as a heretic for all his errors and the Qadarites [Indeterminists] declare him a *kāfir* [non-believer] for his assertion that God is the Creator of the acts of mankind. The various divisions of our community therefore coincide in charging him with unbelief.[19]

Doubts about the mercy of God were also expressed by the blind poet Abū al-'Alā' al-Ma'arrī.[20] Deeming that slaughtering animals caused undeserved and unjust pain, he decided to stop eating meat and eggs. According to historians, al-Maʿarrī lived for more than eighty years, forty-five of these as a vegetarian. The Ḥanbalī theologian and jurist Ibn al-Qayyim (d. 751/1350) called him 'the one whose eyes and heart are blind' (*aʿmā al-baṣar wa al-baṣīra*).'[21] Contrary to Ibn al-Qayyim, the late Egyptian scholar, Aḥmad al-Sharabāṣī (1918–1980), although disagreeing with al-Maʿarrī on this point, opined that al-Maʿarrī took this decision out of his tenderness, mercy and compassion for animals.[22] Like al-Maʿarrī and for the same reasons, Abū ʿĪsā al-Warrāq wrote the book *Al-Nawḥ ʿalā al-ḥayawānāt* (Lamenting the Animals) in which, according to Ibn al-Qayyim, he disclosed his clear infidelity (*al-zandaqa al-ṣurāḥ*).[23] As for Ibn al-Rāwandī, he was accused of making a jeering personal attack on God by claiming that He is vindictive, quarrelsome, weak at arithmetic, etc.[24] Ibn al-Jawzī said that Ibn al-Rāwandī,

> added his ill manners and tasteless humour, and spoke of the Creator in a way in which it would be inappropriate to speak even of one of the common people. We have not heard of any one who spoke of the Creator with such disrespect and jeering as this cursed one.

In another place, Ibn al-Jawzī described him as 'the pillar of heresy' (*muʿtamid al-malāḥida wa al-zanādiqa*).[25]

Certain Sufis also crossed the red lines. Contrary to the first group who were declared heretics and infidels for their views, the Sufis were usually permitted to a certain extent to express criticism of God and were not placed beyond the boundaries of Islam as a result. That is because they criticized the divine government but continued to submit with resignation to what God had ordained and decreed. Additionally, their claimed intimacy with God was so well founded and secure that it could not be disturbed by occasional audacities, just as reproaches and disputes can occur between lovers without disturbing their friendly relations.[26] Apart from this class of God's friends, there were also the saintly or religious fools whose ostensible lunacy gained them the special privilege of speaking to God more audaciously than other people. Some of them complained and criticized the actions of God. The story of the well-known mystic al-Shiblī (d. 334/945)[27] and the young madman in the lunatic asylum serves as a clear example here. The young madman begged al-Shiblī to ask God why He was tormenting him so much, why he was keeping him in a place away from home, far from his parents, hungry and shivering with cold. When al-Shiblī was about to go, the young madman cried, 'No, do not tell God anything! Otherwise He will make it worse. I shall not ask Him for anything. For nothing can impress Him. He is self-sufficient.'[28] The German orientalist Hellmut Ritter (d. 1971) commented on such stories by saying,

> Whatever happens to them is, in their eyes, always a direct action of God or on His behalf. Always they have to deal with God directly. And this direct and intimate relation to God characterizes them as genuinely mystic, as *mystical* fools, and distinguishes them from heretics and philosophers who

have become alienated from God altogether like Ibn al-Rāwandī and Abu al-'Alā al-Ma'arrī.[29]

Apart from such exceptional cases, the main line in Islamic theology continued to be belief in God's perfect and flawless character, expressed by all the divine names and attributes reflecting this character. Scholars of Islam remained unanimous on the fact that the existence of pain in life cannot be a valid reason for casting doubt on the perfect character of God. Two groups of Muslim scholars, namely Sufis and philosophers, regarded the phenomenon of pain, evil or affliction in general as no *real* problem. Their views in this regard are summarized below.

2.1.1 Sufis

The method adopted by the Sufis was highly spiritual and focused on the nature of God and the spiritual relationship that creatures can develop with Him as Creator. The most elaborate and comprehensive presentation of this approach was given by Abū Ḥāmid al-Ghazālī (d. 1111). Al-Ghazālī's starting point was that a proper knowledge of God and a spiritual relationship with Him, based mainly on mutual love, would eliminate any sense of being in trouble. The distinction between good and evil would be meaningless since everything coming from God was good.[30]

In God's eyes, an important sign of loving His servant was to make him an object of affliction and difficulty (*ibtilā'*). The Prophet is reported to have said, 'When God loves a servant, He will visit him with afflictions. When He loves him, with a fully fledged love, He will preserve him.' Being asked what 'preserve him' means, the Prophet said, 'God does not leave for him family or property.' One of the scholars said, 'When you love God and notice that He is visiting you with afflictions, know that He wants to purify you.' One of the mystic teachers advised his student by saying, 'O my son, do not aspire for love as He does not give it to anybody without testing him with afflictions first.'[31]

From the point of view of the human being, always characterized as a servant (*'abd*), an important sign of being in love with God is to love what his Beloved (God) loves. Al-Ghazālī related the story of one of the Companions of the Prophet who, on the eve of a battle, called on God to give him a strong man to fight who would cut off his nose and ears and pierce his stomach. The purpose of this invocation was clarified by the Companion as follows: 'When I meet you tomorrow [on the Day of Resurrection], You will ask me, O servant of God! who cut off your nose and ears? I will say, for the cause of You and Your Messenger. You will say, you have spoken the truth.'[32] It is clear here that disability is invoked because in the Hereafter it will prove the servant's sincere love for God.

Such mutual spiritual love strengthens the bonds between the lover (servant) and the Beloved (God). When in physical pain, someone experiencing such a relationship finds himself in one of two main states. *First*, being immersed in love of God would remove the sense of physical pain. When severe afflictions befall a lover, they cannot cause him pain. In order to rationalize this argument, al-Ghazālī recalled here the example of a warrior on the battlefield who, at the time of fear and wrath, does not feel pain because his mind is fully engaged. The same holds true for the case of one so immersed in love with his beloved that he cannot feel physical pain. For example, the Qu'rān (12.31) mentions the ladies who wounded their hands with knives and remained unconscious of the pain because they were in deep love with the Prophet Joseph.[33] The common rationale here is that when the mind is fully engaged with one thing, it cannot grasp another at the same time.

In the *second* state, one would feel the pain but be satisfied with it at the same time and even be willing to experience it although one could detest it by nature. A mystic leader said in this respect, 'The one who sees the rewards of afflictions will not desire to avoid them.'[34]

Al-Ghazālī was aware of the eccentricity of experiencing these two states while enduring pain and trouble. To prove the validity and practicality of this rationale, he quoted a long list of statements and stories of pious figures. Here we mention just one example which has direct relevance to the case of disability. The well-known mystic Bishr al-Ḥāfī (d. 226/840)[35] is related to have met, at the beginning of his religious life, a man afflicted with blindness, elephantiasis, madness and epilepsy. Seeing that ants were eating the man's flesh, Bishr put his head in his lap and tried to speak to him. The man recovered his consciousness and wondered, 'Who is this curious man who interferes between me and my Lord. Had He cut me into pieces, it would have done nothing but increase my love for Him.'[36]

While some mystics were content to pursue a pious life motivated by the love of God, others became involved in esoteric and even antinomian practices through which they hoped to experience oneness with God or to be 'annihilated in His unity', as expressed in the mystic doctrine of *fanā'* (lit. passing away, effacement).[37] In such a state, in which the Sufi experiences the passing away of the consciousness of all things, including him/herself, and the annihilation of the imperfect attributes of the creature and their replacement by the perfect attributes of God,[38] the question about the wise purposes of evil in life becomes irrelevant. That is because such an experience will leave no room for experiencing evil, let alone asking why it exists.

The *real* disability which men should deem as a *real* problem, according to this approach, is the type of disability afflicting one's heart and soul rather than one's body. One of the mystic authorities explained this point by saying: 'What heartbreak . . . would be greater than seeing the one with blindness in this life as a sighted person in the Hereafter, while the sighted one in this life will be blind?!'[39] This is a reference to the Qur'anic verses (20:124, 125) speaking about the person who suffered this *real* disability which diverted him from the right path to God in this life. As a punishment, this person, who was sighted in the worldly life, will be afflicted with blindness on the Day of Resurrection.[40] Modern Muslim scholars paid considerable attention to this type of disability. As mentioned above, the Syrian scholar Sa'dī Abū Jayb said that the disability which impairs one's soul and thus drives a person away from God is the real (*ḥaqīqiyya*) disability. One's status and dignity in Islam are damaged by this type of disability rather than that afflicting one's body.[41]

2.1.2 Philosophers

A number of Muslim philosophers shed light on the necessity of understanding the general nature of suffering or evil on the one hand and the life we are living on the other hand. To them, comprehending these two dimensions would demonstrate that actually there is no *real* problem.

In this vein, suffering is simply an inevitable concomitant of existence in this life. So it is something that must happen rather than something that could happen.

Ibn Sīnā (d. 429/1037), the most influential Muslim philosopher, will be the main focus in this respect. First of all, he seems to have been the first of the philosophers to concern himself with the problem of evil.[42] Additionally, to my knowledge, he is the main, if not the only, philosopher to focus on disability within the broader framework of evil. I depend principally on Shams Inati's study of Ibn Sīnā's theodicy of evil to review Ibn Sīnā's discussions on disabilities.[43]

Ibn Sīnā advanced a Neoplatonic ontological analysis of the problem of evil, which aims to prove that God, the absolutely good First Cause, produces a good world.[44] He said in this respect,

> There is nothing whatsoever in the entire world, and in all its high and lower parts, which is excluded from the statement that God is the cause of its being and its origination in time, that God has knowledge of it and disposes it and that God wills it to exist. . . . For if this world were not compounded of the effects of good and evil forces and of the produce of both righteousness and corruption in its inhabitants, the world order would never have been fulfilled completely.[45]

As for specific disabilities such as the absence of an arm or of sight, Ibn Sīnā classified them under the category of essential evil (*al-sharr bi al-dhāt*)[46] because they imply the lack of perfections that are inherent in the nature of human beings.[47] Some of the examples of inherent perfection given by Ibn Sīnā are organs, such as the human eye; some are capacities or powers, such as human sight; and some are the act or fulfilment of such powers, such as the act of seeing. The real perfection among these three is the *act:* what is the human eye or its capacity to see, if it does not actually see?[48] This type of evil, according to Ibn Sīnā is evil in all respects:

> As for the lack of perfection and health [of the harmed thing], it is evil not only in relation to [the harmed thing] so that it would have a presence by virtue of which it is not an evil. Rather, its very presence is nothing but an evil in it, and in the manner of being evil. Thus, blindness cannot be except in the eye; and, inasmuch as it is in the eye, it cannot but be evil, with no aspect to it by virtue of which it would be other than evil.'[49]

In his bid to justify the existence of such evils, Ibn Sīnā placed himself within the aforementioned limits by assuring his firm belief in God's absolute goodness which leads to providence (*'ināya*) whose presence is evident.[50] Thus, the explanation should not be at the expense of the divine perfection of God. The question now is: how can we understand the reality of this world including evil in the light of God's absolute goodness?

Ibn Sīnā advanced three main arguments, all of which are applicable to the case of disabilities. *First*, essential evil, to which the phenomenon of disability belongs, is privation of being. For instance, disability is privation of ability which is being and blindness is privation of seeing which is being. Because essential evil is non-being, it is uncaused. In other words, it cannot have a cause for a cause is always the cause of something. 'Cause' here means an agent or efficient cause, not just any principle required for the production of an effect. The agent or efficient cause always produces something and not nothing. It follows that no being, including God, can be a cause of essential evil.[51] However, whether considered as being or non-being, human beings still experience suffering because of disability. This criticism was expressed by Fakhr al-Dīn al-Rāzī (d. 606/1210). He countered Ibn Sīnā's ontological and cosmological theodicy with the very human experience of suffering. This is what 'minds and hearts are perplexed by' and consequently what any attempted theodicy ought to address. Ibn Sīnā's theodicy merely circumvented the real problem of evil. Al-Rāzī wondered why Ibn Sīnā attempted a theodicy in the first place, given that he is not a moral realist and that he did not consider the Creator to be a voluntary agent, in which case He cannot be morally responsible for His acts. His introduction of the terms 'good' and 'evil' into the context of ontology is superfluous (*fuḍūl*) and inept. Instead, al-Rāzī added, Ibn Sīnā should have left the attempt to justify evil in this world to those for whom it is a real problem, namely the Mu'tazila.[52] However, this argument and the one described below are meant to minimize the problem rather than to solve it. It is to be noted here that the mystic Muḥyī al-Dīn Ibn al-'Arabī (d. 638/1240) supported this argument of Ibn Sīnā in his work *Tāj al-rasā'il* (The Crown of Epistles) written in 600/1203. He said in this regard, 'Existence in general is purely good and non-existence is purely evil. However, such evil that may exist is imbued with good. . . . For one cannot appreciate anything without relating it to its opposite. . . . The whole world then enjoys complete happiness.'[53] This approach is rejected by the modern researcher Adīb Nāyif Diyāb (PhD Cambridge University, 1981). He criticized Ibn al-'Arabī for following in the footsteps of traditional philosophy which seems to be incompatible with the conventions of common sense and with the reality of human suffering, quite apart from the obscurity of 'nonthingness' as a concept.[54]

The *second* argument advanced by Ibn Sīnā in this regard is that there is more good than evil in the universe: 'Evil only strikes individuals, and at certain times. The species are preserved. Except for one kind of evil [i.e. accidental evil], real evil does not extend to the majority of individuals.'[55] This is of course easily applicable to people with disabilities who represent a minority among the people on earth. However, Ibn Sīnā's view in this respect was not generally accepted by other philosophers. For instance, Abū Bakr al-Rāzī (d. 313/925) opined that evil is prevalent in this world, a contention which follows from his notion that pleasure is purely relief from pain.[56] Now, suppose that the evils are few, why should not this life be free of these *few* evils?

Here is the *third* argument of Ibn Sīnā, namely, that the universal order cannot be sustained without the occurrence of evil.[57] 'This was not possible in a mode of existence such as this, even though it was possible in the absolute existence, since that mode of absolute existence free from evil is other than this one.'[58] By extending this notion to disability, one could say that being human necessitates being prone to both ability and disability. In the absence of disability, human beings will no longer be human beings. In this vein, although God's unrestricted power is not denied explicitly, it is denied implicitly. If God is the cause of everything, including this sphere, and if this sphere cannot be other than it is, it would follow that its cause has no power to make it other than it is. Everything that God does is done necessarily. It is 'necessity' that seems to have the upper hand in every action in the universe, including the divine ones. God, like everything else, is an instrument in the hands of necessity. It is true that Ibn Sīnā speaks of God's will and sometimes of God's choice, but even God's will runs by necessity.[59] Despite his disagreement with Ibn Sīnā in the aforementioned arguments, Fakhr al-Dīn al-Rāzī was inclined to concede the logicality of this specific argument in his *Al-Mabāḥith al-mashriqiyya* (Oriental Themes).[60]

2.2 Anti-theodicy approach

This approach stressed that the perfect character of God can be seen first and foremost in one specific side of God's character, namely God's self-sufficiency and omnipotence. In the case of disabilities and other forms of misfortunes in life, judging God's acts in accordance with the same criteria used for judging human acts would diminish God's unlimited power and thus tarnish His perfect character. In this sense, no attempts should be made to search for wise purposes (*ḥikam*) for God's acts, including pain and all that can be deemed evil. In short, theodicy cannot be practised. This approach was mainly theorized in the Ash'arī theological manuals. For instance, the founder of the school, Abū al-Ḥasan al-Ash'arī (d. 324/935–6),[61] wrote a chapter in his book *Al-Ibāna* (Illumination) entitled 'Question Concerning the Torture of Infants.'[62] In his book *Al-Mawāqif* (Viewpoints), the well-known Ash'arī theologian 'Aḍud al-Dīn al-Ījī (d. 757/1355) also wrote a whole chapter on theodicy (*ta'līl*).[63] Lately, the contemporary Egyptian scholar Muḥammad al-Sayyid al-Julaynid (Cairo University) treated the issue of theodicy in the Ash'arī school in his book on good and evil.[64] Finally, G. Legenhausen (Texas Southern University, USA) wrote an article elaborating and to some extent advocating the Ash'arī view on the theodicy.[65]

Exposing the main articles of the Ash'arī school, Abū al-Ḥasan al-Ash'arī elaborated this theme as follows,

> We assert that God has prowess (*quwwa*), as He says 'Saw they not that God who had created them was mightier than they?' (Qur'ān 41:14). . . . and that there is not good nor evil on earth, save what God wills and that things exist by God's will and that not a single person has the capacity to do anything until God causes him to act and we are not independent of God nor can we pass

> beyond the range of God's knowledge; and that there is no creator save God and the works of human beings are things created and decreed by God. He has said 'God has created you and what you make' (Qur'ān 37:94). Human beings have not the power to create anything but are themselves created. . . . Human beings do not control for themselves what is hurtful or what is helpful, except what God wills and that we ought to commit our affairs to God and assert our complete need and dependence upon Him.[66]

Abū Ḥāmid al-Ghazālī (d. 505/1111), one of the towering personalities in the Ash'arite School, reiterated this theme by affirming that God can inflict pain on man – indeed He can torment man – without hope of reward and for no reason.[67] In this sense, all sorts of disabilities and by default sufferings and evils are to be traced back to God. He is the one who created them and willed them and man has no role in this regard. The question then is: why does God create and will all these evils? What is the wise purpose (*ḥikma*) behind all this? Where is the justice of God in this case?

The Ash'arites in fact condemned posing questions to God because He is the Almighty who runs His own kingship (*mulk*) as He pleases and thus is not to be questioned.[68] This point is also made by the Ẓāhirī scholar Ibn Ḥazm (d. 456/1064).[69] Furthermore, searching for the wise purposes (*ḥikam*) of God's actions is not only meaningless, but also grave disobedience to Him.[70] The Ash'arites considered this contrary to the perfect and flawless character of God. Defending their contention, the Ash'arites advanced more than one argument.[71]

First, if God's act is precipitated by a cause (*'illa*), then that cause is originated (*ḥāditha*) and requires a cause, and so on *ad infinitum*. If God acted or originated on account of a cause or wise purpose, this would entail an endless chain or infinite regress (*tasalsul*) of causes, which the Ash'arīs deem impossible.

Second, it implies need in God. They argued that one acting by virtue of a specific cause will be perfected by it, because if the occurrence of the cause were not better than its nonexistence, it would not be a cause. One who is perfected by another is imperfect in himself. This is impossible for God. It is clear that the Ash'arīs' concern to deny need in God is rooted in their belief that God's acts are completely free and unbound by any necessity. A God who acts for a wise purpose must be acting out of prior lack and imperfection.

The *third* argument was directed specifically against the Mu'tazilī account which maintained that God acts for a cause that is disjoined (*munfaṣil*) from His essence. The Ash'arīs countered that this cause must have some impact on God; otherwise it would not be a cause. If then it is disjoined from God, His acting for its sake implies that the cause – which is something outside Himself – perfects Him. Conversely, if the cause is 'subsisting in Him' (*qā'im bih*), the Ash'arīs argue, 'It necessarily follows that He is a substrate (*maḥall*) for originated events (*ḥawādith*).'

It is noteworthy to state here that by denying the wise purposiveness of God's acts, the Ash'aris did not deny the name of God, *al-Ḥakīm* (All-Wise). To them, God was undoubtedly All-Wise but they had their own specific understanding of this name. Al-Ghazālī explained it by saying, '*Al-Ḥakīm* is the one who has wisdom. Wisdom is equivalent to knowledge of superior things through the highest modes of knowledge. . . . He is the truly wise because He knows the most sublime things by the most sublime modes of knowing.'[72] Thus God's wisdom was, to the Ash'arīs, knowledge and does not necessarily entail purposiveness in His acts. The same holds true for the name *al-'Adl* (All-Just). They did not deny the name but they had their own understanding of its purport, i.e. justice, which they saw as an expression of God's will. The prominent Ash'arī scholar 'Abd al-Qāhir al-Baghdādī (d. 463/1071) defined this term as 'what the doer can do' (*mā li al-fā'il an yaf'alah*). On the other hand, the antonym of justice, i.e. injustice, is 'Dispose of someone else's property without his consent' (*taṣarruf fī milk al-ghayr bi ghayr idhnih*).[73] In this sense, it is inconceivable to classify any of God's acts as injustice because He runs His own kingship as He pleases and He is in no need of others' permission to act.[74]

Another important point in this regard, on which the Ash'arites disagreed with the Mu'tazilites, was that God's acts are not subject to the human intellect and thus cannot be measured thereby. For instance, the value of justice, injustice and so forth are to be specified solely by the Lawgiver, i.e. God. Accordingly, God does not command an act *because* that act is just and good; it is His command (*amr*) which makes it just and good.[75] One of the main advocates of this argument at the present time is the Syrian scholar Muḥammad Sa'īd Ramaḍān al-Būṭī (b. 1929).[76]

In this theological framework, the Ash'arites do not have much trouble in explaining the existence of disabilities, evil and suffering. For instance, speaking about infants in this life suffering the torture of leprosy which makes their hands and feet drop off, Abū al-Ḥasan al-Ash'arī stressed that the Mu'tazilī theology cannot explain the justice of God in such a case. However, such an act is just and wise, according to the Ash'arī theology, because God is running His own Kingship.[77] Recently, this approach was advocated by G. Legenhausen, stating that this way 'solves the problem of evil not by limiting God, but by exalting Him above human morality'.[78]

2.3 Pro-theodicy approach

Contrary to the previous approach which stressed God's omnipotence, the proponents of this approach argued that the divine perfection of God's character is to be measured by His oneness and justice, wisdom and solicitude for the welfare of His creatures. The proponents of this approach tried to explain or justify the existence of evil, pain and suffering in a way that would not harm God's justice or wisdom. They said that man, because of his freedom to act in life, is the agent of a large part of the evil and pain in this life. Such evils are to be ascribed to their agent, namely man, who is liable to do just and unjust acts. God is not responsible for these evils and cannot be questioned for their existence in our life. However, another part of the pain and suffering of life are beyond human choice, such as being afflicted with blindness, leprosy and other illnesses. God alone is responsible for these pains and they are just and wise. They have been created by God for specific benefits and wise purposes (*ḥikam*). In this sense, the proponents of this approach refused to call such acts 'evils' and say that they are to be classified as forms of *fitna* (temptation) or *ibtilā'* (test).[79] Whether disability results from man's action, other people's action or directly from God and thus is beyond human control, there should be a specific wise purpose that can be discerned by the human intellect.

In this framework, very detailed and sometimes extremely complicated attempts were made to search for these possible wise purposes. The advocates of this approach came basically from the Mu'tazilī theological school. The broad lines of their doctrines in this respect found proponents in the circles of Twelver Shī'ism (Shī'a Imāmiyya) such as Ibn Bābawayh known as al-Shaykh al-Ṣadūq (d. 391/1001),[80] al-Shaykh al-Mufīd (d. 413/1022),[81] al-Sharīf al-Murtaḍā (d. 436/1044)[82] and al-Muṭahhar al-Ḥillī (d. 726/1325).[83] They all held largely similar opinions about suffering and its compensation.[84] Keeping in mind that the Mu'tazilī presentation of issues relevant to this approach was one of the most detailed and elaborated in Islamic history, their doctrines have been taken as the main points of discussion. Cross-references to Shī'ī sources have been given so that their origins can be traced and their conformity to Mu'tazilī thought assessed. The main source which theorized and developed this approach in the Mu'tazilī school was the famous encyclopedia of al-Qāḍī 'Abd al-Jabbār (d. 415/1025),[85] *Al-Mughnī fī abwāb al-'adl wa al-tawḥīd* (The Sufficient on Themes of Justice and Oneness), which recorded Mu'tazilī theology in its entirety.[86] Mu'tazilī contentions, especially as elaborated in *Al-Mughnī*, on pain and suffering in general have recently been studied by the Dutch researcher Margaretha Heemskerk. She wrote her PhD dissertation on pain and compensation in the Mu'tazilite doctrine,[87] and it was later published under the title *Suffering in the Mu'tazilite Theology*.[88] Heemskerk's is the basic study upon which the discussions in this respect are based. As for the Shī'ī sources, three main ones give a general overview on this issue: Ibn Bābawayh's *Risālat al-i'tiqād* (Treatise on Creed),[89] al-Shaykh al-Mufīd's *Awā'il al-maqālāt fī al-madhāhib wa al-mukhtārāt* (The First Treatises on Chosen Doctrines),[90] and al-Ḥillī's *Al-Bāb al-ḥadī 'aṣhar* (The Eleventh Chapter).[91] However, the centrality of the image of God in the theology of this approach escaped the attention of Heemskerk. To compensate for this lack, two main studies were consulted, introducing the viewpoints of the advocates of this approach on the perfect character of God. These two studies are *The Islamic Conception of Justice* by Majid Khadduri (1908–2007) and *God and His Attributes: Lessons on Islamic Doctrine*[92] by the Shī'ī scholar, Sayyid Mujtaba Musavi Lari (b. 1314/1935).[93]

Because of their emphasis on divine oneness and justice, the Mu'tazila derived their name from these two qualities: the Partisans of Justice and Oneness (*Ahl al-'Adl wa al-Tawḥīd*). Justice is even more central in Mu'tazilite thought, for if Oneness describes God's existence as One, justice is His very essence. It is His unique nature that distinguishes Him from everything else.[94] This holds true to the extent that the Mu'tazila were also known as *al-'Adliyya* (Advocates of Justice).[95] Like the Mu'tazila, the Shī'a have selected justice, out of all attributes, to be a principle of their creed. They believe that justice is the basis of God's acts, both in the ordering of the universe and in the establishment of laws.[96]

In the Shī'ī tradition, justice naturally included the avoidance of oppression and all foolish acts. *Imam* Ja'far al-Ṣādiq (d. 148/765) explained God's justice by saying, 'Justice in the case of God means that you should not ascribe anything to God that if you were to do it would cause you to be blamed and reproached.' Al-Shaykh al-Ṣadūq defined justice as rewarding a good act with a good act and an evil act with an evil act.[97] Besides avoiding injustice and foolish acts, justice also implies benefiting others.[98] Doing service for others also appears to be an important element of justice in Mu'tazilī thought. The prominent theologian 'Abd al-Jabbār (d. 415/1025) defined a just act as an act performed by man not necessarily for his own advantage but for the advantage of another man for whom the act is intended. Thus just acts may, generally speaking, be defined as those acts which promote the welfare of other men, and the man who performs them would be called a just man.[99]

Wisdom has always been seen as closely connected with justice. The modern Shī'ī scholar, Sayyid Mujtaba Musavi Lari (b. 1314/1935), says in this regard, 'When we see that God is just, it means that His all-knowing and creative essence does nothing that is contrary to wisdom and benefit.'[100] In this sense, all God's acts are both just and wise.[101] The Mu'tazilites unanimously declare that God does nothing without wisdom, and in all He does, He intends benefit.[102] The Mu'tazilites affirm that God acts for wise purposes (*ḥikam*), otherwise He would be aimless and foolish. However, they also tried to uphold God's complete lack of need by clarifying that the sole beneficiaries in purposive divine acts are His creatures. God created human beings to benefit them. God does not act through self-interest because He has no need.[103]

The other side of God's character, mainly revealed in His omnipotence, occupied a subsidiary role in the thought of this approach. Attributes indicating God's omnipotence were seen by Mu'tazilī scholars as something implied in the fact that God exists and they do not represent a separate category of attributes. Abū al-Hudhayl al-'Allāf (d. 226/840–1)[104] argued that the mere fact that God exists implies that He is knowledgeable and powerful. Other Mu'tazilites like Ḍirār b. 'Amr (d. *c.* 200/915) and al-Naẓẓām (d. *c.* 231/845)[105] said that God's essence implies knowledge and power, as it is inconceivable that God is ignorant and powerless.[106] At any rate, this divine omnipotence cannot supersede or deviate from the divine justice and wisdom. Some of the Mu'tazilites such as al-Naẓẓām and al-Jāḥiẓ (d. 255/868–9)[107] denied that God has the capacity to do injustice. However, 'Abd al-Jabbār and later Mu'tazilites pointed out that this would be inconsistent with God's omnipotence. However, it remains inconceivable that God would ever do injustice because it is contrary to His perfection to associate His name with injustice.[108] Thus in one way or another, God's omnipotence is allowed to work only within the realm of His justice and wisdom. For instance, divine wisdom as an essential attribute of God precludes His committing any bad act (*qabīḥ*), a premise which leads to the conclusion that it is impossible (*muḥāl*) for a wise God to commit such acts. By the same token, what is impossible in a specific case means that it cannot be done (*ghayr maqdūr*). The Shī'ī perspective reiterates the same theme by opining that the Divine Might relates only to things which are possible. Things that are rationally impossible are entirely outside the sphere of His power. It is related that someone asked 'Alī b. Abī Ṭālib, 'Is your Lord able to fit the whole world into a hen's egg?' He answered: 'God Almighty is, indeed, able to do anything, but what you ask is something impossible.' So, although God's sacred essence is utterly free of all impotence and inability, it is meaningless and irrational to ask whether God can do something inherently impossible.[109] Daud Rahbar (b. 1927, Pakistan) is a good example of modern figures who support this tendency. He believes that God's justice is the dominant theme of the Qur'ān.[110] In Rahbar's theodicy, the world exists to demonstrate the justice of God. To him, the full display of justice requires both good and evil, the former for reward and the latter for punishment.[111] When criticized for limiting God's power by making room for human responsibility for evil, he countered, 'God Himself exercises self-restraint from evil and thus limits His own power. To know Him as a moral Being in Qur'anic terms we must know Him as such, and not as a Force "let loose".'[112]

Finally God's justice and wisdom are to be measured by the same scale as the one applied to human actions. This is based on the analogy to be drawn between the Present world (*al-shāhid*) and the Absent (Divine) world (*al-ghā'ib*) because of which the justice, wisdom and goodness of God's acts can be recognized by the human intellect.[113]

According to these doctrines, whether disability or afflictions in general occurred due to man's action, to other people's action or directly to God and so are beyond human control, there should be a specific wise purpose that can be discerned by the human intellect. The main question will thus be: what are the wise purposes of besetting people with affliction? For a systematic presentation of answers to this question within this approach, a distinction will be made between persons with legal liability (*mukallafūn*)[114] who thus can be responsible for the evils they committed and those without legal liability (*ghayr mukallafūn*) such as children, people without mental capacity and animals.

*2.3.1 Afflictions befalling those with legal liability (***mukallafūn***)*

According to Mu'tazilite doctrines, disabilities occurring in this life can be divided into three main categories: (1) self-inflicted; (2) inflicted by humans or animals; and (3) inflicted by God. Each of the disabilities is to be judged as (a) good (*ḥasan*) and just (*'adl*); or (b) bad (*qabīḥ*), which can be further categorized into (1) unjust (*ẓulm*) or (2) a useless act (*'abath*).

To the Mu'tazilites, inflicting pain in general is bad (*sharr*) but it is still possible to inflict harm in a way that may be judged as good. This means that doing harm can be good only by exception. 'Abd al-Jabbār (d. 415/1025) pointed this out by stating that doing harm is an injustice unless this harm:

- involves a benefit greater than the harm;
- averts a harm greater than the inflicted harm;
- is deserved;
- is inflicted on the assumption that one of the above three conditions applies;[115]
- if inflicted on someone else, is intended to bring a benefit; and
- is done to an adult of sound mind who has consented to be harmed for the sake of profit.[116] However, in the case of living beings who are not in full possession of their mental faculties and are in one's care, it is deemed good if one harms them when one is assuming that this will lead to a profit for them in the future or that it will avert an expected harm.[117]

Thus self-inflicted disability or disability inflicted by others is good as long as such conditions are fulfilled. However, the infliction of disability to avert the suffering of an equal harm is deemed a useless act (*'abath*).[118] Based on what has been stated above, the three sorts of affliction can be analysed as follows.

The first type, self-inflicted, which does not involve gaining benefit or averting harm greater than the harm suffered, is deemed by the Mu'tazilites to be a bad act because it is a form of injustice (*ẓulm*) to oneself and thus not to be compensated by God or anyone else.[119] However, such pain is to be compensated if it is inflicted with the intention of averting harm, because a person in that case does not obtain a profit that can take the place of compensation. Also self-inflicted harm is to be recompensed if it is done on the assumption that it will yield a benefit in the future but fails to do so. In these two cases pain is to be compensated by God.[120]

As for the second type, harm inflicted by others, the main rule is that the initiative to inflict pain or cause disability determines who compensates. Thus both *mukallaf* and non-*mukallaf* must compensate for the pain they inflict on another living being even if he/she does not know that they are entitled to compensation equal to the pain suffered.[121] However, humans cannot know precisely how much compensation they must make for pain. This means that they are unable to fulfil the obligation to compensate for pain.[122] Thus it is God who will mediate in executing the process of compensation. God is Omniscient and therefore knows exactly how much compensation must be given for each pain. 'Abd al-Jabbār opined that this mediation is obligatory for God: after having enabled a wrongdoer (*ẓālim*) to wrong someone else and not having prevented him from doing so, God is obliged to pass a verdict and to administer justice between the wrongdoer and the wronged (*maẓlūm*).[123]

God administers justice in this case by taking the required quantity of compensation from the person who inflicted the pain and transfering it to the person who suffered the pain.[124] It is to be noted that administering justice in this respect does not mean that God may take part of a wrongdoer's reward and transfer it to the person wronged by him. That is because reward can be earned only by fulfilling a difficult task.[125] Administering justice in this regard will be done by transferring the compensation from one account to another. 'Abd al-Jabbār explained this by saying that every living being is entitled to divine compensation for the pain and harm that God made him suffer. This theory implies that God is a sort of bookkeeper, who keeps the accounts of the compensation that each creature is entitled to receive from Him and transfers amounts from one account to another.[126] However, in the light of this theory, what would happen in the case of the malicious person who has inflicted so much pain and harm on other living beings that he/she does not have enough 'credit in the Hereafter' to be transferred to all those who have been wronged by him/her? Three main answers to this question are provided by Mu'tazilite theologians, all stressing the fact that people who are wronged must be compensated somehow.

First, if people who have been wronged cannot get compensation from the perpetrator, God will ensure that they are compensated by Him as His donation (*tafaḍḍul*).[127] *Second*, if wrongdoers do not have enough compensation to compensate for crimes that have been committed on their orders, they must compensate only for crimes they have committed with their own hands. In that case, others who acted on their command must themselves make compensation for these acts unless they were committed under constraint.[128] *Third,* it is exaggerated to think that some people, tyrants for example, could have insufficient divine compensation for all their acts of injustice. 'Abd al-Jabbār advocated this idea by saying that we cannot know how much sorrow, pain, misfortune and terror has beset this wrongdoer and how much compensation will be given by God for these sufferings.[129]

The only exception to the obligation to compensate for pain inflicted is when the pain is not inflicted on one's initiative.[130] Thus, if a judge wrongly decreed that someone's hand be amputated in a *ḥadd* punishment and the executor carried out this decree, then it is the judge who must compensate the wrongly condemned person and not the executor because the amputation was made on the initiative of the judge.[131] Also pain that leads to a greater profit need not be compensated because the profit acquired replaces the compensation.[132] Thus, a surgeon who excises a patient's gangrenous hand is not obliged to pay compensation because the benefit acquired – saving the patient's life by preventing the gangrene affecting other parts of the body – is greater than the harm caused by the disability inflicted.

The purpose of establishing the aforementioned conditions (on p. 30) was to draw an analogy between the Present world (*al-shāhid*) and the Absent (Divine) world (*al-ghā'ib*) and finally to confirm that the third type of affliction, those inflicted by God, are always good: the good that can be recognized by human intellect.[133] However, this analogy is not always exact or without problems. For instance, three prominent Mu'tazilite theologians, 'Abd al-Jabbār (d. 415/1025), Mānkdīm (d. 425/1034) and Ibn Mattawayh (d. *c.* 468/1075), put aside the second and fourth conditions in the list on p. 30, in the case of pain imposed by God. They eliminated the possibility that God's infliction of pain is good because it averts a greater harm, pointing out that this would be in conflict with God's Omnipotence.[134] They also eliminated the possibility that God's infliction of pain is good because it is done *on the supposition* that it involves benefit or averts harm because Allah's Omniscience implies that supposition (*ẓann*) is impossible for Him.[135]

Also, the analogy between the Present world and the Absent world placed the Mu'tazila in an awkward position. How could God's imposition of illness on adult people of sound mind be deemed good when they had not given Him their consent to the harm? Mu'tazilite scholars provided three answers to this question.

The *first* answer was that the relation between God and humans is like the relation between a carer and children in his custody. The carer is entitled to inflict pain on them without their consent if this leads to greater benefit than the pain or averts harm greater than the pain, because they have been put into his care and he knows what is best for them. Hence God does not have to ask for humans' consent when He inflicts pain on them. That is because it is God who created them and gave them life and He is therefore in the best position to know what is good for them.[136]

This solution is rejected by other Mu'tazilite scholars. For instance, 'Abd al-Jabbār thought that this solution was in conflict with the theory that God imposes obligations on humans. He argued that this presupposes that they are adults and of sound mind, otherwise it would be wrong to impose obligations on them. That they are adults of sound mind implies that they should give their consent.

The *second* answer is based on imagining a situation in which it is good to harm an adult of sound mind even if he has not given his consent beforehand. Such a situation would be one in which the compensation for the harm is so great that all adults of sound mind (*mukallaf*), different as they are, would certainly choose to bear the harm to obtain the compensation awarded for it, and those who do not make this choice must be considered as not being of sound mind.[137]

The *third* answer was suggested by Ibn Mattawayh who believed that those who are *mukallaf* have given God some kind of silent permission to inflict pain on them. His opinion is that if they know God, they also know that God will certainly compensate them for the pain He inflicts on them, and that He will make the compensation so great that each of them would choose to bear the pain for it. To him, this amounts to giving permission to God to inflict pain.[138]

Apart from such nuances, Mu'tazilite scholars agree that disability – or harm in general – inflicted by God on the *mukallafūn* is good because either (1) it is deserved punishment; or (2) it involves a profit or benefit (*maṣlaḥa*).[139]

*2.3.1.1 Wise purposes (*Ḥikam*)*

2.3.1.1.1 DESERVED PUNISHMENT

Inflicting pain as a deserved punishment is a point of disagreement among the Mu'tazilite theologians. There are two main opinions in this respect. The *first,* articulated by Abū 'Alī al-Jubbā'ī (d. 303/915),[140] is that pain can be a divine punishment that God inflicts in advance, like the prescribed punishments (*ḥudūd*). *Ḥadd* punishments are only given to Muslims, so it is also possible that illnesses which unbelievers suffer are punishments inflicted on them instead of *ḥadd* punishments.[141] However, he made an exception for illnesses suffered by living beings who, according to his doctrine, cannot have deserved punishment, such as prophets and animals. Prophets cannot have deserved punishment from God because they do not commit grave sins and animals are not legally responsible (non-*mukallafūn*).[142] Abū ʻAlī therefore believed that the prophets' illnesses are a trial (*miḥna*) imposed on them by God and not a *luṭf* (Divine Assistance).[143] The difference between the two is that a *luṭf* can motivate not only the person who suffers but other persons as well, whereas a trial only concerns the person who suffers.[144]

The *second* was held by Abū Hāshim (d. 321/933)[145] and ʻAbd al-Jabbār (d. 415/1025). In this regard ʻAbd al-Jabbār was initially keen to reject the idea that illnesses and pain are deserved punishments, as was believed by those whom he called the adherents of the transmigration of souls (*aṣḥāb al-tanāsukh*),[146] those who believed that living beings suffer in this life because of bad acts in their previous lives. Consequently, those who had sinned less and obeyed more were given a body more beautifully formed and their sufferings were less. Those whose sins were more were given a body less beautiful in form and suffered more.[147]

The two main proponents of this opinion stated that illnesses in general cannot be intended as punishment. They cited two arguments in support of this contention. First, it is wrong to punish someone who does not know what he/she is being punished for. Someone who is ill does not know whether the illness is a punishment, and even if he did understand that it was a punishment, he would not know what offence he was being punished for.[148] Such a person may think that an injustice is being done to him and this may prompt him to do bad acts. This makes it clear, they say, that illnesses are not a punishment from God.[149] Even the illnesses of people who are aware that they have failed to fulfil the obligations of God's *taklīf* (charge) and know that they deserve punishment are not a punishment. Inflicting illnesses on them as a punishment conflicts with the theory of God's *taklīf*. According to this theory, God threatens those who fail to fulfil their obligations with severe punishment. This means that their punishment must be more than merely illness in this world. It implies that they will be punished in the Hereafter.[150] Second, prophets and pious people fall ill, although they cannot have deserved punishment from God. This is an indication that illnesses are not a punishment.[151]

However, ʻAbd al-Jabbār – one of the proponents of the second opinion – does not deny that there is pain in this world inflicted by God, or on His command, that is meant as a deserved punishment. However, in these cases the punished persons know why they are being punished. An example of such a deserved punishment from God is a *ḥadd* punishment: although it is carried out by humans, it is considered to come from God because it is done on His command.[152]

In this regard it was asked what God would do in the case of a believer whose hand had been cut off and who then apostatized, and conversely in the case of an infidel whose hand had been cut off and who then came to believe. The simplest response was that he would be compensated by God; another hand would be substituted. Other Muʻtazilites held that the hand of the apostatizing believer would be attached to the repentant infidel, while the infidel's hand (which had been amputated while he still disbelieved) would be attached to the apostate. Still others rejected this on the ground that the believer and disbeliever are not 'the hand and the leg'.[153]

2.3.1.1.2 DIVINE ASSISTANCE (*LUṬF*)[154]

As for the nature of the benefit (*maṣlaḥa*) ensuing from God's infliction of pain, opinions in the Mu'tazilī School fluctuate between *luṭf* (Divine Assistance) and *'iwaḍ* (Compensation). Broadly speaking, several of God's actions towards humans have a relation to God's *taklīf* (charging).[155] God imposes obligations on all adults of sound mind (*mukallafūn*) with the purpose of giving them the opportunity to earn a reward.[156] This means that if God's purpose is to give people the opportunity to earn a reward, He must impose on them something difficult but not so difficult as to be impossible, because it is bad (*qabīḥ*) to impose an impossible task and of course God does not do anything bad.[157] Thus God is *obliged to do* certain things and acts to enable people to fulfil that which He has imposed on them.[158] These acts are performed with the purpose of (1) informing people about which obligations are imposed on them; or (2) motivating them to fulfil these obligations. These acts of God are deemed *alṭāf* (the plural of *luṭf*). For instance, God's sending prophets to the people to inform them of the obligations imposed on them is a *luṭf*.[159]

In this sense, pain sent by God is both an important *luṭf* and a warning (*i'tibār*). Abū Hāshim argues that God's infliction of pain would be a useless act (*'abath*) if it was not a warning.[160] Mānkdīm added that the warning may be intended for the person in pain or for others or for both.[161] By this, Mu'tazilite scholars could mean that pain in this life warns people that there will be a painful punishment in Hell if they fail to fulfil the obligations imposed by God.[162]

2.3.1.1.3 COMPENSATION (*'IWAḌ*)[163]

As stated above, whether the initiative to inflict pain or cause disability is taken by a *mukallaf* or a non-*mukallaf* determines who compensates.[164] As usual, by drawing an analogy between the present and the transcendent (divine) world, Mu'tazilite theologians stated that pain inflicted by God or by His command or permission is compensated by Him. God gives the compensation in order to ensure that His infliction of pain is not a bad act. Without such compensation God's act would be an injustice.[165]

As for the time of giving compensation, some Mu'tazilites such as al-'Allāf (d. between 227 and 235/841 and 849)[166] and Abū 'Alī al-Jubbā'ī (d. 303/915)[167] stated that it must be in the Hereafter[168] whereas some others including 'Abd al-Jabbār and Abū Hāsim opined that compensation can be given by God in this life or in the Hereafter.[169] But in any case God gives the compensation after the harm is done and not before.[170] However, in some particular cases compensation for pain cannot be given in this world. For instance, those who suffer pain while dying can be compensated for it only after their death.[171] Broadly speaking, it is God who determines whether a person will be compensated in this world or in the Hereafter. Being Omniscient, God compensates each creature at the best moment for him.[172] However, compensation to be given by God in the Hereafter cannot be remitted by the person entitled to it. That is because the possibility of remitting compensation is related to the possibility of claiming it and compensation to be given in the Hereafter cannot be claimed in this world.[173]

'Abd al-Jabbār stressed that God's giving of compensation in the Hereafter should not lead to a situation where someone who has not fulfilled the obligations of the *taklīf* receives something that amounts to a reward from God.[174] But this does not negate the fact that even people in Hell will receive the compensation they are entitled to. The fact that these people deserve punishment does not nullify their right to be compensated for the pain and illnesses they have suffered. That is because compensation, unlike reward, is not due to honour or respect for the recipient. Hence, there is no reason to think that people in Hell will not be compensated.[175] However, compensation given to people in Hell cannot be the same as what is given to people in Paradise. Rationally, giving pleasure can be equated with taking away pain. It is therefore possible that God diminishes the punishment of people in Hell in proportion to the compensation they are entitled to receive.[176]

*2.3.2 Afflictions befalling those without legal liability (non-***mukallafūn***)*

Broadly speaking, the Mu'tazilites devoted much ingenuity to the problem of the seemingly unmerited suffering, particularly that of infants and animals.[177] As stated above, in the Mu'tazilite view God does nothing without purpose, and in all that He does He intends only benefit. How might this belief be reconciled with the sufferings of the non-*mukallafūn,* especially innocent children? More than one answer was given to this question. Here opinions may be categorized into two main groupings, namely the *aṣḥāb al-tanāsukh* (those who believed in metempsychosis or the transmigration of souls) and the majority view maintained by the Mu'tazila.

*2.3.2.1 Adherents of metempsychosis (*aṣḥāb al-tanāsukh*)*

That disabilities, illnesses and misfortunes afflicting children, people without mental capacity and animals constitute deserved punishment was a view advocated by those Mu'tazilīs who believed in metempsychosis.[178] They said that the pain and illness suffered in this life are the result of one's sins committed in a previous life.

They held that God created men healthy, sound in body and mind, in an adult state, and in a world other than the one in which they now live. He created in them the full knowledge of Himself and showered on them His blessings. God then placed them under an obligation to show gratitude to Him. Some of them obeyed him and some disobeyed in all that he had commanded while a third group obeyed in some things and disobeyed in others. God allowed those who obeyed in all things to remain in Heaven. Those who were disobedient in all things God cast out of Heaven and put in a place of punishment, namely Hell. Those who were partly obedient and partly disobedient God sent to this world and clothed them in gross human bodies. He also subjected them to adversity, suffering, hardship and comfort, pain and pleasure. In this life, too, He gave them different forms, some having the form of men and some of animals according to the measure of their sins. Those who had sinned less and obeyed more were given a more beautiful body and their sufferings were less. Those whose sins were greater were given a less beautiful body and suffered more. Henceforward, those who are animals will not cease to be animals in one life after another, as long as their acts of obedience and disobedience continue.[179]

Furthermore, the adherents of this doctrine claimed that all species of animals are charged with the duty of observance (*taklīf*), and have received ordinances and prohibitions in accordance with their diverse forms and methods of expression.[180] Moreover, they added, God will endlessly continue to send His message to every kind of living being, even bugs, lice and fleas, while His charge to living beings will always remain.[181]

2.3.2.2 The majority view

The Mu'tazilites could not comfortably claim that children suffered pain as a means of *luṭf*. Nor could they claim that children's suffering was the requisite tribulation through which reward might be won. That is because children possess no juridical status of responsibility (*taklīf*) under Islamic jurisprudence. Various solutions were offered to this seemingly insoluble problem.[182]

Some Mu'tazilites denied that God caused any undeserved pain.[183] Thus, they said, children feel only pain inflicted on them by humans and not pain inflicted by God.[184] 'Abd al-Jabbār refuted this opinion by pointing out that every adult experienced pain during childhood just as they do during adulthood.[185] Children become ill just as adults do. From this 'Abd al-Jabbār concluded that children suffer illnesses sent by God.[186] Others, including al-Naẓẓām (d. *c.* 231/845),[187] held that children's suffering is, indeed, God's doing but occurs through 'the necessary course of events'.[188] However, in the majority view, God inflicted pain on infants for the two main purposes described below.

2.3.2.2.1 DIVINE ASSISTANCE (*LUṬF*)

Each illness is a *luṭf*. Adults of sound mind can profit from the motivation contained in illnesses and deserve a reward for fulfilling the obligations of God's *taklīf*. Thus, after having reached maturity, children become *mukallaf* so that they also can profit from the *luṭf* contained in their illnesses. However, children who die before reaching maturity cannot do this: they cannot deserve a reward, as they never become *mukallaf*. However, such children's suffering is not useless: adults living near them can profit from the *luṭf* contained in their illnesses. Generally speaking, pain suffered by a non-*mukallaf* can be a *luṭf* for a *mukallaf*. Children's illnesses and disabilities serve as a clear example here because they are a sort of *luṭf* for parents.[189]

2.3.2.2.2 COMPENSATION (*'IWAḌ*)

Being a *luṭf* for the *mukallafūn* around them does not fully justify the disabilities and sufferings of children who die before reaching maturity. There must be a benefit for the children as well. It would be bad, Mu'tazilites argued, if God inflicted illnesses on them from which others can profit and they themselves cannot.[190] The benefit that children can get from their illnesses is a compensation (*'iwaḍ*) given to them by God.

The majority of the Mu'tazila stated that it is inevitable that God will revive those children who have not received all their compensation in this world, together with the *mukallafūn,* on the Day of Resurrection so that they can receive their compensation in the Hereafter.[191]

2.4 A median approach

The advocates of this approach represented the majority of early and late Muslim scholars within the circles of theologians (*mutakallimūn*), jurists (*fuqahā'*), traditionists (*ahl al-ḥadīth*), interpreters of the Qur'ān (*mufassirūn*), Sufis, early and late philosophers such as Abū al-Barakāt (d. *c*. 550/1155) and a large number of the late Ash'arites who diverged from their school in this specific respect.[192] In his book *Kitāb al-tawḥīd* (Book of Oneness), Abū Manṣūr al-Māturīdī (d. *c*. 333/944)[193] contributed to this approach in a chapter entitled *al-Dalīl 'alā anna li al-'ālam Muḥdith* (The Evidence that the Cosmos Has One Who Gave It Temporal Existence). Apart from al-Māturīdī, four main scholars played important roles in theorizing this approach and elaborating its doctrines. Throughout his different works, Ibn Taymiyya (d. 728/1328)[194] constantly treated the issue of the theodicy and the divine acts. He also issued a detailed and lengthy fatwa on the theodicy.[195] Recently, Ibn Taymiyya's various statements were collected and analysed in Jon R. Hoover's PhD dissertation defended at the University of Birmingham[196] and published in 2007 under the title *Ibn Taymiyya's Theodicy of Perpetual Optimism*.[197] Ibn al-Qayyim (d. 751/1350) also devoted a large portion of his writings to theodicy. His main work on this issue was *Shifā' al-'alīl fī masā'il al-qaḍā' wa al-qadar wa al-ḥikma wa al-ta'līl* (Healing the Sick on Issues of Fate, Predetermination, Wisdom and Theodicy).[198] The third figure was al-'Izz b. 'Abd al-Salām (d. 660/1066) who wrote a book on afflictions, calamities and misfortunes (*Al-Fitan wa al-balāya wa al-miḥan wa al-razāyā*) in which he counted about seventeen benefits (*fawā'id*) deriving from them.[199] It is noteworthy that al-'Izz b. 'Abd al-Salām used the term 'benefits' (*fawā'id*) rather than 'wise purposes' (*ḥikam*). This may be because of his support of the Ash'arī viewpoint that God cannot be questioned and that the wisdom behind His divine acts should not be investigated.[200] Anyhow, what al-'Izz termed 'benefits' and others 'wise purposes' were studied to present a logical justification for the calamities and suffering taking place in this life. Finally, the Yemeni scholar Ibn al-Wazīr (d. 840/1436) studied the issue of theodicy in his famous book *Īthār al-ḥaqq 'alā al-khalq* (Preferring the True [God] to the Creatures).[201]

Abū Ḥāmid al-Ghazālī was a controversial figure in this regard. According to Ibn al-Wazīr, he was one of the main proponents of this median approach.[202] Sherman Jackson (Professor of Arabic and Islamic Studies, University of Michigan) also argued that Ash'arīs such as al-Ghazālī and later theologians did not reject rational considerations of utility but only Mu'tazilī objectivism.[203] Muḥammad al-Sayyid al-Julaynid (Cairo University) said there were two Ghazālīs. The first Ghazālī was the Ash'arī theologian who accepted the main doctrines of the Ash'arī school and belonged to the anti-theodicy approach. The other Ghazālī was the free thinker who had his own independent views and thus spoke about the wise purposes (*ḥikam*) of the divine acts.[204] In response to al-Julaynid, Hoover stated that

> a careful reading of al-Ghazālī's text reveals that while purpose and causality indeed seem to pervade the discussion, the key term *'illa* does not appear, and the text could be interpreted to exclude causality in God's will. Also, al-Ghazālī explains that, while mercy involves pain and tenderness from the merciful, this does not apply to God whose perfection does not involve feeling pain for one in need. This fits well with the traditional Ash'arī understanding of God.[205]

Hoover supported his point by citing Richard Frank's opinion that al-Ghazālī explicitly denied that God acts for a purpose (*gharaḍ*) or for compensations (*'iwad*).[206] To my mind, it is unfair to enshrine al-Ghazālī within the traditional Ash'arī viewpoint concerning theodicy although he unequivocally advocated this position in some of his works. He has, as al-Julaynid indicated, expressed other views which can easily be placed within this median approach. One of the treatises attributed to al-Ghazālī deals with the divine wisdom to be traced in the created beings (*Al-Ḥikma fī makhlūqāt Allāh 'Azz wa Jall*).[207] However, al-Ghazālī's writings show that he can still be classified, as shown above, among the Sufis who adopted a no-problem approach.

In modern times, the median approach has also been advocated by a number of scholars and researchers. In his book *Fī 'ālam al-makfūfīn* (Inside the World of the Blind), the late Egyptian scholar Aḥmad al-Sharabāṣī (1918–1980) asked the question: Why did God create blindness although it is bad and disliked? The possible answers advanced by al-Sharabāṣī cover twenty-five pages, most of them concerned with medical interpretations rather than theological wise purposes.[208] The Saudi researcher Muḥammad Rabī' Hadī al-Madkhalī wrote his MA thesis on the wisdom and theodicy of the divine acts (*Al-Ḥikma wa al-ta'līl fī af'āl Allāh ta'ālā*).[209] Zuhayr Muḥammad al-Zamīlī made the question 'Why Did God Make diseases?' the title of his book *Limādhā ja'ala Allāh al-amrāḍ*.[210] Apart from these two studies, modern Muslim scholars such as Yūsuf al-Qaraḍāwī (b. 1926)[211] and Muḥammad Sa'īd Ramaḍān al-Būṭī (b. 1929)[212] have treated the issue of theodicy while studying the broad topic of God's fate and predestination (*qaḍā'* and *qadar*). The late Egyptian scholar Muḥammad Mutwallī al-Sha'rāwī (1911–1988) also tackled the issue of theodicy in his book on good and evil.[213]

Other than these figures, a huge relevant literature is available in commentaries on the Qur'ān and Ḥadīth and sometimes also in juristic sources. Although there is almost no mention of the term 'theodicy' (*ta'līl*), the scholars discussed calamities, misfortunes and other issues of direct relevance to the subject. If we classified this extensive material as theodicy related, then the comments, made by more than one researcher, on the rarity of theodicy texts and the non-centrality of this issue in Islamic thought should be taken with reservation.[214]

As for their main ideas, the advocates of this approach pondered over the clashing arguments presented by the first two groups and contended that truth lies in a balance between these two. The pro-theodicy group was criticized because their understanding of divine justice ultimately placed the sayings, actions and movements of angels, human beings and jinns beyond God's power, will and creation. The anti-theodicy group was criticized for overemphasizing the divine omnipotence by which they almost negated the freedom of human beings to act in life according their own will.[215]

Combining divine names and attributes expressing God's omnipotence with those indicating His justice and wisdom was seen as a Qur'anic phenomenon. For instance, the name indicating divine omnipotence, *Al-'Azīz* (the Powerful), occurs eleven times in the Qur'ān in combination with the name indicating God's mercy, *Al-Raḥīm* (the Merciful).[216] This combination occurs for instance in the context of afflicting previous nations and peoples with severe punishments for disobeying God's Messengers (Qur'ān 26:09, 86, 104, 122, 140, 159, 175, 191). The same name, *Al-'Azīz*, occurs also in the Qur'ān twenty-nine times in combination with the name *Al-Ḥakīm* (the All-Wise).[217] A trawl through a number of these verses shows that some references are relevant to disability. For instance, the seventh instance of this combination (3:06) refers to the shaping of embryos in the womb according to God's Will. Thus the wide range of differences among new-born babies – white, black, healthy, sick and disabled – is not an expression of one side of God's character. It is an indication of both His Omnipotence and His All-Wisdom. The fourteenth instance of this combination (5:38) conveys the divine order of amputating the hands as a punishment for committing the crime of robbery. That the verse ends with these two names, was read by some scholars as indicating that the order for such punishment indicates that God is both All-Powerful and All-Wise.[218] In this vein, when Sulaymān b. 'Abd al-Wahhāb (1786–1818) wrote a commentary on *Kitāb al-tawḥīd*, which was written by his grandfather Muḥammad b. 'Abd al-Wahhāb (d. 1703–1792), he gave it the title *Taysīr al-'Azīz al-Ḥamīd fī sharḥ kitāb al-tawḥīd* (The Facilitation of the Powerful the Worthy of Praise: A Commentary on the Book of Unity).[219] This indicated that the phenomenon of combining names that would at first seem contradictory was common among the advocates of this approach.

As for the perfect and flawless character of God, advocates of this approach believed that the aforementioned two approaches ultimately portrayed an inadequate view of God. The retributive justice advocated by the Mu'tazilites and the voluntaristic divine justice promoted by the Ash'arites were both criticized. The Ash'arites' denial of the wise purposiveness of God's acts and the Mu'tazilites' promotion of wise purposiveness as measured by human standards are also both rejected.[220] The standpoint adopted in this third approach is encapsulated in the following statement by Ibn Taymiyya:

> Injustice is putting something in other than its proper place (*waḍ' al-shay' fī ghayr mawḍi'ih*). Justice is putting [every]thing in its proper place. He – Glory be to Him – is a wise arbiter and just, putting things in their places. He puts everything in its place, which corresponds to it and which wise purpose and justice require. He does not differentiate between two identical things, and He does not equate two different things. He punishes only whomever deserves punishment and puts it in its place on account of the wise purpose and justice in that. As for the righteous and God-fearing, He does not punish them at all.[221]

Although they uphold in principle the Mu'tazilī view that God's acts always have a wise purpose (*ḥikma*), the advocates of this approach have their own reservations in this respect. Ibn Taymiyya accused them of ending up in a contradictory position when they said that God acts for a wise purpose that is separate from Him and that benefits creatures but not Himself.[222] For him, it is irrational for any agent to do good to others without some judgement (*ḥukm*), profit or praise accruing to him himself. Someone who is ultimately indifferent to praise and beneficence – as God is in the Mu'tazila view – is acting aimlessly. This, ironically in Ibn Taymiyya's view, is precisely what the Mu'tazila seek to avoid by attributing purpose to God's Will.[223]

As for the notion of theodicy, they also tried to find middle ground by saying that behind every divine act there must be one or many wise purposes but these are not necessarily always detectable by the human intellect. Basing themselves mainly on scriptural texts from the Qur'ān and Sunna on the one hand and making use of rational arguments on the other, they counted a number of possible wise purposes for the existence of disabilities and other forms of suffering in life. According to the advocates of this approach, the theodicy of divine acts can be characterized by four main elements. The *first* element was the ongoing emphasis that no justification for the existence of evil and affliction should impair the perfect and flawless character of God. Contrary to the Ash'arites who stressed divine power at the expense of divine justice, and to the Mu'tazilites who did the opposite, this approach strove for a middle ground by maintaining balance between all the attributes of God and seeing that emphasis on one of them should not be at the expense of the other.[224] They found it necessary to extract what is useful and appealing from both approaches and to cast aside what they deemed harmful.[225]

The *second* element was that attempts to search for the wise purposes behind the divine acts do not represent an eccentric phenomenon or an innovation in Islam. Recalling the prophetic tradition relating that Adam, having seen the blind, dumb and afflicted among his progeny, asked God, 'Why did not you make all my progeny equal?',[226] they concluded that what is inadmissible in Islam is only to make such attempts in order to cast doubt on the wise purposes of God.[227]

The *third* element was the firm belief that no aspect of this world, however insignificant it may seem, is without a redeeming reason.[228] This holds true to the extent that the wise purposes (*ḥikam*) of the pain befalling different creatures are too many to be fully enumerated.[229] However, this belief should never lead to the idea that all the wise purposes (*ḥikam*) of divine acts are always traceable by the human intellect. That is because the human intellect is finite and limited whereas God's wisdom is infinite and unlimited.[230] Thus, when there is a case or incidence whose wisdom cannot be understood, it should be attributed to the incapable mind of humans, not to the All-Wise God.[231]

After mentioning the example of amputating a gangrenous hand and the possible goodness implied in it, al-Ghazālī elaborated on this point by saying,

> Now, if a particular evil occurs to you without your seeing any good beneath it or you should think that it is possible that a particular good be achieved without being contained in evil, you should query whether your reasoning might not be deficient in each of these two trains of thought. . . . So accuse your reasoning in both ways and never doubt that He is *the most merciful of the merciful* or that 'His mercy takes precedence over His anger'.

Concluding this discussion with a mystic touch, al-Ghazālī says, 'Beneath all this lies a secret whose divulgence the revelation prohibits, so be content with prayer and do not expect that it be divulged.'[232] The famous mystic Muḥyī al-Dīn Ibn al-'Arabī (d. 638/1240), in his *Al-Futūḥāt al-makkiyya* (Meccan Illuminations), shared al-Ghazālī's viewpoint, stressing that there is a wise purpose for every mode of being which, if still hidden from our vision, will appear through deeper insight in the course of time.[233] In this vein, 'Azīz al-Nasafī, a thirteenth-century mystic, compared the person who does not realize that the world is perfect to a blind man who enters a house and complains that everything is in his way.[234]

In modern times, Abū al-A'lā al-Mawdūdī (d. 1903–1978) condemned those who argue that the existence of widespread suffering is inconsistent with the image of a Wise, Merciful and All-Powerful God. In his article, *Kotah nazari* (Short Sightedness), al-Mawdūdī replied to this argument by drawing attention to two familiar cases. First, governments which take measures which may involve some unavoidable suffering for a few to promote the general welfare: had the sufferers been aware of the government's real purpose, they would not complain and condemn it. Another example al Mawdūdī gives is that of a gardener. In order to maintain his garden properly and make it look more beautiful, the gardener must trim some plants, change their locations, even throw some out. Had the plants that are affected in the process had tongues, they would certainly have complained. But if they could look at the whole garden and understand the entire planning of the gardener and his work, they would not raise an objection. Al-Mawdūdī argued that our position in this infinitely vast, immensely complex and extremely beautiful world is no better than that of a few sufferers among the masses of a country or some plants in a garden. We are, he added, in no position to scan the entire universe, let alone to comprehend its workings. If we use the presence of evil in the world to deny the existence of God, we will be like the sufferers who complain about their government or plants in the garden who complain about the gardener.[235]

The same line of argument was adopted by the Syrian scholar Sa'īd Ḥawwā (1935–1989)[236] who accused such people not only of short-sightedness, as did al-Mawdūdī, but even of madness.[237] Adopting a less harsh tone, Yūsuf al-Qaraḍāwī (b. 1926) speaks of a sacred or inviolable area (*manṭiqa ḥarām*) of God's predestination that should not be encroached on, and of inscrutable meanings (*asrār*) that should not be investigated. To him, understanding the wise purposes of pain and suffering in life is a thorny issue on which questions cannot be satisfactorily answered. What cannot be known in this regard is much more than what can be known.[238]

The *fourth* element which characterized the median approach was the priority of revelation over reason. The *ḥikma* propounded by revelation cannot be contradicted by rational argument or thought.[239] That is because revelation is infallible whereas reason is prone to err.[240] By the same token the *ḥikma* proposed by the mind should not oppose any of the basic tenets of Islamic belief.[241]

As was the case with the pro-theodicy approach, the wise purposes for the existence of disabilities, within the broad framework of pain or suffering, will be divided into those related to the *mukallafūn* and those related to the non-*mukallafūn*. Contrary to the pro-theodicy approach, categorization here is highly subjective and not always based on a strict separation between the two categories by the advocates themselves. Thus the possibility of overlap between *ḥikam* classified in these two categories should be kept in view.

*2.4.1 Afflictions befalling those with legal liability (***mukallafūn***)*

2.4.1.1 Disabilities: punishment for sins committed?

In the introduction to her recent study *Disability in Islamic Law*, Vardit Rispler-Chaim (University of Haifa) said:

> It is never proclaimed that the disease is predestined by Allah so that the ill Muslim has an opportunity to repent, or that disease is a way of punishment for certain sins. Nowhere in the Qur'ān, Sunna or fiqh is a clear causality established between Allah and the onset of a disease and/or disability in a believer.[242]

Such a statement might find support among a number of the Mu'tazilī scholars, as noted above, who refused to see a link between sin and the infliction of pain. However, the statement remains blatantly contradictory to clear texts in the Qur'ān and Sunna, not to mention the writings of scholars advocating the median approach. The possibility of a cause–effect link between committing sins on the one hand and disabilities or diseases in general on the other cannot be denied. For instance, of the early scholars, Ibn Taymiyya and Ibn al-Qayyim regarded people's sins as the main cause of misfortune, pain and disease in this worldly life.[243] This is also the case among many modern scholars such as the late Egyptian Aḥmad al-Sharabāṣī (1918–1980),[244] the Syrian Muḥammad Sa'īd Ramaḍān al-Būṭī (b. 1929)[245] and the Iraqi 'Abd al-Karīm Zaydān.[246] More than one Qur'anic verse were understood to support this viewpoint (e.g. 4:79, 123, 8:53 30:41, 42:30). Take for instance, the Qur'anic verse, 'Whatever misfortune happens to you, is because of the things your hands have wrought, but for many [of them] He grants forgiveness' (42:30). Some commentators interpreted 'misfortune' (*muṣība*) as illness, punishment or any other form of affliction in this life[247] and 'the things your hands have wrought' as one's sins and misdeeds.[248] Upon the revelation of this verse, the Prophet is reported to have said, 'No scratch of a stick, shudder of a vein or stumble of a foot befalls a man but because of a sin, but what Allah forgives is more.'[249] The same purport is also encountered in the Qur'anic verse, 'Whatever good (*ḥasana*) befalls you, it is from God; and whatever ill (*sayyi'a*) from yourself' (4:79). *Ḥasana* (good) and *sayyi'a* (bad) in this verse are interpreted respectively as favours, e.g. prosperity, health and wellness, and misfortunes, e.g. infertility and calamity.[250] 'From yourself' here means because of your sins.[251] It is to be noted that 'you' and 'yourself' here originally referred to the Prophet Muḥammad but the purport of the verse is applicable to every Muslim and according to some scholars to all humans.[252] Finally, it is related that on the revelation of the Qur'anic verse 'Whoever works evil, will be requited accordingly' (4:123), Muslims found it too hard and conveyed their complaint to the Prophet. Asking him if it was true that the purport of the Qur'anic verse would be precisely applied, the Prophet replied in the affirmative. However, he pointed out that such requital will not inevitably take place in the Hereafter, but could take the form of calamities and afflictions visiting one's body or property in this life.[253]

The purport of these verses was also vivid in the minds of early Muslims, as reflected in many reports about them. For instance, the Companion 'Imrān ibn Ḥuṣayn (d. 52/672)[254] was afflicted with a physical disease. Some of his friends paid him a visit and said, 'We feel sorry for what you suffer.' He said, 'Do not feel sorry. This all happens because of a sin but what Allah pardons is much more.' Then he recited verse 42:30 (quoted above).[255] Afflicted with facial paralysis while performing the Ḥajj, the Companion Mu'āwiya b. Abī Sufyān (d. 60/680)[256] conceded that this could be because he had committed a sin.[257] Likewise, al-Qāḍī Shurayḥ (d. between 76/695–6 and 80/699–700)[258] was asked about an ulcer in the palm of his hand. He said that this was because of what 'your hands have wrought, but for many He grants forgiveness'.[259]

A number of these traditions regarding disabilities in particular were reported to have developed during the lifetime of the Prophet, disability appearing to be concomitant with committing grievous sins such as lying to the Prophet or showing him disrespect out of arrogance and pompousness. Some of the perpetrators recorded in this context include a woman called Jamra bint al-Ḥārith b. 'Awf, who was afflicted with leprosy,[260] Yazīd b. Bahrām, who was afflicted with paralysis and therefore became known as *al-muq'ad* (the seated) because he could not walk any more,[261] and Busr (in another reading Bishr) al-Shuja'ī, whose hand was paralysed.[262] These traditions also paved the way for other stories with the same message said to have happened after the death of the Prophet and related by well-known Muslim scholars such as Ibn al-Jawzī (d. 597/1200),[263] Shams al-Dīn al-Dhahabī (748/1348)[264] and Ibn Ḥajar al-'Asqalānī (d. 852/1449).[265]

Although such traditions are extremely few compared with others promoting forgiveness and tolerance towards people who commit sins, their purport of a possible link between disabilities, diseases or misfortunes in general and committing sins cannot be ignored. However, a thorough survey of Islamic sources on this issue clearly shows that a general assumplion of a disabilities–sins link is mistaken. To provide a well-balanced presentation, two points are in order.

In the first place, the abovementioned traditions indicate that disabilities *may be* but need *not necessarily be* the result of committing sins. For instance, when Mu'āwiya b. Abī Sufyān was afflicted with facial paralysis, he mentioned three possible reasons, i.e. gaining reward, receiving punishment and finally receiving a disciplinary reproach.[266] According to this view, in the normal course of events disobedient people receive more than one warning before being punished. Disabilities or misfortunes as punishment befall those who insist on paying no attention to such warnings, make no effort to return to the straight path, declare no repentance to God and continue their disobedience.[267]

But even as a form of punishment, disabilities must have a beneficent function. They may have a cathartic function by purging the sinner of his sins and bringing him relief from greater torment in the Hereafter. A great number of prophetic traditions stress the expiatory role of suffering and its purging effect on the life of the faithful.[268] To give just a few examples, according to one of these traditions, 'No calamity befalls a Muslim but God expiates some of his sins even if it were being pricked with a thorn.'[269] Another tradition stated, 'The calamity continues to afflict the believing man and woman in body, property and progeny until he/she meets God [on the Day of Resurrection] without any sins cleaving to him/her.'[270] Based on the aforementioned traditions, Ibn Ḥajar al-'Asqalānī (d. 852/1449) characterized misfortunes as divine medicine by which man is cured from the disease of fatal sins.[271] In the same vein, another authority said, 'Had there been no worldly afflictions, we would have come insolvent [with bad deeds outnumbering the good ones] on the Day of Resurrection.'[272]

Understanding disability as a punishment in this context was seen as a sign of God's mercy and benevolence rather than of His anger and wrath. As a comment on the aforementioned Qur'anic verse (4:123), the Prophet is reported to have said,

> Whatever befalls you of illness, punishment or misfortune in the worldly life is because of what your hands have wrought, but God is more tolerant than doubling the punishment [by inflicting it again] in the Hereafter. As for what God has pardoned in [the worldly] life, [one should know that] God is more bountiful than reverting [to punishing] after His pardon.[273]

No matter how extreme they could be, the Qur'ān repeatedly confirms (13:34, 20:127, 39:26, 41:16, 68:33) that the punishments in this life are much more lenient than those in the Hereafter. Commenting on such traditions, Zuhayr Muḥammad al-Zamīlī wondered what grace can be greater than this.[274]

Another sign of God's mercy mentioned in the tradition in this regard concerns the rewards for good deeds that the afflicted person did before the affliction hindered him/her from continuing to do them. In ḥadīth collections, one finds separate chapters on the reward of the sick (*ajr al-marīḍ*). These chapters comprise a number of prophetic traditions purporting that the rewards for such deeds continue to be recorded as if they were still being done.[275] One of these traditions said,

> No Muslim would be visited with an affliction in his body save God would order the Guardians [angels] who guard him by saying, 'Write down for My servant every day and night the equal [reward] of the good (*khayr*) he was doing as long as he is confined in My fetter [i.e. sickness].'[276]

By extension to disability, we may conclude that a person who used to listen to a specific portion of the Qur'ān every day and later on was hindered from doing so by deafness is a further example. The divine rewards accorded for this pious act would go on being counted as if he were still in the habit of listening to the Qur'ān every day.

In the second place, people cannot be afflicted with disabilities as a punishment for sins committed by others. This thesis is advanced by the Qur'ān which repeatedly states that everyone is responsible for his/her own acts and cannot be burdened by the consequences of others' sins (e.g. 6:164, 17:15, 35:18, 39:07, 53:38). Commentaries on these Qur'anic verses show that this is a point of agreement not only among the advocates of the median approach but among Muslim scholars in general.[277] On the Qur'anic verse 6:164, the well-known Qur'ān exegete Abū 'Abd Allāh al-Qurṭubī (d. 671/1272) said that the occasion of revelation was to rectify the pre-Islamic (*jāhilī*) custom of punishing people for offences committed by their parents, children or allies.[278] According to Ibn al-Qayyim, one of the main tenets of Islamic belief is that no one is punished if they have not committed a sin.[279] Hence, punishing someone for someone else's sins is injustice and it is impossible for God to be unjust (*ẓālim*).[280] Interestingly, a number of noted scholars such as Ibn Ḥazm (d. 456/1064) and the Ḥanbalī theologian Mar'ī b. Yūsuf al-Karmī (d. 1033/1624)[281] ridiculed those who maintained that children might be afflicted with disabilities so that their parents could gain more rewards from God. They said that it is impossible for God to do so because it would be injustice (*jawr*) and futility (*'abath*).[282] Consequently, the belief among some Muslim parents that their disabled child is a punishment for sins committed by one or both of them is contrary to the clear text of the Qur'ān. Where does this common belief come from?

It could perhaps come from the references in a number of Islamic sources, although very few, to this possibility. Vardit Rispler-Chaim was right when she described the viewpoint expressed in a publication from Iran as an 'exception' in modern Islamic literature. The author of this book, a certain Qudsiyah Hijazi (a psychologist or sociologist, according to Rispler-Chaim), claimed causality between the parents' misconduct and their offspring's disability and regarded this outcome as a punishment from God.[283] Ignoring the divine laws, the author elaborated, concerning proper sexual conduct leads to the birth of retarded children. To her, the parents' genes are influenced by their emotions, thoughts, moods and actions and thus immoral behaviour is bound to affect the fetus.[284] The viewpoint, as recorded by Rispler-Chaim, is really an 'exception' in the sense that it contradicts the abovementioned quotations from the Qur'ān and the contentions of Muslim scholars. However, it is not an 'exception' in the sense that Qudsiyah Hijazi is not the only person to hold this view. The late Egyptian scholar, Aḥmad al-Sharabāṣī (1918–1980), also stated explicitly that sinful parents may be punished by having blind children. To him, such a punishment is a disciplinary warning to parents always to avoid disobeying God because His punishment may strike the children who are most beloved to them.[285] Interestingly, the same author rejected a historical report maintaining that someone went blind because his grandfather angered a pious man who entreated God to make him and his offspring blind. Al-Sharabāṣī cast doubt on the authenticity of this report and commented, 'Then what is the guilt of the children as long as the sinner is the father himself?!'[286] Al-Sharabāṣī's question remains unanswered both by him and by all those who claim that children's disability may be a punishment for sinful parents.

*2.4.1.2 Gaining reward (*taḥṣīl al-thawāb*) and gaining an elevated rank (*raf' al-darajāt*)*

Besides expiating sins, two other closely interrelated *ḥikam* were mentioned: gaining reward and upgrading one's level of faith, and enabling the person who suffered to attain a lofty rank in Paradise.[287]

As for gaining reward (*taḥṣīl al-thawāb*), a number of prophetic traditions clearly indicated that afflictions can be a source of bountiful reward from God. For instance, the Prophet is reported to have said, 'The magnitude of reward is contingent upon the magnitude of the affliction.'[288] In another tradition, he said, 'Nothing befalls the believer even if it were being pricked with a thorn but Allah records thereby [the reward of] a good deed (*ḥasana*) for him or expiates a sin for him.'[289]

As for 'gaining an elevated the rank', disability as a form of affliction and concomitant suffering were seen as possible means of attaining a lofty rank in Paradise that would have been unattainable by good deeds only. A large number of prophetic traditions were also said to carry this meaning and some traditionists collected these traditions in a discrete chapter entitled '*Bāb bulūgh al-darajāt bi al-ibtilā*' (Chapter on Attaining the [Honourable] Ranks by Affliction)[290] or *Dhikr anna Allāh yarfa' darajāt al-mu'min bimā yuṣībuh min al-balā'* (Mentioning that Allah Elevates the Status of the Believers by the Afflictions that Befall them).[291]

In his commentary on the aforementioned Qur'anic verse (42:30), al-Bayḍāwī (d. *c.* 685/1286)[292] said, 'This verse applies only to people who indulged in guilt and misdeeds. As for the others, misfortunes befall them for other reasons such as gaining the great reward.'[293] Al-Suyūṭī (1445–1505) added elevation through the ranks.[294] On the same lines as al-Bayḍāwī, another authority said, 'Allah visits people He loves with affliction so that He will give them reward in return.'[295]

However, al-Qāḍī 'Iyāḍ (d. 544/1149)[296] claimed that some scholars maintained that sickness only expiates sins, excluding the possibility that it could lead to reward or elevation through the religious ranks. According to al-Nawawī (d. 676/1277), such scholars reached this conclusion because they were unaware of the aforementioned prophetic traditions which explicitly indicated that sickness can also be a cause of rewards and elevation through the religious ranks.[297] In a bid to reconcile these two contradictory claims, Ibn Ḥajar al-'Asqalānī said that it is possible that sickness and pain are means of atonement for the sinful and means of gaining rewards and a high religious rank for those who have committed no sins. Because the overwhelming majority of humans err, Ibn Ḥajar added, some scholars said that sickness can be conceived as a means of expiating sin only.[298]

The most famous examples of people whose affliction gained them greater reward and a higher rank in Paradise rather than expiation of sins, are the prophets.[299] They are sent by God to symbolize obedience and piety among humans and thus their sins are minimal.[300] That is why some scholars excluded the possibility that the sufferings of the Prophet Job (*Ayyūb*) could be interpreted as a means of expiation for the sins he had committed.[301] It is noteworthy in this regard that Muslim scholars do not agree on whether prophets can be afflicted with disabilities.[302] Beyond their disagreements on various details, Islamic sources spoke of a number of Prophets who were visited by afflictions, some of which could be classified as disabilities.[303] For instance, in their commentary on the Qur'anic verse 12:84, a number of Muslim scholars said that the Prophet Jacob (*Ya 'qūb*) suffered from extremely weak eyesight and according to some was even blind for six years, after which his eyesight was miraculously restored.[304] According to some scholars, the Prophet Shua'yb was also afflicted with blindness.[305] Ibn Ḥajar al-'Asqalānī related that the Prophet Job (*Ayyūb*) was the first victim of smallpox.[306] In their commentary on the Qur'anic verses 20:25–28, a number of Qur'ān exegetes opined that the Prophet Moses had a speech disability, lisping according to some traditions. Being commanded by God to go to the Pharaoh and convey the message of the faith to him, Moses asked God to cure this disability.[307]

2.4.1.3 A test of faith

Testing people to find out whose faith is true and strong is one of the central themes in the Qur'ān (2:214, 3:141, 154, 9:126, 21:35, 29:02, 49:03, 76:02, 89:15, 16) and thus in Islamic sources as well.[308] Words such as *fitna, miḥna, tamḥīṣ, ibtilā'* and *imtiḥān* and their derivatives are used interchangeably to convey this concept. The primary meaning of these terms revolves around 'putting to the proof, a discriminatory test as gold is tested by fire'.[309] A sagacious statement was, 'O my son! Gold and silver are to be examined by fire but the believer is to be examined by affliction.'[310]

In this vein, interpreting disability as one of many afflictions that may befall people as a test by God of His servants' faith is the most obvious answer provided by early and late Muslim scholars.

The Prophet is reported to have said,

> Truly God may test you with an affliction (*balā'*) the same as you may test your gold with fire. As a result, some people will come out of it [i.e. affliction] as pure gold. These are the persons whom God has guarded against doubts (*shubuhāt*). [Others] will come out [with a result] less than this. These are the ones who had doubts. The last will come out like black gold. These are the ones who failed the test.[311]

According to Ibn al-Qayyim, one of the main functions of this life was to serve as a transient abode for *taklīf* (charging) where people are tested by means of various difficulties, ups and downs, pains and pleasures, etc. to establish to what extent they are obedient to the commandments of their Creator in different situations. On the basis of such tests, people are admitted to Paradise (the abode of pure pleasure) or Hell (the abode of pure pain) in the Hereafter.[312]

Ibn al-Jawzī divided people, on the basis of their response to affliction (*al-balā'*), into four main categories arranged in ascending order. First are those who consider *al-balā'* an easy test compared with its ensuing reward. Second are those who compare God's imposing *al-balā'* on people with an owner disposing of his own possessions as he wants – something to which they have to submit without objection. Third are those who are so overwhelmed by the love of God that they do not even ask for *al-balā'* to be lifted. Finally, the highest group comprises those who savour *al-balā'* because it comes from the Will of God.[313]

The magicians of the Pharaoh who believed in the God of Moses and publicly declared their disbelief in the Pharaoh as god are central to the theme of disability. The Pharaoh, according to the Qur'ān (e.g. 7:124, 10:83, 20:71), tried to test the strength of their faith by his threat to cut off their hands and feet on opposite sides. According to some Qur'ān exegetes, the Pharaoh was the first person in history to impose such a punishment. However, the magicians stood fast and the Pharaoh's threats did not make them change their faith. These people, the exegetes added, started their day as magicians and finished it as martyrs.[314]

The test of faith argument is also very common among modern Muslim scholars.[315] In his study on the wise purposes of creating diseases, Zuhayr Muḥammad al-Zamīlī mentioned *tamḥīs al-mu'minīn* (testing the believers) as the first possible wise purpose (*ḥikma*).[316] In al-Būṭī's presentation, it was classified as the second *ḥikma*. Had life been created free of calamities and misfortunes, al-Būtī explained, man's *taklīf* (legal liability) would be meaningless. The sincere believer and the hypocrite would then both be able to proclaim their love of God in the absence of any serious instrument to test the sincerity of their love. Calamities and misfortunes are the main instruments by which one's endurance for the sake of God and submission to His will can be measured.[317] However, al-Zamīlī broadened the scope of the test of faith (*ibtilā'* or *tamḥīs*) to include not only those afflicted with calamity but those living with it, including their immediate families and society at large. A sick person is a test for his own family and society to find out who will take the responsibility of care for such a dependent person and who will give him a helping hand. Sick people constitute a criterion by which the goodness of their society can be measured.[318]

*2.4.2 Afflictions befalling those without legal liability (non-***mukallafūn***)*

Advocates of the median approach were sometimes very timid in their search for the *ḥikam* of disabilities and other afflictions befalling the non-*mukallafūn* such as children and animals. Some of them said that providing discursive reasoning and justifications is possible only for what befalls the *mukallafūn*. As for pain and illnesses afflicting the non-*mukallafūn*, it is sufficient to state that inscrutable wisdom and unknown wise purposes lie behind them but they cannot be discerned by the human intellect. Delving into this fraught issue, they continued, could entail serious misunderstandings, aberrations, deviations and perversities.[319] However, such arguments did not stop other advocates of this approach from investigating this subtle issue in a search for possible wise purposes.

2.4.2.1 A proof of God's existence and oneness

The existence of evil and abnormalities in life is a proof that God exists and that He alone has created this life and all creatures therein. This argument is peculiarly Maturidian and, according to some researchers, no earlier philosophers or theologians are known to have advanced such an argument.[320]

In his book *Kitāb al-tawḥīd* (Book of Oneness), Abū Manṣūr al-Māturīdī (d. *c*. 333/944) elaborated this argument in a chapter entitled *Al-Dalīl 'alā anna li al-'ālam Muḥdith* (The Evidence that the Cosmos Has One Who Gave It Temporal Existence). We quote here what is of particular interest to our topic:

> And the second proof that the world has one who gave it temporal existence is that, if the world existed by its own essence, no instant in it would be truer *(aḥaqq)* than any other, no state *(ḥāl)* more appropriate *(awlā)* than any other, no characteristic *(ṣifa)* more seemly *(alyaq)* than any other. But, since it exists with instants, states and characteristics which differ from one another, it is proven that it does not exist by its own essence. Furthermore, if it did, it would be possible that each thing would create for itself such states and characteristics as are the best and most beautiful, and so, by doing this, it would be false to say that moral and physical evils exist. But the fact of their existence shows that the existence of the world came about by something other than itself *(bi-ghayrih)*.[321]

Thus, what proves to al-Māturīdī that the cosmos is not self-existent is the presence of 'more' and 'less' degrees therein. The presence of forms of imperfection shows that the universe is not self-existent, i.e. eternal, but rather exists temporally. If it were self-existent, everything would simply be perfect in regard to points of time, states of being and qualities of being. But, in the world as it is, al-Māturīdī noted, this is not the case.[322] No being which had complete control of its own existence would want for itself anything other than the best in all respects. Now, if it were true that each thing were in control of its own existence, it would follow that no one would choose painful disabilities, sufferings or evil in general to take place in life. Since they do, it must mean that beings are not in control of their own existence. Thus the existence of evil, moral and physical, is made the explicit basis for coming to know that there is a God and that He is a Creator.[323]

As for the oneness of God, al-Māturīdī found evidence for this in the fact that there is no single substance whose existence can be related to one quality only, such as harmfulness or benefit, evil or good, or blessing or trial. Rather, each thing is characterized by evil which then can be judged as good from another perspective. Created beings are neither beneficent nor harmful in every state. This, al-Māturīdī added, is proof that whoever directs it all must be one because he can combine aspects of the harmful and the beneficial in the created beings:

> You also see that all substances fall under the category of material and are an assemblage of mutually opposed natural elements whose real nature should lead to mutual aversion and estrangement because mutual hostility exists among them. Were it conceivable that their nature abandon their being together, that would cause the destruction of the whole. Thus, it is proven that the one who directs the union among them must be one, joining them together because of his benevolence toward the world and keeping the potential harm of each one from the other by an act of remarkable wisdom which human imagination cannot comprehend.[324]

In another place, he added,

> Thus, in that creation of things which combine the beneficial and the harmful, there is the wondrous manifestation of His wisdom, that He combines the harmful and the beneficial in one being, as well as good and evil, in spite of the mutually contradictory natures of both, as the indication for His oneness and the testimony that His Lordship is one.[325]

By extension to disability, one may reformulate al-Māturīdī's argument as follows. Man did not create himself, otherwise he would have chosen the best and most perfect form of being which would naturally have been free from any physical or moral defect. Keeping in mind that this is not the case, it is proved that man is created rather than a creator. Additionally, mankind in general comprises able-bodied as well as people with disabilities and each human being can have some body parts which work properly whereas others do not because of a disability. These seeming contradictions which can exist simultaneously in one single being indicate that there must be a higher power that can combine these contradictories in a coherent form which does not lead eventually to the destruction of this being. According to al-Māturīdī, this higher power is God who is the Creator of this world.

In an article published in 1984, Jerome Meric Pessagno said that his research had not discovered any thinker after al-Māturīdī who took up the thread and the style of this argument.[326] However, statements closely related to this argument can still be traced. Al-ʻIzz b. ʻAbd al-Salām (d. 660/1066) opined that knowing the glory and omnipotence of God is the first benefit of being visited by calamities and afflictions.[327] The same meaning may also be clearly traced in the recent writings of more than one Muslim scholar, for example Aḥmad al-Sharabāṣī (1918–1980).[328] Speaking about the wise purposes of the existence of disabilities in life, Muḥammad Mutwallī al-Shaʻrāwī (1911–1988) said,

> The second purpose is for us to recognize that no organ of our bodies acts by its own abilities but only because God has subjected it to us to act as it does. We say 'I see with my eyes.' So God Almighty brought into existence someone who has two eyes but cannot see so that you know that you only see by the power of God, who has given the eye the property of sight. The same applies to walking. God brings into existence people who have two feet but cannot walk, so that we will know that we only walk by the power of God.[329]

The same point is also stressed by al-Būṭī[330] and al-Zamīlī.[331]

2.4.2.2 Realizing God's threats and promises in the world to come

One of the general beliefs in Islam is that God created three abodes: one is composed of pure goodness and pleasure and this is Paradise; the second is composed of pure evil and pain and this is Hell; the third, however, that of worldly life, is composed of contraries and opposites such as good and evil, pain and pleasure, illness and health and so forth.[332]

The advocates of this approach state that one of the aims of creating this worldly life is to give people an idea of the pain prepared for the disobedient and infidels in Hell and the pleasures awaiting the obedient in Paradise.[333] Speaking about children in particular, Ibn al-Qayyim argued that enduring pain and suffering in this life would intensify children's experience of the pleasures of Paradise in the Hereafter. He said,

> Testing pleasures, joys and delights in Paradise after undergoing pains and illnesses in this life is much more pleasant and enjoyable than getting such pleasures without prior experience of pains in this life. For instance, the enjoyment of eating and drinking after extreme hunger and thirst is much greater than the enjoyment of eating and drinking without prior hunger and thirst.[334]

The same argument has been reiterated by modern scholars. For instance, al-Būṭī opined that suffering and pain in this life serve as a recurrent warning to the living that this life is not eternal and that there must be another sort of life which is free from such opposites of health and sickness, richness and poverty, etc.[335]

2.5 Summary

Within the broad framework of evil and pain in life, Muslim theologians have been concerned to explain the logic and rationale of the existence of disabilities although Islam postulates an All-Powerful, All-Just and All-Wise God. The interpretations and justifications provided by Muslim theologians to explain this paradox show a wide range of views. At one extreme, some figures found it almost an insoluble problem and gave statements which were seen by the majority of Muslim scholars as heretical because they detracted from the flawless and perfect character of God. At the other extreme, a group of Sufis and philosophers did not see this issue as a real problem. The Sufis opined that one who knows God well and experiences loving Him will not feel disturbed by having a disability. On the contrary, disability was seen sometimes as a sign of God's love. According to them, the real disability is not listening to the message of God and not following the Straight Path as shown by His messengers and prophets. Philosophers focused on the nature of human life and stated that it is composed of opposites such as richness and poverty, health and sickness, pain and pleasure, etc. Any attempt to remove one of these opposites will make the other meaningless. In short, this life cannot exist without evil, pain or disabilities.

Between these two extremes, the majority of Muslim scholars conceded the existence of a theological problem and thought that attempts should be made to explain and justify the existence of disabilities in life. However, the starting point of all these scholars was that God is perfect and the existence of disabilities or evil in life does not injure this divine perfection. Although they agreed on this general principle, they differed on further details, constituting three main groups.

One group, mainly comprising the Ash'arites, saw the perfection of God in His omnipotence. Within this framework, they opined that the only explanation for the existence of disabilities and all forms of pain and suffering in this life is God's omnipotence. They said that this universe is His own Kingdom and He runs it as He wills. Nothing and no one can stand against His will. To ask Him, why did You do so and why did You not do so is tantamount to breaching the omnipotence and the lordship of God. The human intellect, which is created by God, cannot question the Creator.

The second group, the Mu'tazilites, stated that the perfection of God is mainly represented in His unmatched justice and wisdom rather than His omnipotence. Because of His justice, He granted people freedom to act in life. As part of this freedom, people can do both good and bad deeds. These bad deeds, whose responsibility lies completely with people rather than with God, are the main sources of evil and pain in life. However, this group did not deny that disabilities can be beyond people's control, for example being born blind. They said that God is responsible for such calamities but they are not 'bad' acts because a just and wise God does not perform 'bad' acts. According to this group, all calamities in life, whether caused by man or by God, have one or more wise purposes. Moreover, these purposes can be discerned by the human intellect. Within this framework, this group tried to understand the possible wise purpose of every form of pain or suffering. They eventually came up with very detailed and complicated theories about the benefits people can gain from pain and suffering.

The third group, represented by the majority of Muslim scholars, tried to find a middle way between the first two groups. They opined that God's omnipotence should not be stressed at the expense of His justice and wisdom or vice versa. They saw no harm in the rational attempts made to seek possible wise purposes which can justify the existence of disabilities and other forms of suffering in life. However, they added, making such attempts does not necessarily mean that every case of disability or every form of suffering can be rationally justified in a convincing way. People should always keep in mind that their capacities are limited while God's wisdom is not. Within this framework, this group provided a number of wise purposes most of which were based on scriptural texts from the Qur'ān and Sunna.

3 Practical theology

The main focus of 'theoretical theology' was God and how to advance the rational arguments which prove that the existence of disability does not put the perfect character of God into doubt. However, in 'practical theology', the main theme is the person who lives with a disability and how to gain spiritual serenity and enjoy life given this condition.

Scholars who were engaged in writing about spiritual serenity and how to achieve it during times of affliction came mainly from the mystic milieux because healing one's soul was one of the main functions of Sufism. However, there is no reason to believe that the means and methods mentioned below were rejected by scholars who advocated other approaches. The two clearest examples in this regard are the mystic Abū al-Qāsim al-Qushayrī (d. 465/1072) who had an Ash'arī background[1] and the Mu'tazilī scholar al-Zamakhsharī (d. 538/1144),[2] whose book, mentioned below, is relevant to our topic here.

To help those afflicted with calamities to achieve this spiritual serenity, Muslim scholars evolved two main genres of psychologically oriented literature. These writings were meant to appease the bitter sorrow and anguish that can be caused by calamities. Some of them spoke of *'ilāj al-muṣība* (curing the calamity),[3] others of *tasliyat ahl al-maṣā'ib* (consoling people with calamities).[4] Some writings focused on specific calamities, the most familiar of which was the death of one's child.[5] Disabilities, especially blindness, did not escape the attention of writers on this topic, as evidenced by titles such as *Tasliyat al-ḍarīr* (Consoling the Blind) by al-Zamakhsharī, *Ta'jīl al-bishāra li man ṣabar 'alā dhahāb al-baṣar* (Accelerating the Good Omen for Those Who have Patience upon Losing their Eyesight) by the Damascene scholar Muḥammad b. Ṭulūn (1475–1546)[6] and *Tasliyat al-a'mā 'an baliyyat al-'amā* (Consoling the Blind for the Affliction of Blindness) by the Ḥanafī jurist Mullā 'Alī b. Sulṭān al-Harawī al-Qārī (d. *c.* 1605).[7] The Meccan scholar Ibn Fahd (d. 1547) concluded his book on people with disabilities with a chapter on the rewards and blessings accorded to those afflicted by calamity.[8]

Besides this genre whose sources are mostly non-extant or unavailable in printed form, there was the broad mystic genre which is also of direct relevance to the topic of spiritual relief in the event of calamity. In this broad mystic genre, Muslim scholars considered calamities and afflictions as among the obstacles that the servant (*'abd*) undergoes on his journey to the Creator. They elaborated a number of states (*aḥwāl*) and stations (*maqāmāt*) that one should pass by. Three main moral attitudes have been repeatedly mentioned as necessary tools to overcome the repercussions of afflictions and tribulations, namely servitude (*'ubūdiyya*), patience (*ṣabr*) and gratitude (*shukr*). In the first genre, patience and to a lesser extent gratitude were the focal points; to my knowledge, servitude did not play an important role.

In his well-known *Al-Risāla fī 'ilm al-taṣawwuf* (Epistle on Sufism), regarded by many as 'one of the most comprehensive compendiums of Ṣufi thought' and the 'Bible of Sufism',[9] Abū al-Qāsim al-Qushayrī (d. 465/1072) divided the Sufi path into (1) states (*aḥwāl*) and (2) stations (*maqāmāt*); the former are always a gift from God whereas the latter can be reached, to a certain extent, by one's own efforts. However, both were indispensable to the Sufi path.[10] Servitude (*'ubudiyya*) was the first state in al-Qushayrī's presentation,[11] and it serves here as the starting point for the seekers of spiritual relief among those afflicted with disabilities or other forms of suffering. Ibn Taymiyya (d. 728/1328) also wrote a short epistle on this topic entitled *Risāla fī al-'ubūdiyya* (Epistle on Servitude).[12] Although he did not classify it as one of the states, the Ḥanbalī theologian and jurist Ibn al-Qayyim (d. 751/1350) studied servitude extensively in his Sufi treatise and opined that all stations and states that one has to pass by are but branches and reflections of servitude.[13] This concept is still prominent among Sufi orders such as the Shādhiliyya which is mainly based on deep immersion in this state of *'ubūdiyya*.[14] Recent interest in this topic is clear from the comments, summaries and elaborations made by modern Muslim scholars of the viewpoints of Ibn Taymiyya and Ibn al-Qayyim in this regard.[15]

According to al-Qushayrī, patience and gratitude belong to the stations.[16] These two moral attitudes were classical topics presented in almost every mystical treatise.[17] The most comprehensive treatment comes from the hand of Ibn al-Qayyim who dedicated a whole book to the two topics.[18] This book is the main source of the following discussion. Patience and gratitude are currently fashionable subjects for religious sermons (*khuṭab*) which are available as audiotapes and sometimes as printed books.[19] A well-known book written recently on the topic of patience is *Al-Ṣabr fī al-Qur'ān* (Patience in the Qur'ān) by Yūsuf al-Qaraḍāwī.[20]

3.1 Servitude (*'ubūdiyya*)

According to al-'Izz b. 'Abd al-Salām (d. 660/1066), realizing one's servitude to God is one of the main benefits of being visited by calamities.[21] The main meaning of servitude is conceding that man in this universe is but a poor servant (*'abd faqīr*) who is always in need of his Lord (*rabb*). Al-Qushayrī quoted his master saying, 'Just as "lordship" is an eternal quality of God (may He be exalted), so is "servitude" a quality of man that stays with him as long as he lives.'[22] Scholars' favourite analogy for this type of relationship is the ordinary man who is always raising objections to the work of physicians or engineers on the grounds that there is no point in doing this and omitting that, because he cannot understand much of what they do.[23] In such a case, a wise person has the right to investigate the efficiency of the physician or the engineer he wants to deal with but once he has made sure that the individual is trustworthy, it is no longer wise, and may even be boorish, to ask stupid questions and make objections about every detail. In the same vein, the servant (*'abd*) should believe in God on the basis of a firm conviction that God is the only and real Lord who can run his affairs and take care of him in the best way. Once the *'abd* has acquired this belief, he would be foolish to think that God has to explain the rationale of every delightful and sorrowful incident in his life. It is sufficient to be sure that it is good (*khayr*). Hard times make it clear who is living in a state of servitude and who is not.[24]

According to al-Qushayrī, a mystical authority is reported to have said, 'Worship is for those who strive, servitude is for those who excel in bearing hardships.' A mystic was asked, 'When is servitude sound?' He replied, 'When a man surrenders himself completely to his Master and has patience with Him in the tribulations He imposes.'[25] This explains the intense fear of the many early pious figures (*salaf*) of falling into the pit of questioning God, out of doubt or objection, about what He had foreordained for them. In this regard, one of them is reported to have said, 'To get my flesh gnawed by scissors, is more beloved to me than saying to something that God predestined, had he better not predestined it!'[26]

Total submission to God's will should be adopted, while investigating one's affairs in the search for possible errors in one's relations with God. When a calamity befalls a Muslim, he should level the first charge against himself, whether he has fallen short in his observance of the Islamic instructions.[27] *Imam* Abū al-Ḥasan al-Qaṭṭān[28] (254–345/868–956) is reported to have said, 'I have been visited with affliction in my eyesight as a punishment for speaking too much[29] during the journey [of searching for knowledge].'[30] To avoid any further deterioration, the sinful person was always advised to make an immediate serious and ongoing attempt to give up such sins.[31] In his book *Al-Kabā'ir* (Grave Sins), Shams al-Dīn al-Dhahabī (748/1348)[32] told a story whose message coincides with the aforementioned thesis. The story is about an unnamed influential person who misused his political position by oppressing a poor fisherman and taking his fish illegally. Feeling the bitterness of this injustice, the fisherman supplicated God by saying, 'O God! This one took advantage of his power and my weakness and unjustly took what you provided me with. Show me what Your Power can do to him.' The unjust person was given a painful bite on the thumb by the fish so he went to the doctor who diagnosed his case as gangrene and said, the thumb must be amputated. Although the infected thumb was amputated, the gangrene continued spreading and consequently the man's palm, forearm and later on his whole arm were amputated one by one. Knowing the background to the man's sickness, some people advised him to go to the fisherman himself and ask forgiveness, lest the gangrene spread throughout his body. He went to the oppressed fisherman, and kissed his foot, cried and asked for forgiveness. Having been forgiven by the fisherman, he also declared his repentance (*tawba*) to God to save himself from such suffering later in his life.[33]

Fearing that servitude would be restricted to passive acts, the Ḥanbalī scholar Ibn Taymiyya stressed that making use of all possible means to combat life's afflictions is an essential element of paying service to God (*'ubūdiyya*).[34] This notion was further elaborated by modern scholars who stressed the importance of positive acts as an essential element of servitude. Speaking about accepting God's predestination of illnesses and afflictions, al-Būṭī reproached those who think that this acceptance of and surrender to God's will implied passivity. Adopting a passive attitude towards affliction and ignoring means of resisting it or minimizing its repercussions amount, according to al-Būṭī, to rebellion against God's predestination and disrespect for the universal norms and natural laws He has enacted in life.[35] According to al-Qaraḍāwī, one of the fruits of belief in God's predestination is moving towards performing more fuitful and constructive activities in life instead of just experiencing passive regret and sorrow.[36] In order to encourage people with disabilities to remain positive and to overcome their disabilities, modern scholars have frequently recalled prominent figures whose disabilities did not stop them participating in the development of their societies. The Moroccan scholar Muṣṭafā b. Ḥamza said, 'So were the disabled Muslims peerless. They gained science, literature, wisdom and virtue and left behind them a good reputation and excellent stories.'[37] The Syrian scholar Sa'dī Abū Jayb said that the number of such prominent figures throughout Islamic history is countless.[38] Recently a separate genre telling the stories of such figures, and depending heavily on a number of early sources in Islamic history,[39] has come into existence.[40]

3.2 Patience (*ṣabr*)

Ṣabr is usually rendered as 'patience', 'endurance'. According to Arabic lexicographers, the root *ṣ-b-r*, of which *ṣabr* is the *nomen actionis*, means to restrain or bind.[41] There is an expression in Arabic, 'so-and-so was killed *ṣabran*', which means that he was captured and detained until he died. In the spiritual sense, patience means to stop ourselves from despairing and panicking, to stop our tongues from complaining, and to stop our hands from striking our faces and tearing our clothes at times of grief and stress.[42]

Practising *ṣabr* at the time of being afflicted with a disability or any other sort of calamity is seen not only as one of the noble principles that man can engage in, showing his chivalry or manliness. It is also a religious duty that every Muslim has to observe.[43] According to Ibn al-Qayyim, patience is *farḍ* (obligatory),[44] God has provided people with ways and means of obtaining and strengthening the quality of patience, for He has never instructed them to do something without providing them with ways and means of achieving it.[45] Here two main means of acquiring patience are quoted from Ibn al-Qayyim.

The *first* means is, if one does not naturally possess the characteristic of patience, to act as if one does, until it eventually becomes second nature.[46] The Prophet is reported to have said, 'Whoever tries to be patient, God will help him to be patient.'[47] The *second* means is to seek the help of God. To possess the characteristic of patience, especially 'patience for the sake of God' which is one of the highest grades of *ṣabr*, one has to seek the help of God. The Qur'ān says, 'And do thou be patient, for thy patience is but from God' (16:127).[48] Thus man should realize that he has no patience himself and no power to acquire patience. Rather, he knows that 'there is no power and no strength except by the help of God.'[49] It would be felicitous to quote here Ibn al-Qayyim's advice on how to maintain patience at times of trial and adversity. According to him, patience during difficult times may be achieved by:

1. Thinking of the good reward that lies ahead. The more one believes in the rewards that are waiting, the easier it becomes to have patience. If it were not for the anticipation of the rewards, no goals or objectives pertaining to this life or the Hereafter would be achieved. Human nature loves instant gratification, but reason and maturity make one think of the long-term outcome. This helps to strengthen patience in enduring whatever one faces, whether or not there is a choice.
2. Expecting and hoping for a time of ease. This hope in itself offers a measure of immediate relief.
3. Thinking of God's countless blessings. When one realizes that one cannot enumerate the blessings of God, it becomes easier for a person to exercise patience in facing the current adversity, because present troubles are like a raindrop compared to the vast ocean of God's blessings and favours.
4. Thinking of previous blessings of God. This will remind one of God's care, and strengthen one's hopes and expectations for a time of ease to come.[50]

Practising patience in general has been elaborated and extolled in myriads of Qur'anic verses[51] and prophetic traditions.[52] Great and matchless rewards are dedicated to those who endure patiently when afflicted by specific sorts of illnesses that could be counted as disabilities such as epilepsy and blindness.

There is the famous story of the epileptic woman who asked the Prophet for his supplication (*du'ā'*) for her healing; he replied to her that, if she refrained from her request and exercised *ṣabr*, paradise would be her portion.[53]

Compilers of prophetic traditions dedicated specific sections to the virtues and rewards of patiently enduring the affliction of blindness.[54] To quote one of the most famous texts in this respect: 'If I test My servant (*'abdī*) by depriving him of his two precious ones [his eyes or eyesight] and he faces that with patient perseverance, I shall compensate him with Paradise.'[55]

It must be pointed out that laudable *ṣabr* in Islam was seen as patience practised at the right time and not after it is too late.[56] At any rate, everyone must exercise patience in order to face difficulties, whether willingly or unwillingly. The noble person, Ibn al-Qayyim elaborated, exercises patience willingly, because he realizes the benefits of patience and he knows that he will be rewarded for his patience and will be criticized if he panics. He is aware that if he does not have patience, panicking and impatience will not help him to regain missed opportunities, and will not take away things he dislikes. Whatever is decreed by God cannot be prevented from happening, and whatever is decreed not to happen cannot be made to happen. So an attitude of impatience and panic actually causes harm. A wise man said: 'A man with wisdom does, as soon as adversity appears, that which a foolish man does after a month [i.e. he resorts to patience].'[57] On the other hand, the ignoble man exercises patience only when he realizes that he has no choice. After wasting a lot of time and energy in panic and struggle, he realizes that his impatience will not help him. Then he exercises patience in the same way as a person who has been tied up to be whipped exercises patience.[58] The patience of such people is as useless as the patience of those people screaming and crying out in Hell, 'Neither panic nor patience will help us now. There is no escape for us' (Qur'ān 14:21).[59]

Within the context of practising patience at times of affliction and adversity and the rewards attached to it, Ibn al-Qayyim spoke of two main misunderstandings that should be pointed out and corrected.

The *first* misunderstanding is that there is no contradiction between being patient on the one hand and crying out and complaining to God on the other.[60] This is not going to diminish the rewards of patience. Several of the Prophets have complained to God at times of affliction. Jacob (*Ya'qūb*) said '*ṣabrun jamīl*', which means 'patience is most fitting for me'; then he said, 'I only complain of my distraction and anguish to God' (Qur'ān 12:86). The Qur'ān also says of Job (*Ayyūb*), 'And (remember) Ayyūb (Job), when he cried to his Lord, "Truly distress has seized me."' (21:83). Ibn al-Qayyim said that even the Prophet Muḥammad, the epitome of patience, prayed to his Lord: 'O God, I complain to You of my weakness and helplessness.'[61] However, complaining to people, either directly through words, or indirectly through the way we look and behave, is contradictory to patience.[62]

The *second* misunderstanding is that a time of good health and ease is better than that of illness and adversity. This does not contradict the prophetic tradition that 'no one has ever been given a better gift than patience' because this means after a trial has befallen a person. But ease is still better.[63] The real spirit of Islam is to ask God to provide you with good health (*al-'āfiya*) in this world and in the Hereafter. In concrete incidents the Prophet guided people to this spirit of Islam. It was related that he paid a visit to a man who was so sick that he looked like a nestling bird. The Prophet asked him, 'What was your supplication [to God]? Did not you ask your Lord for good health *(al-'āfiyah)*?' The man said, 'I used to say, "O God, what you are going to punish me with in the Hereafter, make it happen rapidly in this world." The Prophet said, "Glory to God! You cannot stand it. Would not you say 'O God! Give us good in this world and good in the Hereafter."'[64] According to some narrations of this ḥadīth, after having performed this *du'ā'*, the man was restored to health in only a few days.[65]

We conclude the discussions on patience by citing the story of 'Urwa Ibn al-Zubayr (d. *c*. 93/711),[66] always regarded as one of the most moving stories in the context of showing patience in the case of calamity. It has been chosen here because it also has something to do with disability in particular.

'Urwa Ibn al-Zubayr got gangrene in his leg, and the doctors suggested that it should be amputated, lest the gangrene spread to the rest of his body and kill him. 'Urwa agreed and the doctors asked him whether he would drink intoxicants to ease the pain. He said, 'God is testing me to see the extent of my patience. How could I go against His commands?'[67] The doctors began to amputate his leg, using a saw. When the saw reached the bone, 'Urwa fainted, and when he came around, sweat was pouring down his face, and he was repeating, 'There is no god but Allah. Allah is the Greatest.' When the operation was over, he picked up his leg and kissed it, then said, 'I swear by the One Who mounted me on you, I never used you to walk to any place of wrong action or to any place where God would not like me to be.' Then he gave instructions that the leg should be washed, perfumed, wrapped in a cloth and buried in the Muslim graveyard. When people went to offer him their condolences, the only reply he made was to quote from the Qur'ān: 'truly we have suffered much fatigue at our journey' (18:62). Later on, one of his friends came to visit him and said, 'May your enemies' fathers perish!' and 'Show me the affliction for which I have come to console you.' 'Urwa uncovered his stump, and his friend said, 'By God, we were not preparing you to wrestle! God has saved most of you: your sanity, your tongue, your eyesight, your two hands, and one of your two legs.' 'Urwa told him, 'Nobody has consoled me as you have.'

3.3 Gratitude (*shukr*)

Shukr denotes a state of feeling gratefulness because of a benefaction or favour (*ni'ma*) and showing the effect of having that *ni'ma*.[68] Thus originally *shukr* is a response to blessings and that is why its opposite is called *kufr* (ingratitude).[69] Consequently, everybody should practise *shukr* when enjoying luxuries. However, showing *shukr* in the case of calamity is something to be practised by those of real piety and real understanding (*fiqh*) and is thus of a higher status. A well-known conversation between two Muslim scholars known for their piety and deep sincerity could elaborate this point.

Shaqīq al-Balkhī (d. 194/809),[70] came from Khurāsān to visit Ibrāhīm b. Adham (d. 162/778)[71] in Iraq. On seeing Ibrāhīm b. Adham, Shaqīq al-Balkhī asked him about the current state of his indigent compatriots. In a bid to praise them, Ibrāhīm b. Adham replied, 'When God sends them something they eat it and are grateful, if not, they endure patiently and refrain from begging.' Whereupon Shaqīq replied, 'This is how I left our dogs in Balkh.'[72] Thereupon Ibrāhīm b. Adham asked him about the state of poor people in Khurāsān. Shaqīq answered, 'When they have anything they prefer others to themselves [i.e. they give it away]. If not, they occupy themselves with giving thanks.' On hearing this answer, Ibrāhīm b. Adham kissed Shaqīq's head and said, 'You are right, master!'[73] This story clearly shows the higher rank of those who offer thanks at times of adversity or calamity.

Although practising gratitude in times of affliction is described as a wild bird that one can hardly catch and fetter, Ibn al-Qayyim confirmed that it can still be made possible by two main means.

First, remember the other untold blessings provided by God that one is enjoying. This principle is experienced in the following story retold by the Companion Salmān al-Fārisī (d. *c*. 36/656):[74]

> There was a man who was given many of the luxuries of this world, and then they were taken away from him. But he continued to praise and thank God

> until everything had been taken from him, even his bed. He then still praised and thanked God. Another man, who had also been given many of the luxuries of this world, asked him, 'What are you praising and thanking God for?' The man said, 'I am praising and thanking Him for blessings which, if others asked me to give them in return for all that they have, I would never give them up.' 'What can they be?' asked the second man. 'Can't you see?' asked the first man. 'I have my eyesight, my tongue, my hands, my feet.'[75]

Muslim scholars also state that man should firmly believe that his deeds cannot pay for even one of the blessings of God, because even the smallest of God's blessings and favours far outweighs the deeds of man.[76]

The *second* means to help man practise gratitude during adversity is to keep in mind that blessings always assume the guise of afflictions. One of the scholars defined gratitude as follows, 'To imagine the rose from the thorn and to imagine the non-visible part to be the whole.'[77] Those who knew this fact and instilled it into the depth of their hearts did not see much difference between those times when they enjoyed luxuries and other times when these luxuries were kept away from them. That is why Sufyān al-Thawrī (97–126/715–743)[78] said, 'He does not understand religion properly who does not count affliction as a blessing and ease as a disaster.'[79]

Attaining such a degree of *shukr* was seen as closely connected with two other highly praised Islamic moral principles: *riḍā*[80] and love of God. *Shukr* is related to *riḍā*, which means not patient tolerance of all the vicissitudes of life but happiness in the bitterness of the affliction. The well-known mystic Dhunnūn (d. 859)[81] said, '*Riḍā* is the joy of the heart in the bitterness of the divine decree.'[82] However, *riḍā* itself, as observed by 'Alī b. 'Uthmān al-Hujwīrī (d. *c.* 1071), is the result of love in the sense of being content with what is done by the beloved.[83] In their love of God, people practise two main types of love, purposive love (*hubb gharaḍī*) and pure love (*ḥubb ḥaqīqī*).[84] In the first type, people love God for the divine beneficence and favours that people cannot even fully count. Ibn al-Qayyim elaborated on this type of love by saying,

> How then would such a one [God] not be loved, and how should man not blush to direct a particle of his love to an object other than Him? Who is more worthy of praise and love than He? This unmerited kindness of which man is the recipient is visible to all and it is the gate through which one must pass to enter into a relationship of love with God.[85]

However, to love God as a benefactor is only a first step on the way and never a destination. That is because love for beneficence alone is inherently inadequate since it comes to an end when the benefactor ceases to bestow his favour.[86] By extension, those who love God only because He provided them with good health will cease to love Him once they fall sick or are afflicted with disabilities.

Hence purposive love should be seen only as a gate to pure love. Based on what he has known of the goodness of the Creator, the lover may infer what he does not know. 'God calls men to Himself through this gate. So that when they enter it, they are called through the other – the Gate of Names and Attributes through which pass only the elite.'[87] There is no doubt that love for God as Perfect and Beautiful is a higher stage than love in response to His kindness.[88] Furthermore, God alone may rightly be loved as an end in Himself. All other objects of love, therefore, must be loved only for the sake of God.[89]

Those who practise this type of love – pure love – are also those who give thanks and show gratitude even at times of affliction because they believe that whatever comes from the lover is something to be loved. The well-known Companion, Sa'd b. Abī Waqqāṣ (d. 55/675), was famous for his accepted supplication to God (*al-du'ā' al-mustajāb*) and people used to ask him to pray for them. People deemed it strange that being blind, he did not pray God to give him back his eyesight. Asked about this seemingly eccentric behaviour, he smiled and said, 'The divine predestination is more beloved to me than my eyesight.'[90]

3.4 Summary

This chapter showed that Muslim scholars did not restrict themselves to theological attempts to answer the question: why do disabilities exist? There was also another practical and pragmatic dimension to dealing with the question: how can we live with disabilities? Proposals provided by Muslim scholars in this respect were mainly psychological in nature. They tried to come up with a practical recipe that would wipe out or at least diminish the sorrow and anguish that people may suffer because of disability. The various discussions have been summed up in this chapter under three main headings, servitude (*'ubūdiyya*), patience (*ṣabr*) and gratitude (*shukr*). Servitude was presented as the starting point by which the afflicted person recognizes that he/she is a servant (*'abd*) created by a Creator who takes full care of His creatures. Practising this type of servitude should make it easy for the afflicted person to progress to patience and then finally to gratitude. Scholars were aware of the fact that taking these moral stances at times of affliction is by no means easy. Hence, they evolved different instruments and devised many practical suggestions to bring these virtues within the reach of common Muslims.

Part II

Islamic jurisprudence

4 Human dignity of people with disabilities

Influence of physiognomy?

The dignity of people with disabilities is very central to current discussions on these people's rights. As early as 1975, the UN Declaration on the Rights of Disabled Persons stressed that,

> Disabled persons have the inherent right to respect for their human dignity. Disabled persons, whatever the origin, nature and seriousness of their handicaps and disabilities, have the same fundamental rights as their fellow-citizens of the same age, which implies first and foremost the right to enjoy a decent life, as normal and full as possible.[1]

The recent UN document on the subject, the Convention on the Rights of Persons with Disabilities, declares in its first principle that 'the purpose of the present Convention is to promote, protect and ensure the full and equal enjoyment of all human rights and fundamental freedoms by all persons with disabilities, and to promote respect for their inherent dignity'.[2]

Broadly speaking, early and modern Muslim scholars have been unanimous on the fact that dignity is a proven right conferred by God on every human being, irrespective of colour, race or religion. For instance, al-Alūsī (d. 1270/1854) stated that 'everyone and all members of the human race, including the pious and the sinner, are endowed with dignity, nobility and honour whose magnificence cannot be exclusively expounded and identified'.[3] The same sentiment can be found in statements attributed both to the Companions of the Prophet and to modern scholars.[4]

The main hypothesis of this chapter is that discussions of Muslim jurists on physiognomy (*firāsa*) were central to their understanding of the dignity of people with disabilities. Concerning physiognomy in general, the late Youssef Mourad (1902–1966),[5] the late 'Abd al-Karīm 'Adiyy (1917–1985),[6] Robert Hoyland (University of St Andrews) and Antonella Ghersetti (Università Ca' Foscari, Venice) are the four main modern researchers who have made valuable contributions to the study of physiognomy as a topic in Arabic and Islamic literature.[7] Recently Simon Swain edited an insightful study on the influence of Polemon's physiognomy from classical antiquity to medieval Islam.[8] Apart from cursory references to juristic sources in the aforementioned studies, this chapter represents the first attempt to combine physiognomy on the one hand and jurists' views of people with disabilities on the other hand.

The focus here is on the standpoints of Muslim jurists towards physiognomy and its influence on the dignity of people with disabilities within two main legal schools, the Shāfi'ī and the Ḥanbalī. The available information has imposed this choice. Outside these two schools, pertinent information was scanty and within the Ḥanafī school it was almost non-existent. However, a note in passing is given at the end of the chapter to clarify the standpoints of other schools in the light of the available information.

As regards the Shāfi'ī school, available sources indicate clearly that a number of Shāfi'ī jurists were impressed by the newly introduced science of Greek physiognomy and its practical benefits. They were advocates of this new science and wrote important books in which they did not fail to find arguments from the Qur'ān and Sunna defending physiognomy or at least its main premise of 'inference from physical makeup about nature/disposition/character' (*al-istidlāl bi al-khalq 'alā al-khuluq*).[9] One of the early texts, which may be an allusion to this premise, was written by the prolific Shāfi'ī scholar, Abū Ḥāmid al-Ghazālī (d. 505/1111):

> The exterior form that is attractive to look at is the surest indication of a virtuous soul, for the light of the soul, when it fully shines, would penetrate the body. That is because the external appearance (*maẓhar*) and the inner nature (*makhbar*) are most often inseparable. This is why the authorities on *firāsa* occupy themselves first with the physical looks when getting to know the internal states of people.[10]

Another context in which al-Ghazālī treated *firāsa* was in his comments on Muslim philosophers such as Ibn Sīnā (Avicenna), who was the first to incorporate physiognomy, *firāsa,* in the Greek sense into the recognized Islamic sciences. In his *Maqāṣid al-falāsifa* (Objectives of the Philosophers), al-Ghazālī mentioned the categorization of the sciences compiled by Ibn Sīnā. However, al-Ghazālī listed them in a different order and omitted some, such as *al-firāsa*.[11] In *Tahāfut al-falāsifa* (Incoherence of the Philosophers), al-Ghazālī mentioned the categorization of sciences including *firāsa* in the Greek sense. Al-Ghazālī's comment was that 'the Sacred Law does not require a dispute over them except on a few points which we have mentioned'.[12] None of the critical points raised by al-Ghazālī tackled *firāsa*.[13] A list of important writers who wrote discrete books or treatises on this science would include Fakhr al-Dīn al-Rāzī (d. 606/1209),[14] Shams al-Dīn al-Dimashqī (d. 727/1327), Ibn al-Durayhim al-Mawṣilī (d. 762/1360)[15] and Zayn al-'Ābidīn al-Ghumrī (d. 970/1562).[16]

The main issue here is a number of 'physiognomic' statements ascribed to al-Shāfi'ī (d. 205/820) which are full of offensive and discriminatory remarks. The attempt here is to check the authenticity of these statements and see if they were included in the *fiqh* manuals.

Concerning the Ḥanbalī school, the views of four well-known Ḥanbalī jurists are discussed. Those of Ibn al-Jawzī (d. 597/1200)[17] and Ibn al-Qayyim (d. 751/1350)[18] are presented under the heading 'Paradoxical standpoints' because their views, as recorded in their own writings, sometimes supported the principle of physiognomy and sometimes opposed it. The views of Ibn Taymiyya (d. 728/1328)[19] and Zayn al-Dīn Ibn Rajab (d. 795/1393)[20] are presented under the heading 'Counterpoise trials' because, at least within the Ḥanbalī school, they counterbalanced the paradoxical standpoints expressed by Ibn al-Jawzī and Ibn al-Qayyim.

The main Arabic terms which correspond to physiognomy are *firāsa*[21] and, to a lesser extent, *tawassum* which was often used as a synonym of *firāsa*.[22] Tracing the term *firāsa* in Arabic literature reveals four main meanings, each of which can be seen as a distinct category or type of *firāsa*. That *firāsa* did not have a single meaning is plainly stated in modern studies but a clear definition and exposition of these four meanings have always been missing. Keeping in view that a distinction between them is crucial to the argumentation below, an explanation of these four meanings will be given first.

The first meaning of *firāsa* that can be encountered in the earliest Arabic lexicons centres on keen intelligence and astuteness used to understand what is mysterious.[23] The active participle (*fāris*) and the comparative adjective (*afras*) also denote adeptness, proficiency and expertise in a specific aspect of life. The expression *ana afras bi al-rijāl* means 'I am more knowledgeable and more experienced about men'.[24] A particularly famous example of this type of *firāsa* was the judge Iyās b. Mu'āwiya (appointed in 99/717),[25] who was proverbial for his perspicacity. His ability to glean information unnoticed by others and his shrewdness are often praised.[26] This is almost the broadest meaning of *firāsa* and made the term usable for other meanings as well.

The second meaning of *firāsa* was *qiyāfa*, read sometimes as *qāfa*. *Qiyāfa* was of two types, namely *qiyāfat al-athar* and *qiyāfat al-bashar*. *Qiyāfat al-athar* means to track birds, animals and humans through minute scrutiny of the traces that they leave behind, most obviously foot-prints. *Qiyāfat al-bashar* means to establish the paternity or maternity of a child by careful observation of its bodily characteristics and comparison with those of its alleged parent.[27] This second type brings *qiyāfa* very close to the fourth meaning of *firāsa* below.[28] The two terms *qiyāfa* and *firāsa* were usually used as synonyms.[29] *Qiyāfa* was presented in Arabic literature as a typically Arabic achievement and as something to be inherited rather than to be learnt and that is why no books were written on this topic.[30]

The third meaning of *firāsa* is the illuminative or mystic one. The core of this type of *firāsa* is detaching oneself from worldly desires by means of seclusion (*khalwa*), austerity (*riyāḍa*), staying awake at night for performing religious practices and fasting. Regular adoption of such habits would produce visionary experiences or revelations (*mukāshafāt*) by which the practitioner could predict or have knowledge of unseen objects and unknown future events.[31] Islamic mysticism played a central role in developing this meaning and in one way or another making it part of the religion so that a typically Islamic type of *firāsa* evolved. This centres on the pious qualities of the practitioner of *firāsa*. It enables him to receive a light from Allah by which he can penetrate a person's hidden depths – his conscience, innermost thoughts and his past and future.[32] A more detailed definition states,

> *Firāsa* is that which God plants in the hearts of his friends (*awliyā'ih*) so that they may know the internal states of people by a sort of miracle and divination (*bi naw' min al-karāmāt wa iṣābat al-ẓann wa al-ḥads*) for the heart has an eye just as sight does, and whoever has a sound heart-eye and is supported by God's light may gain confirmation of the true essences of things and understanding of the upper world while he remains in the lower world. He perceives what no eye has seen, no ear has heard, and what has never occurred to the heart of any human.[33]

This type of *firāsa* was seen as a talent possessed only by few people, namely the purest of heart.[34] This also meant that any figure renowned for his/her piety or devotion must have been in possession of *firāsa*, a fact immediately obvious from Islamic religious literature.[35] It was called *al-firāsa al-īmāniyya* (intuitive knowledge produced by belief)[36] or *al-firāsa al-ilāhiyya* (intuitive knowledge produced by God)[37] and sometimes in the Sufi literature *al-mukāshafa* (unveiling).[38] This meaning was a product of the religious dimension added to this term by Islam. Its sense has gradually been integrated into the denotations of *firāsa* and its main synonym *tawassum*, just as many other Arabic words were given a new dimension by Islam, such as *ṣalāh, zakāt, ḥajj* and so forth.

They key citation in this context was 'Beware the *firāsa* of the believer for he sees with the light of God.' This adage was classified as a prophetic tradition by the scholars of Ḥadīth but it does not appear in written form until the time when the great collections of the sayings of the Prophet were being put together in the third/ninth century. It seems to be first noted, very cursorily, by the famous compiler al-Bukhārī (d. 256/870) in his *Al-Tārīkh al-kabīr*, and then by his younger contemporary and fellow compiler al-Tirmidhī (d. 279/892), who adds a few brief thoughts of his own:

> The Messenger of God said: 'Beware the *firāsa* of the believer, for he sees with the light of God', and then he recited [the Qur'anic verse]: 'In that are signs for the discerning.' Abū 'Īsā: 'This tradition is rare; we only know of it in this context. It is transmitted on the authority of a number of knowledgeable people regarding the exegesis of this verse "In that are signs for the discerning" [meaning those who practise *firāsa*].'[39]

However, though the saying was not written down until the mid-ninth century, it is evident from Tirmidhī's comment about its explication by 'knowledgeable people' (*ahl al-'ilm*) that it was already known in his day.[40] This meaning was later integrated as one of the main denotations of the term *firāsa*. For instance, the adage 'Beware the *firāsa* of the believer' is also found in the Arabic lexical entries on *firāsa* and *tawassum*.[41] Additionally, this meaning is included in literally hundreds of legal and theological works, particularly those with Sufi leanings.[42] In fact, within Sufi milieux, this type of *firāsa* was the object of the most systematic attempts to define it, establish the conditions to gain it and also divide it into different types.[43]

The fourth meaning is almost identical with the Greek concept of physiognomy. Etymologically, it is derived from three Greek words, *physis* (nature), *nomos* (law) and *gnomon* (judge or interpreter),[44] and conveys assessment of the relationship between physical attributes and personality traits. *Firāsa* in this sense is a tool by which one can determine what a person's corporeal features might tell us about his or her innate character.[45] This type was known as *al-firāsa al-ṭabīʿiyya* (natural physiognomy),[46] *al-firāsa al-insāniyya* (human physiognomy)[47] or *al-firāsa al-ḥikmiyya* (judicious physiognomy).[48] Unlike the Islamic *firāsa*, this type is more readily available to all, since it consists simply of an enumeration of the particular characteristics that are associated with specific bodily features.[49] The comment on this particular meaning in the article in the *Encyclopaedia of Islam* article on *firāsa*, '*Firāsa* is an Islamic science',[50] cannot be taken without reservations. It can be accepted only in the sense that it became Islamic at a later stage, as is shown below. The only researcher who regards, albeit with reservations, physiognomy as an originally Arabic and Islamic science is ʿAbd al-Karīm ʿAdiyy. This is despite the fact that he concedes that *firāsa* in early Arabic lexicons never appears in the Greek sense.[51] He goes even further to assert that Greek physiognomy was influenced by this Arabic science and not vice versa. ʿAdiyy bases his opinion on what has been related about al-Shāfiʿī's adeptness in this science. At the end he presents his conclusion in the form of a hypothetical question that still needs confirmation or negation.[52] The issue of al-Shāfiʿī is discussed in detail below and I believe Adiyy's question should clearly be answered in the negative.

At any rate, it is clear that this meaning of *firāsa* is neither originally Arabic nor Islamic. Early Arabic lexicons do not make any reference to it as one of the meanings of *firāsa*.[53] This does not necessarily mean that the idea of a possible link between one's physical appearance and personality traits could not have been current among the Arabs before they heard or read about Greek physiognomy. But the majority of specialists in this field are of the opinion that this type of *firāsa* had a definable and distinct existence only after, and thanks to, the translation of the Greek treatises on this science.[54] However, possible Indian and Persian influences should not be ignored. Cursory references to the Indian and Persian *firāsa* were made by Ibn Qutayba (213/828–276/871)[55] and in the treatise attributed to al-Jāḥiẓ (d. 255/868–9) which discusses the Persian view of *firāsa* among other topics. The treatise also quotes Jawbar al-Hindī (the Indian) as the author of a work on *firāsa*.[56] It seems, however, that this initial Indian and Persian influence faded quickly when the Greek sources were translated.

Three main Greek sources were of crucial importance in this regard, namely two books attributed to Aristotle and one book attributed to Polemon.[57] The two books attributed to Aristotle are *Sirr al-asrār* (Secret of Secrets)[58] and *Kitāb Arisṭāṭalīs fī al-firāsa* (The Book of Aristotle on Physiognomy).[59] The first book purports to be the advice given by the famous Greek philosopher to the equally famous general Alexander the Great while on campaign in Iran.[60] This book raised a huge number of scholarly questions, the most important of which centre on whether the origin of the book was Arabic or Greek and the date at which it was written or translated. Many theories have been presented in the attempt to answer these questions and to my mind none of them gives decisive answers.[61] Just two points need concern us here. First, the book contains a section on physiognomy whose categories, style and vocabulary, if not so much the statements themselves, owe much to Polemon.[62] Thus the Greek origin of this specific part should be unquestionable. The second point, which still remains equivocal, is the date at which the Arabic versions of this book appeared. The earliest date suggested was during the Umayyad reign (41/661–132/750)[63] whereas the latest was in the seventh/thirteenth century, not before 1220.[64] The date proposed for the text of the section on physiognomy in particular was 330/941.[65] To sum up, in the absence of definite proof, a wide range of dating possibilities remains open.[66]

The second book was translated by the well-known physician, philosopher, author and translator Ḥunayn b. Isḥāq (192/808–260/873) around the middle of the third/ninth century.[67]

Polemon's book *Kitāb al-firāsa* seems to have been the most influential of all of these books.[68] Its translator and the exact date of translation are unknown.[69] The well-known historian al-Ya'qūbī (who died sometime after 292/905)[70] notes that Polemon, 'the master of physiognomy' (*aflīmūn ṣāḥib al-firāsa*), wrote a book in which he explained what physiognomy can teach about innate disposition, repute and character, giving proof.[71] But it seems that al-Jāḥiẓ (d. 255/868–9) was the earliest Arabic writer to quote Polemon, in his book *Al-Ḥayawān*.[72] However, al-Jāḥiẓ's quotations were on the physiognomy of the dove (*firāsat al-ḥamām*) and none of them can be found in the extant Arabic version of Polemon's physiognomy.[73] Accordingly, it seems that Polemon's book began to circulate around the third/ninth century.[74] By this time, it was widely used and became extremely influential on the development of *firāsa* in the Greek sense.[75]

Gradually, Greek physiognomy in general became one of the main meanings of *firāsa* in Arabic and Islamic culture. One of the main reasons is that contrary to Islamic *firāsa* which was exclusively for pious people, Greek physiognomy could be learned and taught by almost every one.[76] Its practical benefits extended to both the common people and the political elite as well as to different social and economic aspects of life. This science helped ordinary people choose those of good character to be their intimate friends and spouses without being misled.[77] As for the political elite, physiognomy was an important tool for a king or ruler to make suitable choices for his retinue.[78] As for its economic benefits, this type of physiognomy acted as an important guide for those buying slaves[79] or animals, especially horses.[80]

At the literary level, after the cursory quotations of al-Jāḥiẓ, we obtain many hints of widespread interest in Greek physiognomy. This is clear from the numerous quotations from Polemon's treatise or imitations thereof, both direct and indirect, which started circulating in Islamic literature around the fifth/eleventh century at the latest, as is clear from the works of al-Zamakhsharī (461/1075–538/1114)[81] and Ibn Ḥamdūn (495/1102–562/1166).[82]

At the scholarly level, Greek physiognomy appeared on the list of recognized Islamic sciences at almost the same time. During the fifth/eleventh century, the first scientific treatise on Greek physiognomy was written by the littérateur Abū Ḥayyān al-Tawḥīdī (d. 414/1023), recording the academic discussions he had with the great scholar Ibn Miskawayh (d. 421/1030).[83] At about the same time, Ibn Sīnā (d. 428/1037) put this type of physiognomy on the list of Islamic sciences and made it one of the secondary divisions of physics after medicine and astrology.[84]

All these developments paved the way for another step at the lexicographical level. Gradually, and at the latest around the sixth/twelfth century, Greek physiognomy was presented in the Arabic lexicons as one of the main meanings of *firāsa*, as is clear from the works of Majd al-Dīn Ibn al-Athīr (544/1149–606/1210)[85] and Ibn Manẓūr (630/1233–711/1312–13).[86]

The popularity of Greek physiognomy went further as it became the main meaning of *firāsa*. In other words, *firāsa* came to convey first and foremost the Greek sense of physiognomy rather than the other three possible meanings. This is clear from a long list of Arabic books written on this science and including the word *firāsa* in the title without adding *ḥikmiyya* (judicious), *ṭabīʿyya* (natural) or any other term to avoid possible misunderstanding or confusion with the other meanings of *firāsa*.[87]

The mystic and Greek meanings of *firāsa* were the main ones of the aforementioned four to receive further theorization and elaboration. Although mystic *firāsa* never became a systematized science with clear and detailed premises and conclusions, as was the case with Greek physiognomy, Islamic mystic literature could present at least a theory in this regard. These two developed systems of *firāsa* had contradictory standpoints concerning people with disabilities.

The main concern of the mystic *firāsa* was the practitioner of *firāsa* rather than the targeted person whose invisible character the practitioner wants to read. The main component of this *firāsa* is to gain the light of God to illuminate, open up and thus reveal the hidden sides of people's characters. As the aforementioned adage states, 'Beware the *firāsa* of the believer for he sees with the light of God.' To obtain this light, a person must dedicate him/herself to the worship and service of God and fulfil a number of conditions:

> Whoever turns his gaze from forbidden things, restrains himself from desires, and suffuses his inner self with constant vigilance and his outer self with adherence to God's law, and accustoms himself to eating only what is permitted, *firāsa* will not fail him.[88]

Sufi literature shows that physical build and outward appearance obviously play no role whatsoever, whether as a prerequisite to gain this divine light or as a determining factor in judging people's characters. People with different disabilities, including blindness, lameness, hemiplegia, paralysis, leprosy, etc., were repeatedly presented in Sufi literature as people with good character and pure hearts which enabled them to attain the ranks of *awliyāʾ* (Friends of God) and thus deserve high esteem and appreciation.[89]

Unlike the mystic *firāsa*, the main focus of Greek physiognomy was the person whose character we want to understand, and the physical build of that person was crucial in the physiognomic process. This focus made Greek physiognomy, especially as represented by the aforementioned three Greek works, produce a negative image of people with disabilities, abnormalities or deformities.[90] The general principle to be deduced from these works is that any malformation in one's body indicates a similar malformation in one's character.[91] The introductory passages of the chapter on physiognomy in the *Sirr al-asrār* are the most obvious in this regard. The author says,

> know that the womb is for the embryo like the pot for the food, therefore the whiteness or blueness or extreme redness [of the face] indicates imperfect coction, and if any physical imperfection (*naqṣ fī al-khalq*) is added to them, then it is a clear proof of the nature being imperfect as well. Therefore beware of such people, blue or very red and smooth, for they must be shameless, perfidious and sensuous . . . and beware of one of a defective make or having some physical imperfection.[92]

In his work of physiognomy translated by Ḥunayn b. Isḥāq, Aristotle depicts the brave man as having an almost flawless and well-proportioned body whereas the coward has an ill-proportioned and to some extent malformed one.[93] The same line is continued in the work of Polemon.[94] This negative image found its way into Arabic literature which made use of or was influenced by such works. For instance, al-Rāghib al-Iṣfahānī (d. 1108) records this statement, 'The blind man is obstinate (*mukābir*), the one-eyed is frequently unjust (*ẓalūm*) and the squint-eyed is regularly arrogant.'[95] Another good example is a passage which crops up in a number of well-known literary works:

> Largeness of the forehead indicates doltishness, breadth of it to poverty of intellect, smallness of it to gracefulness of movement, and roundness of it to anger. If the eyebrows are joined straight across, it indicates effeminacy and slackness. If they are driven downwards to the edge of the nose, it indicates grace and intelligence; and if they are driven towards the temples, it indicates derision and mockery. If the inner corner of the eye is small, it indicates a wicked inner nature and bad character traits. If the eyebrow falls down to the eye, it indicates envy. The medium-sized eye is an indication of acumen, fine character, and valour; the projecting eye of a confused intellect; the hollow eye of sharpness; the eye that stares much of impertinence and stupidity; and the eye that looks long of levity and inconstancy. Hair on the ear indicates a good listener, and a big erect ear indicates stupidity and folly.[96]

The ascending popularity of Greek physiognomy did not remain within the boundaries of common people and literary sources. Two main factors pushed it into the realms of Islamic jurisprudence. First, Muslim jurists who deal with ordinary people's lives and their daily affairs appear to have taken up this science, which thereby penetrated many aspects of life in the Muslim community.

Second, some of the statements on physiognomy had religious and legal implications. For instance, al-Rāghib al-Iṣfahānī (d. 1108) quotes Aristotle as saying, 'The testimony of humpbacked and short people should not be accepted even if [their credibility was] recommended because of their maliciousness. He was asked why. He said "because their heads are close to their hearts".'[97] Another statement ascribed to al-Shāfi'ī is: 'a little and short palm combined with long thin fingers indicates theft and treachery.'[98] Such statements have direct relevance to issues discussed extensively in Islamic jurisprudence. This meeting-point will be elaborated below with the main focus on the Shāfi'ī and the Ḥanbalī schools of law.

4.1 The Shāfi'ī school

A number of sources written by scholars belonging to the Shāfi'ī school, including those of Fakhr al-Dīn al-Rāzī (d. 606/1209),[99] Shams al-Dīn al-Dimashqī (d. 727/1327), Ibn al-Durayhim al-Mawṣilī (d. 762/1360)[100] and Zayn al-'Ābidīn al-Ghumrī (d. 970/1562),[101] played a significant role in diffusing the idea that the founder of this legal school, al-Shāfi'ī, was an important authority in this *firāsa*.[102] They quote a number of statements claiming to come from al-Shāfi'ī himself.[103] These statements convey the same negative attitude adopted by the aforementioned Greek literature towards people with disabilities and are the topic of the following analysis.

4.1.1 Muḥammad b. Idrīs al-Shāfi'ī's controversial statements

Muḥammad b. Idrīs al-Shāfi'ī (d. 205/820) was regarded as one of the seven main authorities on the science of physiognomy in the Greek sense.[104]

Different sources[105] enumerating the virtues of al-Shāfi'ī (*manāqib*),[106] ascribe statements to him which fall into the category of *firāsa* in the Greek sense. However, these sources also include other statements which fall into the category of *firāsa* in the other three meanings. Robert Hoyland (University of St Andrews) examined the sources on *firāsa* in general and found for instance that the comprehensive work on *firāsa* by Shams al-Dīn al-Dimashqī (d. 727/1327) contains sixty-four physiognomical sayings attributed to al-Shāfi'ī. Just a few of the sayings ascribed to al-Shāfi'ī by al-Dimashqī are also reported by other sources in the same category, such as the work of Ibn Zakariyya al-Rāzī (two sayings), Ibn 'Arabī (six sayings) and Fakhr al-Dīn al-Rāzī (eight sayings).[107]

'Abd al-Karīm 'Adiyy made two more comparisons: first, between the statements mentioned in the *manāqib* works and those quoted in the sources on *firāsā* in general, and he concluded that similarities are there but few; second, between the statements ascribed to al-Shāfi'ī by Shams al-Dīn al-Dimashqī and those ascribed to the Greek authorities in this science. 'Adiyy found that out of the sixty-four statements ascribed to al-Shāfi'ī, forty-five are solely Shāfi'ian, one is also ascribed to Polemon and two to Aristotle.[108]

As stated earlier, people with disabilities in the contemporary sense were included in a broader category in early Arabic and Islamic literature, i.e. among those with any form of physical deformity or abnormality.[109] Hence, we will notice that the statements in the abovementioned sources which generally denigrate the image of people with disabilities come as part of the material concerning all those within that broad category. For instance, the statements ascribed to al-Shāfi‘ī include: ‘a little and short palm combined with long thin fingers indicates theft and treachery’[110] or ‘indicates bad ethics and beguilement’;[111] ‘the face with protruding cheeks combined with thick lips indicates fondness of corruption and perversity’;[112] ‘thick lips indicate foolishness and brusqueness’;[113] and ‘the forehead that protrudes in its middle indicates precipitancy and silliness.’[114]

A large number of these statements deal with physical disabilities that are known in our present time. They convey the general message that one should be on one’s guard when dealing with these people. The statements imply a negative and sometimes even a discriminatory attitude to people with disabilities. However, the statements vary in the degree of rejection they advocate. Some of them are mainly warnings whereas others go further, declaring that these people are malicious and even devilish. Below, I give a translation of the statements attributed to al-Shāfi‘ī:

1 ‘Beware of the lame, the cross-eyed, the one-eyed and everyone with a physical defect (*bihī ‘āha aw nāqiṣ al-khalq*). They are extremely difficult to deal with.’[115]

2 ‘If you see a beardless person then beware him. I have never seen anything good from a [person with] blue [eyes] (*azraq*).’[116]

3 It is related that al-Shāfi‘ī once sent a man to buy him perfume. When he came back, al-Shāfi‘ī asked him, ‘Did you buy [it] from a beardless person (*kawsaj*) who is fair and ruddy in complexion (*ashqar*)?’ On receiving a reply in the affirmative, al-Shāfi‘ī asked him to return it and he did so.[117] Other versions of this story add al-Shāfi‘ī’s justification for the refusal: ‘I have never seen something good from a person who is fair and ruddy in complexion (*ashqar*).’[118]

4 ‘Beware of the one-eyed, the lame, the cross-eyed, the fair and ruddy in complexion (*ashqar*), the beardless (*kawsaj*) and everyone with physical defect (*nāqiṣ al-khalq*). He is a person with cunning and difficult to deal with.’[119]

5 ‘Beware of the one-eyed, the cross-eyed, the lame, the hump-backed, the fair and ruddy in complexion (*ashqar*), the beardless (*kawsaj*) and everyone with a physical defect (*nāqiṣ al-khalq*). Beware of such a person because he is a man with cunning and difficult to deal with. On another occasion, he said, “They are people full of malice”.’[120]

6 ‘Beware of everyone with a physical defect because he is a devil. Ḥarmala asked “Who are those?” He [al-Shāfi‘ī] replied, “The lame, the cross-eyed, the paralysed and the like”.’[121]

7 It is also maintained that al-Shāfi‘ī composed verses advising people to be on guard against nine sorts of people, namely the cross-eyed, the hunchbacked,

> the one-eyed, the beardless, a person with a long nose, a man who is fair and ruddy in complexion, a sunkeyed person, a person with a bulging forehead and finally a person with blue eyes.[122]

These statements also found their way to sources other than the ones quoted above. In literary circles, we find for instance that Muḥammad Diyāb al-Itlīdī (d. after 1100/1689) concludes his historical book *I'lām al-nās*[123] with the aforementioned verses with just slight changes in the types of physical defects mentioned[124] and presenting the poet as anonymous.[125] The verses also appear on the cover of a manuscript of this work completed in 1238/1822, a fact which would suggest that these verses had the status of sage advice.[126]

However, these statements seem to have been disseminated much more widely among ordinary people than in literary circles and sometimes they were even elevated to the rank of prophetic traditions. One example, on people with a physical feature depicted in Arabic literature as a defect (*'āhāt*), is the negative statement on a person who is fair and ruddy in complexion (*ashqar*) and with blue eyes (*azraq*). The statement appears as a prophetic tradition in the ḥadīth collection, *Firdaws al-akhbār* (Paradise of Traditions), by Abū Shujā' al-Daylamī (d. 558/1115).[127] Another statement, on people with disabilities and those with physical defects in general, warns, 'Beware those with physical defects (*ittaqū dhawī al-'āhāt*).' This statement became known among the public as a prophetic tradition and thus appeared regularly in the compilations belonging to the genre of *al-aḥādīth al-mushtahara* (lit. well-known prophetic traditions). In such writings, scholars of Ḥadīth collected traditions widely circulated among the Muslim masses in order to examine their authenticity according to the norms of ḥadīth criticism.[128] As a result, they questioned their authenticity and were inclined to qualify them as non-prophetic statements.[129] In an attempt to discover the origin of such statements, they cited al-Shāfi'ī as a possible source and quoted some of the statements mentioned above. These scholars did not, however, question the authenticity of the attribution of the statements to al-Shāfi'ī.[130] In the light of the available information, a critical study of this attribution is due.

To my knowledge, only three of our contemporaries have studied, although incidentally, the aforementioned statements. Youssef Mourad[131] and 'Abd al-Karīm 'Adiyy did not raise doubts about their authenticity.[132] The only one who has tentatively questioned the statements' authenticity is Robert Hoyland. After discussing the statements mentioned in the sources of *firāsa*, he said, 'without knowing anything about their transmission, it is difficult to say anything secure about their provenance.'[133] Here Hoyland is referring to one type of source, namely those written on *firāsa*, and it is true that the statements are mentioned there without chains of transmission. However, as shown above, sources speaking about the *manāqib* of al-Shāfi'ī mentioned similar statements with almost the same meaning and sometimes even more extreme. Chains of transmission are usually given for such statements. The main question to be tackled here is whether these statements really were made by al-Shafi'ī or whether they are not authentic and were just ascribed to him for some specific end, and if so, what. For a balanced analysis of this highly complicated issue, factors both supporting and opposing the authenticity of the statements will be presented.

4.1.2 Materials that seem to advocate authenticity

The statements mentioned above were quoted in the context of commending al-Shāfiʻī rather than defaming him. Thus one would not think of deliberate fabrication to tarnish his image. The earliest written source in which these statements appear is the book of the traditionist Ibn Abī Ḥātim al-Rāzī (d. 327/938) on al-Shāfiʻī's virtues (*Ādāb al-Shāfiʻī wa manāqibuh*).[134] Ibn Abī Ḥātim grouped the statements ascribed to al-Shāfiʻī in a chapter entitled, 'A Chapter on What Has Been Mentioned about al-Shāfiʻī's *firāsa* and Intelligence (*fiṭna*), May Allah Have Mercy on Him!'[135] The Shāfiʻī scholar Fakhr al-Dīn al-Rāzī (d. 606/1209) in his book about the virtues (*manāqib*) of al-Shāfiʻī cited the second harsh statement listed above and then commented, 'Know that what he said is based on solid grounds in the science of physiognomy (*'ilm al-firāsa*).' He then went on to explain the nature and logic of this science.[136] Another example comes from the Ḥanbalī scholar Ibn al-Qayyim (d. 751/1350) who, in the context of refuting what he considered defamatory information about al-Shāfiʻī, quoted most of the aforementioned statements. He said that such statements indicate al-Shāfiʻī's knowledge of *firāsa* and 'this is what befits his solemnity and high position'.[137]

Identical views were expressed by almost all those who wrote on the virtues of al-Shāfiʻī and those who wrote on *firāsa*. This made the statements very popular, so they were taken by default as coming from al-Shāfiʻī. For instance, when Jurjī Zaydān (1278/1861–1332/1914) wrote at the beginning of the twentieth century on the science of modern physiognomy, he mentioned al-Shāfiʻī as one of the main early authorities.[138] The same is the case with 'Abd al-Karīm 'Adiyy.[139]

A trawl through the two abovementioned categories of sources, especially those on his virtues, gives the impression of al-Shāfiʻī' as an encyclopedic scholarly figure who masters almost every science including not only Islamic jurisprudence but also physiognomy.[140] This is reinforced by the fact that al-Shāfiʻī was also known as an expert in the fields covered by the other three meanings of *firāsa* mentioned above.

The enormous number of references to al-Shāfiʻī's intelligence and quick-wittedness depict a legendary person. In the *manāqib* works, we find a separate chapter dedicated to this side of al-Shāfiʻī's character. Many statements recorded there state that al-Shāfiʻī's mind was matchless.[141] Under the heading *al-firāsa*, we also find statements ascribed to al-Shāfiʻī which indicate his astuteness. Once, while al-Shāfiʻī was issuing fatwas in the mosque of Baghdad, a man came in and asked him, 'What do you say about a person who castrated a turkey?' On the basis of the question, al-Shāfiʻī could immediately identify the questioner and knew that he was the well-known man of letters al-Jāḥiẓ, although, according to the anecdote, al-Shāfiʻī had never seen al-Jāḥiẓ before. Another anecdote makes al-Shāfiʻī's shrewdness more visible and more complicated. While he was sitting in the Holy Mosque with his disciple al-Rabīʻ b. Sulaymān, a man came in and started wandering among the sleeping people. Looking at the man and observing his movements, al-Shāfiʿī could conclude that he was looking for a black slave with a defect in one of his eyes! Ultimately, al-Shāfiʿī's guess proved correct and was confirmed by the man himself.[142]

As for *qiyāfa*, it was no unfamiliar science for al-Shāfiʿī either. As a jurist, he was an advocate of the validity of this science. Contrary to Abū Ḥanīfa, al-Shāfiʿī opined that *qiyāfa* can produce legitimate and valid evidence for establishing one's lineage.[143] In addition, reports ascribe a treatise on this science (*Al-Tanqīḥ fī ʿilm al qiyāfa*) to al-Shāfiʿī.[144]

Al-Shāfiʿī's adeptness concerning the mystic *firāsa* was also clearly demonstrated by the anecdotes told about him under the heading *firāsa*. When al-Shāfiʿī was on his deathbed, four of his disciples came to see him. After scrutinizing the four for a while, he said to the first, 'You will die in iron fetters'; to the second he said, 'You will have repeated failures in Egypt and one day you will be the best [jurist] of your time practising *qiyās* [analogy]'; to the third, 'You will return to the [juristic] school of your ancestor [the Mālikī school]'; to the fourth, 'You will be the most beneficial for me in publicizing my books.' All of what he said came true.[145] Naturally, no observer from a later period would dare to propose that anyone had as much expertise in the fourth meaning of *firāsa* (Greek physiognomy) as al-Shāfiʿī, particularly as it was claimed that he knew Greek medicine and philosophy in their original language.[146] What would have prevented him from mastering Greek physiognomy as well?

4.1.3 Materials that seem to oppose authenticity

In the first place, the fact that the statements are mentioned by pro-Shāfiʿian sources does not mean that they are authentic by default. It is known that whole books on *firāsa*, not to mention just statements, were falsely attributed to people who did not write them.[147] Furthermore, none of the statements attributed to al-Shāfiʿī in these sources is accompanied by a chain of transmitters.[148]

The other sources are those on the virtues (*manāqib*) of al-Shāfiʿī. For a better understanding of this issue, we should say something about this genre in Islamic literature. The plural substantive, *al-manāqib* (sing. *manqaba*), features in the titles of a quite considerable number of biographical works of a laudatory nature, which have gradually become part of a corpus of hagiographical literature. Works belonging to the *manāqib* genre give prominence to the merits, virtues and remarkable deeds of the individual concerned.[149] A great number of books belonging to this category were dedicated to the founders of the juristic schools (*madhāhib*). The main objective of such works is to present the *manāqib*, the qualities (*shamā'il*) and the virtues (*faḍā'il*) of the founders of these schools, so that the disciples can take them as models and imitate their ideas.[150] Al-Shāfiʿī alone is the subject of more than thirteen collections on his *manāqib*.[151] Such books have already been criticized for including inauthentic information. The main example is the claim that al-Shāfiʿī was an expert in astrology, Greek medicine and the Greek language. This claim was refuted by Ibn al-Qayyim (d. 751/1350)[152] and also rejected by the late Egyptian scholar Muḥammad Abū Zahra (d. 1974).[153]

As stated above, *firāsa* in the fourth sense (the relationship between immutable physical attributes and inherent personality traits) is derived from Greek origins and was never developed into an independent science before the translation of the Greek sources.[154] Thus one would expect al-Shāfi'ī's adeptness in this respect to be based on these sources: this would explain the similarity in approach and even in wording between the statements ascribed to him and those ascribed to the Greek authorities in this science such as Aristotle and Polemon. The question, then, is: did al-Shāfi'ī have access to the main Greek sources for this science translated into Arabic?

As mentioned earlier, three main sources were of central importance, two attributed to Aristotle and one to Polemon. The dating of the book entitled *Sirr al-asrār*, falsely attributed to Aristotle as discussed above, is too controversial to give us precise information about its translation or dissemination. The second book, *Kitāb Arisṭāṭalīs fī al-firāsa* (Aristotle's book on physiognomy) was translated by Ḥunayn b. Isḥāq (192/808–260/873) who was twelve years old when al-Shāfi'ī died. Whatever the truth of the matter, it seems to have come too late for al-Shāfi'ī (d. 205/820), as the earliest date attributed to it is in the third/ninth century. The third book, the most influential in this field, was Polemon's *Kitāb al-firāsa*. As stated above, neither the translator nor the date of translation is precisely known.[155] The only possible clue is that the literary author al-Jāḥiẓ (d. 255/868–9) cites a certain Polemon, 'the master of physiognomy' (*Aflīmūn ṣāḥib al-firāsa*), on matters relating to pigeons. It is usually assumed on this basis that Polemon's treatise must have been translated before the mid-ninth century.[156] However, this supposition is not above criticism. First of all, al-Jāḥiẓ's quotations from Polemon on pigeons have a zoological rather than a physiognomical character and this does not accord with any of the known versions of Polemon's *Physiognomy*. Besides the possibility that al-Jāḥiẓ would have used a recension of the work of Polemon which has not been preserved, it could also indicate that that work was not yet available and that al-Jāḥiẓ depended on oral anecdotes about the tradition of the Greek sages (*ḥukamā'*).[157] This possibility seems all the more likely given that when al-Jāḥiẓ wrote an independent treatise on the topic of physiognomy, if we assume that it is not a pseudonymous attribution,[158] and spoke about the Greek side of this science, he made use of a source attributed to Hippocrates and translated by Ḥunayn b. Isḥāq (d. 260/873) but made no mention of Polemon's *Physiognomy*.[159] The fact that Ibn Qutayba (d. 276/871) did not make any reference to Greek sources when speaking about *firāsa* although he referred to an Indian source[160] also raises doubts about the dissemination of Greek physiognomy at this time, including that of Polemon. Thus it is highly improbable that al-Shāfi'ī could have made use of any of these three Greek works.

But a shred of possibility may remain, in the light of the aforementioned information, that the translated Greek sources were available in Baghdad, the capital of the Islamic state, or any of the nearby cities such as Basra where al-Jāḥiẓ lived. The only explicit reference to al-Shāfi'ī's acquaintance with physiognomy in the Greek sense mentions a trip he made to Yemen in search of books on *firāsa* during which he copied and collected them.[161] The question now is, why Yemen and not Baghdad, which would be more logical, and what kind of books on *firāsa* were there? Why were they not mentioned by others? This story might, however, be interpreted as a counterpart to the numerous stories relating the quest by the Abbasid Caliph al-Ma'mūn and others for Greek books among the Christians in Byzantium. It seems that the story of al-Shāfiʿī's quest for books in Yemen underlines that he was *not* looking for *Greek* books or using books of *Greek* origin but was interested in *Arabic and Islamic* materials.[162]

On the other hand, writings from the hand of al-Shāfiʿī himself do not contain any reference to his adeptness in Greek physiognomy or to the negative statements quoted earlier. On the contrary, al-Shāfiʿī's writings indicate a completely different standpoint towards people with disabilities. To start with an easy task, we find no trace of the verses attributed to al-Shāfiʿī in the known collection of poems (*dīwān*) attributed to him or any of the available sources that record passages of his poetry.[163] Hence, that al-Shāfiʿī composed poetry hostile to people with disabilities is by no means a historical fact.

The monumental work of al-Shāfiʿī, *Al-Umm*, should be highly expressive of his standpoint in this respect.[164] First of all, neither the term *firāsa* and its derivatives nor the synonym *tawassum* and its derivatives appears in the text at all. On the contrary, the term *qāfā* (another word for *qiyāfa*) appears sixty-four times in the context of valid evidence to prove one's lineage.[165]

Examining all the terms used in the aforementioned statements, along with their derivatives, shows that none of the derogatory statements appear in the text. This is despite the fact that such terms were extensively used throughout the book. For instance, *aḥwal* (squint-eyed) appears 12 times,[166] *aʿraj* (lame) 86 times[167] and *aʿwar* (a person with one eye) 17 times.[168] Moreover, the contexts in which these terms were used give a positive rather than a negative image. For instance, words like *al-aḥwal* (12 times),[169] *al-aʿraj* (65 times)[170] and *al-aʿwar* (twice)[171] are used to characterize a narrator of a prophetic tradition, a traditionist or a religious scholar, all authorities who have been used in the book.[172] This indicates that people with such disabilities were seen by al-Shāfiʿī as trustworthy authorities rather than as people whose evil character should be avoided.

Now, one question remains in the context of our sources. What about the book on *firāsa* that is said to have been written by al-Shāfiʿī himself?[173] First of all, earlier authorities such as Ibn al-Nadīm do not mention this book among the works written by al-Shāfiʿī[174] and so modern scholars tend to be sceptical.[175] Furthermore, the scientific bibliographer Ḥājjī Khalīfa (d. 1067/1657), in whose time a clear distinction was made between *qiyāfa* and *firāsa* (as is clear from his *Kashf al-ẓunūn*), spoke of a book on *qiyāfa* rather than on *firāsa*.[176] Keeping in mind that *qiyāfa* was never developed into a systematic science and was thus never the sole topic of a single book,[177] one would think that this book must have been a juristic treatise in which al-Shāfiʿī presented and defended his opinion that *qiyāfa* can be valid evidence, particularly as we know that, as a jurist, he was an advocate of the legitimacy of *qiyāfa* for establishing a person's lineage, unlike Abū Ḥanīfa for instance.[178] Looking at the manuscript of this work, which is in Mūṣil (Iraq), could clarify a lot of these ambiguities.[179]

Besides the sources written by or about al-Shāfiʿī, many aspects of his personal life and his career as a jurist and scholar militate against the possibility that he adopted a negative attitude towards people with disabilities. We find among the circles of al-Shāfiʿī's teachers and students a number of people who had disabilities. The clearest example among al-Shāfiʿī's teachers is Yaḥyā b. Saʿīd al-Qaṭṭān[180] who was squint-eyed.[181] Al-Shāfiʿī learnt Ḥadīth from Yaḥyā although he was the younger man.[182] In addition, we find Ḥammād b. Zayd al-Baṣrī who was blind[183] and Ḥusayn al-Althagh who, as his nickname indicates, had a lisp (*althagh*).[184] Among the students, no example could be better than al-Rabīʿ b. Sulaymān al-Azdī who was lame,[185] and according to some reports his father was lame as well.[186] Al-Rabīʿ was Egyptian and thus came into contact with al-Shāfiʿī during the last period of his life. In fact, we also find that al-Shāfiʿī was mixing with such people in his daily life. For instance, it is reported that he had a female and a male slave both fair and ruddy in complexion (*ashqar*),[187] an attribute which is abhorred in the aforementioned statements. Additionally, the word *al-ḍuʿafāʾ* (lit. weak people), according to the language used by al-Shāfiʿī himself, would also include those with disabilities such as the lame.[188] It is reported that al-Shāfiʿī was very friendly with the weak (*al-duʿafāʾ*), and used to give them charity every day.[189]

4.1.4 Origin of these statements

It is clear that these statements were ascribed to al-Shāfiʿī out of love and glorification rather than enmity or malice. The process of attributing them to al-Shāfiʿī started within his circles in the context of *firāsa*. The attribution appeared in written form for the first time in the fourth/tenth century in the work of Ibn Abī Ḥātim al-Rāzī (d. 327/938) on al-Shāfiʿī's virtues (*Adāb al-Shāfiʿī wa manāqibuh*).[190] As illustrated above, the reputation of Greek physiognomy was in the ascendant among the general public as well as the scholarly elite. Thus depicting al-Shāfiʿī as a specialist in this science would have enhanced his scholarly image at this time. Two main factors made al-Shāfiʿī a good candidate to be a specialist in Greek physiognomy; first, his fame as a good practitioner of *firāsa* (*mutafarris*) in its other three meanings, mental acuity, *qiyāfa* and in the mystic sense; second, the stories depicting al-Shāfiʿī as having encyclopedic knowledge and as having mastered Greek medicine and philosophy in the original language.[191]

It is clear that the statements ascribed to al-Shāfiʿī were double-edged. On the one hand, they indicate his adeptness in physiognomy but on the other they convey a negative attitude towards people with physical defects. The double-edged character of these statements divided Shāfiʿī scholars into two main groups. The first group welcomed the science of physiognomy and made use of such statements to depict al-Shāfiʿī as an important authority in the science. The other group was aware of the negative side of these statements. In a bid to cover up or at least minimize their severity, a number of Shāfiʿī scholars added their own comments and clarifications although available information shows that these were very scarce.

The earliest explanation comes from the author of the earliest written source in this respect, Ibn Abī Ḥātim al-Rāzī (d. 327/938). Commenting on the pseudo-Shāfi'ī statement

> Beware of the one-eyed, the cross-eyed, the lame, the hump-backed, the fair and ruddy in complexion (*ashqar*), the beardless (*kawsaj*) and everyone with a physical defect (*nāqiṣ al-khalq*). Beware of such a person because he is a man with cunning and difficult to deal with. On another occasion, he said, 'They are people full of malice'.[192]

Ibn Abī Ḥātim says, 'This holds true for people born with disabilities. There is no harm, however, in mingling with those born without disabilities who later become afflicted with them.'[193] Ibn Abī Ḥātim minimized the severity of the statement by restricting its meaning, though without any clear justification for doing so. Ibn Abī Ḥātim's explanation suggests an influence from the Greek tradition which also made a distinction between congenital disabilities and those acquired in later life through disease, accident, warfare or debauchery. However, in the Greek tradition, congenital disability was not interpreted as divine punishment and thus should be treated with compassion when responsibility for it does not lie at the sufferer's door. However, acquiring disabilities in later life was regarded as shameful.[194]

A long time later, other scholars such as al-Sakhāwī (d. 1497) and Ibn Fahd al-Makkī (d. 1547) tried to place the statements in the broader context of Islamic teachings. Attempting to reach a better reading, al-Sakhāwī and those who agreed with him quote a well-known prophetic tradition: 'Run away from the leper as you run away from the lion!'[195] This applies, they add, to those who fear being infected and it does not indicate any negative feeling about people with physical defects, as common people may think.[196] However, one might still wonder what lameness or strabismus has to do with infection.

Ibn Fahd was more apposite in clearly rejecting the idea that people with physical defects are in principle bad. On the contrary, being afflicted with such calamities is an indication of man's firm belief. As a supporting argument, he quoted the prophetic tradition telling that when the Prophet – peace be upon him – was asked, 'O Messenger of God, who among men are visited with the greatest affliction?', the Prophet said,

> The Prophets, then those with most exemplary character and so forth. A man gets visited with affliction in accordance with his faith (*dīn*). If his faith is durable, his affliction gets harder but if his faith is fragile, then his affliction is lightened accordingly. Calamity continues to afflict the servant until he walks on earth without any sin cleaving to him.[197]

Ibn Fahd al-Makkī added another historical argument. He stated that God's messengers and prophets, who are placed in the highest ranks of humanity, are living examples in this regard. Their afflictions did not lower their status but rather elevated it. The main example presented by Ibn Fahd was the Prophet Job (Ayyūb). All parts of this Prophet's body were heavily afflicted, except for his heart and tongue with which he could practise *dhikr* (remembrance of God).[198]

At any rate, it is clear that the statements did not influence the juristic trend of the Shāfi'ī school. This is evidenced by three main points. First, the Shāfi'ī school continued to include jurists with disabilities, a fact that indicates that this category of people did not encounter any contempt within this school. This group of Shāfi'ī jurists included, for instance, a long list of people afflicted with blindness,[199] lameness,[200] kyphosis[201] and hemiplegia.[202] Second, the juristic works produced by the Shāfi'ī school remained free of prejudice against people with disabilities. On the contrary, a trawl through the Shāfi'ī texts, to be elaborated below, shows a rather positive attitude towards people with disabilities. In addition, the first attempt in the history of Islamic jurisprudence to dedicate a specific chapter to blind people was made in the Shāfi'ī school by al-Ghazālī (d.505/1111) in a book ascribed to him entitled *Al-Rawnaq* (Glamour).[203] Third, *firāsa* in the sense of the astuteness and intelligence, let alone Greek physiognomy, held no legitimacy as valid evidence in the Shāfi'ī works. We know, through the Mālikī jurist Ibn al-'Arabī, that the well-known Shāfi'ī jurist Abū Bakr al-Shāshī (d. 507/1114)[204] wrote a treatise against the use of *firāsa*, to conclude a legal judgment.[205] Priority was always given to *qiyāfa* rather than *firāsa*, a mere continuation of what al-Shāfi'ī started in this regard.

A single passage (of about 150 words) relevant to Greek physiognomy appears in the work of the Egyptian Shāfi'ī jurist Sulaymān al-Bujayramī (d. 1221/1806). This passage comes in the chapter on marriage and in the context of the parts of his fiancée's body that a man is allowed to see, that is, the face and hands. Giving his reader advice on how to use these two body parts in order to deduce information about the parts he cannot see, al-Bujayramī quotes masters of physiognomy with expertise on women (*ahl al-firāsa wa al-khibra bi al-nisā*). For instance, the breadth of a woman's mouth would indicate a similar breadth in her vagina: a thin lower lip indicates a small vagina, for example.[206] The passage is, however, free from any reference to people with disabilities. Passages from the same work indicate that the author adopts a positive attitude towards people with disabilities. For instance, al-Bujayramī states that blindness does affect one's religion. What is harmful, he added, is blindness in one's heart, moving it away from God. The author then quoted the Qur'anic verse, 'Have they never journeyed through the land? Have they no hearts to reason with or to hear with? It is their hearts and not their eyes that are blind.' (22:46).[207]

To conclude, the aforementioned derogatory statements ascribed to al-Shāfi'ī remained, at least within the Shāfi'ī circle in which they originated, at best personal inclinations without any juridical authority. However, further discussions on these statements and on making use of *firāsa* as a valid tool in Islamic jurisprudence took place in the Ḥanbalī school. This will be the focus of the discussions to folllow.

4.2 The Ḥanbalī school

The Ḥanbalī jurist Ibn Mufliḥ (d. 763/1361) made reference to the pseudo-Shāfiʿī statements. He quoted the first harsh statement and also an abridged version of Shāfiʿī's alleged trip to Yemen on which he encountered a person with physical defects whose mean behaviour corroborated his convictions about physiognomy.[208] The context of Ibn Mufliḥ's quotations was typically physiognomic, namely, how to choose your friend and who to choose and who to avoid. This was one of the main advantages of physiognomy.[209] However, the context gives the statements an advisory rather than a juristically binding character. Ibn Mufliḥ may have been the only Ḥanbalī jurist who incorporated the pseudo-Shāfiʿī statements into the school's legal texts. But surely he was not the only person who discussed these statements, or *firāsa* in general, in the Ḥanbalī juristic sources. In this regard the viewpoints and relevant arguments of four well-known Ḥanbalī jurists will be presented under two main headings: paradoxical standpoints as adopted by Ibn al-Jawzī (d. 597/1200) and Ibn al-Qayyim (d. 751/1350); and what can be termed counterpoise trials made by Aḥmad Ibn Taymiyya (d. 728/1328) and Zayn al-Dīn Ibn Rajab (d. 795/1393).[210]

4.2.1 Paradoxical standpoints

To start with Ibn al-Jawzī, his standpoint in this regard is highly paradoxical and confusing. On the one hand, he unequivocally supports the main premise of Greek physiognomy and makes statements with much the same meaning as those ascribed to al-Shāfiʿī. On the other hand, he stressed the triviality of outward physical appearance and attaches great importance to the soul.

Although Ibn al-Jawzī did not quote the pseudo-Shāfiʿī statements verbatim, he clearly showed that he believed them by saying, 'Beware everyone with a physical defect such as the bald, the blind and the like because their souls are evil.' This statement comes in a context known to be typical of Greek physiognomy. Ibn al-Jawzī is stressing the importance of lineage (*aṣl*) and outward physical appearance (*ṣūra*) as determining factors to judge character. His advice is to check these two points before mixing with people as friends or spouses. A strong and well-proportioned figure indicates in most cases good character and the opposite holds true.[211] Keeping in mind that such rules could have exceptions, Ibn al-Jawzī said that people should be tested before one mixed with them even after checking these two points.[212] Stressing the importance of a well-proportioned figure, Ibn al-Jawzī opined that God chooses his Friends (*Awliyā'*)[213] only from among those with a well-proportioned body free of physical defects.[214]

On the other hand, Ibn al-Jawzī severely criticized those who boast about the beauty of their figure (*ṣūra*) and forget that the goodness of the soul (*rūḥ*) is the determining factor. He explains,

> If the soul was enhanced by etiquette (*adab*), disciplined by knowledge, knew the Creator and fulfilled the duties imposed by Him, then it will not be harmed

> by a defect in the structure [in reference to physical defects]. But if it remained ignorant, then it will resemble the mud but may get even lower.[215]

This paradoxical standpoint of Ibn al-Jawzī is not unique. He has been known as a scholar who adopts sometimes inconsistent and contradictory standpoints on a topic. He would even forget that he said or adopt contradictory standpoints because he did not revise what he wrote.[216] This can be attributed to his extreme thirst for learning and mastering every branch of knowledge.[217] It seems that Ibn al-Jawzī could not always detach himself from these different branches of knowledge or come up with a coherent conclusion since they give contrary or inconsistent information. Thus one should not exclude this possibility regarding his discussions on *firāsa*.

The first element of his approach was the influence of Greek physiognomy. This is clear in Ibn al-Jawzī's literary works on the intelligent (*adhkiyā'*) and the foolish (*ḥamqā*) which drew on clear Greek physiognomic notions.[218] For instance, the physical type of the intelligent person (*al-rajul al-fāhim*) reflects more or less faithfully the Aristotelian concept of the proper mean, the Greek *mesotes*, an expression of ethical virtue. The physical characteristics of the man gifted with good intelligence and good nature refer also to the concept of measures and balance between the two extremes which is surely Aristotelian.[219] The Aristotelian concept of a link between physical build and moral traits was duly elaborated and systematically set out by Galen.[220] When Ibn al-Jawzī gave a catalogue of the signs of stupidity, he based his arguments on Galen:

> Galen says that a small head never fails to be a sign of bad conformation of the brain. If the neck is short, this is a sign of a weak and inadequate brain. Whoever has a badly proportioned physical build is one of little value in both his intentions and his intellect.[221]

As the second element of Ibn al-Jawzī's analysis, the mystic influence is indisputable. For instance, it is known that Ibn al-Jawzī was strongly influenced by the Shāfi'ī mystic Abū Nu'aym al-Iṣfahānī (d. 430/1038/9), as is clear from his mystic historical work *Ṣifat al-ṣafwa* (The Character of the Elite).[222] In this book, Ibn al-Jawzī presents a list of those he considered *ṣafwa* (elite, chosen and purified by God) although they clearly do not meet the requirement of having a well-proportioned body or a beautiful physical appearance. On the contrary, they suffered various sorts of disability such as lameness, leprosy, blindness and the like but they could still belong to the rank of *awliyā'*, as stated by Ibn al-Jawzī himself.[223] To sum up, Ibn al-Jawzī's acquaintance with *firāsa* in both the Greek and the Islamic senses is clear. However, it seems that he could live with both senses despite their contradictory attitudes to people with disabilities.

Ibn al-Qayyim's contribution in this respect was much more detailed than that of Ibn al-Jawzī. A trawl through Ibn al-Qayyim's available works shows that he treated, to varying degrees, *firāsa* in the four senses mentioned above.

Firāsa in the aforementioned first meaning occupied the greatest part of Ibn al-Qayyim's discussions on this topic. The main body of his contribution was recorded in two books, *Al-Fawā'id* (Benefits)[224] and *Al-Turuq al-ḥukmiyya fī al-siyāsa al-shar'iyya* (Means of Governing according to the Religious Policy).[225] Discussing *firāsa* was the main focus of the second book and occupied such a substantial part of it that the book is also known as *Al-Firāsa al-marḍiyya fī al-aḥkām al-shar'iyya* (The Accepted *Firāsa* in Religious Rulings). Ibn al-Qayyim's main purpose in these two books was to broaden the traditional concept of proof that can serve as the basis of a valid judgment. There are three main types of proof: confession, testimony and the defendant's refusal to take an oath to affirm his denial of the plaintiff's claim.[226] Ibn al-Qayyim hoped to make *firāsa* a fourth type of proof that could be used by a judge to underpin his judiciary decrees. By *firāsa* here, Ibn al-Qayyim meant that the judge should use his mental and perspicacious faculties to discover, produce and interpret signs and circumstantial evidence (*al-amarāt wa al-qarā'in*) to reach a sound judgment.[227] Ibn al-Qayyim considered that this *firāsa* should head the qualifications needed by judges to practise their judiciary activities.[228] Those who neglect this *firāsa*, Ibn al-Qayyim adds, paralyse many legal norms and cause legal claims to perish.[229] At the same time, he warns against the negative repercussions of overuse of this *firāsa*.[230] The synonym of *firāsa*, *qiyāfa,* considered as eventual legal evidence in specific cases, was used by Ibn al-Qayyim as a supporting argument.[231] He mentioned more than once that his opinion here was shared by the Ḥanbalī jurist Abu al-Wafa' Ibn 'Aqıl (d. 513/1119). Whereas Ibn 'Aqīl did not call it *firāsa*, Ibn al-Qayyim did not see any harm in using the term.[232]

Firāsa in the Islamic sense was discussed by Ibn al-Qayyim in a number of his books,[233] the most important of which is *Madārij al-sālikīn* (Grades of the Walkers), considered to be the masterpiece of Ḥanbalī mystical literature.[234] *Firāsa* was presented in this book as one of the grades that the walker has to pass in his journey to God.[235] The same meaning of *firāsa* was explained in a concise commentary on the same theme by the earlier Ḥanbalī scholar, 'Abd Allāh al-Anṣārī al-Harawı (d. 481/1089), in his celebrated Sufi treatise, *Manāzil al-sā'irīn* (Stations of the Wayfarers).[236] According to Ibn al-Qayyim, this type of *firāsa* is the most honourable and the most beneficial for one's life and for the Hereafter.[237] He opined also that the Companions of the Prophet stand in the first rank of the practitioners of this type of *firāsa*.[238]

Ibn al-Qayyim also advocated the Greek sense of *firāsa*. He believed at least in its main premise, that malformation in the body indicates a similar malformation in the character and spirit.[239] However, Ibn al-Qayyim made two main reservations. First, this premise should not be taken as an absolute rule and thus possible exceptions should be taken into consideration.[240] Second, the negative effect of physical defects on the soul and character is curable and recoverable by means of education, training and habituation.[241] Ibn al-Qayyim warned that attention should be paid to this point, otherwise practitioners of *firāsa* could make numerous misjudgements.[242] In Ibn al-Qayyim's opinion, al-Shāfi'ī was one of the main proficient practitioners of this type of *firāsa* and he said that miracles were attributed to him in this regard.[243] Besides being a proficient practitioner, Ibn al-Qayyim added, al-Shāfi'ī was also one of the main theorists who wrote books on this science.[244] Ibn al-Qayyim was aware of the statements ascribed to al-Shāfi'ī and he did not cast any doubt on their authenticity. He even commended them, and considered them as evidence of al-Shāfiʿī's shrewdness and adeptness in this type of *firāsa*.[245]

Although the two reservations mentioned by Ibn al-Qayyim against making use of *firāsa* in the Greek sense would counterbalance the negative attitude towards people with disabilities, Ibn al-Qayyim's standpoint remains highly controversial.

First of all, he advocated two types of *firāsa*, the mystic and the Greek, which stand at opposite poles concerning their view on physical disabilities.

Second, Ibn al-Qayyim's commendation of al-Shāfiʿī's adeptness in the Greek type of *firāsa* comes in the context of his long refutation of and comprehensive attack on astrology, considered to be the most elaborate and comprehensive attack, or the culminating point in the history of systematic religious attacks, on astrology in Islam.[246] In this context Ibn al-Qayyim refuted what he considered spurious information about al-Shāfiʿī's knowledge of astrology as recorded in the *manāqib* works. Ibn al-Qayyim made a highly critical study on reports mentioned in these works concerning the chain of transmission (*isnād*) and the text (*matn*), concluding that such reports present inauthentic information.[247] This critical approach is completely missing in his study of the statements ascribed to al-Shāfiʿī concerning Greek physiognomy or his alleged adeptness in that field. At any rate, Ibn al-Qayyim's critique of astrology comes as part of his violent opposition to and rejection of the idea that the occult sciences constitute part of the sciences inherited by Islam particularly from the Greeks and known as the rational sciences (*al-ʿulūm al-ʿaqliyya*) or sciences of the ancients (*ʿulūm al-awāʾil*).[248] A popular belief in these occult sciences was seen as endangering the religious basis of Islamic society.[249] Interestingly, a strong link was always claimed to exist between astrology and Greek physiognomy. For instance, when physiognomy was incorporated into the list of the recognized sciences by Muslim scholars, it was placed in the same category as astrology. This had already been done before Ibn al-Qayyim by Ibn Sīnā,[250] al-Ghazālī[251] and Ibn Rushd.[252]

Furthermore, the two sciences share the idea that the disposition of heavenly bodies influences the formation of elemental traits shaping human character.[253] In addition, Arabic works on Greek physiognomy, both before and after the time of Ibn al-Qayyim, show that *firāsa* was known in Greek literature as *ʿilm al-nujūm* (lit. science of the stars or astrology).[254] That is why attacking astrology and simultaneously praising physiognomy without any further explanation remains almost an inexplicable puzzle.

It is possible that the social dimension could solve this puzzle or at least minimize its mysteriousness. In his severe attacks on astrology, Ibn al-Qayyim was primarily concerned with a social phenomenon that he saw as endangering people's religion. In Mameluke society where Ibn al-Qayyim lived, astrology was almost completely removed from the scientific field and approached ever closer to magic, divination and charlatanism. Such astrology could penetrate the different aspects of Mameluke society and astrologers had clients not only in the streets but also sometimes in the citadels of the military class.[255] This would imply that the influence of physiognomy in creating a bad image for people with disabilities had not permeated society as fully as astrology. In other words, at the time of Ibn al-Qayyim, people would not have made use of this type of *firāsa* to degrade or demean people with disabilities, so this might not have attracted his attention while dealing with this science. This would be especially true given the two reservations he made for the applicability of this science, which kept open the possibility that people with disabilities could possess or develop a good character.

4.2.2 Counterpoise trials

Two main Ḥanbalī scholars brought a clear equilibrium to the image of people with disabilities. They were Ibn al-Qayyim's main master Aḥmad Ibn Taymiyya (d. 728/1328) and his main disciple Zayn al-Dīn Ibn Rajab (d. 795/1393).

Initially, Ibn Taymiyya shared with Ibn al-Qayyim three main views relevant to this topic. First, the aforementioned first meaning of *firāsa* developed by Ibn al-Qayyim came originally from Ibn Taymiyya. However, Ibn Taymiyya focused only on developing the theory of evidences and proofs and did not make use of the term *firāsa*.[256] Second, Ibn Taymiyya conceded the validity of the mystic *firāsa* and condemned those who refused to use it as possible evidence in the absence of other clear and authentic testimony. By the same token, Ibn Taymiyya blamed those who overused or misused it as evidence.[257] Finally, Ibn Taymiyya also expressed his anti-astrology attitude in a number of his fatwas.[258]

The main divergence between the master and his disciple lies in their attitudes to Greek physiognomy or its premise at least. Although Ibn Taymiyya did not handle Greek physiognomy in as much detail as his disciple, the available cursory references indicate that he was in the first place sceptical of the validity of Greek physiognomy which he called *al-firāsa al-badaniyya* (lit. physical physiognomy) because it lacked any solid scientific basis.[259] As for the main premise of Greek physiognomy – that people's characters can be judged on the basis of their physical form – Ibn Taymiyya was much more critical. In one place he severely attacked those who judged people and claimed to know their ranks and positions in the sight of God in any way other than that revealed to the Prophet of Islam. Making such judgements would place a person outside Islam. One who also claims, Ibn Taymiyya added, to know people's ultimate destinies without the word of God or of his Messenger would incur God's wrath.[260] It is clear that such statements subvert the premise of physiognomy and its related sciences, which judges character on the basis of, for instance, bodily marks and movements and lines on the hands and feet.[261] *Al-firāsa*, which avoids such pitfalls, Ibn Taymiyya adds in an indirect reference to the mystic one, is true and acceptable.[262]

In another place, Ibn Taymiyya elaborates further on the Islamic criterion by which people's ranks may be measured. He says,

> Texts available in the Qur'an and the Sunna judge justly. Allah favours, in the Qur'ān, nobody on the basis of poverty or richness, *health or sickness*, residence or travel, the position of governor or governed, the position of *imām*

> or that of a follower. On the contrary, He said, 'The most honourable among you is the most pious' and thus he favours them on the basis of good deeds (*al-a'māl al-ṣāliḥa*) including belief, its pillars and branches such as Certainty (*al-yaqīn*), Spiritual Knowledge (*ma'rifa*), love for God, returning to Him, dependence on Him, hoping in Him, fearing Him, thanking Him and practising patience for the sake of Him.[263]

He quotes two main Qur'anic verses and one prophetic tradition supporting this viewpoint.[264] The first verse says, concerning hypocrites, 'And when you see them, their figures (*ajsām,* lit. bodies) will please you' (Qur'ān 63:04). The second verse states, 'And how many of the generations have We destroyed before them who were better in respect of goods and outward appearance (*ri'ya*)!'(Qur'ān 14:74).

The two verses show examples of people whose looks are very pleasing and thus whose bodies are free from physical defects but this outward physical perfection did not protect them from God's wrath because they had bad characters. The prophetic tradition reads, 'Allah does not look at your bodies (*ṣuwar*) or your properties (*amwāl*) but He looks at your hearts and deeds.' Thus the main criterion of favouring one person over another is what he has in his heart and what he does rather than how his body looks.[265]

Available works by Ibn Rajab do not contain any discussions of *firāsa* in any sense. However, some passages from his hand develop and elaborate the ideas of Ibn Taymiyya concerning the disconnection between one's physical appearance and character and the conviction that *taqwā* (piety) is the main criterion by which people's worth can be measured. Commenting on the aforementioned ḥadīth by Ibn Taymiyya, Ibn Rajab says,

> Thus it could happen that the hearts of many of those who have a good figure (*ṣūra ḥasana*), property (*māl*), prestige (*jāh*) or a governing position (*riyāsa*) in this life could be void of *taqwā*, and it could happen that the heart of someone who possesses none of such things be full of *taqwā* and thus more dignified by God. This is what in reality happens in most cases.[266]

Ibn Rajab supported his argument by quoting four prophetic traditions according to which people in Paradise in the Hereafter are mainly those who were not physically and socially powerful but were even weak (*ḍu'afā'*) in this life, whereas powerful people, in the physical and social sense, usually end up in Hellfire.[267]

4.3 Other schools

Beyond the detailed information given in the Shāfi'ī and Ḥanbalī schools, it is generally agreed that the believer can make use of his own *firāsa* in his own private affairs as long as this does not lead to an illegal act (*maḥẓūr shar'ī*).[268] The main disagreement is whether *firāsa* can be a legal proof used by a judge (*qāḍī*). The most well-known judge who made use of *firāsa*, in the first meaning, to conclude his legal judgments is Iyās b. Mu'āwiya (d. 121/739) who was appointed in 99/717 as the judge of Basra during the caliphate of 'Umar b. 'Abd al-'Azīz and thus before the establishment of legal schools (*madhāhib*).[269]

As for the Sunni legal schools, the Ḥanafī jurist, Burhān al-Dīn al-Ṭarābulsī (d. 922/1516), as well as the two Mālikī jurists, Abū Bakr Ibn al-'Arabī (d. 543/1148) and Ibn Farḥūn (d. 799/1397), do not consider *firāsa* – the context suggests the first meaning – a valid tool to conclude a legal judgment.[270] Ibn al-'Arabī supports his argument by quoting a treatise elaborating this point by the Shāfi'ī jurist, Abū Bakr al-Shāshī (d. 507/1114).[271] The same opinion is also given by the well-known mystic Muḥyī al-Dīn Ibn al-'Arabī (d. 638/1240) concerning mystic *firāsa*.[272] Another Mālikī jurist, al-Shāṭibī (d. 709/1388), states that mystic *firāsa* can be valid evidence and one can behave accordingly provided that this will not violate any of the established Islamic regulations.[273] A certain al-Shāmī al-Mālıkī who was the chief judge of Baghdad and a contemporary of Abū Bakr al-Shāshī (d. 507/1114) may be the most famous Mālikī jurist to have opposed the standpoint advocated by Abū Bakr Ibn al-'Arabī and the others. He made use of *firāsa* to reach his legal judgments, as did the earlier judge of Baṣra Iyās b. Mu'āwiya (d. 121/739).[274] Outside the Sunni legal schools, the Ibāḍī school is also against using *firāsa* as legal evidence.[275]

4.4 Summary

One of the interesting findings of this chapter which, to my knowledge, has escaped the attention of previous modern researchers, was the role of Greek physiognomy, according to which a physical deformation indicates a similar one in the spirit and character. By the third/ninth century, important Greek sources had been translated into Arabic and gradually became very popular and sometimes even authoritative in Arabic and Islamic culture. The popularity of this science penetrated juristic circles, as is most clearly indicated by a number of statements which are physiognomic in nature and thus very offensive to people with disabilities, ascribed to the well-known jurist, Muḥammad b. Idrīs al-Shāfi'ī (d. 205/820). After a thorough study of these statements and their dissemination in juristic circles, we conclude that their attribution to al-Shāfi'ī was incorrect. Although such statements found some support among a number of jurists, their general meaning never gained predominance among jurists and it had almost no influence on the main body of Islamic jurisprudence. Thus, people with disabilities were theoretically able to enjoy, within juristic circles, the same status as that guaranteed for human beings in general.

5 The ethics of writing on people with disabilities

5.1 Controversial attempts

Al-Haytham b. 'Adiyy (d. 821) is the first known writer on the topic of people with disabilities in Islam.[1] As described by his biographers, al-Haytham was an expert on people's flaws (*mathālib*) and exploits (*manāqib*).[2] Among his compilations is *Kitāb al-Haytham b. 'Adiyy*, in which he recorded a number of luminaries categorized on the basis of their disabilities. The version of this compilation currently available is in the form of an appendix to the book on the same topic by the well-known man of letters, al-Jāḥiẓ (d. 868–69).[3] Al-Jāḥiẓ criticized al-Haytham's approach of mentioning the names or retelling the stories of people with disabilities for the sole purpose of entertainment.[4] Writing on people with disabilities, al-Jāḥiẓ confirms, should rather have edifying goals, such as demonstrating their spirit of challenge and elaborating the lessons and admonitions to be learnt from their life experiences.[5] It seems that al-Jāḥiẓ was not the only critic of al-Haytham's approach. He was accused by other contemporaries of having malicious intentions in describing and revealing people's defects and drawbacks. However, according to some historians, this accusation was groundless and was levelled against him unjustifiably due to others' personal grudges. At any rate, the accusation was effective in that it made people hate him and impugn his lineage. Al-Haytham was also imprisoned by Caliph Hārūn al-Rashīd (d. 809) for a number of years because he attributed a defect to the Companion al-'Abbās b. 'Abd al-Muṭṭalib. But the next Caliph, al-Amīn (d. 813), freed him upon his succession.[6] Unfortunately, there is no available information to give us more details in this regard. For instance, how did jurists react to al-Haytham's book and how did he defend his book and his opinions?

After al-Haytham b. 'Adiyy, a vast literary genre composed mainly for the sake of entertaining the reader developed. It involved retelling pleasing stories and anecdotes (*nawādir*) containing wit, humour, jocularity and repartee.[7] These stories always contained a chapter on people with physical abnormalities (*dhawū al-'āhāt*).[8] Other books adopted the same approach but focused on people with mental disabilities.[9] Two main points were raised about this type of literature: first, the legal ruling on humour and jocularity in principle;[10] second, the legal ruling on using people's physical or mental defects as a source of entertainment and even occasionally sarcasm. These points were quite controversial and a lot of justificatory material was written on the issue in order to avoid legal or religious embarrassment.[11] However, juristic criticism was given in chapters entitled *Ghība*, as is explained below. No actual incidents about a specific book or a specific author who was attacked are recorded after al-Haytham b. 'Adiyy.

Seven centuries after al-Haytham's death, a book written in 1541 on people with disabilities triggered a vigorous two-year debate, mainly between the author of the book, Ibn Fahd, who was a historian, and a well-known contemporary jurist, Ibn Ḥajar al-Haytamī. A question was posed to the Shafi'ī scholar Ibn Ḥajar al-Haytamī about a book entitled *Al-Nukat al-ẓirāf fīman ibtuliya bi al-'āhāt min al-ashrāf* (Cute Anecdotes on Luminaries Afflicted with Disabilities). Ibn Ḥajar issued a fatwa ordering that the book be destroyed. The debate went beyond these two figures to include destroying the book and the issuing of various fatwas from different Islamic cities.

The discussion here makes use of the manuscript of Ibn Fahd and the two-page fatwa published in the collection of Ibn Ḥajar entitled *Al-Fatāwā al-fiqhiyya al-kubrā* (Grand Juridical Fatwas).[12] *Al-Zawājir 'an iqtirāf al-kabā'ir* (Restraints against Committing Grave Sins), in which Ibn Ḥajar treated the theme of *ghība* (backbiting), is useful for comparative purposes. That is because, as indicated by the author in the introduction, *Al-Zawājir* was written after 1546, i.e. at least five years after the fatwa under discussion was issued.[13]

5.2 Main contributors

As mentioned above, the first main figure participating in this polemic was Ibn Fahd, whose full name was Jār Allāh Muḥammad Taqiyy al-Dīn b. al-'Izz b. al-Najm b. 'Umar b. Taqiyy al-Dīn, Muḥammad b. Fahd al-Makkī al-Hashimī al-Shafi'ī. He was born in July 1486 and died in the same month in 1547.

Ibn Fahd was descended from an elite Meccan family known for their scholarly prestige for three centuries. He himself represented the fourth generation in an unbroken chain of traditionists (*muḥaddithūn*). The family is also known for a general unwillingness to assume political or religious positions.[14] They had their own *waqf* (endowment) in Mecca. Ibn Fahd gained access to this *waqf* after a dispute with his brother and recorded the whole story in one of his books.[15]

Ibn Fahd memorized the Qur'ān and learned Ḥadīth from his father, whom he accompanied on knowledge-seeking trips throughout the Arabian Peninsula. Ibn Fahd's first trip outside the peninsula was in 1507 when he travelled to Cairo to learn Ḥadīth. He visited Cairo whenever he travelled to Syria or to Ottoman cities such as Istanbul or Bursa.[16] Ibn Fahd was better known as a historian and traditionist than as a jurist. However, his biography shows that he studied jurisprudence with more than one shaykh. For instance, he studied *Al-Minhāj*[17] with his father and later on with two other shaykhs, 'Abd Allāh Bākathīr and Shihab al-Dīn al-Yusrī.[18]

Ibn Fahd wrote forty-nine books, mainly historical in nature and some others on ethics and Ḥadīth.[19] Four of these books told the laudable deeds of the Ottoman sultans and a fifth book extolled the Meccan sharīf, Abū Zuhayr Barakāt.[20] But in contrast to these books, Ibn Fahd expressed criticism of the Ottomans and their policy in Mecca and its vicinity in his historical book on Mecca entitled *Nayl al-munā*. However, he maintained a tone of praise for the Meccan sharīfs but tempered it with some indirect criticism of their policy. Interestingly, *Nayl al-munā* remained in draft form till the death of the author and he did not refer to it in any of his other books. The book was not known to his contemporaries. All this would indicate that Ibn Fahd might have wanted to keep his critical remarks beyond the reach of the public during his lifetime.[21]

The second participant in this polemic was Ibn Ḥajar (1504–1567), whose full name is Abū al-ʻAbbās Aḥmad b. Muḥammad b. Muḥammad b. ʻAlā' b. Ḥajar Shihāb al-Haytamī. Unlike Ibn Fahd, Ibn Ḥajar was a specialist in Islamic jurisprudence and well known as a prolific writer of the Shāfiʻī school. He received his elementary school education in the sanctuary of al-Sayyid al-Badawī in Tanta, a province in northern Egypt. In 1518, he went to al-Azhar to continue his education and at the end of 1523 his teachers gave him, on their own initiative, the *ijāza* (authorization or licence) to issue fatwas. He went to Mecca for the ḥajj in 1527 and again in 1531, each time spending a year there. During his first visit, he began writing books after seeing the well-known mystic al-Ḥārith al-Muḥāsibī (d. 857) in an inspiring dream. In 1533, he made his third pilgrimage and settled permanently in Mecca, devoting himself to writing and teaching.

Besides the religious and spiritual benefits of being in the vicinity of the Holy Mosque, Mecca was also an attractive place of residence for Muslim scholars at this time. The province of al-Ḥijāz in general and Mecca in particular were much more economically privileged than the other provinces of the Ottoman Empire. Its inhabitants were, for instance, exempted from paying personal or real estate taxes. Furthermore, al-Ḥijāz used to receive an annual allocation of money and grains.[22] The Ottomans clearly made efforts to establish and develop the institutions of religious learning, funding educational activities and paying for the scholars of the two Holy Mosques and the retirees there through the charities of *Jawālī*.[23] This economic environment had positive effects on the scholarly community, attracting a great number of well-known Muslim scholars to come and live permanently in Mecca.[24]

Although Ibn Ḥajar's reputation spread far and wide, his authority in Mecca was not entirely undisputed and he engaged in a series of vigorous polemics with Ibn Ziyād, the Shafiʻī mufti of Zabīd, on the financial issue of sponsorship and debts. By the time of his death, Ibn Ḥajar had compiled more than forty books, most of which are juristic and theological in nature. It is reported that two of these books concerned the juristic rulings that rulers and kings should abide by.[25] However, Ibn Ḥajar seems to have been quite untouched by the political upheavals that occurred during his lifetime.[26]

5.3 Encounters preceding this polemic

It is useful to examine the nature of the relationship between the two protagonists before the polemic of 1541 to see if personal rather than scholarly issues could have played a role in it. It is not impossible that the two met earlier than 1533, whether during the scholarly visits of Ibn Fahd to Egypt which began in 1507 or during Ibn Ḥajar's visits to Mecca for pilgrimage in 1527 and 1531. However, it is certain that they were both resident in Mecca for at least fourteen years from 1533, when Ibn Ḥajar settled there permanently, staying till his death in 1567.

There is no mention that either of the two scholars assumed an official political or religious position during his lifetime. Thus a struggle for power is not in question. Although they are both recognized as religious scholars, the men belonged to different fields of knowledge: Ibn Ḥajar specialized in *fiqh* and Ibn Fahd in history – thus jealousy or envy of each other's fame would have been minimal. Available historical records are silent on any kind of encounter or relationship between the two scholars before 1537. In that year, Ibn Fahd himself made the first reference to Ibn Ḥajar in his historical record on Mecca, *Nayl al-munā*. In this book, Ibn Ḥajar is mentioned five times as a scholar participating in Meccan life, but no story or incident between the two is told.[27] Ibn Fahd always preceded Ibn Ḥajar's name with honorific titles such as *Mufti of Muslims*,[28] *al-shaykh al-mudarris* (the teacher shaykh)[29] and the like. Unfortunately, *Nayl al-munā* ends in 1539, two years before the polemic took place, and thus makes no reference to this incident. The editor of the book raised the question, 'Where are the historical reports of the last eight years (1539–1547) until the death of Ibn Fahd? Did he write them only in draft form and were they lost? Did he stop writing these reports for a specific reason?' The editor concludes that available texts do not provide us with a satisfactory answer.[30] To sum up, available reports show that before this incident the two main figures taking part in the polemic were neither intimate friends nor vigorous enemies – thus personal issues did not play a role.

The main historical source for what happened next is again Ibn Fahd himself in *Al-Nukat al-ẓirāf*. He said that although Ibn Ḥajar belongs to *dhawū al-'ahāt*, because he was squint-eyed, he did not include him in the old version of the *Nukat*. However, Ibn Ḥajar did issue a fatwa against the *Nukat,* thus giving a helping hand to Ibn Fahd's adversaries. Following the principle of an eye for an eye, Ibn Fahd listed him among the squint-eyed in the new version, likewise giving a helping hand to Ibn Ḥajar's adversaries. Ibn Fahd recalls in this regard the well-known Arabic aphorism, 'Obscurity is a blessing but everyone rejects it whereas celebrity is wrath but everyone desires it.'[31]

5.4 A controversial book

The story of *Al-Nukat al-ẓirāf* started in 1541 when Ibn Fahd wrote the first version of it. It triggered a series of harsh reactions, primarily led by a group of bald people whom Ibn Fahd had mentioned by name in his book. Ibn Fahd and his relatives became the object of malicious attacks on his honour and he was said to have various faults and diseases. Ibn Fahd declared himself and his relatives innocent of any such defects and diseases.[32]

The hostile campaign culminated in Ibn Ḥajar issuing a fatwa declaring that the book fell into the forbidden category of *ghība* (backbiting):

> The author has to repent for what he did by having his book destroyed. If he refuses to do so, then those in charge among scholars and rulers are to reproach him for what he did in whatever way they see fit until he repents. They are to erase the offensive pieces included in this book and even tear it up.[33]

Ibn Ḥajar was aware that an objection could be expected to imposing such a punishment on a prestigious scholar like Ibn Fahd. Islamic sources and Muslim scholars state that the lapses of prestigious scholars are to be forgiven. Ibn Ḥajar responded to this objection by saying, 'This is true in the case of minor sins only. However, the aforementioned book encompasses a grave sin, nay, grave sins for which I ask God to grant me and the author repentance out of His favour and generosity. Amen!'[34]

The aforementioned bald people took the initiative, destroying the book by washing its text away.[35] This happened towards the end of 1541, less than one month after the book was written.[36] In response, Ibn Fahd decided to remove this group from the new version of the *Nukat* on the grounds that he paid them no attention or concern.[37] Ibn Fahd reminded his adversaries of the Day of Judgment when they would stand together in front of God and the oppressed would regain their rights from the oppressor.[38]

The incident also had a social impact. About twenty days later, a great flood swept through Mecca. It flooded the Holy Mosque and the copies of the Qur'ān (*maṣāḥif*) therein. Ibn Fahd deemed this flood a clear admonition. His view was shared by a poet who wrote a poem expressing his sympathy with Ibn Fahd.[39]

The year 1542 was quite a decisive one for Ibn Fahd; he had to defend his book in it. One of his main methods of defence was writing to creditable Muslim scholars in Egypt and Syria asking their legal opinion on the writing of such a book. Five of these scholars answered positively, saying there was no harm in this. Ibn Fahd also wrote a refutation of the arguments used by his adversaries against his *Nukat,* entitled *Al-Nuṣrā wa al-is'āf fī al-radd 'alā al-muntaqidīn lī mu'allafī al-nukat al-ẓirāf* (Advocacy and Succour against the Critics of my Book, the Cute Anecdotes).[40] After gaining the support he wanted, Ibn Fahd embarked upon a new and enlarged version of the *Nukat* entitled *Al-Nukat al-ẓirāf fīman ibtuliya bi al-'āhāt min al-ashrāf* (Cute Anecdotes on Luminaries Afflicted with Disabilities).[41] This new version was almost double the size of the original.[42] It was finished towards the end of 1543 and told the whole story.

The book is divided into an introduction, two chapters and a conclusion. The introduction starts by describing how the book came to be written, a word saying something about the author's predecessors and their writings in this field, and giving an overall description of it. The main body of the introduction is dedicated to the prophetic traditions, anecdotes and verses about people with disabilities. The author started with those traditions that appeared to convey negative attitudes towards people with disabilities. After analysing them and denying their negative implications, the author presented the traditions that extol people with disabilities. The story of Job was presented in detail as an exemplary model for those who show patience and thus eventually gain great rewards. The introduction was supplemented with about five folios dedicated to defending his work against those who attacked it on the grounds that it fell into the forbidden category of *ghība* (backbiting). The author made a detailed refutation of this claim, basing his arguments on a book written by the well-known mystic al-Ḥārith al-Muḥāsibī (d. 857)[43] entitled *Al-Ghība*. He also mentioned the question he posed to the scholars of al-Azhar in Cairo and gave a verbatim account of the fatwas issued by the muftis of the four Sunni schools of law stating that there is no harm in such a book. He also referred to the letter he received from the Damascene scholar Muḥammad b. Ṭulūn (1475–1546).[44]

The first chapter reviews in detail those with disabilities in general and the well-known among them in particular. Ibn Fahd started with a long quotation from *Mufīd al-'ulum wa mubīd al-humūm* (Provider of Sciences and Eliminator of Worries) by Abū Bakr al-Khuwārizmī (d. 1012), which enumerated the prophets and other noble figures known for being afflicted with blindness or the loss of one eye. Ibn Fahd continued by presenting Muslim scholars' discussions on the possibility that a prophet could be blind. This was followed by retelling the stories of those well-known figures afflicted with these two disabilities, in particular the author's contemporaries. Ibn Fahd also retold the stories of how the Prophet healed those afflicted with various disabilities and how others became afflicted with disabilities because they disobeyed or lied to the Prophet.

The second chapter discusses other sorts of *'āhāt* (disabilities) especially the loss of an eye, having a squint, being bald or lame and having leprosy. The author mentioned those who had these disabilities, quoting from al-Khuwārizmī's book and focusing on the author's contemporaries. The author paid special attention to baldness, emphasizing that earlier scholars did not recognize it as grounds for shame. Thus, he added, bald people were not right to have gotten angry because he mentioned them in the first version of the *Nukat*. He concluded this chapter by mentioning supplications that could be said to protect against certain afflictions.

The conclusion focused on the rewards and blessings that accrue to those afflicted with calamities. The author based his work here on Qur'anic verses, prophetic traditions, scholars' statements, anecdotes and poems, all of which promote the beneficial aspects of suffering and adversity.

The contents of this book show that Ibn Fahd attempted to give a balance of entertaining and edifying elements. Besides retelling the entertaining anecdotes about people with disabilities, he also included admonitions and narratives intended to console the afflicted. This explains the statement he made when defending his position that his book was meant for *al-tasliya* (entertainment) and *al-maw'iẓa* (admonition).[45] Keeping in mind that the available version is the enlarged one, we cannot be sure if this balance also existed in the original, smaller, version.

5.5 Identity of the 'demagogues'

According to Ibn Fahd, the main catalyst for the tumult against him was a number of bald men who were angry because he mentioned them in his book. A careful reading of the question upon which Ibn Ḥajar issued the fatwa indicates that the questioner could in fact have been one of those angry bald people. For instance, the questioner was clearly hostile to the author and even suggested a punishment – that the book should be torn up.[46]

Why were the bald upset by what Ibn Fahd wrote rather than the others he mentioned – the blind, the lame, etc.? Apart from the possibility of a pre-existing enmity before the book was written, listing the bald was in a sense revealing a sensitive private issue, because covering the head with an *'imāma* (turban) was a common practice at this time.[47] Ibn Ḥajar wrote a book on this topic, stating that wearing the *'imāma* is one of the signs of a scholar.[48] Ibn Fahd also wrote a book in the same vein and called the *'imāma* the crown of the Arabs.[49] One way of humiliating a person and specifically a scholar was forcing him to take his *'imāma* off.[50] Ibn Fahd would probably have found out that the men were bald in the mosque because they would have to wipe their heads with water as one of the pillars of ablution (*wuḍū'*).

Precisely identifying the members of this group is not possible, mainly because the old version of the *Nukat,* which included a list of them, is unavailable. Available sources recording the history of Mecca during this period are also silent in this respect.[51] However, Ibn Fahd mentioned three characteristics that can help us. They lived in Mecca and held important positions there (*min akābir baladī*)[52] but they were simultaneously the profligates of the age (*fujjār al-'aṣr*) and thus known for their corruption and immoral acts.[53] Third, they were *qur'ān* rather then *ṣul'ān*. According to Ibn Fahd, *qur'ān* means those who are bald in the middle of the head because of an ailment whereas *ṣul'ān* are those who are bald at the front of the head and have no ailment.[54] This specific characteristic could indicate that these people probably belonged to the Mālikī or the Ḥanafī juristic schools rather than the Shafi'ī or the Ḥanbalī, because jurists of the former two schools have to take their turban off completely and wipe their whole bare head during ablution.[55] On the other hand, Ḥanbalīs could just wipe their turban instead of their head.[56] Shafi'īs could wipe the front of the head only without taking their turban off.[57] Thus Ibn Fahd would only have been able to see who was bald in the middle of their head if they were Mālikīs or Ḥanafīs, on the assumption that he found out that they were bald while they were performing ablution. However, we cannot eliminate the possibility that Ibn Fahd could have seen who was bald in a public bath (*ḥammām*). In this case, it would be more difficult to establish their juristic affiliation.

Furthermore, Ibn Ṭulūn's letter[58] to Ibn Fahd gives an indication that those 'demagogues' were known as men of letters (*udabā'*). Learning the lesson from this incident, Ibn Ṭulūn decided to avoid mentioning any of the *udabā'* in his forthcoming book *Ta'jīl al-bishāra lī man ṣabar 'alā dhahāb al-baṣar* (Accelerating the Good Omen for Those Who were Patient Upon Losing their Eyesight).[59]

5.6 The polemic in focus

The key question in this polemic was whether *Al-Nukat al-ẓirāf* fell into Islam's forbidden category of backbiting (*ghība*). Ibn Ḥajar was of the opinion that this was the case but Ibn Fahd insisted that his book had nothing to do with *ghība* and was just written for the sake of admonishment and entertainment.

Before the details of this polemic are examined, two brief notes are in order. First, as indicated by the extensive use of arguments and statements attributed to Shāfi'ī jurists, the two scholars participating in this debate belonged to this school of law. Second, Ibn Fahd based all juristic arguments he used concerning *ghība* on a work of the same title, *Al-Ghība*,[60] by al-Ḥārith al-Muḥāsibī (d. 857), giving him preference over other Shāfi'ī jurists who are more authoritative such as al-Ghazālī (d. 1111).[61] Ibn Fahd may have done this on purpose, in the knowledge that his main interlocutor, Ibn Ḥajar, did not dare start his scholarly career as a writer until he saw al-Muḥāsibī in a dream encouraging him to do so. It seems that this story was well known, especially to those living in Mecca, and it was mentioned by Ibn Ḥajar's Meccan student.[62] In other words, Ibn Fahd is sending the indirect message 'You, Ibn Ḥajar, run the risk of going against the convictions of the authority who first inspired you to embark on your scholarly career.'

*5.6.1 Backbiting (*Ghība*)*

Ghība, according to both Ibn Ḥajar and Ibn Fahd, is to say something, even if it is true, about someone that he or she would *dislike*.[63] After giving that definition, Ibn Ḥajar embarked upon refuting the argument that mentioning the physical defects of the Companions of the Prophet (*al-ṣaḥāba*) in particular does not fall into the category of *ghība* thus defined. This would be because the Companions were too noble to be offended by their defects being mentioned. In short, it is not something they would have disliked. Ibn Ḥajar deemed this argument groundless and invalid, stating that being offended by such things is innate and has nothing to do with being noble or ignoble.[64]

However, the prohibition on *ghība* as defined above is not applicable to six exceptional cases on which Ibn Fahd and Ibn Ḥajar agreed. These are:

1. complaining about oppression or injustice by a wronged or oppressed person;
2. seeking others' assistance for addressing an injustice – for instance, informing the ruling authorities that a specific person is a thief in order to catch him;
3. seeking religious advice (fatwa), for instance asking a scholar about the legal position of living with a spouse doing immoral things;
4. warning Muslims against bad people, those, for example, who invent traditions and ascribe them to the Prophet of Islam. In such an event, one is obliged to declare that such people are liars and untrustworthy;
5. informing on people who practise immoral and dissolute deeds in public;
6. introducing someone by a well-known epithet which incidentally indicates a defect such as 'the lame' (*al-a'raj*), 'the deaf' (*al-aṣamm*) or 'the bald' (*al-aqra'*).[65]

Ibn Ḥajar was convinced that the *Nukat* did not belong to any of the exceptional cases. He refuted the only possibility, that the book could belong to the sixth case, by saying, 'The author did not restrict himself to epithets that are well known in public but went further, to defects that would be known only through his book. Thus it is forbidden (*ḥarām*) by consensus.'[66]

After presenting these six cases, Ibn Fahd claimed that his book belonged to one of them without specifying which. He added that he did not intend to besmirch luminaries. His aim was rather to present an amusing admonition and entertainment. He wondered: 'How could my intention be to besmirch the people mentioned in my work when I included myself among the bald, my maternal grandfather among the lame and a number of my noble masters among the blind?!'[67]

In response to the argument that he intended admonition, Ibn Ḥajar exclaimed,

> This is an empty allegation. I have never known of anyone who listed this as a reasonable ground to legitimize *ghība*. This author should be informed that what he believes is not true. If he insists on his contention, he should receive a grave disciplinary punishment. Ultimately, such a conviction could drag him into a difficult situation.[68]

Ibn Ḥajar continued to say that compiling such a book had nothing to do with admonition. It was rather the result of devilish temptation so that the ignorant would see it as a good work. He cited the Qur'ān in this regard: 'Is he whose foul deeds seem fair to him like the man who is rightly guided?' (35:08).[69] Ibn Ḥajar added,

> Even if we overlooked the truth and supposed that there is admonition, this admonition is accompanied by an untold number of harms and evils. Giving assumed benefit [i.e., admonition] precedence to a definite harm would be done by none except one ignorant about the Qur'ān, Sunna and consensus.[70]

As for the enormity of *ghība* as a sin in Islam, it was sufficient for Ibn Fahd to concede that it is forbidden. However, he added that a number of jurists opine that *ghība* is forbidden only in cases where religion is slandered, rather than a person's honour or physical characteristics.[71] This would mean that his book, according to those scholars, would fall outside the scope of forbidden *ghība*. In a bid to support this argument, Ibn Fahd quoted a tradition relating that the Prophet Muḥammad was asked about two groups of people. To identify them for the questioner, he referred to physical defects, saying that some were red-haired beardless people and the others had short black beards.[72] For the same reason, Ibn Fahd cited the dialogue between two prominent Companions, 'Umar b. al-Khaṭṭāb, who was then caliph, and 'Abd Allāh b. 'Abbās. In this dialogue the former commented on some of the prominent Companions, explaing what deterred him from nominating them for the position of caliph after him. These comments reveal a number of their defects such as being over-humorous, quick-tempered, lenient and so forth. Ibn Fahd comments on this dialogue by saying, ' 'Umar's intention was absolutely not to defame these people. He merely wanted to tell people about their characteristics so that they would choose a caliph among them from a position of knowledge.'[73]

For Ibn Ḥajar, *ghība* was not just a normal sin but one of the *kabā'ir*, the grave and major sins in Islam, when its target is scholars of religion and memorizers of the Qur'ān or anyone who is attacked unjustifiably. Ibn Ḥajar based his argument here on al-Qurṭubī (d. 1272) who transmitted the consensus (*ijmāʿ*) of scholars on this point.[74]

To support his argument, Ibn Ḥajar referred to a statement by the Companion Ibn ʿAbbās, who participated in the aforementioned dialogue: 'The one who hurts a jurist, in fact hurts the Messenger of God, and one who hurts the Messenger of God, in fact hurts God the Sublime.'[75] Ibn Ḥajar even referred to al-Shāfiʿī (767–820) himself.[76] The Prophet is reported to have said that had his daughter Fāṭima stolen something, he would have cut off her hand. When telling this story, al-Shāfiʿī used the expression 'a certain woman (*fulāna*)' instead of naming the Prophet's daughter, in view of the negative context of the story. Commenting on this, Ibn Ḥajar said, 'Had this author reflected on this noble politeness of al-Shāfiʿī, he would have realized that the enormity of what he did cannot be repaired in a lifetime.'[77]

Remarkably, five years later Ibn Ḥajar expressed a more lenient opinion on the enormity of *ghība* in his book, *Al-Zawājir ʿan iqtirāf al-kabāʾir*. He conceded that opinions ascribed to credible jurists such as al-Ghazālī categorize *ghība* as a minor sin. Anyhow, 'Even if no consensus can be demonstrated in this regard, we should at least differentiate between the different sorts, categories, and harms of each *ghība*.'[78] On *ghība* which targets physical defects, as Ibn Fahd's book would have done, Ibn Ḥajar does not negate the possibility of categorizing it as a minor sin (*ṣaghīra*).[79]

Did Ibn Ḥajar adopt this more lenient opinion because he had revised his previous convictions on the basis of new information he came across in the five years between his issuing the fatwa and writing the book? Was he, at the time of issuing the fatwa, simply under the influence of a particular milieu that pushed him to adopt that harsh opinion, compared with the other one expressed in the book? This is an open question. However, the implication is that had this incident happened in another context and at a later date, the fatwa might have been less harsh.

5.6.2 Precursors

One of the main arguments put forward by Ibn Fahd in this polemic is that he had precursors in the field and thus his book did not create new ground. It seems that this point was central in that it was mentioned by the questioner who asked Ibn Ḥajar to elaborate on it. Ibn Fahd also used it in his question sent to the scholars in Egypt.

Ibn Fahd was aware of four precursors. He referred to three of them: Ibn Qutayba (828–889) in *Kitāb al-maʿārif* (Entertaining Information);[80] Salāḥ al-Din al-Ṣafadī (1297–1363), who wrote *Nakt al-himyān fī nukat al-ʿumyān* (Extracting the Precious on the Anecdotes of the Blind) and *Al-Shuʿūr bī al-ʿūr* (Feeling for the One-Eyed People)[81]; and Abu ʿUthman ʿAmr b. Bahr al-Jāḥiẓ (776–868/9), who wrote *Al-ʿUrjān wa al-burṣān wa al-qurʿān* (The Lame, the Lepers and the Bald).[82] The fourth and, to Ibn Fahd, most important precursor was Abū Bakr Muḥammad b. Musā al-Khuwārizmī (d. 1012), who dedicated three chapters of his *Mufīd al-'ulūm wa mubīd al-humūm* (Provider of Sciences and Eliminator of Worries) to prominent people afflicted with disabilities. Ibn Fahd presented al-Khuwārizmī as the jurist of Baghdad, one of the senior ascetics (*zuhhād*) and the fourth-century[83] renewer of religion (*mujaddid al-dīn*).[84]

Ibn Ḥajar did not recognize this argument as valid and put forward two main counterarguments. The first was about the identity of the precursors:

> Are they exemplary figures in the same league as Aḥmad b. Ḥanbal (780–855),[85] Yaḥyā b. Ma'īn (775–847),[86] Abū Zur'a al-Rāzī (d. 878)[87] and their counterparts who came after or before them? If the precursor is any of those then you have to name him. If he was one of those worthless people whose sayings and deeds are negligible, then Allah would not care in which valley you will die away.[88]

The second point was that Ibn Ḥajar believed that the predecessors' context would not involve ascribing dishonour to luminaries. However, the context of Ibn Fahd would encourage the populace to misuse such information and thus degrade the honourable status of those luminaries, including the Companions. Consequently, 'The author of this book would bear the burdens of the sins committed in this respect until Doomsday.'[89]

Important information is still missing concerning the issue of precursors. Ibn Ḥajar avoided any reference to al-Khuwārizmī, the main model for Ibn Fahd. It seems that Ibn Fahd was also not aware of many other precursors in this field. He made reference to only four of them and he seems to have only seen al-Khuwārizmī's book. He missed important sources, some of which would have given support for his argument. To mention the most important, Ibn al-Jawzī (1126–1200)[90] discussed the same subject in his historical work *Talqīḥ fuhūm ahl al-athar fī 'uyūn al-tārīkh wa al-siyar* (Fertilizing the Perceptions of the Traditionists Concerning the Fountains of History and Biographies) in which he listed notable people who had different disabilities.[91] The importance of Ibn al-Jawzī as a precursor in this regard lies in his being a very well-known and venerated Muslim jurist. Furthermore, Ibn Ḥajar himself used Ibn al-Jawzī as a creditable reference more than once in his books.[92]

5.6.3 Juristic authorities

Ibn Ḥajar reproached Ibn Fahd for not consulting the specialized jurists before embarking upon his work. To Ibn Ḥajar, this indicated malice and bigotry to the extent of untruthfulness.[93] Ibn Ḥajar quoted the Qur'anic verse: 'If they had only referred it to the Messenger, or to those charged with authority among them, those among them who can search out the knowledge of it would have known it' (Qur'ān 4:83).

To avoid falling into the same trap, Ibn Ḥajar based the reasoning for his fatwa to destroy the book on a previous fatwa issued by the well-known Shāfi'ī jurist, al-Suyūṭī (1445–1505) on the destruction of houses used for illegal and immoral actions.[94] Thus, fountainheads of corruption were to be devastated whether they took the form of houses or books.

Rather than indulging in defending his juristic background, as shown above, Ibn Fahd took a short cut and consulted the juristic authorities in Egypt. In 1542, he sent the following question to the scholars in Cairo:

> What do you say – May God be pleased with you – of a student who read a book entitled *Mufīd al-ʻulūm* (Provider of Sciences) by the well-known Ḥanafī scholar Abū Bakr Muḥammad b. Mūsā al-Khuwārizmī. The student saw chapters on the physical defects of noble people. The author mentioned a group of the early and late prominent figures of this nation who were known for their defects such as the lame, the bald, the blind and the like. Seeing this, the student composed a book on this issue using the same justification proposed by the author of the aforementioned book, namely, promoting admonition, learning, and entertainment. Would this intention legitimize embarking upon such an act? Give us the fatwa, asking that God would make Paradise your reward![95]

Ibn Fahd recorded verbatim the fatwas issued by four scholars, each of whom belonged to one of the four juristic schools, the Ḥanafī (Abū al-Fayḍ b. ʻAlī al-Sulamī), the Ḥanbalī (Aḥmad b. al-Najjār), the Mālikī (Nāṣir al-Laqqānī) and the Shāfiʻī (Aḥmad al-Bulqīnī). They all responded to the question in the affirmative, stating that there is no harm in compiling such a book with these intentions.

In the same year, Ibn Fahd received a supportive letter from his intimate friend,[96] the well-known Damascene scholar Abū ʻAbd Allāh Muḥammad b. Ṭulūn (1475–1546). Ibn Ṭulūn referred to the contention that *ghība* is only forbidden if a person's religiosity is besmirched. It does not include mentioning a person's physical characteristics or honour unless with the intention of defaming his or her character.

5.7 Who won this debate?

The reader may have received the overall impression that Ibn Fahd won the debate. He rewrote the revised version of *Al-Nukat* after gaining the support of religious authorities through the fatwas of the Syrian and Egyptian scholars. The new version has remained intact until the present day.

However, it seems that the incident was not without adverse consequences. The main example here is Ibn Ṭulūn, who expressed his support for Ibn Fahd. Ibn Ṭulūn was busy at the time of the controversy with writing a book on blind people entitled *Taʻjīl al-bishāra liman ṣabar ʻalā dhahāb al-baṣar* (Accelerating the Good Omen for Those Who had Patience Upon Losing Their Eyesight). Because of the fuss raised by Ibn Fahd's work and fearing that he could face the same consequences, Ibn Ṭulūn decided not to list any men of letters afflicted with disabilities in his book.[97]

We have neither concrete nor comprehensive information on whether the repercussions of this incident ended with Ibn Ṭulūn's book or whether they went further to create a hostile atmosphere for those who wanted to write on this topic. Bearing in mind that current scholarship on disability is still in its initial phase, future findings may tell us more.

Anyhow, this incident indicated clearly that the dignity of people with disabilities was a high priority among Muslim jurists. This is proved by the fact that harsh consequences could follow if it was felt that their dignity had been seriously infringed.

5.8 Further developments

Writing on people with disabilities did not come to a halt after this incident. However, the focus shifted slightly from a literary approach aiming at entertaining the reader to compiling the juristic rulings (*al-aḥkām al-fiqhiyya*) relevant to people with disabilities. For instance, the Ḥanafī jurist Ibn Nujaym (d. 1563) wrote a chapter on the rulings relevant to blind people. This chapter was later expounded upon by his student Aḥmad b. Muḥammad al-Ḥamawī (d. 1687).[98] Another Ḥanafī jurist, Mullā ʻAlī b. Sulṭān al-Harawī al-Qārī (d. *c.* 1605), wrote *Tasliyat al-Aʻma min Baliyyat al-ʻAma* (Consoling the Blind from the Affliction of Blindness).[99] This tendency intensified with the passage of time, especially in the twentieth century. For instance, Aḥmad al-Sharabāṣī (1918–1980) wrote *Fī ʻālam al-makfūfīn* (In the World of the Blind) and made a call for researchers to write on the juristic rulings on blind people. He did this himself in the second volume when he received no response to his call. The juristic rulings on people with disabilities has recently become a favoured topic for MA and PhD researchers in the Arab world. Although the literary works have decreased in number, they have not vanished completely.[100]

5.9 Summary

This chapter has provided an overview of the discussions among Muslim scholars, especially within Islamic jurisprudence, about the ethics of writing on people with disabilities. The main focus was on a previously unstudied manuscript written in the sixteenth century on people with disabilities. The Meccan author, Ibn Fahd, gave the names of famous people, from the time of the Prophet Muḥammad till his own time, enumerating their disabilities. Some of the contemporaries of the author were offended because they were mentioned in the book. Consequently, a fatwa was issued that the book must be destroyed because it had transgressed boundaries and infringed the dignity of people with disabilities. The book was eventually destroyed. The author did not surrender quickly and insisted that he had no bad intentions in writing the book. To protect his reputation, the author contacted five well-known Muslim scholars in Egypt and Syria and described the main objective of his book. The scholars replied that there was no harm in it. The author rewrote and expanded the book and his manuscript copy remains intact to this day. The story of this book is highly informative about the social position of people with disabilities and also about the role of Muslim jurists in protecting this position. For instance, the book was destroyed because of a fatwa against it and the author rewrote it after receiving fatwas approving it. This implies a dynamic relationship between people with disabilities, their society and Muslim jurists.

6 Employability of people with disabilities

In discussing employment, this chapter tackles one of the fundamental rights of people with disabilities. According to the ILO, work of decent quality is the most effective means of escaping the vicious circle of marginalization, poverty and social exclusion.[1] The United Nations report published in August 2006 states that unemployment among people with disabilities is as high as 80 per cent in some countries. Often employers assume that people with disabilities are unable to work. However, an estimated 386 million of the world's working-age population have disabilities.[2] This large-scale unemployment costs the global economy an estimated US$ 1.9 trillion per year.[3] The ILO has appealed for the barriers obstructing disabled people from getting jobs and taking their place in society to be dismantled through a variety of policy measures, regulations, programmes and services.[4] To this end, article 8 of the recent UN Convention on the Rights of People with Disabilities calls for the skills, merits and abilities of persons with disabilities and their contributions to the workplace and the labour market to be recognized.[5] The Optional Protocol of this convention was opened for signature by all states and by regional integration organizations at the United Nations Headquarters in New York on 30 March 2007. The list of signatories includes a number of Islamic countries such as Algeria, Egypt, Turkey, Morocco, Sudan and Yemen.[6]

In the Islamic sources, we find that *'amal*, the best-known equivalent for 'work', is one of the most often repeated words in the Qur'ān. The different derivatives of this word are mentioned in it almost 330 times. If we count references to the notion of work without being limited to the term *'amal*, this number will easily double.[7] However, this Qur'anic term, which is now standard usage in modern Islamic and Arabic literature for work, work opportunities and workers' rights,[8] does not help us to trace juristic discussions on this topic. The two chapters entitled '*Ijāra*' and '*Ji'āla*' in classical *fiqh* manuals represent the main access to relevant juristic discussions on the employability of people with disabilities.

Ijāra is derived from *ajr* (remuneration) and means 'a contract to hire'. In the juristic sense, it is a contract by which one person makes over to someone else the enjoyment, by personal right, of a thing or an activity, in return for payment.[9] In the case of hiring persons for specific services, this type of contract would involve two main parties, the one hired (*ajīr*), in modern usage the employee, and the one hiring (*musta'jir*), now equivalent to employer. The first party (employee) provides a specific service for the second (employer) against a specific remuneration usually called *ujra* or *ajr*, now known as wage, salary, stipend, etc.[10]

Ji'āla, sometimes also read as *ja'āla* and *ju'āla*, comes very close to the notion of *ijāra*. It means the matter given to a person for doing a specific work or service. The same notion is also covered by other relevant terms such as *ju'l* and *ja'īla*. In the juristic sense, it means fixing a specific wage, pay or stipend (*'iwaḍ*) for a specific or non-specific work or service.[11] Thus the employee, the period of work or the amount of remuneration can remain unidentified in such a contract. In the case of an unidentified employee, the first party (employer) would designate a specific *ajr* (stipend) against a specific service without specifying who was going to do this service. *Ji'āla* in this case becomes a sort of open competition and the person who does the service as required by the employer will be entitled to the remuneration designated in advance.[12] Discussions on the second party, namely the employee, and on the service or work, in juristic texts named *manfa'a* (lit. benefit), to be done in these two types of contracts are directly relevant to this topic and thus become the main focus here. The main question is: are people with disabilities in principle employable according to these two main types of contract?

People with mental or physical disabilities are seen as employable in principle in the case of *ji'āla* contracts. Some jurists have limited this unconditional employability to the case where the employee is not designated in advance.[13]

As for *ijāra*, jurists have stipulated that for this contract to be valid the two parties involved, i.e. employer and employee, should be of sound mind (*'āqil*) and capable of discernment (*mumayyiz*).[14] People with disabilities which do not affect these two conditions were thus in principle employable.

Concerning the *manfa'a* (benefit, work or service) whose achievement would make the employee entitled to remuneration, jurists stipulated that the employee should be able to do it. Hence, it is not acceptable for instance to employ a blind person as a guard, a dumb person as an interpreter or a person with amputated hands as a tailor and so forth.[15] Thus people with disabilities are not employable for jobs whose tasks cannot be correctly achieved because of the disability. The main rationale here is guaranteeing the quality of work; it is not discriminating against people with disabilities. The same ruling is, for instance, applicable to able-bodied people who lack the skills to reach the required standard.[16]

The aforementioned two principles are endorsed by all schools of law with one main exception. An opinion within the Shāfi'ī school contends that the financial transactions of a blind person, including sale, purchase and *ijāra*, are not valid. The sole argument advanced for this opinion is that in case of sale and purchase, the blind cannot see the product and thus may be deceived. By way of analogy, employing a blind person is also prohibited. Despite the good intention of protecting the rights of the blind as expressed by the advocates of this opinion, it has been rejected by the majority of jurists.[17] First of all, no evidence from the Qur'ān or the Sunna supports such an opinion.[18] Second, forbidding blind people to sell, buy or work causes real damage to their daily life, greater than the damage caused by any deception during such dealings. Third, deception can be avoided in many other ways such as by a precise description of the product in the case of selling and the type of work and expected remuneration in the case of employment.[19] Fourth, people with analogous sorts of physical disabilities such as dumbness are allowed to conclude such transactions by means of writing or gesture.[20]

This generally agreed broad principle of being able to carry out the required tasks must be traced in its implementation in specific jobs which have attracted the attention of Muslim jurists. The jobs to be discussed below are those with high prestige especially in religious milieux. The list is limited to the positions of muezzin (one who makes the call or *adhān* for prayer), *imām* (one who leads the ritual prayer), judge and the head of the state.

6.1 Muezzin

The muezzin (in Arabic, *mu'adhdhin* or sometimes *munādī*) is the person designated to announce prayer time by chanting a special religious formula called *adhān*. The holder of this office has always enjoyed religious, social and sometimes even political prestige in the Muslim community.[21]

Some jurists have objected to paying the muezzin, considering calling to prayer a devotional practice which should be done for the sake of God, not for the sake of money. Other jurists have permitted this practice in view of the need to have qualified people for this office.[22] Historical reports indicate that muezzin became a paid job during the reign of 'Utmān b. 'Affān (r. 644–656). Later on, muezzins were known to receive sometimes large amounts of money, as was the case during the reign of Aḥmad b. Ṭūlūn (835–884). Muezzins also received a share in the endowments, often by a special provision in the documents establishing the foundations.[23]

Among the qualifications required for holders of this office, jurists mentioned the possession of a sound mind (*'āqil*). A call to prayer (*adhān*) made by a person without mental capacity is invalid according to the majority of jurists because such a person would be unaware of what he is saying and thus would not have the intention (*niyya*) of proclaiming *adhān*. Because intention is not essential according to the Ḥanafīs, they considered a call to prayer made by such a person as merely reprehensible (*makrūh*).[24] Keeping in mind the main task of the muezzin and the aforementioned principle of being able to carry out the required tasks for the job, it could easily be concluded that a dumb person cannot be employed as muezzin. Other disabilities such as lameness and amputated limbs were not mentioned by jurists as barriers to holding this office.

Blindness was the most discussed disability as regards the office of muezzin. According to all jurists, the main purpose of the call to prayer (*adhān*) is to inform people that prayer time is due.[25] This purpose has two main aspects, namely informing people (*i'lām al-nās*) and knowing the prayer times (*mawāqīt al-ṣalāt*). The first aspect was compatible with a blind office-holder whereas the second was not. Here we start with discussions on the second aspect because they started earlier.

On the second aspect, knowing the times of prayer was dependent on observing the day–night cycle and, to guarantee precision in this regard, some jurists elaborated that the muezzin should be proficient in the stations of the moon (*manāzil al-qamar*).[26] A blind muezzin would be unable to fulfil this qualification. In consequence, a blind muezzin might announce the call to prayer before or after the precise time. Thus an important element of the main purpose of the call to prayer could not be guaranteed. This made the issue of employing a blind person in the office of muezzin a point of disagreement. A minority of jurists including the Shāfiʿīs and the Ḥanbalīs opposed making the blind eligible for this office, arguing that they cannot know the time at which the call to prayer should be made.[27] However, the majority of jurists thought employing a blind person for this office was permissible as long as he could be informed by a sighted person when it was the exact time for prayer.[28]

As for the first aspect, informing people of the time for prayer, jurists stated that the muezzin should do his best to make his voice heard by as many people as possible. Different prophetic traditions indicate the rewards of raising one's voice during the prayer call, stating, for instance, that the sins of the muezzin will be forgiven, he will be rewarded for every person who responds to the prayer call and comes to prayers, and all who hear the prayer call will testify for the muezzin on the Day of Resurrection.[29] It was always recommended that ideally *adhān* should be called from a high place so as to be audible to the largest possible number of people.[30] During the lifetime of the Prophet, *adhān* was proclaimed from the top of the highest house near the mosque. After its height was raised for this specific purpose, *adhān* was proclaimed from the roof of the mosque itself.[31] Later on, *adhān* was proclaimed from a high place, generally a turret of a mosque called a 'minaret' (in Arabic *manāra* or *mi'dhana*). According to some jurists, this new system was introduced during the reign of Muʿāwiya b. Abī Sufyān (r. 41/661–60/680).[32] Climbing the minaret, however, enabled the muezzin to see into the private space of neighbouring houses, a practice which is absolutely forbidden in Islam.[33] To overcome this problem, jurists came up with a number of precautionary measures. For instance, a number of Mālikī jurists stipulated a minimum distance between the minaret and the houses near the mosque, otherwise the muezzin would not be allowed to climb it. This minimum distance had to be far enough for a person looking from the minaret to be unable to differentiate between male and female figures in nearby houses.[34] Jurists also focused on specific characteristics in the muezzin himself to help him to lower his gaze and thus not look into the private space of others. Righteousness, being married and being advanced in years were the characteristics most often mentioned.[35] Other jurists said that in addition the muezzin should promise not to spy on the neighbours or allow others to go up the minaret.[36] But it seems that all these measures did not solve the problem. For instance, the Shāfiʿī jurist Ibn Ḥajar al-Haytamī told the story of a muezzin who, despite his well-known righteousness, watched a Christian lady from the minaret and fell so deeply in love with her that he converted to Christianity in order to marry her. On the day of the marriage, Ibn Ḥajar added, the former muezzin fell from the roof of his house and died, thus lost to his religion and to his beloved lady.[37]

The most practical solution to this problem was to employ blind people and thus they were preferred to the sighted for this specific office.[38] Blindness was sometimes cited, in practice, as one of the qualifications that a muezzin should possess.[39] Documents of some *waqf* records also add credibility to this fact. The large *waqf* foundation instituted in 1774 in Mameluke Egypt, which funded a large mosque and educational centre, serves as a clear example in this regard. Among the daily and annual disbursements allocated for mosque personnel, a stipend was reserved for five *blind* men as muezzins.[40] According to some anecdotes, the popularity of employing blind men only for this office made many sighted people feign blindness in order to become muezzins of wealthy mosques.[41]

It is worth mentioning here that introducing the office of *al-muwaqqit*, a professional astronomer whose primary responsibility was the regulation of the times of prayer, must have had important repercussions, because knowing prayer times ceased to be among the tasks of the muezzin and so blindness was no longer an obstacle. The exact date when the office of *al-muwaqqit* was introduced is not known but it was well established by the seventh/thirteenth century.[42]

6.2 Prayer leader (*imām*)

One of the main meanings of this term is the one appointed to lead ritual prayers. As a sign of the importance of this position, the chief political leader or caliph was the person who held it from the earliest days of Islam. If it was not the caliph himself, *imāms* always had to be chosen from among those learned in religious matters, beginning with the most versed in the Qur'ān and, failing him, the eldest.[43]

The juristic controversy over whether to pay the muezzin was repeated for the office of *imām* because it is a religious service and thus belongs to the category of devotional practices.[44] In fact, appointed *imāms* were paid from the public treasury (*bayt al-māl*).[45]

As in the case of the muezzin, people with mental disabilities were not deemed eligible for holding the office of *imām*.[46] People with other disabilities could hold this office as long as they were not thereby prevented from performing any of the essential parts of the prayer. For instance, according to the majority of jurists, the blind could be employed as *imām* since blindness, like loss of the sense of smell, need not affect the performance of prayer.[47] The Shāfi'īs stated that the blind would be more eligible for this office than the sighted because they could concentrate more fully on the prayers.[48] The Ḥanafīs were against employing the blind as *imām* because of their lack of awareness of impurities, unless they were better qualified in the Qur'ān and religious knowledge.[49] During the lifetime of the Prophet, two persons were known to hold this position, 'Abd Allāh b. Umm Maktūm and 'Itbān b. Mālik.[50]

People with speech disabilities such as a lisp or the dumb, those with hearing disabilities such as the deaf, or physical disabilities such as amputated arms or legs and also people suffering from epilepsy were generally considered ineligible for the job of *imām*. Jurists believed these disabilities would have a negative effect on the ideal performance of prayer.[51] The case against employing people with such disabilities as *imāms* is based on two main considerations. First, he would be *imām* for people who do not suffer from the same disability. Second, there are other qualified people who do not suffer from these disabilities. If one of these two conditions did not apply, people with the aforementioned disabilities would be allowed to be prayer leaders.[52] Thus, in centres for people with disabilities, one of them may be appointed to lead the other residents in ritual prayers. On 21 February 1983, a question was posed to Dār al-Iftā' in Egypt as to whether a man with amputated legs could lead the ritual prayer. The late Muftī of Egypt, 'Abd al-Laṭīf Ḥamza, issued a fatwa stating that this would be reprehensible (*makrūh*), based on earlier Ḥanafī and Mālikī authorities who held the same opinion.[53]

The Ẓāhirī (literalist) jurist Ibn Ḥazm (d. 456/1064)[54] had a different opinion which deserves to be recorded. Basing his argument on the Qur'anic verse, 'The noblest of you in God's sight is he who is most righteous' (Qur'ān 49:13), he said that defects that might count against employability in this office are those which affect their religion rather than their bodies or lineages. Thus, Ibn Ḥazm adds, physical disabilities can never be a decisive factor in selecting people to hold the office of *imām*.[55] In practice, deaf people also held the position of *imām,* such as 'Alī Ibn 'Irāq (1501–1556) who was appointed *imām* and preacher of the Mosque of the Prophet Muḥammad in the holy city of Medina, where he died.[56]

6.3 Judge (*qāḍī*)

The judge, known in legal texts as the *qāḍī*, was broadly speaking a representative of the authority invested with the power of jurisdiction (*qaḍā'*). He was seen as a direct or indirect delegate (*nā'ib*) of the head of the state, the caliph. The religious nature of this office has led to its accumulation with administrative functions of the same nature, such as the administration of mosques and endowments.[57] Islamic history also knew the office of *qāḍi al-quḍāt* (lit. the judge of the judges, chief judge). Besides being a judge, the holder of this office was entrusted with judicial administration: the nomination, control and dismissal of other judges.[58] In the Ottoman Empire, the authority of the judge was extended beyond the usual legal matters to include confidential posts to which judges were appointed by the government which expected them to report from time to time on the activities of high-ranking officials, the general situation and the mood of the population. They had to see that craftsmen were attached to the army before it set off for war, that roads were safe, and that goods needed for domestic consumption were not exported. They also had to supervise the public affairs of the cities, the suitability of buildings, the guilds, the quality of goods and their prices. They were also responsible for seeing that foodstuffs were sold at officially fixed prices. Judges were also important as public notaries; their function was to issue different kinds of certificates and documents concerning sales, contracts, loans and the occasional manumission of slaves, to witness private and public documents, and to supervise the accounts of the endowment incomes and endorse them with an authentication clause.[59] The decrees of the judge were generally binding and without appeal other than in exceptional cases.[60]

Employing a qualified person as a judge against a specific stipend is permissible, according to the majority of jurists. They base their argument on practical cases of people holding this office at the time of the Prophet Muḥammad. Other jurists state that it is reprehensible (*makrūh*) because this office falls into the category of pious acts.[61] To guarantee the competence of the appointed judge, jurists established a long list of qualifications which an employable person should possess.[62] Here the focus will be on conditions relevant to disabilities.

Jurists are in agreement that people with mental disabilities are not eligible for this position because the tasks entrusted to a judge demand shrewdness and intelligence.[63] Other disabilities were points of disagreement among jurists. For instance, the majority of jurists stated that deaf, blind or dumb people must not be employed as judges and if a judge is afflicted with any of these disabilities he should immediately be dismissed.[64] According to Mālikī jurists, if a blind, dumb or deaf person was appointed as a judge, his decrees would be valid and binding as long as they were correctly concluded. They also agreed that if the appointed judge was afflicted with all of the aforementioned three disabilities, his decrees would not be valid. However, they disagreed if he was afflicted with just one of these disabilities.[65] Other jurists, including a number of the Shāfi'īs, Ḥanbalīs, Shī'īs and Ibādīs, contend that a judge may be blind. They base their opinion on the fact that the blind Companion Ibn Umm Maktūm was the delegate of the Prophet many times and this would imply that he could have practised as a judge. And the Prophet Shua'yb was blind and acting as a judge, one of the main tasks of Prophets.[66] The well-known Shāfi'ī jurist, Abū al-'Abbās b. Surayj (d. 306/918),[67] opines that a dumb person (*akhras*) may be employed as a judge as long as he can express himself by means of understandable signs.[68]

If a person is afflicted with a mild form of one of these three disabilities, such as nyctalopia (night blindness), loss of one eye, a stammer or hearing difficulties, then he would remain eligible for the office of judge. Their main argument was that such mild disabilities would not drastically affect the work of the judge. As for a slight speech disability, they recalled the case of the Prophet Moses who was known to lisp.[69]

Jurists also stipulated the need for sound organs for those employed as judges, but without specifying which organs were meant.[70] According to the Shāfi'ī jurist Ibn Ḥabīb al-Māwardī (d. 450/1058),[71] a person whose limbs have contracted, whose hand has been amputated or who has a protracted disease (*zamāna*) may be employed as judge.[72]

In modern studies, two main opinions can be traced. The first supports the view of the majority of early jurists and states that people with hearing, sight and speech disabilities are not qualified to hold this office.[73] The second opinion sees no harm in appointing a blind person as a judge as long as he is qualified.[74]

In practice, people with disabilities have managed to hold the office of judge and sometimes of chief judge throughout Islamic history, proving their eligibility for such a position. Ṣalāḥ al-Dīn al-Ṣafadī (d.1297–1363)[75] mentioned a number of well-known judges who were blind.[76] It was also possible for men with hearing disabilities to receive high-level juridical appointments, for example Muḥammad b. Dawūd, known as Riyāḍī al-Uṭrūsh al-Rūmī, who was appointed chief judge in 1617.[77] Well-known blind judges in modern times would include the two Saudi judges ‘Abd Allāh b. Ḥumayd (d. 1402/1985) and ‘Abd al-‘Azīz b. Bāz (d. 1999).[78]

6.4 Head of state (Caliph)

The highest authority in the Islamic state was the *imām* (lit. leader), *khalīfa* (caliph) or *amīr al-mu'minīn* (the emir of the believers).[79] The office itself was called *imāma* or *khilāfa*. Jurists gave it the title *al-imāma al-kubrā* or *al-'uẓmā* (grand leadership) whereas *al-imāma al-ṣughrā* (minor leadership) meant leadership in prayer.[80] Jurists summed up the tasks entrusted to the caliph as ‘guarding issues pertaining to religion and administering the worldly affairs’ (*ḥirāsat al-dīn wa siyāsat al-dunyā*).[81]

Given that this was the highest position in the state, the qualifications stipulated by jurists were stricter and more detailed than for all the other aforementioned jobs. As regards disability, apart from insanity, jurists contend that hearing, sight and speech disabilities are defects that affect a person's eligibility for this office.[82] According to some jurists, if the caliph himself was afflicted with a hearing or speech disability, he could still remain in office as long as he could express himself through understandable signs or writing. However, the majority of jurists argue that the caliph should be dismissed in such cases.[83] If someone is not blind but just suffers from nyctalopia (night blindness) or weak eyesight, he may still hold this office as long as he recognizes people once he sees them.[84] The same applies to losing an eye or suffering a slight form of speech disability such as a stammer because this need not have a negative effect on executing the tasks entrusted to the caliph.[85]

That amputated hands or legs are also barriers to a person's eligibility to be a caliph is maintained by the great majority of jurists. However, a number of jurists say that if the caliph lost a hand or a leg, he should not be dismissed on this basis. They argue that such a disability would prevent him from carrying out some tasks but not all of them.[86]

Ibn Ḥazm, the Ẓāhirī jurist, is unique in this respect, saying, ‘There is no harm in the *imām* having a physical defect such as blindness or deafness. The same holds true for a person whose nose, both hands or both legs have been cut off.’ According to Ibn Ḥazm, preventing such a person from holding this office is not supported by any evidence from the Qur'ān, Sunna or consensus.[87]

I could find only two opinions in the modern studies which have tackled this point. The first maintains that any of the aforementioned disabilities would prevent a person from being employed as a caliph or head of state.[88] According to the second opinion, if a caliph becomes dumb while in office, the Muslim community should study the case and then decide if his dismissal would be in the public interest. If not, the caliph should remain in office.[89]

6.5 Summary

This chapter has investigated the juristic sources in the search for an answer to an important question: how can people with disabilities earn their living? This chapter first discussed the possibility of employment, the first available means of earning money. We found that juristic sources were full of detailed information about the rulings relevant to people with disabilities in this regard. We also studied the possibility of people with disabilities being employed in the highly prestigious jobs in Islamic society. The general attitude was that this group of people can in principle be employed in any job as long as their disabilities do not affect the quality of the work they are required to do. Interestingly, disability sometimes brought privilege in the sense that people with disabilities were preferred for specific jobs over other candidates. The case of blind people who were appointed as muezzins is a clear example. Because *adhān* (the call to prayer) was made from the top of a minaret, enabling the muezzin to look into neighbouring houses, blind muezzins were always preferred. This is borne out by the fact that some people pretend to be blind so as to get this job, which was sometimes well paid.

These discussions show that early jurists were practising *ijtihād* (personal reasoning)[90] with the main aim of safeguarding the common interest of the Muslim community. In the absence of scriptural evidence from the Qur'ān, Sunna or practical incidents during the lifetime of the Prophet, jurists made use of one main rational argument. They argued that disabled people were not employable for specific jobs if their disabilities would not allow them to execute the tasks entrusted to them properly.

The case of employing blind people as muezzins serves as a clear example in this regard. At first, blind people were not preferred because they could not observe the day–night cycle. Later on, with the introduction of minarets, blind people were preferred because their blindness guaranteed that they would not look into other people's private spaces from the vantage point of the minaret. In the light of available computer programs which inform everyone of the exact time of each prayer, the skill of following the day–night cycle is no longer necessary for the muezzin. On the other hand, with the availability of mechanical amplifiers such as loudspeakers, blindness is not an advantage any more because the muezzin does not have to climb the minaret in order to make the call to prayer.

The same rule holds for the office of judge. Jurists who objected to a blind judge saw no harm in appointing an illiterate person. This is because blindness was seen as hindrance whereas writing skills were not essential for a qualified judge because knowledge was based on orality.[91]

Of course this is all based on arguments which remain relative, elastic and open to different interpretations. That is why in almost every case we find disagreement as to whether a specific disability would affect eligibility for a job. Interestingly enough, the minority of jurists who opposed the idea that eligibility for work might be affected by disability could find scriptural references in the Qur'ān and Sunna, and also practical examples, to support their opinion. The main protagonist of this group, Ibn Ḥazm, made it clear that the opinion advocated by the majority is not based on any clear or authentic evidence.

This situation clearly indicates that there is an area for practising *ijtihād*. Unfortunately, this *ijtihād* is still waiting for new, qualified jurists. Apart from a few studies which have tackled this issue, whose authors incline most of the time to the early authoritative juristic opinions, noted jurists of the modern age have remained almost silent on this topic. In view of the new technological facilities available for people with disabilities, which create new contexts and work opportunities, modern jurists should re-examine and revise earlier opinions and practise a fresh *ijtihād* in this new situation. The position of the caliph or head of state has attracted more attention. Due to the religious and political importance attached to this office, a large number of studies have been carried out by well-known modern jurists. However, the case of people with disabilities still remains outside their main focus.[92]

7 Medical treatment of people with disabilities

This chapter reviews the juristic sources in a search for viewpoints and attitudes towards treating disabilities. These sources made reference to two main methods. The first method, termed in juristic sources 'physical medicine', is based on using medicines and drugs known to medical science at the present time. The second method, called 'spiritual medicine', makes use of specific religious formulas including texts from the Qur'ān, words attributed to the Prophet of Islam, etc. This chapter gave a detailed overview of these two methods in Islamic jurisprudence, the attitudes of Muslim jurists towards these two methods, and finally 'treatments' developed within each method to prevent the occurrence of disability or to cure it.

Among the immense literature available on medicine in Islam,[1] it is difficult to find anything specific on treating disabilities. The only book I am aware of on this topic is *Al-I'āqa fī al-turāth al-'arabī al-islāmī* (Disability in the Arabic Islamic Literature) which collected together the scattered passages and information on different mental and physical disabilities in medical sources written by early Muslim physicians.[2] Mental disabilities may have received more attention mainly due to the writings of Michael Dols (d. 1989).[3] Studies which treated disability within Islamic jurisprudence (*fiqh*) are virtually silent on the issue of the treatment of these disabilities.[4] Muṣṭafa al-Quḍāt (Jordan University) could be the main exception since, under the heading 'the right of people with disabilities to live', he referred to two main points: abortion and organ transplants.[5] The same points are discussed by Vardit Rispler-Chaim (Haifa University) in *Islamic Medical Ethics in the Twentieth Century*.[6] The present chapter, by studying opinion within early and modern Islamic jurisprudence on different methods of treating disabilities, tackles almost untrodden ground in modern literature.

Through trust in the unlimited power of God, according to Ibn Taymiyya, disabilities and diseases in general can be cured without medicine.[7] A vast genre in Islamic literature discussed miraculous healing without medicine, through the power of a Prophet or a Friend of God (*walī*).[8] The Qur'ān speaks in more than one place (3:49, 5:110) of Jesus' miraculous healing of the blind and the lepers. For their part, Muslim scholars also wrote on the miracles of the Prophet of Islam whereby people with different disabilities were healed. Some of them enumerated more than thirty such cases.[9] Similar miraculous powers were also attributed to the Friends of God (*awliyā'*) who were thought to be able to bestow fertility on the barren, food on the hungry and comfort on the distressed. Some such stories told of curing people of disabilities such as deafness.[10] In the Shī'ī tradition, similar healing powers were attributed to the *imāms* and, for instance, to the soil of the grave of al-Ḥusayn b. 'Alī b. Abī Ṭālib.[11] The main focus of Muslim jurists remains, however, on the use of medicine to cure disabilities or diseases in general.

A note on the terminology used in this field is indispensable for a better understanding of the discussions and analyses to follow. First of all, one should be aware of terms like *tadāwī* (lit. taking up or making use of *dawā'* (pl. *adwiya*); medicine) and its synonyms *ta'āluj* (making use of *'ilāj* (pl. *'ilājāt*); medicine, remedial medicine or therapy)[12] and *taṭbīb* (lit. making use of *al-ṭibb;* the science of medicine).[13] For surgery, one comes across terms like *al-'amal bi al-yadd* or *'amal al-yadd* (lit. work or action performed with the hand or by hand). This expression gradually lost ground over the centuries and was ultimately replaced by *jirāḥa* (the art of healing wounds or surgery).[14] The term *jarā'iḥī* (surgeon) was often used by jurists for the person practising this art.[15]

It is to be noted that terms relevant to this topic, e.g. *dawā'*, *'ilāj* and *ṭibb,* were used in their broadest sense by Muslim scholars. First, *dawā'*, in its juristic use, could mean not only a simple or compound medical drug but also a Qur'anic verse or specific religious formula to be recited or chanted in specific situations for healing purposes.[16] Second, *dawā'* was not exclusively used to mean curing physical diseases. Spiritual diseases affecting one's soul and heart and thus weakening one's faith also need *dawā'* and the healing process called *tadāwī* leads to *shifā'* (recovery). For instance, the Ḥanbalī jurist, Ibn al-Qayyim (d. 751/1350), wrote at the beginning of his *Al-Ṭibb al-nabawī* (Prophetic Medicine) a chapter on diseases of the heart, as opposed to diseases of the body, and their medicines.[17] The same author dedicated a whole book to the issue of medication for the heart and the disease of disobeying God in a book entitled *Al-Jawāb al-kāfī liman sa'al 'an al-dawā' al-shāfī* (The Satisfying Answer for the One who Asked about the Curing Medicine), abridged to *Al-Dā' wa al-dawā'* (The Ailment and the Medicine).[18] That is why the definition given for *adwiya,* 'every substance which may affect the constitution of the human body, every drug used as remedy or a poison',[19] although relatively broad, is not exhaustive. The same holds true for *'ilm al-ṭibb* (the science of medicine). Muslim jurists made it clear that this science is to be divided into two branches, *al-ṭibb al-jusmānī* or *al-jismānī* (corporeal or physical medicine) and *al-ṭibb al-ruḥānī* (spiritual medicine).[20] Below, we give a detailed overview of juristic discussions on these two branches of medicine, the standpoints adopted in each branch, and finally 'treatments' developed within each branch of this science with relevance to disabilities.

7.1 Physical medicine

Physical medicine and Islamic jurisprudence were not rivals nor did they stand at opposite poles. First of all, the history of Islamic scholarship records a considerable number of Muslim scholars who were well versed in both fields – Islamic jurisprudence and physical medicine.

Well-known physicians who also mastered Islamic jurisprudence include Ibn Sīnā (d. 428/1037),[21] Fakhr al-Dīn al-Rāzī (d. 606/1209),[22] Ibn Rushd (1126–1198)[23] and Ibn al-Nafīs (d. 1288).[24] Names like Muḥammad ʻAlī al-Bār[25] and Haytham al-Khayyāṭ[26] show that the phenomenon of combining medicine and Islamic jurisprudence has not disappeared in the modern era. The earliest jurist whose name was attached to the science of medicine is Muḥammad b. Idrīs al-Shāfiʻī (d. 205/820). Writers on his virtues (*manāqib*) would dedicate a chapter to his knowledge of Greek medicine and some of them claimed that he mastered this science in its original language.[27] According to the Ḥanbalī jurist Ibn al-Qayyim (d. 751/1350), al-Shāfiʻī's knowledge of medicine was based on the Arabian rather than the Greek tradition.[28] Furthermore, biographical sources on jurists of various schools of law include many references to those jurists who were well versed in the science of medicine, some of whom were also authors in this field.[29]

In addition, early and modern jurists are unanimous on the importance of medicine as an essential science for maintaining human life. Learning and teaching this science was seen as a collective duty (*farḍ kifāya*).[30] At times when medical professionals were in short supply, learning this science became obligatory (*farḍ ʻayn*) for those with the capacities to do so.[31] Al-Shāfiʻī is reported to have said: 'Do not live in a place where you have no scholar to inform you about your religion and no physician to inform you about your body.'[32] The well-known scholar Shams al-Dīn al-Dhahabī (1274–1352/3) considered medicine to be one of the important means to bring one closer to God. He said in this regard, 'After carrying out the religious rites and desisting from actions He has prohibited, the most beneficial means of getting closer to God is that which benefits man in preserving his health and in curing his illness.'[33] Al-Dhahabī's contention is shared by other authors who considered writing on health and medicine to be an essential part of their piety and religiosity.[34] Similar standpoints were also adopted within Shīʻī Islam. *Imām* ʻAlī, the first *imām* of the Shīʻa and the son-in-law of the Prophet Muḥammad, was said to put medicine on a par with the study of Islamic jurisprudence.[35] Modern Muslim scholars condemned the new trend among a number of Muslim youngsters of seeing the study of religious sciences rather than of the exact sciences including medicine as more important for a practising Muslim. The scholars insisted on the religious merit of learning such sciences.[36] They reiterated that carrying out and developing scientific research in the field of medicine represented important ways of achieving the first objective of Islamic Sharīʻa, namely protecting human life.[37]

Notwithstanding the high value attached to medical science, the treatment of disabilities or diseases in general is not similarly encouraged. A clear distinction should be made in this respect between early and modern jurists.

Fazlur Rahman, basing himself on various quotations from a single source, speaks of a Shīʻī trend maintaining that the use of medicine must be avoided as much as possible because medicines produce and can themselves constitute disease. People were strongly advised to bear the pain and discomfort of disease and have recourse to a doctor only if it threatened to become incurable and the pain unbearable.[38] However, Rahman's assessment should be qualified. First, he conceded, 'Of the Shīʿa, only one work I have mentioned earlier, viz., *Ṭibb al-a'imma* or 'The Medicine of the *Imāms*' is available to me.'[39] Second, Andrew Newman (University of Oxford) rejected Rahman's assessment and asserted that no big difference between Shīʿī and Sunni traditions is apparent in this regard. He stated that the folk medicine of the Arabian Bedouin, the borrowing of Galenic concepts and the over-arching principle of divine supernatural causation found favour within the Shīʿī community as much as the Sunni.[40] The main difference between these two traditions could be the high value attached to the importance of the twelve *imāms* believed to be designated by God to govern the Muslim community and to be in direct contact with God as was the Prophet himself for the purpose of guiding the community.[41] That is why the Shīʿī genre on this topic carries the title *Ṭibb al-a'imma*. Researchers counted at least thirteen works of this genre bearing this title.[42]

A limited number of Sunni jurists believed that recourse to medicine became obligatory only when its effectiveness was certain and ignoring it would put a patient's life in danger.[43] The majority, including the Ḥanafīs and Mālikīs, adopted a neutral position and opined that use of medicine (*tadāwī*) was permissible (*mubāḥ*).[44] The rest were divided into two groups. The first group was mainly represented by the Shāfiʿīs, a number of the Ḥanbalīs including al-Qāḍī Abū Yaʿlā b. al-Farrā' (d. 458/1066), Ibn ʿAqīl (d. 513/1119) and Ibn al-Jawzī (d. 597/1200), and the Zaydī school from the Shīʿa. These all can be categorized as the pro-*tadāwī* group who opined that it was recommended (*mandūb* or *mustaḥabb*) to make use of medicine.[45] The second group, represented mainly by the majority of Ḥanbalīs, was not anti-*tadāwī* per se but still believed that practising *tawakkul* (dependence on God)[46] was better than making use of medicine to heal diseases.[47]

This last group in particular demands more detailed discussion because of its direct relevance to the current situation. A typical complaint from workers in the health sector and especially in the disability field is that some Muslims at present refuse to follow up a medication process for a family member who has a disability or to send him/her to a rehabilitation centre. Justifications advanced by these Muslims always revolve around trust in God (*tawakkul*) who is the real 'Healer'.

The question now is about the extent of this group which saw a potential contradiction between trust in God and resignation to His will (*tawakkul*) on the one hand and seeking medical treatment (*tadāwī*) on the other.

This group always remained a minority among early jurists. It included the majority of the Ḥanbalīs, and Ibn ʿAbd al-Barr and Ibn al-Ḥājj (d. 1336) from the Mālikīs. Although they saw no harm in making use of medicine, they still opined that trust in God's power and mercy was more meritorious.[48] A clear influence of Sufism is apparent here.[49] For instance, when the noted Sufi woman, Rābiʿa al-ʿAdawiyya (d. 185/801), fell sick and was asked to pray to God to ease her sufferings (making use of spiritual medicine), she refused, stating that her sickness was God's will and thus her prayer would contradict His will.[50]

However, this standpoint has been refuted by a majority of jurists including a number of the Ḥanbalī school such as Ibn al-Qayyim (d. 751/1350),[51] al-Dhahabī (d. 1352–3)[52] and Manṣūr al-Buhūtī (d. 1051/1641).[53] After citing a number of prophetic traditions encouraging people to make use of medicine, Ibn al-Qayyim (1998a:11) comments:

> These sound Prophetic traditions contain the command to carry out treatment, and this does not negate trust in God (*tawakkul*), any more than does the repelling of hunger, thirst, heat and cold by their opposites. Moreover, the reality of divine unity (*tawḥīd*) is only made complete by direct use of the means which God has appointed as being essential to bring about certain effects, according to the Decree and the religious Law.

This standpoint holds true for many other jurists, some of whom were also known for their Sufi leanings such as Abū Ḥāmid al-Ghazālī (d. 1111)[54] and Abū al-ʿAbbās al-Qasṭallānī (d. 923/1517),[55] and also for Sufi scholars such as al-Ḥārith al-Muḥāsibī (d. 243/857).[56] Fazlur Rahman adds that most Sufis made use of both types of medicine, physical and spiritual, when they were ill and also recommended both to their followers. It is therefore, he continued, not legitimate to make generalizations for all Sufis from the practice of some sufi ascetics.[57]

A third group of jurists preferred a more nuanced approach. They divided medicines on the basis of their effectiveness into certain (*qaṭʿī*), doubtful (*ẓannī*) and fictitious (*mawhūm*). They placed most of the known physical medicines in the category of the doubtful. Cauterization (*kayy*) was placed among the doubtful medicines and no concrete examples were given for the certain medicines. In their view, making use of medicines belonging to the first and second categories did not contradict *tawakkul* whereas using medicines of the third category would. Making use of medicines whose effectiveness is certain, jurists add, is obligatory in case of an illness endangering one's life.[58]

New developments in pharmaceutical science and strict regulations on bringing a medicine to market have brought the controversy on the inexactness of medicine to an end and thus no trace of this discussion is encountered in any of the modern jurists. This new situation is also responsible for the considerable change in the tone of modern juristic discussions. First of all, taking medicine is now seen obligatory (*wājib*), without reservations on the certainty of its efficacy. During its seventh session held in Jeddah in 1992, the International Islamic Fiqh Academy (IIFA),[59] which includes Sunni as well as Shīʿī scholars, issued decision no. 7/5/67 on medication, stating that it is: (1) obligatory (*wājib*) if neglecting it may result in the patient's death, loss of an organ or disability, or if the illness might spread to others, as in the case of contagious diseases; (2) recommended (*mustaḥabb*) if neglecting it might weaken the body without entailing the consequences mentioned in the first case above; (3) permissible (*mubāḥ*) if not covered by the preceding two cases; and (4) undesirable (*makrūh*) if there is a risk that the action to be taken may provoke complications that are worse than the illness being treated.[60]

Hence, whether making use of medicine is contradictory to *tawakkul* is no longer an issue among modern jurists.[61] Some even condemn those who abstain from medication on the grounds that they prefer to trust in God. 'Umar Sulayman al-Ashqar (University of Jordan) describes such a standpoint as one of the great drawbacks besetting the Muslim mentality.[62]

In the light of the above discussion and the clear curve in juristic opinion concerning medication, one can easily trace the standpoints of those Muslims who refuse to make use of some or all medical facilities. These practices, in most if not all cases, can be traced back to early opinion favouring *tawakkul* over *tadāwī*. However, patients of the present time and their families are unaware that those earlier arguments were advanced by a minority of jurists and in a specific context which has no further relevance in the present time. Explaining this issue to such patients can bring a considerable change to their behaviour.[63]

7.1.1 Preventive measures

According to Ibn al-Qayyim (d. 751/1350), one of the main deficiencies of physical medicines is that they are therapeutic rather than preventive. On the other hand, 'divine medicine can either prevent the occurrence of these causes or work to ward off the full force of their effect.'[64] This may have been the case at the time of Ibn al-Qayyim but it is surely not the case any more. One of the main objectives of physical medicine now is to prevent the occurrence of disease or disability – a specific branch of medicine called preventive medicine (*ṭibb wiqā'ī*) has been in existence for some time.[65]

Preventive measures whose main aim is to prevent the occurrence of disability will be presented in three levels: discouragement of consanguineous marriage; during pregnancy by aborting a disabled fetus; and after birth by vaccination.

7.1.1.1 Consanguineous marriage

The term generally used for consanguineous marriage by Muslim jurists is *nikāḥ* or *zawāj* (marriage) *al-qarāba* (lit. kinship). This term can be translated as close-kin marriage, intra-familial marriage, or – and this is the most commonly used term – consanguineous marriage. In anthropological studies, consanguineous marriage is defined as 'marriage in which the two partners have at least one ancestor in common, with the ancestor being no more distant than a great great grandparent'.[66] In clinical genetics, it is 'a union between a couple related as first cousins or closer'.[67] As we shall see below, both the anthropological definition which broadens the scope of consanguineous marriage and the medical definition which narrows it are used in juristic discussions.

The prevalence of close-kin marriage exceeds 50 per cent in many Muslim countries of the Middle East and Pakistan.[68] Records show that this type of marriage is also common among migrant – including Muslim – communities in Western Europe, North America and Australia.[69] Religion exerts a major influence in this regard. However, medical researchers complain of an ambiguity concerning attitudes towards this type of marriage within Islam.[70] In a bid to clarify this ambiguity, a survey of early and modern juristic discussions will be given. But first, a short presentation of medical standpoints is in order.

The first question to be raised here is whether consanguineous marriage is, medically speaking, dangerous for the health of the prospective children. As early as 1902, scientific researchers discussed such marriages and specifically cautioned against unjustified speculation about the overall health status of first-cousin progeny.[71] However, the first comprehensive investigations into the effects of inbreeding in human populations commenced in the late 1940s, with the classic studies of Neel and Schull into the outcome of cousin marriages in Hiroshima and Nagasaki, Japan.[72] Ever since then, many scientific voices have affirmed that there is a relationship between consanguineous marriage and specific physical defects and behavioural and psychiatric disorders.[73] Different studies and experiments show that disabilities among the progeny of such marriages could include deafness, blindness and mental retardation.[74] However, such results are still far from certain because the majority of these studies did not check potentially important non-genetic variables.[75]

As for the Islamic perspective, we see that the Qur'ān states clearly that specific family members are not allowed to marry each other:

> Prohibited to you (for marriage) are: Your mothers, daughters, sisters; father's sisters, Mother's sisters; brother's daughters, sister's daughters; foster-mothers (who gave you suck), foster-sisters; your wives' mothers; your step-daughters under your guardianship, born of your wives to whom ye have gone in, – no prohibition if ye have not gone in; (those who have been) wives of your sons proceeding from your loins; and two sisters in wedlock at one and the same time.
>
> (Qur'ān 4:23)

Beyond this forbidden circle, a Muslim may in principle marry other blood relatives. In a clear reference to the permissibility of first-cousin marriage, the Qur'ān says,

> O Prophet! We have made lawful to thee thy wives to whom thou hast paid their dowers; and those whom thy right hand possesses out of the prisoners of war whom Allah has assigned to thee; and daughters of thy paternal uncles and aunts, and daughters of thy maternal uncles and aunts, who migrated (from Mecca) with thee.
>
> (Qur'ān 33:50)

However, Muslim jurists from early times to the present are not in agreement as to whether consanguineous marriage is reprehensible (*makrūh*) or remains just permissible (*mubāḥ*). A group of jurists including the Shāfi'īs, Ḥanbalīs and Zaydīs prefer marriage with a distant relative or non-relative rather than with a close relative because the potential children will be physically and mentally healthier.[76] As regards physical health, it is related that the second Caliph 'Umar b. al-Khaṭṭāb

(r. 13/634–23/644) advised an Arab tribe known for marrying close relatives to marry people from outside the tribe to avoid feebleness in their prospective offspring.[77]

Concerning mental health, al-Shāfiʿī is reported to have opined that marrying within one's own *ʿashīra* (family) would result in an idiot child (*aḥmaq*).[78] A piece of evidence used by this group is a saying traditionally attributed to the Prophet: 'Marry with the non-relatives so that [the offspring of] you do not get feeble.' However, most scholars have declared this tradition inauthentic.[79] Muḥammad ʿUthmān Shubīr (lecturer in Islamic jurisprudence at Jordan University) is one of the modern jurists who advocate this opinion, basing his argument on the medical dangers of such a marriage as stated by physicians.[80] On the other hand, the well-known Saudi scholar Ibn Sāliḥ al-ʿUthaymīn (d. 2001) is one of the modern jurists who objected to the aforementioned opinion. In a response to the question, 'Is it true that consanguineous marriage will result in malformed or disabled children, as physicians say?', Ibn ʿUthaymīn stated that it is not true,[81] adding 'the issue is in the hands of God, besides malformation has other causes'. He also said that jurists who are against consanguineous marriage are wrong. According to him, the main factor in selecting a partner must be religion and ethics. Additionally, Ibn ʿUthaymīn confirms, a lot of people who married their cousins found nothing but good, for example ʿAlī b. Abī Ṭālib who married the daughter of his cousin, Fāṭima, the daughter of the Messenger of God – peace and blessings be upon him.[82]

A pre-marriage medical check-up for both spouses is one of the measures suggested by modern Muslim scholars to avoid the possibility of contracting genetic, hereditary or contagious diseases whether by one of the spouses or by the prospective children. To my knowledge, the Saudi Mufti Ibn Bāz (d. 1999) was the only opponent – or at least one of very few – of such check-ups. In answer to the question, 'I wish to marry my cousin. Some friends advised me to have a medical check-up before the marriage to investigate the hereditary genetics. Would this be interference in God's predestination (*qaḍā' wa qadar*) and what is the religious ruling on conducting such a medical check-up?', Ibn Bāz said, 'There is no need for a check-up. You both should just expect the best of God as He says "I am as My servant thinks of Me" as narrated by His Prophet – peace and blessings be upon him.'[83] Medical check-ups are, however, favoured by the majority of modern jurists and represents a midway solution because it will also achieve a higher degree of certainty as to whether the consanguineous marriage would result in disabilities or other health dangers for the potential progeny.[84]

The question that remains is whether the state authorities should be allowed to make a pre-marriage medical check-up compulsory for the spouses and consider it one of the obligatory preliminaries to the marriage. Modern jurists are divided into two groups, one advocating this measure and the other opposing it.[85]

If a medical check-up was not carried out, and one of the spouses came to know that the other was a carrier of a genetic disorder, would this be a sufficient reason to bring the marriage to an end? Fatwas recommend that the marriage continues as long as carrying the genetic disorder does not hinder safe sexual intercourse. As an alternative, the spouses can resort to contraceptives in order to prevent the birth of malformed children.[86] Some muftis even spoke of possible sterilization or a temporary form of it.[87] If the carrier of the genetic disorder intentionally deceived his/her spouse, she/he would have the right to ask for the marriage to be ended.[88] It is to be noted that this applies to consanguineous and non-consanguineous marriages.

7.1.1.2 Abortion of the disabled fetus

Broadly speaking, abortion may be spontaneous (known in juristic terms as *saqṭ*, *ilqā'*, *ṭarḥ* and *imlāṣ*[89]), i.e. an unplanned occurrence due to some physiological factor, or deliberate (*ijhāḍ*), a premeditated intervention intended to end the life of the fetus. When it is spontaneous, a miscarriage is interpreted as the will of God and no blame is attributed to any individual.[90] As for deliberate abortion, Muslim jurists have frequently discussed the rulings on this practice.

Early jurists were in agreement that abortion was forbidden after 120 days of pregnancy, by which time ensoulment (*nafkh al-rūḥ*) had already taken place.[91] As for abortion before 120 days, various opinions have been expressed which can be summed up into three or four main categories: unconditionally permissible; permissible if there is an excuse (*'udhr*); generally reprehensible; and forbidden.[92] Each of these opinion has its own advocates among modern Muslim jurists.[93]

Among excuses for aborting the fetus, some jurists counted the poverty of the two parents, making them unable to afford the necessary milk or food for their prospective child. They also counted medical excuses such as illness causing the mother to take medicine which eventually leads to the abortion.

Modern scientific advances have produced a new possibility not encountered by the early jurists, namely the case of the disabled fetus. Prenatal screening and other scientific advances have made it possible to identify genetic disorders in the fetus while still in the womb. Some of them can be cured in the womb. For those that are incurable, the parents can choose either to let the fetus complete its term and be born, or to abort it. Is it permissible for the parents to abort a disabled fetus to avoid having a disabled child?

Although they may not have said anything directly on this issue, the probable opinions of some jurists can be predicted in specific cases. For instance, before 120 days, abortion would be permissible for those who said it is unconditionally permissible, reprehensible for those who opine that it is generally reprehensible, and forbidden for those who forbid abortion in every case. The same holds true for those who maintain that abortion after 120 days is forbidden in all cases. However, it is impossible to predict the likely opinion of those early jurists who permitted abortion when there was an excuse. Would having a disabled fetus be a sufficient excuse for terminating the pregnancy? Here we must refer to modern jurists who have had to address this new situation.

Two main factors played a central role in the formulation of fatwas on this subject: the duration of the pregnancy and the seriousness of the defect or disorder that the potential child would suffer. The majority keep the two factors in view and thus permit abortion in case of extreme and incurable disorders as long as it takes place before 120 days[94] and, according to some, not before forty days.[95] Although 'severity of disorders' remains in principle vague and at best subjective and relative,[96] specific disorders such as blindness and deafness are explicitly excluded from the acceptable excuses.[97] The rationale for this generally anti-abortion stance on the part of Muslim jurists can be summed up in the following points. First, every human being is God's creation and no one may 'play God' and decide to terminate another human life. Second, happiness and the quality of life are subjective terms and no one can speak for another.[98] Maḥmūd Shaltūt said, 'Who knows whether the retarded child or Down's syndrome child is unhappy as he is? It is often the projection of the healthy on the life of the handicapped, but this is not necessarily true.'[99] As for blindness, deafness and the like, al-Qaraḍāwī states that many people have lived with such disabilities throughout human history and were not thereby prevented from participating actively in life.[100]

7.1.1.3 Vaccination

According to the WHO, the two public health interventions that have had the greatest impact on the world's health are clean water and vaccines.[101] One of the main benefits of vaccines, which is especially relevant to disability, is the prevention of poliomyelitis.[102]

Despite the great benefits of vaccines as prevention against many fatal diseases and disabilities, they were not without opponents, usually termed 'antivaccinationists', belonging to a movement known as 'antivaccinationism'. A vociferous antivaccination movement emerged as early as in the 1830s, after an initial generation had been vaccinated and the incidence of smallpox had declined markedly in the United States and Europe.[103] Sometimes antivaccinationists protested against what they considered intrusion into their privacy and bodily integrity. Many working-class Britons, for example, viewed compulsory vaccination laws, passed in 1821, as a direct assault on their communities by the ruling class.[104] In addition, by the mid-eighteenth century the rise of irregular medicine and unabashed quackery encouraged antivaccinationism. In addition, antivaccinationists, who abhorred animal experimentation, sometimes joined forces with antivaccinationists.[105] While nineteenth-century fears of vaccination might have been based on anecdotal horror stories of other infections, the statistical risks of vaccine-induced infection in that era would not be medically acceptable today. Until quite recently, historical studies frequently depicted all antivaccinationists as irrational and antiscientific. Commenting on this, Alexandra Stern and Howard Markel (University of Michigan), say: 'This characterization was misguided. If we interpret antivaccinationists on their own terms and by applying historical context, we can see that many behaved as rational actors who were weighing the pros and cons of inoculation.'[106] Some of the criticisms were raised because of a putative link between vaccination and neurological problems. In the past decade in particular, parents and their watchdog groups have raised important questions about the alleged link between a noticeable rise in autism and the preservative thimerosal (previously used in diphtheria, tetanus, pertussis, *Haemo-philus influenzae* type b, or Hib, and hepatitis B vaccines). The series of scientific studies which have demonstrated that there is no causal connection between thimerosal and autism could not always allay people's fears, especially because such claims were sometimes sensationalized by the media. Not surprisingly, the suggestion that vaccinating their child might lead to developmental disorders has fostered unease among many parents.[107]

Some of the protests against vaccines also had a religious dimension[108] and this was the case with some requests to Muslim jurists for fatwas. A clear example is a fatwa issued by Yūsuf al-Qaraḍāwī on 15 March 2004 in response to the following question posed from Nigeria:

> What is the Islamic point of view regarding vaccinating children against specific diseases? Scholars of Kano in northern Nigeria issued a fatwa to the effect that it is not lawful to vaccinate their children against polio. According to them, the vaccine contains chemicals and hormones that may cause women to be infertile or impure elements that should not enter the body. People of Kano abode by the fatwa and this resulted in the spread of polio among the children of the state. About 335 children have become paralysed by polio. Moreover, travellers have carried the poliovirus to eight other Muslim countries. What is your point of view on this?

Al-Qaraḍāwī expressed his astonishment at the antivaccinationist attitude adopted by the scholars of Kano. He unequivocally disapproved their opinion, for the lawfulness of the vaccine in terms of Islam is as clear as day. However, he still understood the motives and good will behind their attitude, and thus besought God to reward them for their good will and to forgive their mistakes. In view of the importance of this issue, al-Qaraḍāwī consulted twelve noted Muslim scholars affiliated to the International Islamic Fiqh Academy (IIFA) as members and experts. They came up with five main conclusions. First, it is the duty of every Muslim to avoid harm as much as possible. One's body is a trust from Allah the Almighty, and thus it is not lawful for one to cause it harm. They quoted Qur'anic verses and incidents from the life of the Prophet to support this point. Second, parents are responsible for giving their children as much protection and immunity against harm and disease as possible to save them suffering during their lives. If there is a certain vaccine that can prevent a disease altogether, parents should try to give it to their children. If parents neglect their duty in that regard, they commit the sin of causing their children life-long ill-health. Third, people in authority in every country should enact laws and take action to protect the health of people in general, and children in particular, against diseases. This includes not only providing treatment for disease but also finding means of preventing them. If people in authority order a certain vaccine to be given to children all over the country, people must abide by this, for it is their duty to obey their rulers as long as they remain in the framework of following what is right. Fourth, things are primarily in a state of purity and thus permissible to make use of. Hence, something cannot be called impure without clear evidence. Likewise, something cannot be ruled unlawful without certain proof. As for the polio vaccine, there is no sign that it contains impurities or causes infertility, hence its use cannot be called unlawful. Furthermore, experts on vaccines affiliated to the Egypt branch of the WHO were consulted. Their answer was that the polio vaccine is not harmful in any way, nor does it include impurities or cause infertility. On the contrary, the experts added, it has been proved in experiments to be highly effective in protecting against polio. Fifth, the polio vaccine has been used for a long time all over the world, including in more than fifty Muslim countries, and has proved to be highly effective in eradicating the disease. No outstanding scholar, whether from Al-Azhar University (Egypt), Al-Qarawiyyīn University (Morocco) or in the Sacred Shrines (Saudi Arabia), has been reported to have objected to the use of the vaccine.

If they maintain their objection to the polio vaccine, the muftis added, those scholars of Kano will make two mistakes. First, they will commit the sin of exposing children to great harm and suffering. Second, they will distort the image of Islam and make it appear hostile to science and medical progress. Islam is completely innocent of such distorted images. On the contrary, it calls for adopting healthy methods and seeking medical treatment when needed. Finally, a call is made to the scholars in Kano to review their attitude and recant the fatwa that they gave without consulting specialists or even collaborating sufficiently. Should the scholars of Kano refuse to follow the advice of their fellow scholars, then the people of Kano are called on to vaccinate their children against polio according to the fatwa of the majority of Muslim scholars in that regard.[109]

7.1.2 Therapeutic measures

Disability through the loss of one limb or part of the body for one reason or another is theoretically curable in two main ways: by reattaching the amputated organ itself or transplanting a similar organ from another source, whether a human being, an animal or an artificial material. Reattaching an amputated body part such as the ear and the nose has been a subject of discussion among Muslim jurists since the second/eighth century.[110] However, organ transplantation is a much more recent phenomenon and only started to preoccupy the minds of jurists from the 1950s.[111] A third possible way which at present remains theoretical is therapeutic cloning.

7.1.2.1 Reattaching

Reattaching, or in juristic terminology rejoining (*i'ādat waṣl*), an amputated limb has been almost completely ignored by modern researchers into medical ethics in Islam. This could be because one would believe that reattaching an amputated limb on its original owner does not raise any juristic problems. However, this is not the case, as we shall see below.

Historical reports indicate that simple forms of reattaching specific parts of the body such as teeth and skin took place centuries ago.[112] In modern times, with advances in microsurgical techniques, severe injuries and amputation do not necessarily have to mean the permanent loss of a limb. In hand surgery, reattachment of totally or partially severed fingers is well established. Since the first successful reattachments of hands in the early 1960s, reattachment of entire limbs has become more common.[113]

Relevant references to this issue in early juristic sources indicate that they were discussing not a hypothetical but a real issue which they knew existed. Such discussions indicate the feasibility of reattaching three body parts only, the ear, nose and teeth.[114]

An introductory comment is indispensable in order to understand the opinions of early jurists in this regard. The starting point adopted by early jurists, with very few exceptions, was that an organ disconnected or separated from the body is regarded as part of a corpse (*mayyit*). The core question which occupied the minds of early jurists and on the basis of which they adopted their standpoints on reattaching or rejoining amputated organs was whether a human corpse is pure or impure. Hence, the main issue here is relevant to purity (*ṭahāra*) and impurity (*najāsa*).

Three main opinions can be traced among the early jurists. The first is the unconditional permissibility of rejoining or reattaching an organ severed from a human body, based on the contention that this amputated organ is pure (*ṭāhir*). This is the authoritative opinion within the Mālikīs, the Shāfi'īs, the Ḥanbalīs and a number of the Ḥanafīs. The second opinion, attributed to al-Shāfi'ī, Aḥmad b. Ḥanbal and a number of Ḥanafī and Mālikī jurists, totally prohibits reattaching severed organs. They base their contention on the argument that the amputated organ is dead and thus impure (*najis*). They added that, if such an organ is reattached, then the recipient is not allowed to use it when praying. The third opinion, which is the one accepted by the Ḥanafīs, makes a distinction between body parts containing blood such as the hand, leg and nose and those without blood such as teeth. They prohibited reattaching the first group because of their impurity and permitted the second type because of their purity.[115] For modern jurists, the purity/impurity issue became irrelevant. Recent medical research has proved that body parts do not die immediately upon being amputated but continue to live for a couple of hours, even after a person is declared dead; that is why reattaching or transplanting these body parts is possible. Basing their contention on these medical findings, modern jurists opine that reattaching such body parts is permissible.[116] It is noteworthy that a small number of early jurists adopted the same standpoint, stating that the possibility of rejoining an amputated body part indicates that it is still alive and thus the purity/impurity issue has no relevance.[117] In its resolution no. 26 (1/4), the International Fiqh Academy stipulated that the benefits accruing from this operation outweigh its harmful effects and that its purpose is to replace a lost body part, reshape it, restore its function, correct a defect or remove a malformation which is a source of mental anguish or physical pain.[118]

7.1.2.2 Transplants

Available Islamic literature does not provide us with any indication that organ transplantation took place during the lifetime of the Prophet. However, early juristic discussions have some implications which are used as starting points by modern jurists. Using a tooth of a dead person or animal to replace a broken tooth and joining fractured bones with the use of animal bones serve as examples here. Opinions on these topics were used for instance by the late grand *imām* of al-Azhar, Shaykh Jād al-Ḥaqq (1917–1996),[119] in his fatwa no. 3372 on organ transplantation issued on 5 December 1979.[120] Besides these early references which escaped the attention of modern researchers,[121] modern jurists used deductive reasoning, drawing on general principles and ethical concepts applied in all fields of life.[122] With the exception of the well-known Egyptian scholar, Shaykh Muḥammad Mutwallī al-Sha'rāwī (1911-1988), who opted for a total prohibition, and the fatwa issued in 1974 in Singapore by the highest Islamic authority of the Muslim minority which also prohibited kidney donation (revised in 1987 and declared permissible), a semi-consensus among modern Muslim jurists can be claimed to agree on the permissibility of organ transplants from one human being to another. Moreover, some scholars have described them as not only permissible but as recommended acts or forms of charity which bring one closer to God.[123]

However, this permissibility is not unconditional. For instance, modern jurists are unanimous on the condition that no compensation may be allowed for the donated organs because the human body is viewed as a trust (*amāna*) from God rather than as one's own property. Thus no sale can legally take place if the property is not fully owned. According to some jurists, it is permitted to make a gift or contribution to the donor of the organ but some of them stipulated that the gift should not be equal to the value of the organ.[124]

Quoting from Isam Ghanem (PhD in Law, London), Vardit Rispler-Chaim (Haifa University) said, 'Ibn Qudāma in the 14th century allowed the sale of an organ of a living person.'[125] First of all, Ibn Qudāma (541/1147–620/1223) lived in the twelfth–thirteenth centuries, not the fourteenth.[126] Checking the encyclopedic *Al-Mughnī* by this Ḥanbalī jurist, I found that the context does not confirm the two authors' conclusion. The context is a discussion on the sale of mothers' milk, which some jurists prohibited on the same basis as selling the sweat of a human being while others opined that it was merely reprehensible and a third group said it was permissible. Ibn Qudāma supported the third opinion and said that 'all parts of the human being can be sold because male and female slaves can be sold. A free person cannot be sold because he is not owned and the sale of an amputated organ is prohibited because it has no benefit.'[127] By 'all parts of the human being', it is clear that Ibn Qudāma does not mean an organ such as an eye, a hand or a kidney because this was not even feasible at that time. This is proved by his statement 'and the sale of an amputated organ is prohibited because *it has no benefit*'. Ibn Qudāma was only speaking about separable parts such as milk and sweat in order to defend his opinion.

Another condition is that the living person who decides to donate an organ must do so of his/her own free will without moral or social coercion or economic pressure.[128] As for minors and people with mental disabilities, some jurists opined that their donations would be legitimate provided the proxy consent of their guardians had been obtained.[129] Other jurists prohibited such donations even with the guardian's consent because a minor is not allowed to donate money, let alone body parts.[130] Additionally, it should be certain that the donation will cause no harm to the donor or to those with a legal claim on him/her such as a husband, wife, children and creditors.[131] Thus a living person may not donate organs of which a person has only one, such as the heart or liver. The same holds true for external parts of the body such as the eye, the hand and the leg or the internal parts of which a person has two such as kidneys, if one of them is diseased or inactive.[132] Some jurists also expressed reservations on transplanting the testicles, which carry many genetic traits, so this could lead to the mixing of lineages.[133]

As for donation by a dead person, jurists legitimated it if the dead person had given instructions for it in his/her will, or if relatives authorized it post mortem. If the deceased indicated in the will that he/she does not allow his/her organs to be donated, then no one is authorized to give permission on his/her behalf.[134] If the deceased has no relatives or if they are unknown, then the state is entitled to remove an organ for transplant. Some jurists favour enacting a code of law permitting the state to do so but only in cases of necessity.[135] However, scholars do not give a precise definition of necessity, which gives the state more space for case by case decisions.

The religion of the donor and the beneficiary has also played a role in the modern discussions. Some jurists state that although it is permissible to receive donations from non-Muslims, donations to them are not allowed.[136] The majority of jurists, however, made no distinction between a Muslim and a non-Muslim in this regard and permitted reciprocal donations between the two as long as the aforementioned conditions are met, as the Muslim donor will be rewarded anyhow for his good deed.[137]

As for transplanting animal organs to human bodies, jurists made a distinction between pure (*ṭāhir*) animals whose flesh may be eaten and impure (*najis*) animals whose flesh may not be eaten. Organs of the first type can be transplanted because they are pure. Organs of the second type such as dogs and pigs were prohibited by some jurists because of their impurity. Yūsuf al-Qaraḍāwī permitted transplanting organs from impure animals such as pigs in case of necessity and when trustworthy Muslim physicians affirm its beneficial effects. He argued that what is forbidden is eating impure animals' flesh whereas transplants have nothing to do with eating. As for its impurity, he added, what counts is touching impure materials with the external parts of the body and not having such material inside the body. Every Muslim may pray, read the Qur'ān and circumambulate the Ka'ba while having many impurities inside his body such as blood, urine and excrement.[138]

Replacing amputated organs with artificial limbs has not been opposed by jurists. The only reservation I came across was from Khālid Rashīd al-Jamīlī (Lecturer in Comparative Islamic Jurisprudence, Baghdad University), who stipulated that they should be made of pure material. Impure material would be permitted in case of necessity and when no other alternative is available.[139] Although men in Islam are not allowed to use gold for ornaments, they are allowed to use artificial limbs made of gold if there is no alternative. This is based on the case of the Companion 'Arfaja b. As'ad, who lost his nose in a military expedition.

First, he used a silver nose but when it oxidized the Prophet allowed him to use a gold one.[140]

7.1.2.3 Cloning

Cloning is simply defined as production of a cell or organism with the same nuclear genome as another cell or organism.[141] It is of two main types: reproductive cloning, by which cloned babies are produced, and therapeutic cloning which is used for treating diseases.[142] The second type can be of relevance, at least theoretically, to treating people who have lost organs such as a hand, leg, ear, eye and so on. Until the end of the twentieth century and, to my knowledge, until the present, only one human organ, namely the skin, could be grown in a laboratory to provide self-compatible skin grafts.[143] In his fatwa on cloning in general, Yūsuf al-Qaraḍāwī tried to hypothesize this issue and stated that if therapeutic cloning were to result in cloning a human being or even a fetus so that the organs could be used as 'spare parts' for others, then it would be absolutely forbidden. However, if therapeutic cloning succeeded in cloning specific organs such as the heart, liver, kidneys and the like, then it would be welcomed and God would reward it because it would benefit people without causing any harm.[144]

7.2 Spiritual medicine

The main sources which theorized and discussed this type of medicine belong to the genre of prophetic medicine (*al-ṭibb al-nabawī*) which arose by the fourth/tenth century and started to attract particular attention in the seventh/thirteenth century. Authors of this genre were religious scholars, most of whom were Sunni Muslims but there were also Shī'ī writers in this genre which became known as *ṭibb al-a'imma,* as indicated above.[145] Almost all the information in these sources is also to be found in the juristic sources but dispersed in different chapters and under many headings.

Al-ṭibb al-rūḥānī (spiritual medicine) had two basic meanings. The first, sometimes also called 'medicine of the heart', was mainly interested in managing, maintaining and healing the spirit, soul and heart. To Muslim scholars, this type of medicine was entrusted to the Messengers of God and there is no means of obtaining it except through their teachings.[146] Ibn al-Qayyim, expressing the high value attached to this medicine, said, 'The connection between the medicine of the Messengers and that of physicians is as tenuous as its connection with the medicine of the village healers.'[147] The main theories developed in this science, which are meant to help the heart and soul of the servant of God to come closer to the Creator, were developed in Sufi literature and thus fall beyond the scope of this chapter.[148]

The second meaning of *al-ṭibb al-rūḥānī* is the science which focuses on physical and mental diseases which attack the body, as in physical medicine, but which uses spiritual rather than physical means to combat and cure them. These spiritual means might include saying Qur'anic verses, chanting prayers and religious formulas and doing good deeds such as giving to charity.[149] *Al-ṭibb al-rūḥānī* in this sense is the main focus of the discussions that follow.

Standpoints adopted by Muslim jurists towards spiritual medicine have undergone considerable changes. It is clear from early juristic discussions that there were opponents of spiritual medicine but they were always seen as a minority[150] comprising two groups. The first group, including a number of Sufis such as Rābi'a al-'Adawiyya (d. 185/801), the Successor Sa'īd b. Jubayr (d. 95/714), and the two Shāfi'ī jurists al-Ḥalīmī and al-Khaṭṭābī, opposes medication in general, whether physical or spiritual, because it contradicts trust in God (*tawakkul*).[151] The second group casts doubt on the effectiveness of this type of medicine. Juristic sources do not name names, describing members of this group sometimes as heretics[152] or as 'the most ignorant, the most veiled one whose soul is so dense that he becomes the furthest from God'.[153]

The majority of early jurists were ardent advocates of spiritual medicine and were always inclined to value it more highly than physical medicine. The most famous statement quoted by early jurists in this regard is from the classical Muslim scholar Ibn al-Tīn:

> Using al-Muw'awwidhāt [the last three Qur'anic chapters 112–114] and other [religious formulas] such as the Names of God, the Sublime is spiritual medicine. If they are chanted by the tongues of the pious, recovery will take place by God's permission. However, because of the scarcity of [qualified specialists of] this type, people rush into physical medicine.'[154]

This standpoint is shared by the majority of the early jurists[155] including the aforementioned Ibn al-Tīn, Ibn Taymiyya,[156] Ibn al-Qayyim,[157] Abū al-'Abbās al-Qasṭallānī (d. 923/1517),[158] al-Munāwī (d. 1031/1621)[159] and the Zaydī jurist al-Shawkānī (d. 1760–1839).[160] Jurists mentioned two main conditions, the fulfilment of which would guarantee the effectiveness of spiritual medicine. The first is related to the practitioner (*mu'ālij*), namely piety and sincerity in religion. The second is related to the patient, namely firm belief in the efficacy of spiritual medicine. Ineffective spiritual medication in some cases may be attributed to the absence of any of the aforementioned conditions.[161] The same emphasis on spiritual medicine can also be traced in Shī'ī circles which placed great value on the healing traits of Qur'anic verses and prayers.[162]

This positive attitude towards spiritual medicine – sometimes even favouring it over physical medicine – became muted over time among the majority of modern Sunni jurists. In this respect, they can be divided into three main tendencies.

The first tendency simply maintained the standpoint adopted by the majority of the early jurists without any significant amendments or changes. Among the main advocates of this trend are 'Umar Sulaymān al-Ashqar[163] and the Permanent Committee for Scientific Research and Issuing Fatwas in Saudi Arabia which issued a fatwa stating that the Qur'ān can be used as a medicine for physical diseases such as cancer.[164] The late Moroccan scholar, 'Abd Allāh b. al-Ṣiddīq al-Ghumārī (1328/1910–1413/1993), was also an ardent advocate of using the Qur'ān as spiritual medicine for physical diseases. He elaborated his arguments in a book entitled *Kamāl al-imān fī al-tadāwī bi al-Qur'ān* (The Perfection of Belief in Using the Qur'ān as Medicine).[165] In this book, al-Siddīq launched a severe attack against those 'reformists' who, in his view, were actually heretics because they denied this aspect of the Qur'ān. His main target in this regard was the late grand *imām* of al-Azhar, Maḥmūd Shaltūt (1893–1963),[166] who was one of the main representatives of the second tendency.

The second tendency, which stood at the opposite pole to the first, limited the effectiveness of the Qur'ān to the first meaning of spiritual medicine, i.e. purifying one's soul and heart from sin and thus bringing them closer to the Right Path of God. The main advocates of this opinion were Rashīd Riḍā (1865–1935)[167] and the late grand *imām* of al-Azhar Maḥmūd Shaltūt.[168] Rashīd Riḍā gave two rational arguments to support his position. The first is that frequent experiments have not proved that the Qur'ān can be used as medicine for physical diseases. Had it been so, people, and Muslims in particular, would have abandoned physical medicines and physicians. The second argument was that curing physical disease was not included by scholars among the miraculous properties of the Qur'ān.[169] Shaltūt stated that using the Qur'ān as medicine for physical disease represents a clear deviation from the proper way of glorifying it, and falls into the category of heresy. He traced this phenomenon back to ignorance and disrespect for the norms of life established by the Creator.[170] As for prophetic traditions which indicated the medical use of Qur'anic verses, and of supplications or religious formulas as incantations (*ruqā*) to treat physical disease, Rashīd Riḍā had his own interpretation. He argues that *ruqya* was originally a tradition from the pre-Islamic period (*Jāhiliyya*), which was forbidden by the Prophet with a few exceptions, namely, the evil eye, snake bites, and stings, and bleeding which cannot be staunched. Besides limiting the scope of permissible incantations, Riḍā adds, the Prophet clarified that making use of incantation is inconsistent with trust in God (*tawakkul*), and this is not the case with making use of physical medicine. That is because using incantation as medicine falls into the category of fictitious (*mawhum*) means of medical treatment.[171] But if so, why did not the Prophet forbid incantation completely? Riḍā suggests that it could be out of mercy for those weak people who were affected by such fictitious things and benefited from them. Thus, incantation remains no more than a legal concession (*rukhṣa*) to be used by people who believed in its effectiveness.[172]

The third tendency is represented mainly by Yūsuf al-Qaraḍāwī and Muḥammad 'Uthmān Shubīr (Lecturer in Islamic Jurisprudence at Jordan University) who tried to find middle ground. On the one hand, the validity of spiritual medicines such as the Qur'ān for treating physical disease is not denied. On the other hand, it is stressed that the main function of the Qur'ān is for purely spiritual purposes rather than treating physical disease. For physical disease, besides spiritual medicine, one should always consult a specialist physician.[173] Bashīr says that the two types of medicine should be used without over- or underestimating either of them.[174]

7.2.1 Good deeds and charity

All sorts of spiritual medicine are covered by two main categories. The first consists of performing supererogatory good deeds, exemplified by giving charity (*ṣadaqa*), with the intention of seeking a cure for disease. The second category is based upon saying specific prayers and religious formulas.

I could trace no more than cursory references to the first category, made by some jurists including the Shāfi'ī al-Ḥalīmī[175] and the Mālikī Ibn 'Abd al-Barr.[176] The most detailed exposition of this category is given by the Shāfi'ī jurist, al-Munāwī, in his comments on four prophetic traditions mentioned by the other Shāfi'ī jurist al-Suyūṭī in his collection of ḥadīth entitled *Al-Jāmi' al-ṣaghīr*. The four traditions enumerate the four main benefits of giving charity: curing diseases, blocking seventy doors of evil, warding off bad death and eliminating afflictions or misfortunes (*'āhāt*, plural of *'āha*).[177] Commenting on the first benefit, al-Munāwī states that giving charity falls into the category of spiritual medicine (*al-ṭibb al-rūḥānī*). In reference to charity, al-Munāwī adds, the Prophet draws attention to other good deeds of a similar nature such as helping those in need or beset by calamity. Emphasizing the effectiveness of this spiritual medicine, al-Munāwī says that experiments by people of success (*al-muwaffaqūn*, in reference to the pious believers) have shown that spiritual medicine can do what physical medicine cannot. For instance, when a person fell sick, such people would slaughter a sheep and prepare a glamorous banquet to which they invited needy people. If the sick person is very dear, they would give the dearest part of their property, for instance a slave girl, a slave boy or a horse, as charity.[178] It is also clear that disabilities are included among the diseases to be cured by this type of spiritual medicine. The fourth benefit of charity, namely eliminating *'āhāt* (afflictions), alludes to this fact as well. As mentioned earlier, one of the main terms used for people with disabilities in early Arabic literature is *dhawū al-'āhāt* (lit. people of afflictions). Al-Munāwī named some specific disabilities such as leprosy (*baraṣ*) and elephantiasis (*judhām*).[179] It is worth mentioning that the authenticity of the aforementioned traditions have been a point of discussion among the scholars of Ḥadīth and many of them consider that they are not authentic.[180]

7.2.2 Prayers and religious formulas

All medicines which fall into this category are covered by the broad Arabic term *ta'wīdh,* which literally means guaranteeing a refuge, protection or preservation. In the technical usage of jurists, it denotes those spiritual means by which protection against sickness, madness, the evil eye and the like can be guaranteed.[181] Within this category, the three main spiritual medicines most frequently mentioned in Islamic jurisprudence are *ruqya*, *tamīma* and *nushra*.

Ruqya (pl. *ruqā*) denotes utterance of, or, according to some opinions writing, a charm or a spell as protection against a misfortune such as fever, epilepsy and the like.[182] The most used English equivalent is incantation.[183] According to some jurists, *ruqya* also means supplication (*du'ā'*) made for the sake of recovery.[184] *Tamīma* means an amulet hung on the human being. It is also said that it signifies certain beads which the Arabs used to hang round their children's necks to ward off the evil eye.[185] Jurists define it as a paper on which verses from the Qur'ān are written and then hung on a human being.[186] *Nushra* means a charm or amulet by which a sick person or one possessed is cured.[187] According to jurists, *nushra* involved writing some of the names of God or an extract from the Qur'ān and then washing it in water which the sick person would drink or use as an ointment.[188] In sum, the three methods are based on using the same material but in different ways: *ruqya* by uttering it, *tamīma* by writing it and hanging it round the neck and *nushra* by using the water in which the written material has been washed.

The question now is whether it is possible to use *ta'wīdh* as a medication for disabilities. A minority among the jurists restricts its permissible use to two cases, namely the evil eye and snake sting. They base their opinion on the prophetic tradition, 'There is no incantation except for the Eye or bites.'[189] The majority opinion, however, is that the three main forms of *ta'wīdh* may be used for any disease, so disability in general would be included.[190] A number of relevant references mention specific complaints such as burns,[191] fever,[192] eye diseases[193] and snakebite. Some disabilities are also mentioned specifically such as epilepsy, especially that caused by evil earthly spirits,[194] mental disabilities, possession and the like.[195] In the interpretation of the majority of jurists, the tradition mentioned above does not mean that the Prophet intended to deny the possibility of using incantation in other cases. It simply means that there is no incantation more fitting and beneficial than that for warding off the evil eye and curing the effect of snakebites.[196] In the Shī'ī tradition, apart from incantations believed to cure every sort of disease,[197] some were also meant to treat specific disabilities such as deafness,[198] semi-paralysis and facial paralysis,[199] mental disorders[200] and insanity.[201]

Now we move to the juristic rulings. As noted above, the linguistic definition of *ta'wīdh*, in all its three forms, does not impose limitations on its content or the formulas used in this process. That is because the aforementioned forms of *ta'wīdh* originated in the pre-Islamic period (*Jāhiliyya*), leaving the drawing of lines between lawful and unlawful practices to Islam.[202] Basing their discussions on relevant prophetic traditions, Muslim jurists have tried to trace these lines.

First, the majority of jurists stipulated that the formulas used must be composed of the Qur'ān or the names or attributes of God. Additionally, they must be in Arabic or in a comprehensible language. Some jurists restricted permissible incantation to the last three chapters of the Qur'ān (*mu'awwidhāt*). Other jurists widened the possibilities to include not only words or names of God but anything else as long as it could be understood. In this contact, the genre of *khawāṣṣ al-Qur'ān* (the prerogatives of the Qur'ān) came into existence, containing discussions and analyses of the miraculously healing effects of certain Qur'anic verses. This genre makes use of some prophetic traditions such as 'The opening chapter of the Qur'ān is a cure for every disease' and others citing practical cases in which the Prophet treated different diseases by reciting specific verses from the Qur'ān.[203] For instance, the Qur'anic chapter 36 (*Sūrat Yāsīn*) was used as a cure for madness.[204] Besides these prophetic traditions, such sources mainly comprise stories of well-known pious figures experiencing Qur'anic verses as spiritual medicine for various diseases.[205] This genre is still thriving in the present time, with a growing list of books elaborating the curative aspects of the Qur'ān.[206] Some writers extended these healing practices to include poems, formulas based on the names of God, angels or prophets, and prayers citing celebrated names.[207] The best-known such poem is *Al-Burda* which Ibn 'Abd al-Salām al-Marrākushī, in his *Khawāṣṣ al-Burda fī bur' al-dā'* (The Peculiarities of *al-Burda* concerning Healing the Disease), divided into several sections and described the beneficial effects of each.[208] Some verses could cure epilepsy whereas others were regarded as medicine for every other sort of disease.[209]

Second, jurists said that one should not believe that such medicine cures diseases by its own power. One should always believe that recovery takes place at any rate with God's permission.[210] It is clear that these stipulations were made in an attempt to draw a clear line between lawful *ta'wīdh* and the magical charms with their potential polytheistic elements which are prohibited by Islam.[211] In this context the jurists cite the following prophetic statement about the use of incantations traced back to the pre-Islamic period, 'Show me your incantations. There is no harm in using incantations as long as they do not involve polytheism.'[212]

In the light of the above discussion, two points are in order. The first is the erroneous categorization of *ruqya* as a magical practice, for instance in the article '*Ruḳyā*' in the *Encyclopaedia of Islam*. *Ruqya* is defined as a magical chant consisting in the pronunciation of magical formulas for procuring an enchantment. The writer adds, 'It is one of the procedures of *siḥr* used by the Prophet himself and, because of this, permitted in exceptional cases, on condition that it brings benefit to the people and does not harm anyone.'[213] Besides stipulating the condition of being beneficial, the writer does not refer to any of the conditions listed by the majority of jurists to distinguish between lawful *ruqya* and unlawful *siḥr* (magic). This also holds true for the Shī'ī scholars who made the condition that incantations should be based on Qur'anic verses only.[214]

The second point is the inaccurate distinction made by some researchers between Islamic therapies approved by 'official Islam' and those already practised within 'popular Islam'. 'Official Islam', they argued, restricts permissible Islamic therapies to those made with the help of Qur'anic texts. However, they added these restrictions are frequently ignored in 'popular Islam'.[215] Although the division of Islam into 'official' and 'popular' remains highly debatable, it is certainly not valid for this case. The above discussions show that Muslim jurists, who are supposed to represent the 'official Islam', are not a single bloc. Although some jurists restricted the scope of permissible incantations to specific chapters of the Qur'ān, the majority of them broadened it to include names and attributes of God as well. A third group allowed anything, even if it was non-Arabic, as long as it was understood, including poems such as *Al-Burda*.

7.3 Summary

This chapter has dealt with treating disabilities. Here juristic discourses adopted a holistic approach. A person with a disability could be treated by regular medicine, in juristic literature called 'physical medicine' (*ṭibb jusmānī*), or by religious formulas from the Holy Scripture, i.e. the Qur'ān or other texts believed to have healing effects. This type of medicine was called 'spiritual medicine' (*ṭibb rūḥānī*). Although early and modern Muslim jurists approved both types of medical treatment, a general preference was given to 'spiritual medicine' by early jurists and to 'physical medicine' by modern jurists. The point agreed among all jurists was the need to relieve or minimize the pain and trouble contingent on disabilities. In this regard we have checked a number of issues which now fall into the category of medical ethics such as abortion, vaccination, organ transplantation and cloning. Although modern jurists have tried always to search for relevant discussions among early jurists on these issues, they mostly had to develop their own independent investigation basing themselves directly on the general principles in the Qur'ān and Sunna. However, it was clear that their standpoint on medical research was the decisive factor for their religious advice. For instance, those who do not trust what physicians say about the efficiency of vaccination discourage people from using it, whereas others who believe in the validity of medicine criticized the antivaccination standpoint adopted by other scholars.

8 Financial aid for people with disabilities

8.1 Revenues within the family

The well-known Arabic terms *usra* or *'ā'ila* now used to mean 'family' are modern. No direct use of these terms can be traced in early juristic texts. Other equivalent terms such as *āl*, *ahl* and *'iyāl* convey the same concept.[1] It is very important to start by pointing out the connotations of the family as an institution in Islam. Islam does not prescribe any specific family organizational type. Traditionally, the Muslim structure has been, and still remains, closer to the extended than to the nuclear family. A Muslim family primarily includes the self, the spouse and the immediate forebears and descendants.[2] Members of the Muslim family may or may not share a residential unit. The residence may be shared by all members, or some or all of them may live separately and independently. In all these cases, the family ties remain intact and reciprocal family obligations must be discharged by all the members.[3] Thus there is mutual responsibility between the individual and his immediate family, as indicated more than once in the Qur'ān (17:23 and 24, 31:14 and 15, 33:06). This mutual responsibility is the foundation that holds the family together and is considered to be its basic building block. It is based on the strong inclinations of human nature, on affection and love and on the requirements of interest and necessity.[4]

This chapter reviews the main financial revenues within a family through which the needs of people with disabilities can be met. As a form of social solidarity among the family, maintenance (*nafaqa*) is incumbent upon the well-off members in order to support the poorer members. People with disabilities, whether parents, children, wives or other relatives, are entitled to receive *nafaqa* from the rich members of the family. As family members, people with disabilities can still enjoy financial support from a bequest (*waṣiyya*) or family endowment (*waqf ahlī*). Detailed juristic discussions on the regulations of these three financial revenues are presented below, with a focus on those relevant to people with disabilities.

8.1.1 Maintenance (*nafaqa*)

Nafaqa, generally translated as 'maintenance', signifies in the juristic sense all those things essential to support life, such as food, clothes, lodging, and toilet requisites, and excludes luxuries like hair dye, kohl, lipstick and similar articles.

Entitlement to maintenance is established through relationship, marriage and property (*milk*), making it incumbent on one person to maintain another.[5] Maintenance of this kind is obligatory (*wājib*) according to the Qur'ān, Sunna and the consensus of jurists.[6] Here discussion will be restricted to maintenance established by reason of relationship or marriage.

In most cases of *nafaqa*, the maintained person has to be *mu'sir* and he/she is to be maintained till he/she reaches *ḥadd al-kifāya*. It is essential to understand these two juridical terms, frequently used in discussions on *nafaqa*.

The exact juristic definition of the term *al-mu'sir*, translated as 'needy' or 'someone who is financially dependent', is a point of disagreement among Muslim jurists. Some Ḥanafī jurists said that *al-mu'sir* is a person who is permitted to receive charity (*ṣadaqa*) and whose money did not reach the *niṣāb* (the prescribed amount) requiring him to pay *zakāt*. Other Ḥanafī jurists stated that the needy person is one short of money. Such a person may even own a house, but he cannot be obliged to sell it. Instead his son must give him enough money.[7] According to the Ḥanbalī school, a needy person is one who has no extra money after meeting his and his wife's basic needs.[8] The jurists of the Ẓāhirī school considered that a needy person is one who has no money after meeting his basic needs, broadly defined, and acquiring clothing.[9] Opinions within the Zaydī school state that a needy person is one who has no income and insufficient food for ten nights after meeting his basic needs for clothes, housing, furniture and servants. Other Zaydī jurists who represent the predominant opinion of the school define *al-mu'sir* as one who has no food for lunch or dinner. However, it is stipulated that the needy are those unable to earn money due to old age, persistent illness and the like.[10] A needy person, as defined by the jurists of the Imāmiyya school, is someone who has no extra money to spend on any given day and night other than the amount sufficient for his and his wife's food.[11] Jurists of the Ibāḍiyya school say that a needy person is one who is destitute and has no money. If he needs money but he owns a house, then he has to sell the house to buy food unless he/she is a father or a mother.[12] In the absence of clear-cut textual evidence supporting any of the aforementioned opinions, defining *al-mu'sir* has remained a point of *ijtihād* (personal reasoning) that has taken place at different times and places. When reasoning thus in modern times the context in which the various individuals concerned lived must be borne in mind.

Broadly speaking, the term *ḥadd al-kifāya* (sufficiency level) denotes reaching the level at which all basic needs are met. Again, defining this level precisely remains a point of disagreement among jurists. One group, including the Shāfi'īs, favours a precise definition, and states that it is two *mudd* (a classical measure of grain, approximately 5 gills) every day for a wealthy husband, one *mudd* for a poor one and one and a half for the middle-class husband. The second group, mainly represented by the Ḥanafīs and supported by the majority of modern jurists, considers that this level must be decided by a judge on the basis of the social and economic milieu in which a couple live.[13] Hence, the flexibility of the term should be remembered when the items needed for maintenance are calculated. In case of people with disabilities, special needs should also be taken into consideration, for instance hearing aids for people with hearing disabilities and sticks or canes for blind people. By the same token, if a person's disability makes him need a wife to look after him or a servant to help him, maintenance of this wife or servant shall be incumbent on the one who is to provide maintenance.[14]

In Islamic jurisprudence, the maintenance system functions within the family structure and thus pertains to one's relatives.The main Qur'anic expression used to signify 'relatives' is *dhawū* or *ulū al-qurbā* (2:83 and 177, 4:8 and 36, 5:106, 6:152, 7:41) (translated as kindred, kith and kin, kinsfolk, relatives). Membership of this category would carry a number of rights and duties as well. For instance, Islam enjoins that spending on poor relatives, by blood or marriage, is obligatory upon their well-off relatives because it is a part of *ṣilat al-raḥim* (upholding family ties), which literally means 'joining of uterus ties'. This is proved by the following verse, 'The mothers shall give suck to their offspring for two whole years, if the father desires to complete the term. But he shall bear the cost of their food and clothing on equitable terms' (Qur'ān 2:233). This means that maintenance of relatives by birth is obligatory. Then Allah said, 'an heir shall be chargeable in the same way' (Qur'ān 2:233). So it is concluded that maintaining forebears, descendants and collaterals is mandatory as the heir may be in one of these categories.[15] However, Qur'anic references to 'relatives' do not identify exactly who falls into this category and who does not. As a consequence, jurists did not agree on which family members belong to the category of 'relatives' or *dhawū al-qurbā,* as indicated by the Qur'ān.

According to the Ḥanafīs, the criterion for a relative's responsibility to provide maintenance for another is the prohibited degree of marriage, meaning that in the case of a male and a female, marriage between them would be considered unlawful.[16] Therefore, generally this responsibility includes fathers – however many generations back – and sons – however many generations forward – and also includes brothers, sisters, uncles and aunts, both paternal and maternal, because marriage between any two of them is prohibited. The closest relative is liable to provide maintenance.[17] *Imām* Mālik and *imām* al-Shāfi'ī said that the only obligatory *nafaqa* in Islam is that of parents and children.[18] The Ja'farī school adopted the same opinion.[19] The Ḥanbalīs stated that it is obligatory that fathers, however many generations back, provide and receive maintenance. Similarly, it is obligatory that sons, however many generations forward, provide and receive maintenance, irrespective of their title to inheritance. Maintenance of relatives not belonging to the two classes is also obligatory if the person liable to provide maintenance inherits from the person being maintained either by *farḍ* (obligatory share) or *ta'ṣīb* (the residual share). But if excluded from inheritance, he will not be responsible for maintenance.[20]

Given that these are the most important three categories of relatives in terms of maintenance in Islamic jurisprudence, the focus below will be on people with disabilities as parents and grandparents, as children, and finally as wives. The last category will be treated seperately and in more detail because the relevant discussions on the marriage of people with disabilities in Islamic jurisprudence will be considered as well.

Parents with disabilities enjoy all financial rights guaranteed by Islam to parents in general. Furthermore, special consideration is given to the fact that they are living with disabilities. For instance, al-Shāfi'ī stated that the needy parent is entitled to maintenance only when he suffers *zamāna* (enduring disease or disability) or madness. Other jurists did not stipulate this condition.[21] Muslim jurists unanimously stated that the parent entitled to maintenance must be sustained from his children's property; according to the majority of jurists, this also applies to the needy grandparent.[22] According to the Mālikīs, a grandson does not have to maintain his needy paternal or maternal grandparents. On the other hand, the Ẓahirī school states that a rich child must maintain the needy among his parents, grandparents, children and grandchildren equally and simultaneously without giving precedence to any of them.[23] In this regard, Muslim scholars did not stipulate that the parent and the child should be of the same religion. That is because *nafaqa* here is to preserve life and this has nothing to do with shared religion.[24]

Muslim jurists are unanimous that a child who has no personal property is entitled to receive maintenance, in the first instance from the father. However, this right is subject to three conditions. First, the child must be in need, i.e. indigent and unable to earn a living.[25] Second, the father must have the means to provide maintenance from capital.[26] Finally, the child must be born free (*ḥurr*), not a slave.[27] Inability to earn a living can be a matter of age, and physical or mental condition. According to the Sunni and Shī'ī schools, a boy with no property of his own loses his right to maintenance on reaching the age at which he can earn a living, even before puberty (*bulūgh*), but retains that right if he cannot work due to illness or disability.[28] The Shāfi'īs state that maintenance of children includes purchasing medicine, doctor's fees and a servant if these are necessary due to chronic disease (*zamāna*) or illness.[29]

8.1.1.1 Marriage of people with disabilities

Before discussing the *nafaqa* of a wife with disability, it is essential to sketch the broad lines of juristic discussions on the marriage of disabled people. Broadly speaking, *nikāḥ* and *zawāj* are the best-known terms used in early and modern legal texts in chapters focusing on issues pertaining to marriage. References to people with disabilities in these chapters are generally infrequent. These scattered references to rulings on marriage collected by five main studies, four in Arabic[30] and one in English,[31] form the basis of the discussions below.

Based on the Qur'anic references to marriage (4:1, 7:189, 30:21, 16:72), Muslim jurists tried to deduce the main objectives of marriage. Vardit Rispler-Chaim (Haifa University) tried to compile a complete list of these objectives.[32] Two main objectives have direct relevance to people with disabilities, namely, enjoying a sexual relationship (*istimtā'*) and enjoying companionship (*'ishra ṭayyiba* or *sakan,* according to the Qur'anic expression). Given that these two elements are prohibited between a man and a woman outside the marital relationship, they become high priorities in marriage. That is why jurists were unanimous in paying great attention to safeguarding these two objectives and agreed in principle that any defect in any of the spouses hindering their realization could be of legal consequence to the validity of the marriage contract. Beyond agreement on this general principle, jurists disagreed on how to apply it to specific cases. Two main criteria govern subsequent discussions on this point. The first criterion is the timing of the onset of a disability or of the discovery that the partner has a disability, whether before or after marriage. The second criterion is the relevance of the disabilities to either of the aforementioned two objectives, a good sexual relationship or good companionship.

8.1.1.1.1 RULINGS PERTAINING TO THE SITUATION BEFORE A MARRIAGE IS CONTRACTED

Marriage of people who have *junūn* (insanity) has preoccupied both early and modern jurists. A few Ḥanbalī and Mālikī jurists regarded a marriage contract involving a mentally retarded person as valid and considered that the consent of the guardian was not required.[33] Other jurists agree that the contracting parties should be of sound mind. Thus, people who are mentally retarded may marry but only with the consent of the guardian. Here jurists distinguished between males and females and between minors and adults. One of the most detailed presentations of this issue is given by the well-known Ḥanbalī jurist, Ibn Qudāma. According to him, jurists agreed that if a girl without mental capacity was still a virgin (*bikr*), her guardian, whoever it might be, could marry her off. In case of a non-virgin (*thayyib*), the character of the guardian was decisive. If the guardian was the father, then he could marry her off, according to Abū Ḥanīfa and al-Shāfiʿī. Other jurists opined that he would not be entitled to do so because a non-virgin could not be married against her will and it would not be possible to know her wishes because of her insanity. If the guardian was the ruler, then he would not be entitled to marry her off. Another opinion contended that it would be permissible only in two cases: if she displayed signs of sexual desire or if physicians (*ahl al-ṭibb*) stated that her sickness could be healed by marriage. A minor boy without mental capacity, on the other hand, could get married with the consent of his father. Al-Shāfiʿī said that the father was not permitted to consent to the marriage as long as there were no signs of a need to do so because marriage implied financial costs.

Ibn Qudāma also considered that in the views of the Shāfiʿī, Ḥanbalī and Jaʿfarī schools marriage of people with a mental disability was not valid without the consent of the guardian. If the person without mental capacity was adult, the father was entitled to marry him off whether he exhibited sexual desire or not, according to the Shāfiʿīs and Ḥanbalīs. Others did not give the father this right whereas a third group said that the father would be entitled to marry off such a son as long as there was a need or desire (*ḥāja*) to do so. Ibn Qudāma opined that restricting the notion of 'need' to satisfying the sensual appetite does not do justice to the term, which implied the need to protect and share a place to live with someone. He added that marriage itself can be a sort of medication.[34]

The contemporary Moroccan scholar, Muṣṭafā b. Ḥamza, said of this:

> It is by no means impossible for people with mental disabilities to marry and establish their own families. Islamic *fiqh* states that a father, guardian or judge can decide to marry off a mentally sick person if he fears that he/she could commit fornication (*zinā*) and if he expects that marriage would be beneficial to that person. The bridal money (*mahr*) in such a case is to be paid from the resources of the father or the guardian who concludes the marital contract. If the person suffers from intermittent insanity, then he himself should conclude his marital contract while he is sane, otherwise his guardian should marry him off.[35]

In a fatwa from Gaza (1998), Sheikh Muḥammad Dīb Qūsa was asked whether mentally retarded people should marry at all. He concluded that they may, but only if they demonstrate attraction to members of the opposite sex. He explained that sanity *('aql)* is not a prerequisite for marriage. In an Egyptian fatwa, the mufti distinguished between *'atah* (mental deficiency) and *junūn* (insanity), claiming that *'atah* is a 'quiet' insanity and *junūn* is a violent extrovert insanity. He permitted the marriage of a *ma'tūh* (one who has *'atah)* only as long as he or she could differentiate between good and evil, and if he or she has his or her guardian's consent to marry. *'Atah,* contrary to *junūn,* is believed to be less hazardous to the partner. In another fatwa dated 24 June 1981, the late grand *imām* of al-Azhar Jād al-Ḥaqq declared an existing marriage null and void on the grounds that the husband had been continuously insane since 1968 – that is, prior to the marriage, which was concluded in 1978. Similarly, Egyptian law no. 462 of 1955 stipulates, in the Ḥanafī spirit of the law, that if both partners are not sane when the contract is made, the marriage is void.[36]

Jurists discussed physical defects affecting sexual ability when speaking of people with no sexual appetite (*shahwa*) due to congenital impotence (*'unna*). Given that enjoying a sexual relationship is one of the main objectives of marriage, some jurists opined that marriage of such people is reprehensible (*makrūh*). Others considered they could still marry because a sexual relationship is not the sole objective of marriage.[37] As for other disabilities which have no effect in this respect such as blindness, lameness, dumbness and the like, early jurists agreed that none of them disqualified a person from marrying and, according to some jurists, such disabled people can also fulfil the role of guardian (*walī*) in the conclusion of a marriage.[38] But should the other partner be informed of the disability before the marriage? They agreed that this should happen in the case of elephantiasis (*judhām*), leprosy (*baraṣ*) and other defects affecting sexual capabilities, as detailed below, while disagreeing on the other disabilities.[39] The majority of jurists did not require the other partner to be told before marriage about disabilities like blindness, paralysis and amputated organs.[40] Other jurists considered concealing such disabilities as an illicit deceit, entitling the partner to end the marriage and claim financial compensation for the harms suffered.[41]

Although the main trend in modern times is towards the promotion, safeguarding and protection of the rights of people with disabilities, voices objecting to the marriage of such people are still heard. In his commentary on the Qur'anic verse on polygamy (4:2), the well-known Qur'ān exegete, Jamāl al-Dīn al-Qāsimī (d. 1332/1914) quoted an article entitled 'Islam and Improving Progeny (*Al-Islām wa iṣlāḥ al-nasl*)' by an anonymous author described as a sociologist and Muslim philosopher. The author's suggested eugenics was based on two procedures which were both first devised by two contemporary western philosophers, one from Germany and the other from England. The first procedure was to prevent people with disabilities, chronic diseases or a serious criminal record from marrying, and so avoid their having offspring, who in most cases would suffer from the same problems. The second procedure was to allow polygamy for people of genius (*nawābigh*), so that their offspring would increase. Al-Qāsimī comments on the article by saying, 'This is a marvellous inference!'[42]

'Umar Riḍā Kaḥḥāla (d. 1905-1988)[43] follows much the same tendency. He concludes that whoever suffers from a contagious disease or chronic illness, and cannot recover from it, may not marry. He even suggests that proper legislation be enacted on this subject. Kaḥḥāla enumerates the following diseases as bars to marriage: gonorrhea, syphilis, pulmonary tuberculosis, alcoholism, nervous diseases, defects in the reproductive organs, a too narrow vagina, physical deformities, heart, liver and kidney diseases and cancer. In his view, 'every couple should be tested prior to getting married, and of course avoid marriage if one of them suffers from any of the above diseases'. In Kaḥḥāla's view, the absence of a test document should render a marriage legally invalid.[44]

On the other hand, other voices today espouse the right of people with disabilities to start a family:

> It is not fair to determine that those who are not perfectly healthy should not marry, because many people who suffered a chronic disease or a birth defect have married, and their marriages have turned out to be as happy as can be imagined.[45]

According to Egyptian law no. 25/1920, the wife has the right to request dissolution if her husband has an incurable disability. But only physicians are authorized to determine whether a condition is curable or not.[46] Since no time limit is stipulated in the law within which the cure must occur, it tends to protect the rights of a disabled man who wants to continue the marriage bond.[47]

8.1.1.1.2 RULINGS PERTAINING TO THE SITUATION AFTER A MARRIAGE IS CONTRACTED

The main question here is whether the disability of one partner entitles the other to ask for the marriage to be dissolved.

An introductory note is in order. If a marriage ends at the husband's request on the basis of the wife's disability, the financial consequences are different from if the wife makes the request on the basis of the husband's disability. Financially, the first alternative favours the husband whereas the second favours the wife.[48] Since in the second case divorce becomes a reality the wife cannot prevent, the best financial terms would be achieved for her through *ṭalāq sharʿī* (repudiation according to the Sharīʿa), in which the husband is required to pay her the postponed part of the dowry (the portion of the dowry that is still to be paid), provided this was stipulated in the marriage contract, as well as paying maintenance during the waiting period of a divorce (the period before a divorce becomes final).[49] The husband is responsible for proving that the disability existed before consummation of the marriage and this should preferably be corroborated by a doctor's opinion. If the husband cannot furnish sufficient proof, the guardian has to swear that he did not know of the disability, hence he was not deceitful.[50] Others claim that if the husband is deemed trustworthy, his statement should be accepted as true. Another view is that if the guardian is a distant relative of the wife such as a third cousin, his word will be valid; if not, the husband's statement will count as the truth.[51]

Now we move back to the main question. One of the requirements for the marriage contract to be binding is that the contracting parties should be 'free from defect'. 'Defect' here refers to physical or mental flaws in one of the parties which make the marriage unfruitful.[52] If one of the parties finds in the other some defect which is impossible to live with, then the marriage is not binding and he or she has the right to dissolve it. This right is not absolute, as there are essential disagreements among jurists.

Jurists have not drawn up an agreed list of defects affecting the first objective, sexual relations. The Ḥanafīs state that such defects are legally significant only when they affect the husband. They named three defects, *jabb* (amputation of the penis and/or testicles), *ʿunna* (impotence, a too small or too large a penis which is unable to penetrate, lack of erection, or lack of sexual desire causing impotence) and *khiṣāʾ* (castration).[53] The majority of jurists did not differentiate between the man and the woman when considering the legal validity of defects affecting sexual relations. However, they disagreed again on what these defects are. To the Mālikīs, they are in the case of a man, *jubb, khiṣāʾ*, *ʿunna* and *iʿtirāḍ* (lack of erection), and in the case of a woman, *rataq* (the meatus of the vagina being sealed by a tissue which prevents penetration), *qarn* (a protruding tissue or bone that blocks the vagina), *ʿafal* (scrotal hernia; a piece of flesh extruding into the vulva, like a man's hernia), *ifḍāʾ* (when the uterine tract and the urinary tract are intertwined) and *bakhr* (bad odour released from the vagina).[54] To the Shāfiʿīs, the defects are, in the case of a man, *ʿunna* and *jubb*, and in the case of a woman, *rataq* and *qarn*. To the Ḥanbalīs, they are *ʿunna* and *jubb* in the case of a man and *rataq, qarn* and *ʿafal* in the case of a woman.[55] Modern scholars state that it should be kept in view that most of the aforementioned defects are now curable since modern surgery is capable of correcting them. Thus, the partner with the defect should be given the opportunity to try medical treatment.[56]

In the category of defects affecting good companionship, the three main disabilities which could affect the man or the woman are, *junūn* (insanity), *judhām* (elephantiasis) and *baraṣ* (leprosy).[57] According to the Jaʿfarī and Zaydī schools, blindness is annexed to the defects legally considered by jurists as bringing a marriage to an end.[58]

Michael Dols and more recently Rispler-Chaim have meticulously noted that *junūn* should be approached carefully and studied in Islamic sources. Dols says that *majnūn* (insane) was often a social rather than a clinical diagnosis.[59] Tracing early jurists' discussions on this point clearly shows that medical diagnosis did not play a central role in defining who is considered *majnūn*. Jurists were more concerned with searching for and studying rulings pertinent to this group of people rather than defining their disease. This overwhelming social-cultural dimension of the term *majnūn* remains up to the present time.[60]

The majority of jurists, including the Mālikīs, Shāfi'īs and Ḥanbalīs, allow either spouse to request dissolution of a marriage when the other becomes mad. The Mālikīs include under the term *junūn* epilepsy and *waswās* (melancholia, delirium, confusion of the intellect). It depends, however, on when the *junūn* first occurred. If it was before the contract, and the other spouse was not aware of it, each has the right to request *radd* (annulment of the contract), whether the revelation of the disability came before or after consummation. If it is a periodic *junūn,* with intermissions of sanity, as in epilepsy (*ṣara'*), then there are no grounds for *radd.* It is worth noting here that epilepsy in the medieval period was viewed as a form of insanity, unlike today when it is treated as a neurological disorder which can largely be controlled by medication.[61]

The question now is whether the aforementioned defects the only ones considered by jurists or whether they are just examples.

In their answers, the jurists can be divided into two main groups. The first group, representing the majority of Ḥanafīs, Mālikīs, Shāfi'īs and Ḥanbalīs, restricts the defects affecting the validity of marriage to the list mentioned above. Thus, disabilities such as blindness, loss of an eye, dumbness and the like do not count in this respect.[62] For instance, Ibn Mufliḥ al-Ḥanbalī (816/1413–844/1440) comments on the aforementioned disabilities saying, 'Based on what has been mentioned, it is known that dissolution of marriage cannot happen on the basis of other defects such as *'awar* (blindness in one eye), *'amā* (full blindness), the loss of one hand, etc.'[63] However, according to the Mālikīs, both spouses are considered to possess the right to stipulate in the marriage contract that the other party must be free from defects like the loss of an eye (*'awar*), lameness, paralysis, gourmandism and the like. Other jurists, including the Ḥanafīs, said that neither party was entitled to make this stipulation. If the husband (who stipulated such a condition) discovered any of these defects before consummation of the marriage, then he had the choice between accepting it and paying all the bride price agreed upon or canceling the marriage without any financial obligations. On the other hand, if the husband found out about the defect after consummation, then the wife was entitled to *mahr al-mithl* (the dowry paid to an equal) unless the bride price agreed upon was less than the *mahr al-mithl.*[64]

The other group is mainly represented by the two Ḥanbalī jurists, Ibn Taymiyya and his disciple Ibn al-Qayyim. They stated that every defect seriously affecting the aforementioned two objectives of good companionship and sexual relations would have the same effect as the other defects previously listed by jurists. Thus defects such as amputated organs, dumbness, blindness and the like would represent, according to this group, valid legal grounds for bringing a marriage to an end.[65]

More problematic are defects believed to have existed before the marriage but concealed from the other spouse and discovered only after consummation. This circumstance calls in question the credibility of the spouse with disability, in addition to the unpleasant discovery of his/her disability.

In principle, a health problem in one partner that existed before the signing of the contract but was not reported to the other is considered a deception with regard to the *sharṭ al-salāma* (lit. the condition of soundness). The impact of such a revelation on the fate of the marriage will depend on the type of health problem, and also on when it was discovered, whether before or after the advance payment of dowry, or before or after consummation of the marriage. Even when the disability does not dramatically affect the fate of the marriage it might reflect on the value of the *mahr,* and possibly lead to a call to apply *mahr al-mithl* instead. Once again we realize that health is an important factor in the estimation of the *mahr.*[66]

One solution to cases where the deception *(tadlīs)* was on the part of the wife and discovered by the husband before consummation was 'sending her back to her parents' home'. The marital contract becomes void and the husband may take back all the gifts and money he has hitherto provided. Disabilities not reported prior to marriage for which a wife may be sent back are only leprosy, elephantiasis, insanity and a non-penetrable vagina (*qarn* and *'afal*), which means that she will never be able to bear children. But she can be sent back only if consummation has not taken place. Once consummated, the marriage cannot be annulled. Only in Shī'ī sources do the wife's blindness and lameness constitute grounds for the annulment, but only if the marriage has not been consummated. If it has, no further grounds for annulment (*radd*) exist, since consummation is legally viewed as an expression of satisfaction or acceptance of the bride as she is.[67]

In all cases, if the husband still feels after consummation that he was tricked into the marriage he may sue the person who introduced the woman to him (her guardian) for the amount of the *mahr* he paid her. The guardian is usually a close relative of the wife, a father or a brother, and is expected to know if she has disability or not, and therefore may be sued. If the guardian is a distant relative, such as a cousin, who claims that he was not aware of her disability, there is no one to sue. If the woman and her guardian shared the deception they will bear the *ḍamān* (compensation) on a fifty-fifty basis. As early as the fifteenth century the Mālikī jurist, al-Wansharīsī, was asked about a case in which the husband charged the wife with being a leper, and her father claimed 'she only had bright spots on her body' (*luma'āt fī jasadiha*). The husband probably intended to claim that the impairment existed prior to the contract, in order to prove that he was tricked into the marriage. The burden of proof lay on him. In the absence of such proof the wife's guardian has to testify that the impairment was not there prior to marriage, and consequently *tafrīq* (dissolution by court) would not be applicable. Only if the impairment was in her sexual organs and penetration was impossible should the wife be returned to her father *(radd)*.[68]

Such questions were also posed to modern scholars. In 1979, a man approached Shaykh Jād al-Ḥaqq, the late grand *imām* of al-Azhar, who was the chairman of Dār al-Iftā' al-Miṣriyya at this time, asking him to terminate his marriage with his epileptic wife.[69] The husband pointed out that he discovered the epilepsy only after consummation of marriage. He suspected her guardian of having concealed relevant information about his future wife's health. Hence the husband wished to terminate marriage through dissolution (*faskh*), and demanded that the guardian return the dowry paid, on the basis that the condition of physical integrity (*sharṭ al-salāma*) in the contract had been breached. Naturally, the husband wished to terminate the marriage on the best terms for himself, that is through *faskh*. The Muftī had therefore to determine the most just legal way of separating the couple.

In his response, Shaykh Jād al-Ḥaqq surveys the range of existing legal opinion on an illness or a disability discovered in one of the spouses after marriage:

- According to the Ẓāhirīs, neither spouse has legal grounds to claim dissolution of a marriage (*faskh*), whether disability appeared before or after marriage.
- Certain disabilities constitute legal grounds for dissolution of marriage (*tafrīq*), a procedure recognized by all four Sunni schools of law. The Ḥanafīs limit the application of *tafrīq* to the case of disabilities found in the husband, while the Mālikīs, the Shāfi'īs, Ḥanbalīs, Zaydīs and Twelver Shī'īs allow the request for dissolution from either spouse. However, within each school, the scholars are divided as to the number and nature of the disabilities which justify the request of dissolution by court.
- Any physical defect in the husband or in the wife is a legal ground for the other spouse's resort to dissolution. If, however, the husband finds after consummation a defect in the wife of which he was not informed prior to marriage, the husband may ask his wife's guardian to return the dowry. This view was supported by Ibn Qayyim and Ibn Qudāma and all the Ḥanbalīs and the Shāfi'īs 'in older times' (*fī al-qadīm*). However, 'recent generations' (*fī al-ḥadīth*) of Ḥanafī and Shāfi'ī jurists do not permit any dissolution after consummation, arguing that by this act the husband has availed himself of his right to sexual intercourse acquired by his payment of the dowry. He may not claim it back thereafter.

Jād al-Ḥaqq concluded that the Egyptian law no. 28/1931, which is influenced by Ḥanafī law, does not acknowledge the right to request dissolution if the husband discovered a disability in his wife only after consummation. Apparently, he sided with the 'recent generations' of Ḥanafīs and Shāfi'īs. Hence, according to Shaykh Jād al-Ḥaqq, the husband who is unwilling to continue living with his epileptic wife may terminate the marriage through *ṭalāq* for which he needs no judicial intervention, but he must provide the wife with the financial rights of a divorcee, that is the postponed portion of the dowry and the waiting period maintenance (*nafaqat al-'idda*).

It is to be noted that epilepsy (*ṣaraʿ*) is not specifically mentioned in the list of defects, mentioned by the Ḥanafīs for instance, that give a spouse the right to request dissolution. The husband in the fatwa under discussion, therefore, has no legal grounds, according to the four Sunni legal schools, for requesting the court to separate him and his wife through dissolution of the marriage. However, epilepsy is an illness known to Muslims since the Middle Ages.[70] According to Rispler-Chaim, this suggests that at least culturally epilepsy could have been considered a sort of madness and under this heading admissible onto the list of a wife's disabilities entitling the husband to request dissolution of the marriage, according to many jurists, as mentioned above. Jād al-Ḥaqq did not make this possible analogy, thereby safeguarding the wife's financial rights.

In a recent fatwa, a mufti was asked about a defect that neither the woman nor her guardian was aware of. From whom should the misled husband request reimbursement of the dowry? The answer provided was that if the guardian did not know, the woman was required to compensate. However, if she did not know either, then no one was at fault and there was no one to sue.[71]

8.1.1.1.3 WIVES WITH DISABILITIES

A general overview of the wife's right to maintenance will be sketched and then the financial consequences of being disabled will be detailed. Initially speaking, there is consensus among all Muslims that marriage is one of the circumstances that make maintenance obligatory. The Holy Qur'ān explicitly mentions the wife's maintenance in the following verse: 'The mothers shall give suck to their offspring for two whole years, if the father desires to complete the term. But he shall bear the cost of their food and clothing on equitable terms' (Qur'ān 2:233). There is also a tradition which says, 'The right of a woman over her husband is that he feeds her, and if she acts out of ignorance, to forgive her.'[72]

The legal schools agree that the wife's maintenance is obligatory if the requisite conditions, to be mentioned below, are fulfilled and that maintenance of the divorcee is obligatory during the waiting period of a revocable divorce.[73] The schools also agree that a woman observing the waiting period following her husband's death is not entitled to maintenance, whether she is pregnant or not, although the Shāfiʿī and the Mālikī schools state that if the husband dies, she is entitled to maintenance only for housing.[74]

The Shāfiʿīs said that if the husband leaves his wife while she is pregnant and he then dies, her maintenance shall not cease.[75] The Ḥanafīs observe that if she is a revocable divorcee and the husband dies during the waiting period, this changes into the waiting period following death, and her maintenance ceases, unless she has been asked by the court to borrow her maintenance and she actually did so. In this case, her maintenance does not cease.[76]

There is consensus that a woman observing the waiting period as a result of 'intercourse by mistake' is not entitled to maintenance.[77] The schools differ over the maintenance of a divorcee during the waiting period of an irrevocable divorce. The Ḥanafīs assert that she is entitled to maintenance even if she has been divorced three times, whether she is pregnant or not, on condition that she does not leave the house provided by her ex-husband for her to live in during the waiting period. According to the Ḥanafīs, the rulings which apply to a woman in a waiting period following the dissolution of a valid contract are the same as those which apply to a divorcee in an irrevocable divorce.[78]

According to the Mālikī school, if the divorcee is not pregnant, she is not entitled to any maintenance except her residence, and if she is pregnant she is entitled to her full maintenance. Maintenance must continue even if she leaves the house provided for the waiting period, because it is intended for the child in the womb and not for the divorcee.[79] The Shāfiʿī, Jaʿfarī and Ḥanbalī schools state that if she is not pregnant she is not entitled to maintenance, and if pregnant she is entitled to it. But the Shāfiʿīs add that if she needlessly leaves the house of the waiting period, her maintenance shall cease.[80] The Jaʿfarīs do not consider the dissolution of a valid contract similar to an irrevocable divorce. They observe that a divorcee during the waiting period of a dissolved contract is not entitled to any maintenance whether pregnant or not.[81]

Would a working wife be entitled to maintenance? Jurists give more than one answer to this question. The Ḥanafīs are explicit that a working woman who does not stay at home is not entitled to maintenance if the husband demands that she stay at home and she does not concede to his demand.[82] This view accords with what the other schools believe regarding the impermissibility of a wife leaving her home without her husband's permission.[83] The Shāfiʿīs and the Ḥanbalīs further state that if she leaves home with his permission in order to meet her own requirements, her maintenance ceases.[84]

But another view draws a distinction between a husband who knows at the time of marriage that his wife is employed and that her employment prevents her staying at home, and a husband who is ignorant about her employment at the time of marriage. If he knew and remained silent and did not include a condition that she leaves her job, he has no right to ask her to do so. If he demands it and she refuses to comply, her maintenance shall not cease, because he concluded the contract in the knowledge that she works.[85] But if the husband did not know that she was working at the time of the marriage, he can demand that she stops working, and if she does not comply, she is not entitled to maintenance.[86]

But what is the criterion for determining the amount of *nafaqa* due to a wife? The schools concur that a wife's maintenance is obligatory in all its three forms: food, clothing and housing. They also concur that maintenance should be determined in accordance with the financial status of the two if both are of equal status.[87] But if one is well-off and the other indigent, the schools differ as to whether maintenance should be in accordance with the husband's financial status or whether the financial status of both should be considered and a median maintenance be fixed for the wife.

The Ḥanbalīs state that if the husband and wife differ in their financial status, a median course should be followed.[88] The Shāfiʿī school, along with some Ḥanafī jurists, hold that maintenance will be determined in accordance with the financial status of the husband as regards food and clothing, but according to her status as regards housing.[89] *Imām* Mālik and *imām* Abū Ḥanīfa state that *nafaqa* should be determined according to the status of the wife.[90] However, if a judge specifies a sum of money, or the spouses make their own agreement instead of waiting for a legal decision on maintenance, it is permissible to increase or decrease it in line with changes in prices or in the financial situation of the husband.[91]

8.1.1.1.4 FINANCIAL CONSEQUENCES OF DISABILITIES

Two important issues are intimately related to the case of a wife with disability: first, the issue of maintenance during sickness; and second, the issue of the medical expenses for curing the wife or at least minimizing the effects of her disability. On the first issue, the question is: does a husband have to pay maintenance for his sick wife? On the second issue, the question is: is a husband compelled to pay the medical and surgical expenses that the disability of his wife may incur?

In answer to the first question, the Ḥanbalī scholar, Ibn Taymiyya (d.728/1328), pointed out that a sick wife is unquestionably entitled to full maintenance by the husband, in the opinion of the four founders of the major schools of law.[92] To trace the different judicial opinions in this respect, a distinction should be made between the wife whose disability does not affect her ability to discharge her household and marital duties, such as sexual intercourse, and a wife whose disability could affect the fulfilment of such duties. In the first case, the disability would be disregarded and so the wife would remain entitled to maintenance according to all the schools of law, as stated in the fatwa of Ibn Taymiyya.

In the second case, jurists have disagreed. The main examples in this respect are defects affecting the woman's ability to perform her marital duties properly, such as *al-rataq* or *al-qarn* (both diseases affecting the sexual organs and preventing sexual intercourse; they are birth defects in which the vulva is blocked or its sides are joined together).[93] If a wife is afflicted with such a disease, her right to maintenance does not cease, according to the majority of jurists including the Ja'farī, Ḥanbalī and Ḥanafī schools. It does not cease according to the Mālikīs if she suffers from a serious disease or if the husband himself is seriously ill, according to all schools.[94] This opinion is based mainly on the juristic principle of *istiḥsān* or preference (a moral and practical consideration that overrules the formalities of law). On the basis of this principle, it is the husband's obligation to provide for her because she is still his spouse, whose companionship he enjoys even though illness may impede her performance in certain respects, e.g. sexual fulfilment.[95] A variant of this doctrine maintains that the *raison d'être* of the wife's right to maintenance is marriage as such or the husband's trusteeship of the wife. This right remains inalienable so long as she is his wife and he is the trustee. Her physical condition is inconsequential in this regard; it neither lightens his obligation nor negates her right.[96]

However, another group of jurists argue that formally, or analogously, a husband is not responsible for the maintenance of a sick wife on the grounds that she is actually unable to meet her marital responsibilities. It has been objected that, being his wife, living in his household and giving him companionship should entitle her to the right of maintenance even though she may be sick and incapable of playing her full role. Advocates of this opinion responded by saying that if the husband is responsible for her maintenance because of the marriage – a contract for which she has already received her bride price (*mahr*) – then she would be acquiring two rights, *mahr* (bride price) and *nafaqa* (maintenance), for one and the same reason, i.e. being a wife, or she would be receiving 'two compensations for one and the same loss'. This is, according to the argument, unlawful and unjust.[97]

In this regard, it is to be noted that the denial of maintenance of a sick wife does not mean that she will be abandoned to destitution or starvation. If she has any property, she must maintain herself from her own assets. Otherwise, the responsibility will be discharged by the nearest consanguine male who can afford it. If not, she becomes a community or state responsibility. Allah the Almighty says,

> Allah commands justice, the doing of good, and liberality to kith and kin, and he forbids all shameful deeds, and injustice and rebellion: he instructs you, that ye may receive admonition. . . . And render to the kindred their due rights, as also to those in want, and to the wayfarer: but squander not your wealth in the manner of a spendthrift.
>
> (Qur'ān 16:90, 17:26)

On the second question raised above, the main point is if medical care is part of maintenance or separate from it. Reference to the canonical sources shows that the Qur'ān makes the wife's food and clothing obligatory. The traditions say that it is for the husband to satisfy her hunger and clothe her.[98] Yet the application of this general principle to the case of a sick wife has stimulated curious arguments, differences of opinions and legal niceties.[99] The majority of jurists agree that the husband is not legally responsible for the cost of medicine, physician's fees, etc.[100] Some jurists, however, maintain that if the husband is financially comfortable and the cost of medical care is modest, he is responsible for it. Others argue that even if he is not *legally* responsible for the cost, it is still his *religious* responsibility out of compassion or courtesy, or in conformity with the social norms.[101] A minority of Ḥanafī and Shī'ī jurists consider medical care a means to save life and preserve health. Hence, it is as essential as food, shelter and clothing; it is therefore part of the husband's responsibility.[102] This is the standpoint adopted by the absolute majority of contemporary jurists, some of whom are impatient with these formalistic interpretations of the law which, on one hand, enjoin the husband to provide his wife with maids – an obvious luxury – but, on the other, exempt him from the responsibility for her medical care.[103] These formal interpretations, they add, contain no explicit authoritative evidence.[104] Other jurists adopt a more lenient approach, saying that the early jurists gave detailed lists of things to be provided as *nafaqa* at the time they were writing. These should be adjusted in the light of modern conditions to suit the circumstances of the countries concerned and their living standards.[105]

It is interesting to note that this position has been adopted by the courts of Syria and North Africa because it was considered to accord with the spirit of the law even though it came from a partisan and traditionally adversary group.[106] In his definition of a wife's maintenance, Jamal J. Nasir, the former Minister of Justice of Jordan, says,

> Maintenance is the lawful right of the wife under a valid marriage contract on certain conditions. It is the right of the wife to be provided at the husband's expense, and at a scale suitable to his means, with food, clothing, housing, toilet necessities, medicine, doctors' and surgeon's fees, baths and also the necessary servants where the wife is of a social position which does not permit her to dispense with such services, or when she is sick.

So he included medical expenses in the definition of *nafaqa* and then stated that all modern Arab codes on personal status more or less repeat this general Sharī'a position with some slight modification.[107]

8.1.2 Bequest (*waṣiyya*)

One of the revenues available in Islamic jurisprudence which can be used to provide financial support for people with disabilities is *waṣiyya*. *Waṣiyya* comes from the Arabic word *waṣṣā* which means 'he conveyed'. In other words, *waṣiyya* means a gift of property by its owner to another, contingent on the giver's death.[108] The law of *waṣiyya* in Islam supplements the compulsory inheritance rulings. An individual is not free to determine the future of his property after his death by favouring or depriving legal heirs. Under the *ultra vires* doctrine, there are two restrictions on wills, one quantitative and the other personal: no more than one-third (net) of the estate after the payment of debts may be bequeathed, and nothing may be bequeathed to a legal heir if the other heirs do not give their consent.[109] Shī'ī doctrine does not include this personal restriction.[110]

Waṣiyya was introduced mainly to cover certain situations in which someone has a connection with a family but is not included as an heir. The *waṣiyya* legislation allows the testator (*mūṣī*) to make provision for such a person, and also gives him scope to distribute some of the legacy as charity.[111] Thus dependent members of a family such as those with disabilities have other financial revenues even if they were not included in the list of heirs.

The beneficiary of a will may be an individual or individuals, a more or less defined group of persons, or an organization, or the proceeds of a bequest may be used for some specific purpose.[112]

8.1.3 Family endowment (*waqf ahlī*)

Waqf literally means 'detention' (*ḥabs*), but its legal meaning is the dedication or charitable gift of property for a good purpose, pious or charitable. The establishment of *awqāf* (endowments), in other words, extinguishes the right of the *wāqif* (dedicator) and transfers its ownership to Allah. *Waqf* property was brought into existence in order to organize and institutionalize voluntary charity. The scriptural basis for it is the ḥadīth related by Muslims that the Prophet said, 'When a human being dies, his work comes to an end, except for three things: ongoing charity, knowledge benefited from, or a pious son who prays for him.' Scholars understand ongoing charity to mean an endowment (*waqf*).[113]

As regards the legality of *waqf*, Muslim jurists are divided into three groups. The first group, whose opinion is considered the most weighty, asserted that it is absolutely and unconditionally permissible (*jawāz muṭlaq*), and legalized *waqf* in houses, lands, slaves, clothes, etc.[114] To this group belong the majority of Shāfiʿīs,[115] Ḥanafīs,[116] Ẓāhirīs,[117] Zaydīs[118] and Jaʿfarīs.[119] The second group, mainly represented by the two Companions, ʿAbd Allāh b. Masʿūd and ʿAlī b. Abī Ṭālib, restricted *waqf* to weapons of war and remote lands (*kurāʿ*).[120] The third group opted for absolute prohibition. This opinion is advocated by Shurayḥ al-Qāḍī, one of the reports attributed to *imām* Abū Ḥanīfa and the majority of the scholars of Kūfa.[121]

8.1.3.1 The main principles of waqf

Seven main principles have been mentioned by jurists which should be observed if an endowment is to be legally valid. First, the founder (*wāqif*) must have the full right of disposal of his property; he must therefore be in full possession of his physical and mental faculties, be of age and be a free man (*ʿāqil, bāligh, ḥurr*). He must further have unrestricted ownership of the object of the endowment. Endowments by non-Muslims are only valid if they are intended for a purpose that is compatible with Islam.[122] Second, the object of the endowment (*mawqūf*) must be permanent[123] and must yield a usufruct (*manfaʿa*), so that it primarily involves real estate.[124] Third, the purpose of the endowment must be a work pleasing to Allah (*qurba*).[125] Fourth, the endowment should concern a particular identified article (*ʿayn*) (it is invalid to make the mere 'right to use something' an endowment, because it is not a particular article).[126] Fifth, the article should have a lawful use.[127] Sixth, the beneficiary should be some particular party, such as the poor around the founder (*wāqif*) himself, whether the endowment is an act of worship, as when the beneficiary is mosques, one's relatives, or the general good, or whether it is merely permissible, such as an endowment that benefits the wealthy, or Jewish and Christian subjects of the Islamic state. Finally, the endowment should be formally established by words that enact it such as 'I make it an endowment', or 'I restrict such and such a thing to benefit so and so', or 'I give such and such as non-saleable charity'.[128]

It is important to emphasize that initially both types of *waqf*, namely family (*ahlī*) and welfare (*khayrī*), were equally considered *ṣadaqa* (a gift made in the hope of heavenly reward) and were viewed together with mixed *awqāf*, as fully accepted variants of the same institution. The challenge to the religious character of *ahlī* endowments and the subsequent differentiation between them and *khayrī* endowments resulted from modernist terminology.[129] There was no hint of this in traditional Islamic *fiqh* books.[130] Shaykh ʿAbd al-Majīd Salīm, the late mufti of

Egypt, in his fatwa of 1932, said: 'We did not find in the compilations of the well-informed jurists that *waqf* was divided into *ahlī* and *khayrī*. This division, however, is a customary (*'urfī*) division.'[131]

Like others, Muslim societies have always been divided into social units according to various criteria. Most important of these social units are those based on kinship or quasi-kinship. The Muslim *waqf* system had an important function in supporting and reinforcing these social units and their cohesion. There can be no doubt that a founder's primary concern for the position and welfare of his or her family and offspring is reflected in the institution of *waqf*.[132]

Waqf ahlī, in particular, is created for the welfare of near relatives of the dedicator (*wāqif*) to ensure that their needs are met by it for all their lives. After their death, it reverts to the welfare of the poor. It can consist of both movable and immovable property.[133]

Muslim jurists said that if the dedicator made the *waqf* for the benefit of the poor in general, then poor relatives should be given precedence over non-relatives as long as they are on an equal level of poverty.[134] This juristic rule has been applied more than once. For example, in a controversy over the administration of the Sayyidnā 'Alī *waqf* (north of Jaffa), when the Supreme Muslim Council claimed that the *waqf* was dedicated for charitable purposes (*'alā wujūh al-birr*), the family replied that even if this were true, they were worthier than anybody else to receive the gifts.[135] In fact the Prophet is quoted as saying, 'The most excellent *ṣadaqa* is that a man bestows upon his family.' This shows that Muslims clearly included such provisions in their understanding of the notion of beneficence (*birr*).[136]

8.1.3.2 The future of family endowment

Waqf ahlī has always been a way of getting closer to Allah (*qurba*) and obtaining His pleasure. This is shown by the example of *waqf ahlī* during the lifetime of the Prophet of Islam and his Companions.[137] However, *waqf ahlī* turned out to be a means of circumventing the Islamic rules of inheritance. A number of unconscientious founders used family endowments as a method of attaining their malicious ends and depriving some of their legal heirs.[138] Undoubtedly, early jurists were aware of this risk. For instance, *imām* al-Shawkānī says in this regard, 'One who makes *waqf* for the sake of injuring the shares of his heirs, then his *waqf* is invalid (*bāṭil*).'[139] Such misuse of family endowment resulted in a number of calls for the annulment of this kind of *waqf*. Some succeeded in ending a *waqf ahlī* whereas others did not.[140] Dr Al-Kubaysī commented, 'If this kind of *waqf* now entails a specific risk, then it is traced back to misuse by unconscientious people, not to the system itself. So what is required now is a reform not complete abolition.'[141]

Our interest here is the fate of people with disabilities in the light of these circumstances. Abolishing this kind of *waqf* would harm disabled family members who could benefit from this kind of *awqāf*. Some jurists stated that it would not be against the spirit of the Islamic Sharī'a for a father to favour one of his children with *waqf* in consideration of his/her disability. For instance, in *Al-Mughnī*, Ibn

Qudāma quotes *imām* Aḥmad as saying that there is no harm in a father favouring one of his children, to whom he gives more money in the form of *waqf* for a specific and important reason such as need (*ḥājah*), chronic disease, blindness, responsibility for a big family, being busy with seeking knowledge or other similar virtues.[142] Still we believe that if this kind of *waqf* were reactivated in a positive way it could be an optimum financial resource for supporting the impoverished and disabled members of a family. It could take the place of a regular source of income.

8.2 Revenues within society

If the family institution fails to meet the financial needs of people with disabilities, it becomes the collective duty of the Muslim community at large to do so. Some members of the society must perform these duties; otherwise all members will be in a state of sin.[143]

First, a note on the most common terms in this context, namely community and society, is in order. 'Community' is defined as a group of people living together and/or united by shared interests, religion, nationality, etc.[144] On the other hand, 'society' has two main definitions. First, it means people in general, considered in the context of the structure of laws, organizations, etc. Second, it denotes a particular broad group of people who share laws, organizations, customs, etc.[145] The well-known contemporary sociologist Anthony Giddens focused on the second rather then the first meaning, arguing that society is one of the most important of all sociological concepts. To him, 'society' is a group of people who live in a particular territory, are subject to a common system of political authority and are aware of having an identity distinct from other groups around them. Some of these societies may be very small whereas others can be extremely large, such as Chinese society which has more than one billion members.[146]

To my knowledge, the Arabic term *mujtamaʿ* used today to express the idea of society or community, was not used by early jurists. Classical terms which may be close to 'society' and 'community' are *umma* (lit. nation) and *dār* (lit. house or abode), especially in discussions on *dār al-islām* (abode of Islam) and *dār al-kufr* (abode of unbelief). One of the modern definitions of 'society' in the Islamic sense states:

> The entire Muslim Umma is one big family held together by the common bonds of belief in one Allah and His last Prophet – Peace and Blessings be upon him. It is one homogenous body and makes no distinctions with regard to color, race or nationality.[147]

All the definitions given above indicate clearly that this is an elusive term, whether in the Arabic or the English sense. However, broad lines are still apparent. First of all, society must be something larger than the family institution. The main idea revolves round a group of people with something in common like land, religion, a specific interest, etc. In the juristic sense, members of this group are collectively responsible for each other in a social and economic sense. As we see below, no main criterion draws a distinct border beyond which people will not belong to this society and thus not be entitled to the common rights and duties of its members. Non-Muslims sharing land with Muslims would belong to the same society and thus, according to different Muslim jurists, should benefit from both *zakāt* and the public treasury for their needs. On the other hand, Muslims living in remote areas again belong to this society because they belong to the same religion and thus should also benefit from the *zakāt* system. Thus one criterion is sufficient to make a society exist.

References in the Qur'ān and ḥadīth can be taken as pointers towards a definition of the rights of various members of a community. For instance, the Prophet is reported to have said,

> One who has a surplus animal to ride should give it to his brother who has no animal to ride, and one who has surplus property should apportion it among those who are propertyless. The Prophet recounted so many kinds of commodities by which his Companions presumed that man has no right to his surplus wealth.[148]

This chapter discusses two main financial resources which people with disabilities can benefit from as members of a society. These are welfare endowment (*waqf khayrī*) and *zakāt*, both of which are intended to meet the financial needs of people with disabilities. If these resources are not sufficient, jurists discussed whether extra financial obligations should be imposed on the rich to fill the financial gap. References to the role of the state, whenever relevant, will also be in order.

8.2.1 Welfare endowment (*waqf khayrī*)

As noted above, *waqf ahlī* (family endowment) was mainly for family members, whereas *waqf khayrē* is mainly for society at large. Broadly speaking, one of the original aims of the *waqf*, if not the main one, was of course to strengthen Muslim society.[149] The institution of *waqf* in Islam has contributed a great deal and played an important role in building up society and is supposed to continue to do so as long as this institution exists.[150]

Basing our argument on modern terminology and dividing *waqf* into *ahlī* and *khayrī*, it is to be noted that the need for every *waqf* to have a permanent nature (*ta'bīd*) is one of the fundamental principles of Islamic endowments. Since families were not conceived of as permanent, the founder of every *ahlī* endowment deed has to name, as the ultimate beneficiary, after the chain of family members, either the poor or a general charity of an equally permanent character.[151] At this stage in its history, what was originally a family endowment (*ahlī*) would no longer benefit specific private individuals but the general interest of Islamic society. Furthermore, this kind of *waqf* chronologically precedes the family endowment. Tracing the origins of the *waqf* institution in Islam, we find that the first examples belong to what is termed as *waqf khayrī* (welfare endowments). Muslims disagree on the first example of *waqf* in Islamic history.[152] The first *waqf* made in the history of Islam, according to some reports, was that of 'Umar Ibn al-Khaṭṭāb.[153] It is reported that the Prophet Muḥammad divided the land of Khaybar among the fighting forces.[154] One plot of land, known by the name Thamgh, fell to 'Umar's share and he set it apart for charitable purposes.[155] 'Umar gave this land as *ṣadaqa* for the poor, needy relatives, slaves, wayfarers, guests and for the cause of Allah (*fī sabīl Allāh*).[156] According to others, the *waqf* of the seven *ḥawā'iṭ* by the Prophet was the first *waqf* made in Islam.[157] A third opinion stated that the first *waqf* in Islam was the 'mosque of Qibā'', which the Prophet of Islam built on his arrival at Medina after the *hijrā* and before entering the city.[158]

Whatever may have been the case, in modern terminology, most previous cases of *waqf* belong to the category of charitable endowments. It is to be noted that the *waqf* of 'Umar also identified relatives as among the beneficiaries.

This practice later gave rise to a social institution known as *waqf* (religious and charitable trusts and endowments), which provided a service analogous to that known in modern times as social security. This term is understood to mean that those who are unable to earn their livelihood on account of old age, sickness or disability are given an allowance to maintain them at a moderate level until such time as they are able to support themselves by their own earnings through lawful means.[159]

In fact *waqf* is an institution very characteristic of Islamic jurisprudence. It has experienced considerable development in all Muslim countries and has played a very important role in society. Until recent times, the income from *waqf* defrayed a certain proportion of public expenses, such as that on the relief of the poor, education, the upkeep of *madrasas*, aqueducts, fountains, etc.[160]

As for its relevance to people with disabilities in particular, Yūsuf al-Qaraḍāwī comments that early Muslims used to allocate a considerable number of *awqāf* (charitable endowments) for benefit of people with disabilities such as blindness, lameness, etc.[161] The Islamic *awqāf* that people with disabilities could benefit from were of two kinds. First, those of a medical nature: a considerable number of *awqāf* were dedicated to setting up hospitals and providing medical care for the sick.[162] The endowment of a hospital with *waqf* constituted a sign of more complete integration with Muslim culture and civilization and it was also a guarantee of the hospital's longevity.[163] As late as the sixteenth century, Muslim hospitals were still being endowed, a fine one having been established in Delhi. Hence it may be concluded that from the standpoint of financial administration, the organization of the hospital as a specialized institution was completed with the Cairo hospital of Aḥmad Ibn Ṭūlūn. So far as is known, the Ṭūlūnid hospital, established in 259/872–261/874,[164] is the first Islamic hospital endowed with *waqf* revenues.[165] The other four earliest hospitals with *waqf* in the chronological order of their foundation are: (1) the Hospital of Badr Ghulām (d. 902), an administrator and army commander of the Caliph Mu'taḍid (892–902) in Baghdad; (2) the Baghkami Hospital of Baghdad built by Amīr 'Abdul Ḥassan Baghkan at Turkf (d. 940), commander of the Caliph Muktafī (902–908); (3) the

Ikhshid Hospital of Cairo built by the Turkish Kāfūr al-Ikhshid in 957; and (4) the hospital built by Mu'izz al-Dawla Ibn Buwayh in Baghdad in or around the year 967 AD.[166] Shaykh Muṣṭafā al-Sibā'ī (d. 1384/1967) states that there were also *awqāf* for psychology in its primitive sense. In Tripoli, Lebanon, there was *waqf* for employing two persons to pass by the sick in the hospitals and speak in a low voice that the patient could hear. One of them says 'I see this person is much better than yesterday.' The other says, 'And I see his face and eyes much brighter than yesterday.' This is to make the patient think that he/she is really getting better.[167] The second category of *awqāf* dedicated to people with disabilities was social in nature. For instance, there were *awqāf* to hire guides for blind people.[168]

Shaykh al-Qaraḍāwī has commented, 'This kind of Islamic *waqf*, i.e. welfare endowment, should be retrieved and reactivated, as it is one of the important ways of taking care of people with disabilities.' By re-establishing this kind of Islamic *waqf*, Qaraḍāwī adds, we can provide computers, spare parts and other tools that the people with disabilities may need.[169]

8.2.2 *Zakāt*

Zakāt was defined by jurists as that portion of a man's wealth which is designated for the poor.[170] In the early days of Islam in Mecca, no limit or restriction was placed on the amount to be donated, for that decision was left to the individual Muslim's conscience and generosity. In the second year of *hijra,* according to the well-known authorities, both the type and quantity of *zakāt* revenues were determined, and detailed illustrations were provided.[171]

Zakāt was mainly for the society rather than the immediate family. The jurists, with the exception of the Mālikīs, agreed that it is not permissible to give *zakāt* to one's father, grandfather, mother or grandmother because payers of *zakāt* are obligated to take care of all such people anyway. When such people become poor, they may draw upon the payer's largess because it is their right. Thus if someone pays *zakāt* to them, he benefits himself by avoiding the obligation of supporting them.[172] In this sense, *zakāt* is mainly directed to those poor members of society who have no family or whose families cannot provide for them. This category of people generally includes the most unfortunate people:

> Those with the most serious financial problems are single and widowed women; and many of them are among those with the most serious social and welfare problems; those without families. Community services tend primarily to reach those without, or with comparatively few, family resources.[173]

Although *zakāt* took the form of financial duty, it also has many other dimensions. First of all, it was seen as a form of *'ibāda* (act of worship) which constitutes one of the five pillars (*arkān*) of Islam. It is associated with prayer (*ṣalāh*) in eighty-two Qur'anic verses.[174] It also had social and moral aims. Shāh Walī Allāh (1110/1698–1176/1762) explains this in mystic language, saying,

> Know that when a need presents itself to the poor person, and he entreats God about it either verbally or through his conditions, his entreaty knocks at the door of the Divine Generosity. Sometimes the best interest will be fulfilled by inspiring the heart of a pure person to furnish the remedy of his want. Thus when the inspiration descends and he is provoked (to respond), he is given success, God is pleased with him, and blessings flow to him from above and below, and from his right side and his left, and God's mercy is upon him.[175]

In this way, *zakāt* is in harmony with the spirit of Islam, which abhors forcing a person to do good deeds by external coercion. On the contrary, the Muslim should give out of his own belief and for his own satisfaction. The Qur'ān criticized those people who give without pleasure: 'The only reasons why their contributions are not accepted are: that they reject Allah and His Messenger; that they come to prayer without earnestness; and that they offer contributions unwillingly' (Qur'ān 9:54).[176]

Zakāt is not considered a favour (*minna*) that the wealthy bestow upon the poor; rather, it is a due (*ḥaqq*) that Allah has entrusted into the hands of the rich to give to the poor and distribute among the deserving.[177] Allah has described this right as a known right (*ḥaqq ma'lūm)*. He says: 'And those in whose wealth is a recognized right. For the (needy) who asks and him who is prevented (for some reason from asking)' (Qur'ān 70:24–25).[178]

Modern Muslim jurists tried to integrate the *zakāt* institution into the social solidarity system. Yūsuf al-Qaraḍāwī says in this regard:

> Some of the central goals of *zakāt* have a social dimension. One of these goals is supporting helpless and dependent people like the poor and the destitute (*masākīn)*. Such support has its effect on those people as individuals and on the whole society at large as well. Actually the limits between individual and society are interrelated concepts. Hence, there is no wonder that giving assistance to the needy is considered as a social goal because this assistance creates a more united and cohesive society. *Zakāt* in this sense is part of the social solidarity system in Islam but it is not the whole system because the system of social solidarity in Islam is very broad. *Zakāt* comprises both 'social insurance' and 'social security'. In social insurance, the individual pays regularly an insurance premium so as to benefit from it when he/she becomes disabled. In *zakāt*, the individual who pays *zakāt* one year may become poor in the second year, so he turns out to be a recipient of *zakāt*. When viewed from this aspect, *zakāt* is social insurance. On the other hand, from a social security perspective, the poor receive financial support directly from the state although they did not pay any premiums. In *zakāt*, it may happen that an individual would benefit from *zakāt* revenues although he has never paid anything for that purpose. In this sense, *zakāt* is social security. But *zakāt* is closer to the concept of security (*ḍamān*) than insurance (*ta'mīn*). This is because the

> individual benefits from *zakāt* not according to what he has paid but according to what he needs, whether his/her needs are great or small, until he/she reaches the level of sufficiency (*ḥadd al-kifāya*). *Imam* al-Shāfi'ī and the scholars who agreed with him stated that *zakāt* should allow the poor to achieve *ḥadd al-kifāya* not only for a month or a year but also for the whole life. Al-Zuhrī wrote to the Caliph 'Umar b. 'Abd al-'Azīz about the recipients of *zakāt*, people suffering from incurable diseases, the disabled poor and the destitute who receive no financial support (neither salaries nor pensions).[179]

Based on what has been stated above, Yūsuf al-Qaraḍāwī concluded that *zakāt* constituted the first organized legislation in the field of social security which does not depend on individual voluntary charity but on systematic and regular aid (which the poor receive directly) from the government.

8.2.2.1 People with disabilities and zakāt

Helping people with disabilities within the *zakāt* system is a high priority. It has been stated explicitly by more than one jurist that people with disabilities, as long as they are poor, must be included among the recipients of *zakāt*. Muṣṭafā Ibn Ḥamza, a contemporary Moroccan scholar of Oujda University, says that Muslim scholars agreed that people with disabilities who cannot earn their living on their own are the first category who should benefit from *zakāt*.[180] Interestingly, some of the Qur'anic interpreters limited the meaning of *al-faqīr* (the poor) to people of disability as against *al-miskīn* (the needy), the able-bodied needy. A saying with this meaning was ascribed to Qatādah by al-Ṭabarī in his *Jāmi' al-bayān*.[181] The same opinion is expressed by 'Abd Allāh b. 'Amr b. al-'Āṣ. Al-Ṭabarī reports that Zuhayr al-'Āmirī met 'Abd Allāh b. 'Amr b. al-'Āṣ and asked him of *zakāt*: 'Whose money is it?' 'Abd Allāh replied, 'It is the money of those people who are lame, blind, or one-eyed, and all other dependent people.' Then Zuhayr said, 'Collectors of *zakāt* and those fighting for the sake of Allah have also a right to it!' 'Abd Allāh said, 'For those fighting for the sake of Allah, it has been made lawful for them. As for the collectors of *zakāt*, it is allowed to them to take only in accordance with their work. *Ṣadaqa* is not lawful for the rich or for the able bodied.'[182]

In this connection, it is apposite to refer to a document prepared by various jurists who, at the behest of 'Umar b. 'Abd a-'Azīz, elaborately specified the religious precepts concerning the eight *zakāt* beneficiaries. We will select only those parts relating to our topic. The document runs as follows:

> The following are the places of *ṣadaqa* and these are eight in number. . . . One half of the share of the poor (*al-fuqarā'*) goes to those who fought for the first time in a battle for God's cause. Then, as the auxiliary troops, they will be allotted a fixed emolument, which they will receive as the first *'aṭā'*, but afterwards, no more *ṣadaqa* is allowed to them. The remaining half is given

> to the poor who have not been able to fight because of disability or chronic disease (*zamāna*).'[183]
>
> One half of the share of the destitute (*al-masākīn*) goes to those stricken with diseases preventing them from doing any job and from moving around the earth. The other half is for those who beg for their food, and for the Muslims in prison who have nobody to care for them.[184]

Among modern scholars, Professor Muḥammad al-Bahiyy, the former director of al-Azhar University, says in his comment on the first category of the recipients of *zakāt*, namely the poor (*al-fuqarā'*), that people of advanced age and those suffering from incurable diseases should be included in this category.[185] Yūsuf al-Qaraḍāwī[186] and 'Abd Allāh b. Bāz[187] also stated that people with disabilities are to be included among the beneficiaries of *zakāt* as long as they are poor.

8.2.2.2 Are there other claims on wealth besides zakāt?

Suppose the amount of *zakāt* collected was clearly insufficient to put an end to the financial dependence of people with disabilities. In other words, suppose the government had given them their due share of *zakāt* but they did not reach *ḥadd al-kifāya*. What is the role of the Islamic state in such a case? The question of extracting money other than *zakāt* from the wealth of the rich was first raised by a number of the Companions of the Prophet such as 'Alī b. Abī Ṭālib, 'Abd Allāh b. 'Umar and the most enthusiastic Abū Dharr al-Ghifārī during the caliphate of 'Uthmān b. 'Affān. They all saw that there were other claims on wealth apart from *zakāt* so long as the poor did not reach the level of *ghinā* or self-sufficiency. They disagreed however, on the amount to be paid after *zakāt*. Abū Dharr, the main protagonist of this drama, promoted his idea publicly in Syria. Abū Dharr's call was met with substantial interest, especially on the part of the poor – so much so that Mu'āwiya b. Abī Sufyān, the ruler of Syria at this time, felt anxious. He wrote to Caliph 'Uthmān and asked him to order Abū Dharr to leave for Medina, and the Caliph did so.[188] The attempt of Abū Dharr was later enhanced and codified by Ibn Ḥazm. In his *Al-Muḥallā*, he states that the rich must take care of the financial needs of the poor in their locality. The sulṭān or the ruler must force them to do so if the *zakāt* collected money is not sufficient to meet the financial needs of the poor.[189] Ibn Ḥazm then quotes a number of Qur'anic verses, prophetic traditions and sayings from the Companions and the Successors.[190]

In the modern era, Shaykh Sayyid Sābiq responded to the problem by saying,

> If the amount of *zakāt* is not enough to alleviate the conditions of the poor and the needy, then the rich can be subjected to further taxation. How much should be taken is not specified. Its quantity will be determined by the needs of the poor. The scholars agree that should a need arise, even when *zakāt* has been paid, the Muslim community is bound to contribute toward the alleviation of the problem.[191]

It should also be known that the rulings concerning *zakāt* applied there are to be applied typically here. *Imām* Muḥammad 'Abduh's comments are: 'The giving of property in excess of the due *zakāt* is considered one of the basic elements of piety (*birr*) and is enjoined like the prescribed *zakāt*.[192] Some contemporary scholars call this extra money the Islamic income tax.[193]

Now there are two points to comment on. First, after mentioning the proponents of this viewpoint, we understand that the main target of *zakāt* is to achieve the *ghinā* of the poor. In other words, all the basic needs of the poor are to be met, if not by *zakāt* alone, then by other financial claims imposed by the state upon the rich, which some modern scholars have called as the Islamic income tax. Second, the specific case of each recipient must be considered. Hence, the case of poor people with disabilities is to be considered from the perspective of these two points. Thereupon, when the state distributes *zakāt* among the beneficiaries, it should be taken into consideration that the basic needs of people with disabilities are different from those of the non-disabled. For instance, health care expenses should be counted. In other words, it is most likely that the basic needs of a person with disability will cost more. Therefore they should be given more even if this necessitates imposing extra taxes on the rich or giving them a share bigger than that of the other recipients of *zakāt*.

8.3 Summary

This chapter has reviewed the possible sources of financial aid for people with disabilities, whether within the family or in society at large, as described by the juristic sources. Concerning the family, this chapter has shown that the system of maintenance (*nafaqa*) played a central role. Within this system, every individual who cannot work to earn his/her livelihood has the right to receive financial support from other well-to-do family members. In juristic sources, we found a highly complicated system elaborating in detail who is responsible for whom and under what circumstances. Detailed information was given about people with disabilities as parents, children or wives within this system. Another financial resource within the family for people with disabilities was family endowment. In this system, endowments may be dedicated to people with disabilities and can guarantee financial support for them on a regular basis. If a family is unable to help its members who have disabilities, society and the state should step in.

As for the financial responsibility of members of a society towards people with disabilities, this chapter has reviewed the juristic discussions on welfare endowment in terms of the two main financial resources which can meet the needs of people with disabilities as members of society. Throughout Islamic history, people with disabilities were among the main beneficiaries of welfare endowment in the form of hospitals and asylums. The second financial resource described in this chapter was *zakāt*. No early or modern jurist objected to paying money to people with disabilities as long as they were poor. Moreover, a number of early and modern jurists considered that poor people with disabilities represented a specific category of their own who are more entitled to receive *zakāt* than other poor people who are not disabled. The modern concept of using charities as means of developing projects and programmes to secure the needs of this category of people on a regular and constant basis had already been expressed by early jurists such as al-Shāfi'ī (d. 205/820).

9 Conclusion

In this concluding chapter, a number of points will be emphasized, some of which represent the core of this study and others of which open up new fields of research.

In the first place, I should clarify a specific point about the main protagonists of this study, namely the Muslim scholars. I did my best to find a balance between early and modern Muslim scholars when discussing ideas about people with disabilities and their rights in the Islamic tradition. However, the reader should have noticed that the early Muslim scholars were more prominent in some parts of this study than the modern ones. To my mind, this is because the relevant discussions of early scholars were much richer and more original than those of the modern scholars. A considerable number of modern scholars either rehearsed what their early predecessors had said or tried to give an Islamic slant to the human rights of people with disabilities as proclaimed by the United Nations, but adding hardly anything new. This does not negate the importance of the modern scholars' contributions as shown in different parts of this study, especially Chapter 7 on medical treatment for people with disabilities.

The terminology used by classical sources to denote people with disabilities also deserves further attention in this Conclusion. That is because almost every term used in these sources to refer to this group or some of its members included other groups as well. In other words, this group of people was always 'integrated' into larger groups. For instance, in Islamic theology, people with disabilities fell within the broad category of 'people with afflictions' (*ahl al-balā'*) whose common characteristic was 'affliction'. The case of the person who had lost a hand or a leg was, in this theological perspective, the same as the case of a parent whose child had died. In Islamic jurisprudence, people with disabilities also fell into the broad category of 'people with excuses' (*aṣḥāb al-a'dhār*), whose common characteristic was having a valid excuse for exemption from specific religious obligations. Also in the *adab* works, people with disabilities were presented as part of a large group of those mainly characterized by their 'abnormality' and 'weirdness'. Thus, people with different disabilities such as the blind and the lame were mentioned in the same context as bald people, for instance, as in the book of Ibn Fahd described in Chapter 5. A possible interpretation for this phenomenon is that people with disabilities were integrated into the main corpus of the broad society and thus cannot be easily offended by terminology. This is simply because the whole range of terminologies referring to them also refers to a wide range of other groups in the society.

A note on the human rights dimension of this issue is also in order. In the light of the discussions reviewed throughout this study, it is clear that currently used terminology such as 'human rights', 'autonomy', 'independence', etc. cannot be traced in the writings of Muslim scholars, especially the early ones. However, the concepts which these new terms imply were not absent from these discussions. As shown throughout this study, intensive discussions took place among Muslim scholars on the rights of this group to have paid work, medical treatment, financial aid when they needed it, etc. The debates among these scholars on the ethics of writing about people with disabilities as elaborated in Chapter 5 also bear witness to the fact that the human rights dimension was not absent from the discussions of these scholars.

Based on this inclusive approach, we can speak of an overall positive attitude towards people with disabilities in Islamic literature. Sara Scalenghe said, 'Preliminary evidence suggests that the physically and mentally disabled were not necessarily stigmatized or marginalized.'[1] Rispler-Chaim concluded her study by saying, 'Against the abusive attitudes to the disabled in the Roman and Byzantine empires as well as in the dark Middle Ages in Europe, the attitudes in Islamic law were in every way enlightened and farseeing.'[2]

This positive attitude recorded in the theological and juristic sources does not negate the existence of negative sides in the Islamic tradition. For instance, Chapter 4 recorded how physiognomic expressions borrowed from translated Greek literature penetrated into a wide range of Islamic sources. Although these expressions, which implied a discriminatory attitude towards people with disabilities, were criticized by various Muslim scholars, it seems they could still find their way into a number of scholarly and public circles. The other negative aspects of the Islamic tradition towards people with disabilities might be more perceptible in the actual society which was not always in line with what these sources pleaded for. This is also true of the current reality of people with disabilities in different parts of the Muslim world. I believe this is an interesting field of study which specialists in different fields could investigate to see to what extent the text was guiding the society or vice versa. Information now available can help them assess this text–reality link. The information given in this study may help them understand specific forms of behaviour by people with disabilities or their families which would otherwise have remained insoluble riddles.

Finally, I hope this study will also be a stimulus to my colleagues, specialists in Islamic studies, to conduct more research on this category of people which still continues to be an under-studied, if not an unstudied, group. I believe that future research can best be directed to more specific topics such as people with disabilities during the lifetime of the Prophet and his Companions, women with disabilities, people with disabilities in a specific period of Islamic history such as the Umayyad or Abbasid dynasties, people with disabilities within a specific geographical location such as Egypt or the Levant, throughout Islamic history and so forth.

Notes

Preface

1 See for instance Ghaly, Mohammed (2007), 'Islam en handicap: praktijkthema's en islamitische ethische opvattingen' in: *Tijdschrift voor gezondheidszorg en ethiek*, jaargang 17, no. 2, pp. 40–45; Ghaly, Mohammed (2008b), 'Visies op mensen met verstandelijke beperkingen binnen de islamitische traiditie', *Nederlands Tijdschrift voor de Zorg aan mensen met verstandelijke beperkingen (NTZ)*, vol. 34, no. 2, pp. 115–126.

1 Introduction

1 United Nations (2006), *Draft Resolution: Convention on the Rights of Persons with Disabilities*, United Nations, General Assembly, 6 December 2006, available at http://www.un.org (accessed 3 August 2007).
2 Robinson, Mary (1998), 'Human Rights and Disabled Persons' in: Rachel Hurst (ed.) *Are Disabled People Included?*, Disability Awareness in Action, UK: Freeways Print, p. 1.
3 Office of the High Commissioner of Human Rights (1971), *Declaration on the Rights of Mentally Retarded Persons*, available at http://www.unhchr.ch/html/menu3/b/m_mental.htm (accessed 18 April 2009).
4 Office of the High Commissioner of Human Rights (1975), *Declaration on the Rights of Disabled Persons*, available at http://www.unhchr.ch/html/menu3/b/72.htm (accessed 18 April 2009).
5 United Nations (1983), *International Year of Disabled Persons: A Document of the UN General Assembly no. A/RES/36/77*, available on http://www.un.org (accessed 3 August 2007).
6 Robinson, Mary (1998), p. 1.
7 Ibid.
8 United Nations (2007), *Convention on the Rights of Persons with Disabilities and* Optional Protocol, available at http://www.un.org/disabilities/default.asp?id=150 (accessed 18 April 2009).
9 United Nations (1994), *Standard Rules on the Equalization of Opportunities for Persons with Disabilities*, New York, United Nations, available at http://www.unhcr.ch (accessed 3 August 2007).
10 For general remarks about religion and disability, see Ghaly, Mohammed (2008c), 'Islam and Disability: Perspectives in Islamic Theology and Jurisprudence', Leiden University, PhD dissertation, pp. 2-5.
11 For the responses of a number of Islamic countries to the last WHO questionnaire on observation of the Standard Rules, see World Health Organization (2001a), *The UN Standard Rules on the Equalization of Opportunities for Persons with Disability:*

Main Report, Geneva: World Health Organization, pp. 92– 93, 115–117, 120–122, 159–160, 164–165, 166–167, 178–180, 193–194, 213–214, 233–235.

12 The list of signatories included a number of Islamic countries such as Algeria, Egypt, Turkey, Morocco, Sudan and Yemen. For a full list of the signatory states and regional integration organizations, see http://www.un.org/esa/socdev/enable/conventionsign.htm (accessed 13 May 2005).

13 See http://cirrie.buffalo.edu/bibliography/MEast3.html . For other similar conferences, see http://cirrie.buffalo.edu/bibliography/MEast2.html; http://www.disabilityworld.org/05-06_01/news/riconf.shtml; http://www.deakin.edu.au/tedca/ncet/issues_and_events/calendar.html; http://www.worldenable.net/beirut2003/journal28may.htm; http://www.worldenable.net/beirut2003/arabicdefault.asp; http://www.dpi.org/en/events/world_summit/06-23-03_summit2004.htm (all accessed 13 May 2005).

14 See ʻAwaḍī, ʻAbd al-Raḥmān ʻAbd Allāh al- and Aḥmad Rajā'ī al-Jundī (eds) (1422/2001), *Al-Mushāwara al-buldāniyya ḥawl tashrī'āt al-ṣiḥḥa al-nafsiyya fī mukhtalaf al-sharā'i' bimā fī dhālik al-sharī'a al-islāmiyya*, Kuwait: Islamic Organization for Medical Sciences, vol. 1, pp. 345–372, 395–443, vol. 2, pp. 481–517, 523–538, 601–636, 725–735, 734–775, 777–833. I hereby submit due thanks to Dr Aḥmad al-Jundī, the general secretary assistant of the Islamic Organization for Medical Sciences, for providing a copy of this publication.

15 An article published by *Ain-al-Yaqeen* magazine on 3 November 2003; an electronic version is available on http://www.ain-al-yaqeen.com/issues/20001103/feat7en.htm (accessed 13 May 2005). For an Arabic version of the same article, see http://www.ain-al-yaqeen.com/issues/20001103/feat7ar.htm (accessed 13 May 2005). All I could get was a general report on the activities and summaries of the papers submitted in the conference: see *Barnāmaj wa al-mulakhkhaṣāt al-ʻilmiyya, al-: al-mu'tamar al-dawlī al-thānī li al-iʻāqa wa al-ta'hīl* (2000).

16 http://www.deakin.edu.au/tedca/ncet/issues_and_events/calendar.html (accessed 13 May 2005).

17 http://leb.net/pipermail/lexington-net/2000-August/002302.html (accessed 13 May 2005). Unfortunately, I could not get access to any of the papers presented in this conference.

18 On him, see http://www.ibn-jebreen.com/book.php?cat=0&book=75&toc=4747 (accessed 7 August 2007).

19 See Shāyiʻ, ʻAbd al-Ilāh b. ʻUthmān b. ʻAbd Allāh (1420/1999), *Ārā' Ibn Taymiyya ḥawl al-iʻāqa*, Riyadh: Dār al-Ṣumayʻī li al-Nashr wa al-Tawzīʻ, pp. 5–6.

20 ʻAwadī, ʻAbd al-Rahmān ʻAbd Allāh al- and Aḥmad Rajā'ī al-Jundī (eds) (1422/2001), vol. 1, pp. 276, 301.

21 For a detailed analysis of these studies, see Ghaly, Mohammed (2008c), 'Islam and Disability: Perspectives in Islamic Theology and Jurisprudence', Leiden University, PhD dissertation, pp. 7–13.

22 See, for instance, the statement by Sara Scalenghe, 'The study of disability in the medieval Islamic world is still in its infancy': Scalenghe, Sara (2007), 'Disability', in: Meri, Josef W. (ed.) *Medieval Islamic Civilization: An Encylopedia*, vol. 1, p. 208.

23 Taftazānī, Saʻd al-Dīn Masʻūd b. ʻUmar al- (n.d.), *Sharḥ al-ʻaqā'id al-nasafiyya*, Karachi, Pakistan: Nashr Nūr Muḥammad, p. 30; Bayāḍī, Kamāl al-Dīn Aḥmad al- (1949), *Ishārāt al-marām min ʻibarāt al-imām*, Cairo: Maṭbaʻat Al-Ḥalabī, pp. 28–29; Bukhārī, ʻAbd al-ʻAzīz b. Aḥmad b. Muhammad al- (n.d.), *Kashf al-asrār sharḥ uṣūl al-Bazdawī*, Beirut: Dār al-Kitāb al-Islāmī, vol. 1, p. 7.

24 See Eliade, Mercea (1987), *The Encyclopaedia of Religion,* New York: Macmillan, p. 455; Hastings, James (1974), *The Encyclopaedia of Religion and Ethics*, Edinburgh and New York: Clark , vol. 5, p. 293; Hodgson, Peter Crafts (1994), *Winds of the Spirit: A Constructive Christian Theology*, Louisville, Ky: Westminster John Knox Press, p. 3; Williams, John Rodman (1996), *Renewal Theology: Systematic Theology from a Charismatic* Perspective, Michigan: Zondervan Publishing House, p. 16;

McGrath, Alister E. (1998), *Historical Theology: An Introduction to the History of Christian Thought*, Oxford: Blackwell, p. 1.

25 See Ibn Khaldūn (1984), *Al-Muqaddima*, 5th edn, Beirut: Dār al-Qalam, vol. 1, p. 466; Wizārat al-Awqāf wa al-Shu'ūn al-Islāmiyya bi al-Kuwayt (n.d.), *Al-Mawsū'a al-fiqhiyya*, Kuwait, vol. 1, p. 12.

26 One of the oldest names given to this science and attributed to *imam* Abū Ḥanīfa. See Bayāḍī, Kamāl al-Dīn Aḥmad al- (1949), pp. 28–29; Shāfi'ī, Ḥasan Maḥmūd al- (1411/1991), *Al-Madkhal ilā dirāsat 'ilm al-kalām*, 2nd edn, Cairo: Maktabat Wahba, p. 26.

27 See Gimaret, D. (2003), 'Uṣūl al-Dīn' in: *EI*, vol. X, pp. 930–931. It is also noteworthy to state that the expression *uṣūl al-dīn* occurs in the titles of many treatises on Islamic theology. For such treatises representing the Ash'arī viewpoint, see Baghdādī, Abū Manṣūr 'Abd al-Qāhir al- (1346/1928), *Uṣūl al-dīn*, Istanbul; Juwaynī, Abū al-Ma'ālī, al- (1969), *Al-Shāmil fī uṣūl al-dīn*, ed. 'Alī al-Nashshār *et al.*, Alexandria. For the Ḥanafī–Māturīdī viewpoint, see Bazdawī, Abū al-Yusr al- (1307/1889), *Uṣūl al-dīn*, Istanbul; Nasafī, Maymūn b. Muḥammad al- (1990), *Tabṣirat al-adilla fī uṣūl al-dīn 'alā ṭarīqat al-imām Abī Manṣūr al-Māturīdī*, Damascus: Al-Ma'had al-'Ilmī al-Faransī li al-Dirāsāt al-'Arabiyya. For the Ḥanbalī viewpoint, see Abū Ya'lā, Ibn al-Farrā' (1974), *Al-Mu'tamad fī uṣūl al-dīn*, Beirut. For the Mu'tazilī viewpoint, see Ibn al-Malāḥımı (1991), *Al-Mu'tamad fī uṣūl al-dīn*, ed. Martin J. McDermott and Wilfred Madelung, London: Dār al-Hudā.

28 Shāfi'ī, Ḥasan Maḥmūd al- (1411/1991), *Al-Madkhal ilā dirāsat 'ilm al-kalām*, 2nd edn, Cairo: Maktabat Wahba, p. 30.

29 Bukhārī, 'Abd al-'Azīz b. Aḥmad b. Muḥammad al- (n.d.), *Kashf al-asrār sharḥ uṣūl al-Bazdawī*, Beirut: Dār al-Kitāb al-Islāmī, vol. 1, p. 7; Wālī, Ḥusayn (1909), *Kitāb al-tawḥīd*, Cairo: Maṭba'at al-Wā'iẓ, p. 123; Jād al-Ḥaqq, 'Alī Jād al-Ḥaqq (1979), 'Dawr al-sharī'a al-islāmiyya fī taḥqīq ahdāf al-mujtama': A fatwa issued on 1 April 1979, no. 1321', in: *Barnāmaj fatāwā Dār al-Iftā' al-Miṣriyya mundh 'ām 1312 A.H.* (a software version). Cairo: Al-Majlis al-A'lā li al-Shu'ūn al-Islāmiyya; Shāfi'ī, Ḥasan Maḥmūd al- (1411/1991), p. 30.

30 Taftazānī, Sa'd al-Dīn Mas'ūd b. 'Umar al- (n.d.), *Sharḥ al-'aqā'id al-nasafiyya*, Karachi: Nashr Nūr Muḥammad, p. 4, Shāfi'ī, Ḥasan Maḥmūd al- (1411/1991), pp. 30–31.

31 Shāfi'ī, Ḥasan Maḥmūd al- (1411/1991), p. 32.

32 Bayḍāwī, 'Abd Allāh b. 'Umar al- (1323/1905), *Ṭawāli' al-anwār bi sharḥ al-mar'ashī*, Cairo, p. 4; Ījī, 'Aḍud al-Dīn 'Abd al-Raḥmān b. Aḥmad al- (1997), *Kitāb al-mawāqif*, ed. 'Abd al-Raḥmān 'Imīra, 1st edn, Beirut: Dār al-Jīl, vol. 1, p. 30; Gardet, L. (2003a), ''Ilm al-Kalām', in: *EI*, vol. III, pp. 1141–1150.

33 Shāfi'ī, Ḥasan Maḥmūd al- (1411/1991), pp. 20–21; Gardet, L. (2003a).

34 Gardet, L. (2003b), ''Akliyyāt', in: *EI*, vol. I, pp. 342–343.

35 *'Al-Qaḍā' wa al-qadar'*: when combined into one expression these two words have the overall meaning of the Decree of God, both the eternal Decree (the most frequent meaning of *qaḍā'*) and the Decree given existence in time (the most frequent meaning of *qadar*). For further details over the meanings and definitions of *al-qaḍā'* and *al-qadar*, see Mudhārī, Ibrāhīm b. Muṣṭafā al-Ḥalabī al- (1358/1939), *Al-Lum'ah fī taḥqīq mabāḥith al-wujūd wa al-ḥudūth wa al-qadar wa af'āl al-'ibād*, ed. Muḥammad Zāhid b. al-Ḥasan al-Kawtharī, 1st edn, Cairo: Maktab Nashr al-Thaqāfa al-Islāmiyya, pp. 32–55. In this book, al-Mudhārī gave sixteen definitions of the term *al-qaḍā' wa al-qadar*. See also Nawawī, Abu Zakariyya Yaḥyā b. Sharaf al- (1392/1972), *Sharḥ al-Nawawī 'alā ṣaḥīḥ Muslim*, 2nd edn, Beirut: Dār Iḥyā' al-Turāth al-'Arabī, vol. 1, pp. 154–155; 'Asqalānī, Ibn Ḥajar al- (1379/1959), *Fatḥ al-Bārī*, ed. Muḥammad Fu'ād 'Abd al-Bāqī and Muḥibb al-Dīn al-Khaṭīb, Beirut: Dār al-Ma'rifa, vol. 11, p. 509; Būṭī, Muḥammad Sa'īd Ramaḍān, al- (2001), *Al-Insān musayyar am mukhayyar*, 2nd edn, Beirut: Dār al-Fikr al-Mu'āṣir and Damascus: Dār

al-Fikr, pp. 37, 38, 210, 217, 221, 233; Gardet, L. (2003), 'al-Ḳaḍā wa'l Ḳadar', in: *EI*, vol. IV, pp. 365–367.

36 This was one of the very knotty issues that has busied the minds of theologians from early Islamic history up to the present time. That is why most of the books and compilations written on *al-qaḍā' wa al-qadar* focused on this point and gave less or no attention to the other point which is our concern here. For those interested in it, see for instance Obermann, Julian (1935), 'Political Theology in Early Islam: Ḥasan al-Baṣrī's Treatise on Qadar', in: *JAOS*, vol. 55, pp. 138–162; Rehman, Mutazid Wali-ur, (1939), 'Iqbāl's Doctrine of Destiny', in: *IC*, vol. 13, pp. 150–175; Watt, W. Montgomery (1948), *Free Will and Predestination in Early Islam*, London: Luzac; Siddiqi, Mazheruddin (1953), 'Islamic Concept of Destiny', in: *Iqbal*, vol. II, no. 1, pp. 46–59; Vahiduddin, S. (1968), 'The Qur'anic Visions of God, Man and his Destiny', *IC*, vol. LX, no. 1, pp. 1–18; Ansari, Zafar Ishaq (1969), 'Taftazānī's Views on *Taklīf*, *Jabr* and *Qadar*: A Note of the Development of Islamic Theological Doctrines', in: *Arabica*: *Revue d'Études Arabes*, Leiden, vol. XVI, pp. 65–78.

37 Ash'arī, Abū al-Ḥasan 'Alī b. Ismā'īl al- (1397/1977), *Al-Ibāna 'an uṣūl al-diyāna*, ed. Fawqiyya Ḥusayn Maḥmūd, 1st edn, Cairo: Dār al-Anṣār, pp. 193–194; Ash'arī, Abū al-Ḥasan 'Alī b. Ismā'īl al- (1940), *Al-Ibāna 'an Uṣūl al-Diyāna: The Elucidation of Islam's Foundation*, trans. Walter C. Klein, New Haven, Conn.: American Oriental Society, pp. 112–113.

38 For the derivatives and meaning of this term, see Fayyūmī, Aḥmad b. Muḥammad b. 'Alī al- (n.d.), *Al-Miṣbāḥ al-munīr fī gharīb al-sharḥ al-kabīr*, Beirut: Al-Maktaba al-'Ilmiyya, pp. 349–350.

39 Ibid., p. 298.

40 Ibid., p. 309.

41 For instance, *muṣība* has been interpreted as disability and sickness in general: see Bayḍāwī, 'Abd Allāh b. 'Umar al- (1416/1996), *Ṭawāli' al-anwār bi sharḥ al-mar'ashī*, Cairo, vol. 5, p. 303; Qurṭubī, Abū 'Abd Allāh Muḥammad b. Aḥmad al- (1372/1952), *Al-Jāmi' li aḥkām al-Qur'ān*, ed. Aḥmad 'Abd al-'Alīm al-Bardūnī, 2nd edn, Cairo: Dār al-Sha'b, vol. 16, pp. 30–31, vol. 17, p. 257, vol. 4, p. 315; Ṭabarī, Muḥammad b. Jarīr al- (1405/1984), *Jāmi' al-bayān fī ta'wīl al-Qur'ān: tafsīr al-Ṭabarī*, Beirut: Dār al-Fikr, vol. 27, p. 234. Also *sayyi'a* has been interpreted as a synonym for *muṣība*: see Ibn Taymiyya (n.d.), *Kutub wa rasā'il wa fatāwā Ibn Taymiyya fī al-'aqīda*, ed. 'Abd al-Raḥmān Muḥammad Qāsim al-Najdī, Maktabat Ibn Taymiyya, vol. 1, p. 42; Alūsī, Abū al-Faḍl Maḥmūd al- (n.d.), *Rūḥ al-ma'ānī fī tafsīr al-Qur'ān al-'Aẓīm wa al-sab' al-mathānī*, Beirut: Dār Iḥyā' al-Turāth al-'Arabī, vol. 12, p. 15. As for *sharr* (pl. *shurūr*), Ibn al-Qayyim named pain and adversities in life as evils (*shurūr*). See Ibn al-Qayyim (1348/1929), *Mukhtaṣar al-ṣawā'iq al-mursala 'ala al-Jahmiyya wa al-Mu'aṭṭila*, ed. Muḥammad Ḥāmid al-Fiqī, Mecca: Al-Maṭba'a al-Salafiyya, vol. 1, p. 376.

42 See Kamali, Muhammad Hashim (2003), *Principles of Islamic Jurisprudence*, 3rd edn, Cambridge: The Islamic Texts Society, pp. 46–51; see also pp. 27, 280, 299, 332.

43 For further information on this usage of *ta'līl* see Hasan, Ahmad (1974), 'Rationality of Islamic Legal Injunctions', in: *IS*, no. 13, pp. 95–109; Kamali, Muhammad Hashim (2003), pp. 46–51; see also pp. 27, 280, 299, 332.

44 Just to mention some of these scholars, we refer to Ibn al-'Izz from the Ḥanafī school (see Zāda, 'Abd al-Raḥmān b. Muḥammad Shaykhī (n.d.), *Majma' al-anhur fī sharḥ multaqā al-abḥur*, Beirut: Dār Iḥyā' al-Turāth al-'Arabī, vol., 1, p. 245), 'Abd al-Malik b. 'Abd al-'Azīz al-Mājishūn and Abū al-Walīd al-Bājī from the Mālikī school (see Ḥaṭṭāb, Abū 'Abd Allāh al- (1412/1992), *Mawāhib al-Jalīl fī sharḥ mukhtaṣar al-Khalīl*, 3rd edn, Beirut: Dār al-Fikr, vol. 6, p. 93) and a third Mālikī jurist, Abū 'Abd Allāh al-Māzirī (see Zayn al-Dīn, 'Abd al-Raḥīm b. al-Ḥusayn al-'Irāqī (n.d.), *Ṭarḥ al-tathrīb fī sharḥ al-taqrīb*, Dār Iḥyā' al-Kutub al-'Arabiyya, vol. 8, p. 100).

45 See, for instance, Ibn Taymiyya (n.d.a), *Majmū' al-fatāwā*, ed. 'Abd al-Raḥmān b. Qāsim and Muḥammad b. 'Abd al-Raḥmān b. Qāsim, Riyadh: Mujamma' al-Malik Fahd, vol. 8, pp. 377–381; Ibn al-Wazīr, Muḥammad b. Ibrāhīm (1987), *Īthār al-ḥaqq 'alā al-khalq fī radd al-khilāfāt ilā al-madhhab al-ḥaqq min uṣūl al-tawḥīd*, 2nd edn, Beirut: Dār al-Kutub al-'Ilmiyya, vol.1, pp. 181–182.
46 See for instance Hasan, Ahmad (1974), pp. 98–101.
47 See Hoover, Jon (2002), *An Islamic Theodicy: Ibn Taymiyya on the Wise Purpose of God, Human Agency and Problems of Evil and Justice*, a thesis submitted to the University of Birmingham for the degree of Doctor of Philosophy, p. 1.
48 See, for instance, 'Abd al-Raḥmān 'Abd Allāh al-'Awaḍī & Aḥmad Rajā'ī al-Jundī (eds) (1422–2001), vol. 2, pp. 577, 582, 587.
49 See Ashqar, 'Umar Sulaymān al- (1413/1991), *Tārīkh al-fiqh al-islāmī*, Jordan: Dār al-Nafā'is, and Kuwait: Maktabat al-Falāḥ, pp.9–18; Wizārat al-Awqāf wa al-Shu'ūn al-Islāmiyya bi al-Kuwayt (n.d.), vol. 1, pp. 11–15, vol. 32, pp. 193–194.
50 See Ashqar, 'Umar Sulaymān al- (1413/1991), pp. 35–36; Goldziher, I. and Joseph Schacht (2003), vol. II, pp. 886, 887. For more differences between *fiqh* and jurisprudence, see Wizārat al-Awqāf wa al-Shu'ūn al-Islāmiyya bi al-Kuwayt (n.d.), vol. 1, pp. 20–22.
51 Ashqar, 'Umar Sulaymān al- (1413/1991), pp. 20–24; Bousquet, G.H. (2003), ''Ibādāt', in: *EI*, vol. III, pp. 647–648; Bernand, M. (2003), 'Mu'amalāt', in: *EI*, vol. II, pp. 255–257.
52 Ashqar, 'Umar Sulaymān al- (1413/1991), p. 21.
53 Ghaly, Mohammed (2008), 'Physical and Spiritual Treatment of Disability in Islam: Perspectives of Early and Modern Jurists', *Journal of Religion, Disability and Health*, vol. 12, no. 2, pp. 107 and 108.
54 Turki, Abdel-Magid (2003), pp. 394–397.
55 Ghaly, Mohammed (2008), p. 108.
56 Ibid.
57 Baqmī, Ṣāliḥ al-Marzūqī al- (2006), *Al-Ta'rīf bi al-Majma' al-Fiqhī al-Islāmī bi Makka al-Mukarrama*, 3rd edn, Mecca: Rābitat al-'Ālam al-Islāmī.
58 http://www.islamset.com/ (accessed 19 April 2009).
59 http://www.e-cfr.org/en/ (accessed 19 April 2009).
60 See Anṣārī, Abū Yahyā Zakariyya al- (n.d.), *Tuḥfat al-ṭullāb bi sharḥ taḥrīr tanqīḥ al-lubāb*, Pekalongan, Indonesia: Maktabat wa Maṭba'at Rajamura Vkālūghān, pp. 140–141; Khalīfa, Ḥājjī (1412–1992), *Kashf al-ẓunūn 'an asāmī al-kutub wa al-funūn*, Beirut: Dār al-Kutub al-'Ilmiyya, vol. 2, p. 1541; 'Abd Allāh, Muḥammad 'Abd Allāh (1422/2001), 'Ḥuqūq al-mu'āqīn nafsiyyan wa 'aqliyyan fī al-islām wa al-qawānīn al-ma'mūl bihā', in: 'Awaḍī, 'Abd al-Raḥmān 'Abd Allāh al- and Aḥmad Rajā'ī al-Jundī (eds), *Al-Mushāwara al-buldāniyya ḥawl tashrī'āt al-ṣiḥḥa al-nafsiyya fī mukhtalaf al-sharā'i' bimā fī dhālik al-sharī'a al-islāmiyya*, Kuwait: Islamic Organization for Medical Sciences, vol. 2, vol. 2, p. 678.
61 This has been stated by those who quoted him such as al-Suyūṭī: see Suyūṭī, Jalāl al-Dīn al- (1403/1983), *Al-Ashbāh wa al-naẓā'ir*, 1st edn, Beirut: Dār al-Kutub al-'Ilmiyya, pp. 251. However, I could not trace this book in either a manuscript or an edited form.
62 Nawawī, Yaḥyā b. Sharaf al- (n.d.), *Al-Majmū' sharḥ al-muhadhdhab*, Cairo: Maṭba'at al-Munīriyya, vol. 9, p. 368.
63 See Suyūṭī, Jalāl al-Dīn al (1403/1983), pp. 251–253.
64 See Ḥamawī, Aḥmad b. Muḥammad al- (1405/1985), *Ghamz 'uyūn al-baṣā'ir fī sharḥ al-ashbāh wa al-naẓā'ir*, Beirut: Dār al-Kutub al-'Ilmiyya, pp. 334–335.
65 See Jurjānī, 'Alī b. Muḥammad b. 'Alī al- (1405/1984), *Al-Ta'rīfāt*, ed. Ibrāhīm al-Ibyārī, 1st edn, Beirut: Dār al-Kitāb al-'Arabī, p. 120; Ibn 'Ābidīn, Muḥammad Amīn b. 'Umar (n.d.), *Al-'Uqūd al-durriyya fī tanqīḥ al-fatāwā al-ḥāmidiyya*, Beirut: Dār al-Ma'rifa, vol. 5, p. 187.

66 Wizārat al-Awqāf wa al-Shu'ūn al-Islāmiyya bi al-Kuwayt (n.d.), vol. 18, p. 7.
67 Ibid., vol. 3, p. 10.
68 See Grīsha, 'Alī (1987), *Ḥurumāt lā ḥuqūq: ḥuqūq al-insān fī ẓill al-islām dirāsa muqārana*, Cairo: Dār al-I'tiṣām, pp. 31–32; Badawi, Mohamed Zaki (2001), in an unpublished lecture, 'Islam and citizenship', delivered at the conference, 'Does the Muslim Citizen Exist?', held in Rotterdam, The Netherlands, in 2001 and organized by the Dutch organization Islam & Burgerschap (Islam and Citizenship). For further details and a critical study on this lecture, see Ghaly, Mohammed (2001).
69 Kamali, Muhammad Hashim (1993), 'Fundamental Rights of the Individual: An Analysis of Haqq (Right) in Islamic Law', in: *American Journal of Islamic Sciences*, vol. 10, no. 3, p. 340.
70 Abū Ghudda, 'Abd al-Sattār (1411/1991), 'Ri'āyat al-mu'awwaqīn fī al-islām' in: *Buḥūth fī al-fiqh al-ṭibbī wa al-ṣiḥḥa al-nafsiyya min manẓūr islāmī*, Cairo: Dār al-Aqṣā/Maṭba'at al-Ḥaramyn, p. 216.
71 See Bukhārī, 'Abd al-'Azīz b. Aḥmad b. Muḥammad al- (n.d.), vol. 4, pp. 134–135; Ibn al-Qayyim (1973), *I'lām al-muwaqqi'īn 'an Rabb al-'Ālamīn*, ed. Ṭāhā 'Abd al-Ra'ūf Sa'd, Beirut: Dār al-Jīl, vol. 1, p. 108; Kamali, Muhammad Hashim (1993), p. 348; Hoexter, M. (1995), 'Ḥuqūq Allāh and Ḥuqūq al-'Ibād as Reflected in the Waqf Institution', in: *Jerusalem Studies in Arabic and Islam*, no. 19, p. 134; Nashmī, 'Ajīl Jāsim al- (1423/2002), 'Al-Ḥuqūq al-ma'nawiyya li al-barāmij wa ahkām naskhihā', in: *SRECFR*, no. 1, (Rabī' Thānī 1423/June 2002), p. 163.
72 Ibn Qudāma (n.d.), *Al-Muqni' fī fiqh imām al-sunna Aḥmad Ibn Ḥanbal*, Cairo: Al-Maṭba'a al-Salafiyya wa Maktabatuhā, vol. 10, p. 218; Nashmī, 'Ajīl Jāsim al- (1423/2002), pp. 164–166.
73 Kamali, Muhammad Hashim (1993), p. 348.
74 Ibid., p. 349.
75 See for instance, Miles, M. (1981), 'Some Historical Notes on Religions, Ideologies and the Handicapped', in: *Al-Mushir*, 1981, vol. XXIII, no. 4, p. 128; 'Awaḍī, 'Abd al-Raḥmān 'Abd Allāh al- and Aḥmad Rajā'ī al-Jundī (eds) (1422/2001), vol. 1, p. 8, vol. 2, p. 472; Such expressions have also been used in the titles of some books and articles: see Ibn Ḥamza, Muṣṭafā (1414/1993), *Ḥuqūq al-mu'awwaqīn fī al-islām*, Casablanca: Maṭba'at al-Najāḥ al-Jadīda; 'Al-Mu'āqūn 'aqliyyan aw nafsiyyan bayn al-islām wa al-qawānīn al-waḍ'iyya wa ḥuqūquhum qibal al-usra wa al-mujtama'', in: 'Awaḍī, 'Abd al-Raḥmān 'Abd Allāh al- and Aḥmad Rajā'ī al-Jundī (eds), (1422/2001), vol. 1, pp. 395–443; Abū Ghudda, 'Abd al-Sattār (2001), 'Mas'ūliyyāt wa ḥuqūq al-mu'āqīn 'aqliyyan wa nafsiyyan', in: 'Awaḍī, 'Abd al-Raḥmān 'Abd Allāh al- and Aḥmad Rajā'ī al-Jundī (eds) (1422/2001), vol. 2, pp. 734–775.
76 Qaysarānī, Muḥammad b. Ṭāhir al- (1415/1994), *Tadhkirat al-ḥuffāẓ*, ed. Ḥamdī 'Abd al-Majīd Ismā'īl al-Salafī, 1st edn, Riyadh: Dār al-Ṣumay'ī, vol. 1, p. 679.
77 The International Classification of Impairments, Disabilities and Handicaps (ICIDH) (1980), that has been replaced by the International Classification of Functioning, Disability and Health (ICF) (2001) adds credence to this fact. See also Devlieger, Patrick J. (1999), 'From Handicap to Disability: Language Use and Cultural Meaning in the United States', in: *Disability and Rehabilitation*, vol. 21, no. 7, pp. 346–354, p. 346.
78 Beneken, M.M. *et al.* (1997), *Social Integration of People with Disabilities in 12 South-Mediterranean Countries*, Utrecht: sDG, Netherlands Foundation for Rehabilitation, p. 5.
79 See http://graham.main.nc.us/~bhammel/INS/disab.html and http://www.accessiblesociety.org/topics/demographics-identity/dkaplanpaper.htm (accessed 15 May 2008).
80 World Health Organization (2001), p. 3.
81 Ibid.
82 Ibid., p. 213.
83 'Activity limitations' replaces the term 'disability' used in the 1980 version of the ICIDH. See World Health Organization (2001), p. 213, fn. 18.

84 'Participation restrictions' replaces the term 'handicap' used in the 1980 version of the ICIDH. See World Health Organization (2001), p. 213, fn. 19.
85 World Health Organization (2001), p. 213.
86 Stein, Scott, http://www.wfthecoliseum.com/articles/sticks%20and%20stones/crippled_words.html (accessed 15 May 2008).
87 Eiesland, Nancy (1994), p. 26; Mairs, Nancy (1986), *Plaintext*, Tucson: University of Arizona, pp. 10, 11.
88 Eiesland, Nancy (1994), p. 26.
89 Rispler-Chaim, Vardit (2007), *Disability in Islamic Law*, Dordrecht, The Netherlands: Springer, p. 2.
90 This is the most common Arabic equivalent for disability. However, some scholars indicate that it is linguistically incorrect and prefer the other two terms: see Ibn Ḥamza, Muṣṭafā (1414/1993); http://www.qaradawi.net/arabic/meetings/shreai-&-hayaa/prog -27.htm (accessed 20 May 2008).
91 See Mūsā, Nāṣir b. 'Alī al- (2001), 'Muṣṭalaḥāt fī al-Tarbiyya al-Khāṣṣa bayn al-Tawḍīḥ wa al-Taṣḥīḥ', in: *Al-Tarbiyya al-khāṣṣa*, (April), no. 2, pp. 20–21.
92 Munaẓẓamat al-Ṣiḥḥa al-'Ālamiyya (2001), *Al-Taṣnīf al-dawlī li ta'diyat al-waẓā'if wa al-'ajz wa al-ṣiḥḥa (ICF)*, Munaẓẓamat al-Ṣiḥḥa al-'Ālamiyya, p. 28. Paging is based on an electronic version. I hereby submit my deep thanks and gratitude to the Regional Office for Eastern Mediterranean, WHO, especially to Dr Muḥammad Haytham Al Khayyāṭ and Dr Qāsim Sāra who provided me with this software version. See also Wazna, Ṭal'at b. Ḥamza al- (1412/2000), *Al-I'āqa wa al-ta'hīl: usus wa mabādi'*, a paper presented to the 2nd International Conference on Disability and Rehabilitation, Markaz al-Amīr Salmān li Abḥāth al-I'āqa, Riyadh, pp. 1–2.
93 Munaẓẓamat al-Ṣiḥḥa al-'Ālamiyya (2001), p. 327.
94 Munaẓẓamat al-Ṣiḥḥa al-'Ālamiyya (2001), pp. 22, 31, 84, 346.
95 Ibid., pp. 31, 37, 193, 346, 354.
96 Ibid., pp. 22, 28, 340, 346.
97 Ibid., pp. 31, 193, 346.
98 Abū Jayb, Sa'dī (1402/1982), *Al-Muw'awwaq wa al-mujtama' fī al-sharī'a al-islāmiyya*, Damascus and Beirut: Dār al-Fikr al-Mu'āṣir/Dār al-Fikr, p. 12; 'Abd Allāh, Muḥammad 'Abd Allāh (1422/2001), vol. 2, p. 665.
99 Ibn Ḥamza, Muṣṭafā (1414/1993), p. 4; 'Abd Allāh, Muḥammad 'Abd Allāh (1422/2001), pp. 665–666.
100 For further information, see 'Abd al-Ḥamīd, al-Sayyid Muḥammad (1418/1998), *Al-Ta'wīq 'al-i'āqa'*, Cairo: Al-Maktaba al-Azhariyya li al-Turāth, pp. 7–8; 'Abd Allāh, Muḥammad 'Abd Allāh (1422/2001), pp. 665–667.
101 For further information on this point, see Qurṭubī, Abū 'Abd Allāh Muḥammad b. Aḥmad al- (1372/1952), vol. 14, p. 151; 'Abd al-Ḥamīd, al-Sayyid Muḥammad (1418/1998), pp. 7–9; 'Abd Allah, Muḥammad 'Abd Allāh (1422/2001), pp. 666–667.
102 Rispler-Chaim, Vardit (2007), p. 4.
103 Ibid., pp. 4–5.
104 Just to give examples of early writers who made use of this term where people with disabilities were included, see Ibn Ḥabīb, Muḥammad (1361/1942), *Kitāb al-muḥabbar*, ed. Elza Lichten Stitter, Hyderabad, pp. 261–382; Ibn Qutayba Abū Muḥammad 'Abd Allāh b. Muslim (1388/1969), *Al-Ma'ārif*, ed. Tharwat 'Ukāsha, 2nd edn, Cairo: Dār al-Ma'ārif, pp. 578–589; Ibn Qutayba Abū Muḥammad 'Abd Allāh b. Muslim (1406/1986), *'Uyūn al-akhbār*, ed. Mufīd Muḥammad Qamīḥa, 1st edn, Beirut: Dār al-Kutub al-'Ilmiyya, vol. 4, pp. 63–68; Ibn Rusta, Abū 'Alī Aḥmad b. 'Umar (1419/1998), *Al-A'lāq al-nafīsa*, ed. Khalīl al-Manṣūr, Beirut: Dār al-Kutub al-'Ilmiyya, pp. 189–192; Khuwārizmī, Jamāl al-Dīn Abū Bakr al- (1327/1909), *Mufīd al-'ulūm wa mubīd al-humūm*, Cairo: Al-Maṭba'a al-Sharqiyya, pp. 296–298; Tha'ālibī, Abū Manṣūr 'Abd al-Malik b. Muḥammad al- (1968), *The Book of Curious and Entertaining Information: The Laṭā'if al-Ma'ārif of Tha'ālibī*, trans. C.E.

Bosworth, Edinburgh: The University Press, pp. 92–95; Ibn al-Jawzī (n.d.), *Talqīḥ fuhūm ahl al-athar fī 'uyūn al-tārīkh wa al-siyar*, Delhi, pp. 229–231.

105 See Ṣan'ānī, Muḥammad b. Ismā'īl al-Kaḥlānī al- (n.d.), *Subul al-salām*, Cairo: Dār al-Ḥadīth, vol. 2, p. 64; Fayyūmī, Aḥmad b. Muḥammad b. 'Alī al- (n.d.), p. 439.

106 Exploring the denotations and connotations of such terms without giving direct English equivalents is done on purpose. Despite some of these terms having English equivalents in dictionaries and lexicons (for instance chronic illness or invalidism for *zamāna*, valetudinarianism for *qi'ād*), none of them conveys the precise meaning intended in this context. Hence adding such equivalents will create only confusion for the reader.

107 Wizārat al-Awqāf wa al-Shu'ūn al-Islāmiyya bi 'al-Kuwayt (n.d.), vol. 24, pp. 10–11.

108 See Ṭabarī, Muḥammad b. Jarīr al- (1405/1984), vol. 3, pp. 121–122; Qurṭubī, Abū 'Abd Allāh Muḥammad b. Aḥmad al- (1372/1952), vol. 3, p. 388; 'Abd Allāh, Muḥammad 'Abd Allāh (1422/2001), pp. 567–569.

109 See Mizzī, Abū al-Ḥajjāj al- (1400/1980), *Tahdhīb al-kamāl*, ed. Bashshā 'Awwād Ma'rūf, 1st edn, Beirut: Mu'assasat al-Risāla, vol. 10, p. 463.

110 See Ibn Abī al-Dunyā (1410/1989), *Al-Riḍā 'an Allāh bi qaḍā'ih*, ed. Ḍiyā' al-Ḥasan al-Salafī, 1st edn, Bombay: Al-Dār al-Salafiyya, vol. 1, p. 89; Ibn Ḥazm, Abū Muḥammad 'Alī (n.d.), *Al-Muḥallā bi al-āthār*, Beirut: Dār al-Fikr, vol. 3, p. 97; Ibn al-Wazīr, Muḥammad b. Ibrāhīm (1987), vol. 1, p. 209.

111 Abū Jayb, Sa'dī (1402/1982), pp. 15–16.

112 Tirmidhī, Abū 'Īsā al- (n.d.), *Sunan al-Tirmidhī*, ed. Aḥmad Muḥammad Shākir *et al.*, Beirut: Dār Iḥyā' al-Turāth al-'Arabī, Ḥadīth no. 2420, vol. 4, p. 603.

113 See, for instance, Nawawī, Yaḥyā b. Sharaf al- (n.d.), vol. 3, p. 31, vol. 4, p. 347; Bukhārī, 'Abd al-'Azīz b. Aḥmad b. Muhammad al- (n.d.), vol. 4, p. 253.

114 See 'Asqalānī, Ibn Ḥajar al- (1406/1986), *Lisān al-mizān*, 3rd edn, Beirut: Mu'assasat al-A'lamī li al-Maṭbū'āt, vol. 1, p. 537.

115 See Ṭabarī, Muḥammad b. Jarīr al- (1405/1984), vol. 5, p. 240; Ibn Kathīr (1401/1980), *Tafsīr Ibn Kathīr*, Beirut: Dār al-Fikr, vol. 1, p. 544; 'Asqalānī, Ibn Ḥajar al- (1412/1992), *Al-Iṣāba fī tamyīz al-ṣaḥāba*, ed. 'Alī Muḥammad al-Bījāwī, 1st edn, Beirut: Dār al-Jīl, vol. 3, p. 491.

116 See Shāfi'ī, Muḥammad b. Idrīs al- (1410/1990), *Al-Umm*, Beirut: Dār al-Ma'rifa, vol. 8, p. 108; Ibn al-Murtaḍā, Aḥmad b. Yaḥyā (n.d.), *Al-Baḥr al-zakhkhār al-jāmi' li madhāhib 'ulamā' al-amṣār*, Beirut: Dār al-Kitāb al-Islāmī, vol. 2, p. 346.

117 Fayyūmī, Aḥmad b. Muḥammad b. 'Alī al- (n.d.), p. 480; 'Illaysh, Muḥammad b. Aḥmad b. Muḥammad (n.d.), *Fatḥ al-'aliyy al-mālik fī al-fatwā 'alā madhhab al-imām Mālik*, Beirut: Dār al-Ma'rifa, vol. 2, p. 341.

118 Ṭaḥāwī, Aḥmad b. Muḥammad b. Salāma al- (1399/1979), *Sharḥ ma'ānī al-āthār*, 1st edn, Beirut: Dār al-Ma'rifa, pp. 123–125.

119 Muṭarrizī, Nāṣir b. 'Abd al-Sayyid Abū al-Makārim al- (n.d.), *Al-Mughrib fī tartīb al-mu'rib*, Beirut: Dār al-Kitāb al-'Arabī, p. 135.

120 'Asqalānī, Ibn Ḥajar al- (1379/1959), vol. 12, p. 295.

121 Ibn Mufliḥ, Ibrāhīm b. Muḥammad (n.d.), *Al-Ādāb al-shar'iyya wa al-minaḥ al-mar'iyya*, Beirut: 'Ālam al-Kutub, vol. 3, p. 574.

122 Wizārat al-Awqāf wa al-Shu'ūn al-Islāmiyya bi al-Kuwayt (n.d.), vol. 24, pp. 10–11.

123 See Rāzī, Muḥammad b. Abī Bakr b. 'Abd al-Qādir al- (1415/1995), *Mukhtār al-ṣiḥāḥ*, ed. Maḥmūd Khāṭir, Beirut: Maktabat Lubnān Nāshirūn, vol. 1, p. 238.

124 Haytamī, Ibn Ḥajar al- (1403/1983), *Tuḥfat al-muḥtāj fī sharḥ al-minhāj*, Beirut: Dār Iḥyā' al-Turāth al-'Arabī, vol. 7, p. 152.

125 For the complete list of these terms, see Ibn Ḥabīb, Abū al-Qāsim al-Ḥasan b. Muḥammad (1418/1998), *'Uqalā' al-majānīn*, Beirut: Dār al-Nafā'is, pp. 43–49.

126 Turmusani, Majid (2001), 'Disabled Women in Islam: Middle Eastern Perspective', in: Gaventa, William C. and Coulter, David L. (eds) (2001) *Spirituality and Intellectual*

Disability: International Perspectives on the Effect of Culture and Religion on Healing Body, Mind and Soul, New York: Haworth Pastoral Press, pp. 77–78.

127 Rispler-Chaim, Vardit (2007), pp. 8–9.

128 For examples of early Qur'ān commentaries, see Ṭabarī, Muḥammad b. Jarīr al- (1405/1984), vol. 1, pp. 146–147, vol. 2, p. 83; Qurṭubī, Abū 'Abd Allāh Muḥammad b. Aḥmad al- (1372/1952), vol. 1, pp. 214–215, vol. 10, p. 333; Ibn Kathīr (1401/1980), vol. 1, p. 54; Bayḍāwī, 'Abd Allāh b. 'Umar al- (1323/1905), vol. 1, pp. 194–195; Suyūṭī, Jalāl al-Dīn al- and Jalāl al-Dīn al-Maḥallī (n.d.), *Tafsīr al-Jalālayn*, 1st edn, Cairo: Dār al-Ḥadīth, vol. 1, p. 5 ; Alūsī, Abū al-Faḍl Maḥmūd al- (n.d.), vol. 2, p. 41, vol. 7, p. 147. For modern commentaries, see, for instance, Ibn 'Ashūr, Muḥammad al-Ṭāhir (1997), *Tafsīr al-taḥrīr wa al-tanwīr*, Tunisia: Dār Saḥnūn li al-Nashr wa al-Twazī', vol. 1, pp. 313–314; Qāsimī, Jamāl al-Dīn al- (1424/2003), *Tafsīr al-Qāsimī al-musammā maḥāsin al-ta'wīl*, Cairo: Dār al-Ḥadīth, vol. 1, pp. 285–286.

129 See, for instance, Ibn Manẓūr, Muḥammad b. Makram (n.d.), *Lisān al-'Arab*, 1st edn, Beirut: Dār Ṣādir, vol. 12, p. 53.

130 It is to be noted that more than one contemporary Muslim scholar found no harm in using the modern terminology – as long as it is understandable and inoffensive – and also used such terminology in their writings on disability in Islam and in the titles of such writings. See, for instance, Abū Jayb, Sa'dī (1402/1982), pp. 11–16; 'Abd al-Ḥamīd, al-Sayyid Muḥammad (1418/1998), pp. 7–10; 'Abd Allāh, Muḥammad 'Abd Allāh (1422/2001), p. 667.

131 Ibid., p. 27; http://www.sacredplaces.org/PSP-InfoClearingHouse/articles/That%20All% 20May%20Worship.htm (accessed 19 September 2007).

132 Ibid., p. 27.

2 Speculative theology

1 See Maqsood, Ruqaiyyah Waris (2000), *The Problem of Evil: A Study of Evil, Fate, Freewill and Predestination, Forgiveness and Love*, Delhi: Adam Publishers & Distributors, pp. 8–44; Ayoub, Mahmoud M. (1977), 'The Problem of Suffering in Islam', in: *Journal of Dharma*, vol. 2, pp. 267–294, p. 267; Julaynid, Muḥammad al-Sayyid al- (1981), p. 55. For people with disabilities, in particular see Muṭawwa', Munīra Khālid al- (1422–2001), 'Waraqat 'amal ḥawl al-'amal al-ijtimā'ı wa dawrih fī ḥimāyat al-mu'āqīn wa al-ḥusūl 'alā ḥuqūqihim muqaddama ilā nadwat ḥuqūq al-mu'āqīn nafsiyyan wa 'aqliyyan fī al-islām', in 'Awaḍī, 'Abd al-Raḥmān 'Abd Allāh al- and Aḥmad Rajā'ī al-Jundī (eds) (1422/2001), *Al-Mushāwara al-buldāniyya ḥawl tashrī'āt al-ṣiḥḥa al-nafsiyya fī mukhtalaf al-sharā'i' bimā fī dhālik al-sharī'a al-islāmiyya*, Kuwait: Islamic Organization for Medical Sciences, vol. 2, p. 642.

2 See Pessagno, J. Meric (1984), 'The Uses of Evil in the Maturidian Thought', in: *SI*, vol. LIX, pp. 59–82, p. 65.

3 Bayhaqī, Abū Bakr Aḥmad b. al-Ḥusayn al- (1410/1989), *Shu'ab al-īmān*, ed. Muḥammad al-Sa'īd Basyūnī Zaghlūl, Beirut: Dār al-Kutub al-'Ilmiyya, vol. 4, p. 107.

4 Ghazālī, Abū Ḥāmid al- (1407/1987), *Al-Maqṣad al-asnā fī sharḥ ma'ānī asmā' Allāh al-ḥusnā*, ed. Bassām 'Abd al-Wahhāb al-Jābī, 1st edn, Limassol, Cyprus: Al-Jaffān wa al-Jābī, pp. 52–53.

5 See Gardet, L. (2003c), 'al-Asmā' al-Ḥusnā', in: *EI*, vol. I, p. 714

6 See, for instance, Bukhārī, Abū 'Abd Allāh al- (1407/1987), *Ṣaḥīḥ al-Bukhārī*, ed. Muṣṭafā Dīb al-Baghā, 3rd edn, Beirut: Dār Ibn Kathīr/al-Yamāma, vol. 6, p. 2691.

7 Among the well-known scholars who wrote on this topic, we mention Ibn Khuzayma (d. 311 /923), Abu Isḥāq al-Zajjāj (d. 311/923), Al-Dāraqutnī (d. 385/995), Al-Bayhaqī (d. 458/1065), Abū Ḥāmid al-Ghazālī (d. 505/1111), Ibn al-Jawzī

(d. 597/1200) and Fakhr al-Dīn al-Rāzī (d. 606/1209). For their books on this topic, see Ibn Khuzayma (1387/1968), *Kitāb al-tawḥīd wa ithbāt ṣifāt al-Rabb 'azz wa jall*, ed. Muḥammad Khalīl Harrās, Cairo: Maktabat al-Kulliyyāt al-Azhariyya; Zajjāj, Abū Isḥāq Ibrāhīm al- (1974), *Tafsīr asmā' Allāh al-ḥusnā*, ed. Aḥmad Yūsuf al-Daqqāq, Damascus: Dār al-Thaqāfa al-'Arabiyya; Ghazālī, Abū Ḥāmid al- (1407/1987); Rāzī, Fakhr al-Dīn al- (1400/1980), *Sharḥ asmā' Allāh al-ḥusnā*, ed. Ṭāhā 'Abd al-Ra'ūf Sa'd, Cairo: Maktabat al-Kulliyyāt al-Azhariyya. For a Ṣufī perspective in this regard, see Qushayrī, 'Abd al-Karīm al- (1968), *Al-Taḥbīr fī al-tadhkīr*, ed. Ibrāhīm Basyūnī, Cairo: Dār al-Kitāb al-'Arabī li al-Ṭibā'a wa al-Nashr. For contemporary studies on the same topic, see Shanqīṭī, Muḥammad al-Amīn al- (1404/1983), *Manāhij wa dirāsāt li āyāt al-asmā' wa al-ṣifāt*, ed. 'Atiyya Muḥammad Sālim, 4th edn, Kuwait: Al-Dār al-Salafiyya; Qaraḍāwī, Yūsuf al- (1426/2005), *Fuṣūl fī al-'aqīda bayn al-salaf wa al-khalaf*, Cairo: Maktabat Wahba, pp. 13–179.

8 See Ibn 'Abd al-Wahhāb, Muḥammad (n.d.), *Mu'allafāt al-Shaykh Muḥammad Ibn 'Abd al-Wahhāb*, ed. 'Abd al-'Azīz Zayd al-Rūmī *et al*., Riyadh: Jāmi'at al-Imām Muḥammad b. Sa'ūd, vol. 1, p. 130.

9 Rāzī, Fakhr al-Dīn al- (1400/1980), p. 47. God's Names are described as *Al-Ḥusnā* four times in the Qur'ān; 7:180, 17:110, 20:8, 59:24.

10 Gardet, L. (2003c), vol. I, pp. 714–715. See also Rāzī, Fakhr al-Dīn al- (1400/1980), pp. 185–186.

11 See Rāzī, Fakhr al-Dīn al- (1400/1980), pp. 47–48.

12 Conrad, Lawrence I. (1999), 'Medicine and Martyrdom: Some Discussions of Suffering and Divine Justice in Early Islamic Society', in: John R. Hinnells and Roy Porter, *Religion, Health and Suffering*, London and New York: Kegan Paul International, p. 229.

13 On him, see Watt, W. Montgomery (2003c), 'Djahmiyya', in: *EI*, vol. II, p. 388.

14 For further information on this sect, see Ash'arī, Abū al-Ḥasan 'Alī b. Ismā'īl al- (1397/1977), *Al-Ibāna 'an uṣūl al-diyāna*, ed. Fawqiyya Ḥusayn Maḥmūd, 1st edn, Cairo: Dār al-Anṣār, p. 143; Baghdādī, Abū Manṣūr 'Abd al-Qāhir al- (1977), *Al-Farq bayn al-firaq*, 2nd edn, Beirut: Dār al-Āfāq al-Jadīda, pp. 199–200; Baghdādī, Abū Manṣūr 'Abd al-Qāhir al- (1920), *Muslim Schisms and Sects: Al-Farq bayn al-Firaq*, trans. Abraham S. Halkin, New York: Columbia University Press, p. 14; Ibn al-Qayyim (1358/1939), *Ṭarīq al-hijratayn wa bāb al-sa'ādatayn*, Cairo: Idārat al-Ṭibā'a al-Munīriyya, vol. 1, p. 239; Frank, Richard (1965), 'The Neoplatonism of Ǧahm Ibn Ṣafwān', in: *Le Muséon*, vol. LXXVIII, 3–4, pp. 395–424; Watt, W. Montgomery (2003c), vol. II, p. 388.

15 On him, see Stern, S.M. (2003), 'Abū 'Īsā Muḥammad B. Hārūn al-Warrāq', in: *EI*, vol. I, p. 130.

16 On him, see Kraus, P. and Vajda, G. (2003), 'Ibn al-Rāwandī', in: *EI*, vol. III, pp. 904–906.

17 Ibn al-Qayyim (1358/1939), vol. 1, p. 251.

18 For an overall idea of this sect, see Ibn al-Qayyim (1358/1939), vol. 1, p. 239; Frank, Richard (1965), pp. 395–424.

19 See Baghdādī, Abū Manṣūr 'Abd al-Qāhir al- (1977), pp. 99–200.

20 Ritter, Hellmut (1952), 'Muslim Mystics' Strife with God', in: *Oriens*, vol. 5, p. 6.

21 Ibn al-Qayyim (1358/1939), vol. 1, p. 251.

22 Sharabāṣī, Aḥmad al- (1375/1956), *Fī 'ālam al-makfūfīn*, Cairo: Maṭba'at Nahḍat Miṣr, vol. 1, pp. 345–346.

23 Ibid.

24 Ritter, Hellmut (1952), p. 6; Stroumsa, Sarah (1987), 'From Muslim Heresy to Jewish–Muslim Polemics: Ibn al-Rāwandī's *Kitāb al-Dāmigh*', in: *JAOS*, vol. 107, no. 4, pp. 767–768.

25 Stroumsa, Sarah (1987), p. 769.

26 Ibid., pp. 7–8.

27 On him, see Sobieroj, F. (2003), 'Al-Shiblī', in: *EI*, vol. IX, pp. 431–433.
28 Ritter, Hellmut (1952), p. 4.
29 Ibid., p. 9. For similar Sufi practices in the Shī'ī tradition, see Navar, Iraj and Chelkowski, Peter J. (1994), 'If You are Merciful, O Bounteous, full of Compassion, Why Make Hell, Punishment, and the Need to Account for each Action', in: Giese, Alma and Bürgel, Christoph (eds) *God Is Beautiful and He Loves Beauty*, Berlin: Peter Lang, pp. 111–129.
30 Kader, Abdel (1954), 'Al-Junayd's Theory of Fanā'', in: *IC*, vol. 1, no. 4, pp. 222–223.
31 Ghazālī, Abū Ḥāmid, al- (n.d.), *Iḥyā' 'ulūm al-dīn,* Beirut: Dār al-Ma'rifa, vol. 4, p. 329.
32 Ibid., vol. 4, p. 330.
33 Ibid., vol. 4, pp. 347–348.
34 Ibid., vol. 4, pp. 347–348.
35 On him, see Meier, F. (2003), 'Bishr al-Ḥāfī', in: *EI*, vol. I, pp. 1243–1246.
36 Ghazālī, Abū Ḥāmid, al- (n.d.), vol. 4, p. 348. For more stories with relevance to disability as well, see ibid., pp. 348–349; Bayhaqī, Abū Bakr Aḥmad b. al-Ḥusayn al- (1410/1989), vol. 4, p. 118; Aṣbahānī, Abū Nu'aym al- (1405/1984), *Ḥilyat al-awliyā'*, 4th edn, Beirut: Dār al-Kitāb al-'Arabī, vol. 2, pp. 319–320, vol. 4, p. 68, vol. 6, p. 156; Ibn al-Jawzī (1399/1979), *Ṣifat al-ṣafwa*, ed. Maḥmūd Fakhūrī and Muḥammad Ruwās Qal'ajī, 2nd edn, Beirut: Dār al-Ma'rifa, vol. 2, pp. 463–466, 501, vol. 4, pp. 18, 19, 60, 86, 282, 283.
37 Otten, Henry J. (1985), 'The Problem of Evil in Islam', in: *The Bulletin of Christian Institutes of Islamic Studies*, vol. 1, p. 7. On the term '*fanā'*', see Ibn Taymiyya (1401/1981), *Al-'Ubūdiyya*, Beirut: Dār al-Kutub al-'Ilmiyya, pp. 44–46; Kader, Abdel (1954), pp. 219–228; Rahman, Fazlur (2003), 'Baḳā' wa Fanā'', in: *EI*, vol. I, pp. 950–951.
38 See Rahman, Fazlur (2003), vol. I, p. 950.
39 Aṣbahānī, Abū Nu'aym al- (1405/1984), vol. 4, p. 214.
40 Alūsī, Abū al-Fadl Maḥmūd al- (n.d.), *Rūḥ al-ma'ānī fī tafsīr al-Qur'ān al-'Aẓīm wa al-sab' al-mathānī*, Beirut: Dār Iḥyā' al-Turāth al-'Arabī, vol. 16, p. 278.
41 Abū Jayb, Sa'dī (1402/1982), *Al-Muw'awwaq wa al-mujtama' fī al-sharī'a al-islāmiyya*, Damascus and Beirut: Dār al-Fikr al-Mu'āṣir/Dār al-Fikr, pp. 17–25; Bazna, Maysaa S. and Hatab, Tarek A. (2005), 'Disability in the Qur'an: The Islamic Alternative to Defining, Viewing, and Relating to Disability', *JRDH*, vol. 9, no. 1, p. 12.
42 Inati, Shams C. (2000), *The Problem of Evil: Ibn Sīnā's Theodicy*, Global Publications, Institute of Global Cultural Studies, New York: Binghamton University, pp. 67–85, p. 65.
43 For an overall presentation of Ibn Sīnā's discussions on theodicizing the existence of disabilities, see ibid. For a modernized presentation of Ibn Sīnā's views on evils in general, see Muṭahharī, Murtaḍā al- (1424/2003), *Al-'Adl al-ilāhī*, trans. Muḥammad 'Abd al-Mun'im al-Khaqānī, Tehran: Dār al-Fiqh li al-Ṭibā'a wa al-Nashr, pp. 153–170, 186.
44 Shihadeh, Ayman (2006), 'Suffering', in: Meri, Josef W. (2006), *Medieval Islamic Civilization: An Encyclopedia*, vol. 2, p. 771.
45 Otten, Henry J. (1985), pp. 8–9.
46 On the reasons for translating this term in that way, see Inati, Shams C. (2000), p. 79. For a full presentation of this notion in Ibn Sīnā's philosophy, see Inati, Shams C. (2000), pp. 67–85.
47 Inati, Shams C. (2000), p. 69.
48 Ibid., p. 70.
49 Ibid., p. 81.
50 Ibid., p. 127.
51 Ibid., pp. 81, 148.
52 Shihade, Ayman (2006a), pp. 163–164.

53 Ibn ʻArabī, Muhyī al-Dīn (1328/1910), ʻTāj al-Rasāʼilʼ, in: *Majmūʻ al-Rasāʼil*, Cairo, p. 610, quoted by Diyāb, Adīb al-Nāyif (2000), ʻIbn ʻArabī on Human Freedom, Destiny and the Problem of Evilʼ, in: *Al-Shajara: Journal of the International Institute of Islamic Thought and Civilization (ISTAC)*, vol. 5, no. 1, p. 36.
54 Diyāb, Adīb al-Nāyif (2000), p. 37.
55 Inati, Shams C. (2000), p. 133; Shihadeh, Ayman (2006a), p. 161.
56 Shihadeh, Ayman (2006a), p. 161.
57 Inati, Shams C. (2000), p. 145.
58 Otten, Henry J. (1985), pp. 8–9; Inati, Shams C. (2000), p. 147.
59 Inati, Shams C. (2000), p. 147.
60 Rāzī, Fakhr al-Dīn al- (1343/1924), *Kitāb al-mabāḥith al-mashriqiyya fī ʻilm al-ilāhiyyāt wa al-ṭabīʻiyyāt*, 1st edn, Hyderabad: Majlis Dāʼirat al-Maʻārif al-Niẓāmiyya, pp. 522–523.
61 On him, see Watt, W. Montgomery (2003d), ʻDjahm B. Ṣafwānʼ, in: *EI*, vol. 1, pp. 694–695.
62 Ashʻarī, Abū al-Ḥasan ʻAlī b. Ismāʻīl al- (1940), *Al-Ibāna ʻan Uṣūl al-Diyāna: The Elucidiation of Islamʼs Foundation*, trans. Walter C. Klein, New Haven, Conn.: American Oriental Society, pp. 112–113.
63 Ījī, ʻAḍud al-Dīn ʻAbd al-Raḥmān b. Aḥmad al- (1997), *Kitāb al-mawāqif*, ed. ʻAbd al-Raḥmān ʻImīra, 1st edn, Beirut: Dār al-Jīl, vol. 1, pp. 422–474.
64 Julaynid, Muḥammad al-Sayyid al- (1981), *Qaḍiyyat al-khayr wa al-sharr fī al-fikr al-islāmī: uṣūluhā al-naẓariyya, jawānibuhā al-taṭbīqiyya: dirāsa ʻilmiyya li masʼūliyyat al-insān fī al-islām*, 2nd edn, Cairo: Matbaʻat al-Ḥalabī.
65 Legenhausen, G. (1988), ʻNotes towards an Ashʻarite Theodicyʼ, in: *Religious Studies*, vol. 24, pp. 257–266.
66 Ashʻarī, Abū al-Ḥasan ʻAlī b. Ismāʻīl al- (1940), pp. 50–51.
67 See Ormsby, Eric L. (1984), *Theodicy in Islamic Thought: The Dispute Over al-Ghazālīʼs ʻBest of all Possible Worldsʼ*, Princeton, NJ: Princeton University Press, p. 237. It will be noticed that *imam* al-Ghazālī himself, in the light of criticism of the Ashʻarites that they had neglected the role of divine wisdom, emphasized the role of wisdom but this was repugnant to many of his fellow Ashʻarites, for whom any attempt to rationalize Godʼs actions was suspect. See Ormsby, Eric L. (1984), p. 47. Cf. Ibn al-Wazīr, Muḥammad b. Ibrāhīm (1987), *Īthār al-ḥaqq ʻalā al-khalq fī radd al-khilāfāt ilā al-madhhab al-ḥaqq min uṣūl al-tawḥīd*, 2nd edn, Beirut: Dār al-Kutub al-ʻIlmiyya, vol. 1, p. 202.
68 Ashʻarī, Abū al-Ḥasan ʻAlī b. Ismāʻīl al- (1988), *Risāla ilā ahl al-thaghr*, ed. ʻAbd Allāh Shākir Muḥammad al-Junaydī, Damascus: Maktabat al-ʻUlūm wa al-Ḥikam, vol. 1, p. 268.
69 Ibn Ḥazm, Abū Muḥammad ʻAlī (n.d.), *Al-Muḥallā bi al-āthār*, Beirut: Dār al-Fikr, vol. 3, p. 41.
70 Rahman, Fazlur (2000), p. 62.
71 The Ashʻarī arguments in this regard are sporadic throughout their sources and manuals. For one of the extensive and detailed presentations of these arguments, see Ījī, ʻAḍud al-Dīn ʻAbd al-Raḥmān b. Aḥmad al- (1997), vol. 1, pp. 422–474. These arguments have been summed up in three main points by the Ḥanbalī scholar Ibn Taymiyya and translated by Jon Hoover. See Ibn Taymiyya (1406/1985), *Minhāj al-sunna al-nabawiyya fī naqḍ kalām al-Shīʻa wa al-Qadariyya*, ed. Muḥammad Rashād Sālim, Muʼassasat Qurṭuba, vol. 1, pp. 144–145; Hoover, Jon (2002), ʻAn Islamic Theodicy: Ibn Taymiyya on the Wise Purpose of God, Human Agency and Problems of Evil and Justiceʼ, a thesis submitted to the University of Birmingham for the degree of Doctor of Philosophy, pp. 85–86. I hereby express my deep gratitude to Jon Hoover who provided me with a copy of his thesis.

72 Ghazālī, Abū Ḥāmid al- (1992), *Al-Ghazālī: The Ninety-Nine Beautiful Names of God: Al-Maqṣad al-Asnā fī Sharḥ Ma'ānī Asmā' Allāh al-Ḥusnā*, trans. David B. Burrell and Nazih Daher, Cambridge: The Islamic Texts Society, pp. 116–117.
73 Ghazālī, Abū Ḥāmid al- (1985), vol. 1, p. 204.
74 Julaynid, Muḥammad al-Sayyid al- (1981), p. 225.
75 Ibn Ḥazm, Abū Muḥammad 'Alī (n.d.), vol. 3, p. 21; Gardet, L. (2003).
76 Būṭī, Muḥammad Sa'īd Ramaḍān, al- (2001), p. 183–187.
77 See Ash'arī, Abū al-Ḥasan 'Alī b. Ismā'īl al- (1940), p. 112; Julaynid, Muḥammad al-Sayyid al- (1981), p. 224.
78 Legenhausen, G. (1988), p. 266.
79 Julaynid, Muḥammad al-Sayyid al- (1981), pp. 63 and 64.
80 On him, see Fyzee, Asaf A.A. (2003), 'Ibn Bābawayh', in: *EI*, vol. III, pp. 226–227.
81 On him, see Madelung, Wilfred (2003), 'Al-Mufīd', in: *EI*, vol. VII, pp. 312–313.
82 On him, see Brockelmann, Carl (2003b), 'Al-Sharīf al-Murtaḍā', in: *EI*, vol. VII, p. 634.
83 On him, see Jafri, S.H.M. (2003), 'Al-Ḥillī', in: *EI*, vol. III, p. 390.
84 See Fyzee, Asaf A.A. (1942); Ḥillī, Ḥasan b. Yūsuf b. 'Alī b. al-Muṭahhar al- (1958), *Al-Bābu 'l-ḥādī 'ashar*, trans. William Mcellwee Miller, commentary by Miqdād-i-Fāḍil al-Ḥillī, London: The Royal Asiatic Society of Great Britain and Ireland; Ibn Taymiyya (1406/1985), vol. 1, pp. 129, 447, vol. 2, pp. 100, 101, 242; Muṭahharī, Murtaḍā al- (1424/2003), p. 64.
85 On him, see Heemskerk, Margaretha T. (2000), *Suffering in the Mu'tazilite Theology: 'Abd al-Jabbār's Teaching on Pain and Divine Justice*, Leiden: Brill, pp. 36–53.
86 'Abd al-Jabbār, al-Qāḍī Abū al-Ḥasan (1380/1960–1389/1969), *Al-Mughnī fī abwāb al-tawḥīd wa al-'adl*, Cairo.
87 Heemskerk, Margaretha T. (1995), *Pain and Compensation in Mu'tazilite Doctrine: 'Abd al-Jabbār's Teaching and its Adoption by Mānkdīm and Ibn Mattawayh*, Nijmegen, The Netherlands: Quikprint.
88 Heemskerk, Margaretha T. (2000).
89 Fyzee, Asaf A.A. (1942).
90 'Ukbarī, Muḥammad b. Muḥammad b. al-Nu'mān al- (known as al-Shaykh al-Mufīd) (1371/1951), *Awā'il al-maqālāt fī al-madhāhib wa al-mukhtārāt*, 2nd edn, Tabriz: Maṭba'at al-Riḍā'ī.
91 Ḥillī, Ḥasan b. Yūsuf b. 'Alī b. al-Muṭahhar al- (1958).
92 Lari, Sayyid Mujtaba Musavi (2003), *God and His Attributes: Lessons on Islamic Doctrine Book One*, trans. Hamid Algar, Qom, Iran: Al-Hadi.
93 On him, see ibid., pp. 5–7.
94 Khadduri, Majid (1984), *The Islamic Conception of Justice*, Baltimore, Md.: The Johns Hopkins University Press, pp. 44–45.
95 Ibn Taymiyya (n.d.a), *Majmū' al-fatawā*, ed. 'Abd al-Raḥmān b. Qāsim and Muḥammad b. 'Abd al-Raḥmān b. Qāsim, Riyadh: Mujamma' al-Malik Fahd, vol. 17, p. 352.
96 Lari, Sayyid Mujtaba Musavi (2003), p. 134.
97 Fyzee, Asaf A.A. (1942), p. 70.
98 Lari, Sayyid Mujtaba Musavi (2003), pp. 134–135.
99 Khadduri, Majid (1984), p. 48.
100 Lari, Sayyid Mujtaba Musavi (2003), p. 134.
101 'Abd al-Jabbār, al-Qāḍī Abū al-Ḥasan (1380/1960–1389/1969), vol. 6, p. 48; Khadduri, Majid (1984), p. 48.
102 Ash'arī, Abū al-Ḥasan 'Alī b. Ismā'īl al- (n.d.), p. 251, Ormsby, Eric L. (1984), p. 244.
103 Hoover, Jon (2002), p. 83.
104 On him see Dhahabī, Muḥammad b. Aḥmad b. 'Uthmān al- (1413/1992), *Siyar a'lām al-nubalā'*, ed. Shu'ayb al-Arna'ūṭ and Muḥammad Nu'aym al-'Arqasūsī, 9th edn, Beirut: Mu'assasat al-Risāla, vol. 10, pp. 542–543.

105 On him, see Dhahabī, Muḥammad b. Aḥmad b. ʻUthmān al- (1413/1992), vol. 10, pp. 541–542.
106 Ashʻarī, Abū al-Ḥasan ʻAlī b. Ismāʻīl al- (n.d.), vol. 1, pp. 166–167; Khadduri, Majid (1984), p. 48.
107 On him, see Pellat, Ch. (2003c), 'Al-Djāḥiẓ', in: *EI*, vol. II, pp. 385–387, vol. II, pp. 385–387.
108 Khadduri, Majid (1984), p. 45.
109 Lari, Sayyid Mujtaba Musavi (2003), pp. 124–125.
110 Rahbar, Daud (1960), *God of Justice: A Study in the Ethical Doctrine of the Qur'ān*, Leiden: Brill, p. 119, quoted by Otten, Henry J. (1985), p. 9.
111 Rahbar, Daud (1960), pp. 79, 80, 81, quoted by Otten, Henry J. (1985), p. 10.
112 Rahbar, Daud (1960), p. xx, quoted by Otten, Henry J. (1985), p. 10.
113 See Heemskerk, Margaretha T. (1995), p. 137.
114 By '*mukallafūn*', we refer here to those who can be punished for violating the laws. In Islamic tradition, a person falls into this category by being a human with his/her sanity (ʻ*aql*) who has reached the age of majority (*bulūgh*). Therefore, animals, children and people without mental capacity fall into the category of non-*mukallafūn*. For further details on the term, legal liability (*taklīf*) and its derivatives, *mukallaf* and *ghayr mukallaf*, see Kamali, Muhammad Hashim (2003), *Principles of Islamic Jurisprudence*, 3rd edn, Cambridge: The Islamic Texts Society, pp. 425–450; Gimaret, D. (2003a), vol. X, pp. 138–139. For further information on the Muʻtazilite theory of *Taklīf*, see ʻUthmān, ʻAbd al-Karīm (1971), *Naẓariyyat al-taklīf: ārā' al-qāḍī ʻAbd al-Jabbār al-kalāmiyya*, Beirut: Mu'assasat al-Risāla.
115 ʻAbd al-Jabbār, al-Qāḍī Abū al-Ḥasan (1380/1960–1389/1969), vol. XIII, pp. 298, 316; Heemskerk, Margaretha T. (1995), p. 135.
116 ʻAbd al-Jabbār, al-Qāḍī Abū al-Ḥasan (1380/1960–1389/1969), vol. XIII, p. 345, 396; Heemskerk, Margaretha T. (1995), p. 136.
117 See ʻAbd al-Jabbār, al-Qāḍī Abū al-Ḥasan (1380/1960–1389/1969), vol. XIII, p. 362; Heemskerk, Margaretha T. (1995), p. 144.
118 See ʻAbd al-Jabbār, al-Qāḍī Abū al-Ḥasan (1380/1960–1389/1969), vol. XIII, p. 314, 331; Heemskerk, Margaretha T. (1995), p. 133.
119 See ʻAbd al-Jabbār, al-Qāḍī Abū al-Ḥasan (1380/1960–1389/1969), vol. XIII, p. 489, 522, 558; Heemskerk, Margaretha T. (1995), p. 174.
120 See ʻAbd al-Jabbār, al-Qāḍī Abū al-Ḥasan (1380/1960–1389/1969), vol. XIII, pp. 490–491; Mānkdīm, Aḥmad b. al-Ḥusayn b. Abū Hāshim al-Ḥusaynī Shashdīw (1965), *Kitāb sharḥ al-uṣūl al-khamsa li qāḍī al-quḍāt ʻAbd al-Jabbār Ibn Aḥmad al-Hamadhānī al-Asadābādī*, ed. ʻAbd al-Karīm ʻUthmān, Cairo: Maktabat Wahba, p. 501 Heemskerk, Margaretha T. (1995), pp. 174, 175–176.
121 ʻAbd al-Jabbār, al-Qāḍī Abū al-Ḥasan (1380/1960–1389/1969), vol. XIII, pp. 484, 492 & 493; Heemskerk, Margaretha T. (1995), p. 167, 168, 182.
122 ʻAbd al-Jabbār, al-Qāḍī Abū al-Ḥasan (1380/1960–1389/1969), vol. XIII, p. 454; Heemskerk, Margaretha T. (1995), p. 182.
123 ʻAbd al-Jabbār, al-Qāḍī Abū al-Ḥasan (1380/1960–1389/1969), vol. XIII, p. 472; Heemskerk, Margaretha T. (1995), p. 183.
124 ʻAbd al-Jabbār, al-Qāḍī Abū al-Ḥasan (1380/1960–1389/1969), vol. XIII, p. 472; Heemskerk, Margaretha T. (1995), p. 183.
125 ʻAbd al-Jabbār, al-Qāḍī Abū al-Ḥasan (1380/1960–1389/1969), vol. XIII, p. 445; Heemskerk, Margaretha T. (1995), p. 189.
126 ʻAbd al-Jabbār, al-Qāḍī Abū al-Ḥasan (1380/1960–1389/1969), vol. XIII, pp. 530, 482; Heemskerk, Margaretha T. (1995), p. 183.
127 ʻAbd al-Jabbār, al-Qāḍī Abū al-Ḥasan (1380/1960–1389/1969), vol. XIII, p. 540; Heemskerk, Margaretha T. (1995), p. 184. This suggestion was rejected by ʻAbd al-Jabbār on the ground that giving compensation as a donation to the person wronged is as if a donation were given to the wrongdoer and then transferred to the person

wronged. It is, ‘Abd al-Jabbār declares, unthinkable that God would make donations to wrongdoers. For further details on this point, see ‘Abd al-Jabbār, al-Qāḍī Abū al-Ḥasan (1380/1389–1960/1969), vol. XIII, pp. 543–544.

128 It is clear that this solution conflicts with the Mu‘tazilite rule that someone who commands someone else to inflict pain on a third person must compensate for this pain himself. See ‘Abd al-Jabbār, al-Qāḍī Abū al-Ḥasan (1380–1960/1389–1969), vol. XIII, pp. 492–493; Heemskerk, Margaretha T. (1995), pp. 167, 182, 185.

129 For further details, see ‘Abd al-Jabbār, al-Qāḍī Abū al-Ḥasan (1380/1960–1389/1969), vol. XIII, pp. 449, 543, 472; Heemskerk, Margaretha T. (1995), p. 184.

130 ‘Abd al-Jabbār, al-Qāḍī Abū al-Ḥasan (1380–1960–1389/1969), vol. XIII, pp. 492–493; Heemskerk, Margaretha T. (1995), p. 167.

131 See ‘Abd al-Jabbār, al-Qāḍī Abū al-Ḥasan (1380/1960–1389/1969), vol. XIII, p. 493.

132 See ibid., vol. XIII, p. 490; Heemskerk, Margaretha T. (1995), p. 167.

133 See Heemskerk, Margaretha T. (1995), p. 137.

134 See ‘Abd al-Jabbār, al-Qāḍī Abū al-Ḥasan (1380/1389–1960/1969), vol. XIII, p. 369; Mānkdīm, Aḥmad b. al-Ḥusayn b. Abū Hāshim al-Ḥusaynī Shashdīw (1965), pp. 485–486; Heemskerk, Margaretha T. (1995), p. 167.

135 ‘Abd al-Jabbār, al-Qāḍī Abū al-Ḥasan (1380/1389–1960/1969), vol. XIII, p. 369.

136 ‘Abd al-Jabbār, al-Qāḍī Abū al-Ḥasan (1380/1389–1960/1969), vol. XIII, pp. 454–455; Heemskerk, Margaretha T. (1995), p. 137.

137 Ījī, ‘Aḍud al-Dīn ‘Abd al-Raḥmān b. Aḥmad al- (1997), vol. 3, p. 290; ‘Abd al-Jabbār, al-Qāḍī Abū al-Ḥasan (1380–1389/1960–1969), vol. XIII, p. 322; Mānkdīm, Aḥmad b. al-Husayn b. Abū Hāshim al-Ḥusaynī Shashdīw (1965), p. 492; Heemskerk, Margaretha T. (1995), pp. 137–138.

138 Heemskerk, Margaretha T. (1995), pp. 138, 166.

139 See ‘Abd al-Jabbār, al-Qāḍī Abū al-Ḥasan (1380/1389–1960/1969), vol. XIII, pp. 369, 417; Heemskerk, Margaretha T. (1995), pp. 161, 166–167. Cf. Ibn al-Qayyim (1348/1929), *Mukhtaṣar al-ṣawā‘iq al-mursala ‘ala al-Jahmiyya wa al-Mu‘aṭṭila*, ed. Muḥammad Ḥāmid al-Fiqī, Mecca: Al-Maṭba‘a al-Salafiyya, vol. 1, p. 324; Ghazālī, Abū Ḥāmid al- (1985), vol. 1, p. 204.

140 He is Abū ‘Alī Muḥammad b. ‘Abd al-Wahhāb al-Jubbā’ī. On him, see Ibn al-‘Imād (n.d.), *Shadharāt al-dhahab fī tārīkh man dhahab*, Beirut: Dār al-Kutub al-‘Ilmiyya, vol. 2, p. 97.

141 This opinion has been articulated by Abū ‘Alī al-Jubbā’ī. See ‘Abd al-Jabbār, al-Qāḍī Abū al-Ḥasan (1380–1389/1960–1969), vol. XIII, p. 431; Heemskerk, Margaretha T. (1995), p. 160.

142 ‘Abd al-Jabbār, al-Qāḍī Abū al-Ḥasan (1380/1960–1389/1969), vol. XV, pp. 300–303; Heemskerk, Margaretha T. (1995), p. 160.

143 ‘Abd al-Jabbār, al-Qāḍī Abū al-Ḥasan (1380/1960–1389/1969), vol. XIII, pp. 431, 104–105.

144 Heemskerk, Margaretha T. (1995), p. 160.

145 He is Abū Hāshim ‘Abd al-Salām ibn Abī ‘Alī al-Jubbā’ī. On him, see Dhahabī, Muḥammad b. Aḥmad b. ‘Uthmān al- (1413/1992), vol. 15, pp. 63–64.

146 ‘Abd al-Jabbār, al-Qāḍī Abū al-Ḥasan (1380/1960–1389/1969), vol. XIII, pp. 379, 381; Heemskerk, Margaretha T. (1995), p. 159.

147 The most well-known Mu‘tazilī theologians who accepted the doctrine of metempsychosis is Aḥmad b. Khābiṭ (according to other readings Aḥmad ibn Ḥā’iṭ; on the different readings of Aḥmad’s father, see Baghdādī, Abū Manṣūr ‘Abd al-Qāhir al- (1920), p. 260 and his followers (al-Khābiṭiyya or al-Ḥā’iṭiyya). See Ījī, ‘Aḍud al-Dīn ‘Abd al-Raḥmān b. Aḥmad al- (1997), vol. 3, pp. 666–667; Baghdādī, Abū Manṣūr ‘Abd al-Qāhir al- (1920), p. 93. Also among the Mu‘tazilīs who advocated this doctrine are al-Faḍl al-Ḥadathī and his followers al-Ḥadathiyya, Aḥmad ibn Ayyūb ibn Yanūsh

and Muḥammad ibn Aḥmad al-Qaḥṭabī: see Baghdādī, Abū Manṣūr ʻAbd al-Qāhir al- (1977), p. 255. See also Ibn Yūsuf, Marʻī (1410/1989), *Rafʻ al-shubha wa al-gharar ʻamman yaḥtajj ʻala fi ʻl al-ma ʻāṣī bi al-qadar*, ed. Asʻad Muḥammad al-Maghribī, 1st edn, Mecca: Dār Ḥirā', vol. 1, p. 58.

148 ʻAbd al-Jabbār, al-Qāḍī Abū al-Ḥasan (1380/1960–1389/1969), vol. XIII, pp. 140, 105, 431–432; Heemskerk, Margaretha T. (1995), p. 160.

149 ʻAbd al-Jabbār, al-Qāḍī Abū al-Ḥasan (1380/1960–1389/1969), vol. XIII, pp. 415–416; Heemskerk, Margaretha T. (1995), p. 160.

150 ʻAbd al-Jabbār, al-Qāḍī Abū al-Ḥasan (1380/1960–1389/1969), vol. XIII, pp. 417–418; Heemskerk, Margaretha T. (1995), p. 160.

151 ʻAbd al-Jabbār, al-Qāḍī Abū al-Ḥasan (1380/1960–1389/1969), vol. XIII, p. 407; Heemskerk, Margaretha T. (1995), p. 160.

152 ʻAbd al-Jabbār, al-Qāḍī Abū al-Ḥasan (1380/1960–1389/1969), vol. XIII, p. 417; Heemskerk, Margaretha T. (1995), p. 161.

153 Ashʻarī, Abū al-Ḥasan ʻAlī b. Ismāʻīl al- (n.d.), p. 252.

154 It is difficult to find an adequate translation for this term. Abrahamov held that translating *lutf* as 'Divine Assistance' is preferable to 'Grace'. See Abrahamov, Binyamin (1993), 'ʻAbd al-Jabbār's Theory of Divine Assistance (*lutf*)', in: *Jerusalem Studies in Arabic and Islam*, vol. 16, p. 43, note 16.

155 ʻAbd al-Jabbār, al-Qāḍī Abū al-Ḥasan (1380/1960–1389/1969), vol. XIII, pp. 293; Heemskerk, Margaretha T. (1995), p. 152.

156 ʻAbd al-Jabbār, al-Qāḍī Abū al-Ḥasan (1380/1960–1389/1969), vol. XIII, p. 420; Heemskerk, Margaretha T. (1995), p. 154.

157 ʻAbd al-Jabbār, al-Qāḍī Abū al-Ḥasan (1380/1960–1389/1969), vol. VI/1, p. 61; Heemskerk, Margaretha T. (1995), p. 154.

158 ʻAbd al-Jabbār, al-Qāḍī Abū al-Ḥasan (1380/1960–1389/1969), vol. XI, pp. 292–293; Heemskerk, Margaretha T. (1995), p. 154.

159 ʻAbd al-Jabbār, al-Qāḍī Abū al-Ḥasan (1380/1960–1389/1969), vol. XV, p. 22, vol. XI, p. 292; Heemskerk, Margaretha T. (1995), pp. 154, 156.

160 ʻAbd al-Jabbār, al-Qāḍī Abū al-Ḥasan (1380/1960–1389/1969), vol. XIII, p. 390; Heemskerk, Margaretha T. (1995), p. 164.

161 Mānkdīm, Aḥmad b. al-Ḥusayn b. Abū Ḥāshim al-Ḥusaynī Shashdīw (1965), pp. 14–17; Heemskerk, Margaretha T. (1995), p. 165.

162 Heemskerk, Margaretha T. (1995), p. 159.

163 For the Shīʻī opinions on this concept, see Ḥillī, Ḥasan b. Yūsuf b. ʻAlī b. al-Muṭahhar al- (1958), pp. 52–53; Mutahhari, Murtada (2002), pp. 80–83.

164 ʻAbd al-Jabbār, al-Qāḍī Abū al-Ḥasan (1380–1389/1960–1969), vol. XIII, pp. 492–493; Heemskerk, Margaretha T. (1995), pp. 167, 182.

165 See ʻAbd al-Jabbār, al-Qāḍī Abū al-Ḥasan (1380/1960–1389/1969), vol. XIII, pp. 390–391; Heemskerk, Margaretha T. (1995), pp. 164–165.

166 He is Abū al-Hudhayl Muḥammad b. al-Hudhayl al-ʻAllāf; on him, see Dhahabī, Muḥammad b. Aḥmad b. ʻUthmān al- (1413/1992), vol. 10, pp. 542–543.

167 He is Abū ʻAlī Muḥammad b. ʻAbd al-Wahhāb al-Jubbā'ī; on him, see Ibn al-ʻImād (n.d.), vol. 2, p. 97.

168 Ījī, ʻAḍud al-Dīn ʻAbd al-Raḥmān b. Aḥmad al- (1997), vol. 3, p. 289.

169 Ibid., vol. 3, p. 289.

170 See ʻAbd al-Jabbār, al-Qāḍī Abū al-Ḥasan (1380/1960–1389/1969), vol. XIII, pp. 520–521; Heemskerk, Margaretha T. (1995), p. 186.

171 ʻAbd al-Jabbār, al-Qāḍī Abū al-Ḥasan (1380/1960–1389/1969), vol. XIII, p. 520; Heemskerk, Margaretha T. (1995), p. 186.

172 ʻAbd al-Jabbār, al-Qāḍī Abū al-Ḥasan (1380/1960–1389/1969), vol. XIII, pp. 526–527; Heemskerk, Margaretha T. (1995), p. 186.

173 See ʻAbd al-Jabbār, al-Qāḍī Abū al-Ḥasan (1380/1960–1389/1969), vol. XIII, pp. 532–533; Heemskerk, Margaretha T. (1995), pp. 187–188.

174 ‘Abd al-Jabbār, al-Qāḍī Abū al-Ḥasan (1380/1960–1389/1969), vol. XIII, p. 545; Heemskerk, Margaretha T. (1995), p. 189.

175 ‘Abd al-Jabbār, al-Qāḍī Abū al-Ḥasan (1380/1960–1389/1969), vol. XIII, p. 524; Heemskerk, Margaretha T. (1995), pp. 191–192. In this respect, some Mu‘tazilites negated the possibility that people would receive any compensation in Hell. That is because in Hell, the pleasures ensuing from receiving compensation and the pains proceeding from the fire of Hell are incompatible. See Ījī, ‘Aḍud al-Dīn ‘Abd al-Raḥmān b. Aḥmad al- (1997), vol. 3, p. 288.

176 ‘Abd al-Jabbār, al-Qāḍī Abū al-Ḥasan (1380/1960–1389/1969), vol. XIII, pp. 486, 523; Heemskerk, Margaretha T. (1995), p. 192.

177 Ormsby, Eric L. (1984), p. 27.

178 See Shahrastānī, Muḥammad b. ‘Abd al-Karīm al- (1416/1996), *Al-Milal wa al-niḥal*, ed. Amīr ‘Alī Mihannā and ‘Alī Ḥasan Fa‘ūd, 5th edn, Beirut: Dār al-Ma‘rifa, vol. 1, pp. 74–77; Shahrastānī, Muḥammad b. ‘Abd al-Karīm al- (1984), *Muslim Sects and Divisions: The Section on Muslim Sects in Kitāb al-Milal wa 'l-Niḥal*, trans. A.K. Kazi and J.G. Flynn, London, Boston, Melbourne and Henley: Kegan Paul International, pp. 53–56.

179 Shahrastānī, Muḥammad b. ‘Abd al-Karīm al- (1416/1996), vol. 1, p. 75.

180 Baghdādī, Abū Manṣūr ‘Abd al-Qāhir al- (1920), pp. 95–96.

181 Baghdādī, Abū Manṣūr ‘Abd al-Qāhir al- (1977), p. 257. It is to be noted that this contention advocated by *aṣḥāb al-tanāsukh* is forcefully criticized and refuted by the other Mu‘tazilī theologians. See ‘Abd al-Jabbār, al-Qāḍī Abū al-Ḥasan (1380/1960–1389/1969), vol. XIII, pp. 379, 381; Heemskerk, Margaretha T. (1995), p. 159.

182 Ormsby, Eric L. (1984), p. 245.

183 Ibid., Ess, Josef van (1971), p. 98.

184 ‘Abd al-Jabbār, al-Qāḍī Abū al-Ḥasan (1380/1960–1389/1969), vol. XIII, pp. 382–383; Heemskerk, Margaretha T. (1995), p. 162. Some of the Mu‘tazilites even claimed that children and animals do not feel pain. See Ījī, ‘Aḍud al-Dīn ‘Abd al-Raḥmān b. Aḥmad al- (1997), vol. 3, p. 290.

185 ‘Abd al-Jabbār, al-Qāḍī Abū al-Ḥasan (1380/1960–1389/1969), vol. XIII, p. 382; Heemskerk, Margaretha T. (1995), p. 162.

186 ‘Abd al-Jabbār, al-Qāḍī Abū al-Ḥasan (1380/1960–1389/1969), vol. XIII, p. 385; Heemskerk, Margaretha T. (1995), p. 162.

187 On him, see Dhahabī, Muḥammad b. Aḥmad b. ‘Uthmān al- (1413/1992), vol. 10, pp. 541–542; Ess, Josef van (2003), ‘Naẓẓām, Abū Isḥāq Ibrāhīm’, in: *EI*, vol. VII, p. 1057, vol. VIII, p. 1.

188 Ormsby, Eric L. (1984), p. 245; Ess, Josef van (1971), p. 98.

189 Ash‘arī, Abū al-Ḥasan ‘Alī b. Ismā‘īl al- (n.d.), p. 253; Ormsby, Eric L. (1984), p. 244

190 Heemskerk, Margaretha T. (1995), pp. 162.

191 ‘Abd al-Jabbār, al-Qāḍī Abū al-Ḥasan (1380/1960–1389/1969), vol. XIII, p. 486; Heemskerk, Margaretha T. (1995), pp. 193, 195. Some Mu‘tazilite theologians also stated that animals can be compensated in life, on the Day of Resurrection or in Paradise. See Ash‘arī, Abū al-Ḥasan ‘Alī b. Ismā‘īl al- (n.d.), p. 254.

192 Māturīdī, Abū Manṣūr al- (n.d.), *Kitāb al-tawḥīd*, ed. Fatḥalla Khulayf, Alexandria: Dār al-Jāmi‘āt al-Miṣriyya pp. 135–136; Ibn Taymiyya (n.d.), *Kutub wa rasā'il wa fatāwā Ibn Taymiyya fī al-‘aqīda*, ed. ‘Abd al-Raḥmān Muḥammad Qāsim al-Najdī, Maktabat Ibn Taymiyya, vol. 8, p. 89.

193 On him, see Madelung, Wilfred (2003a), ‘Al-Māturīdī’, in: *EI*, vol. VI, pp. 846–847.

194 On him, see Bazzār, Abū Hafṣ ‘Umar b. ‘Alī b. Mūsā al- (1400/1979), *Al-A‘lām al-‘aliyya fī manāqib Ibn Taymiyya*, ed. Zuhayr al-Shāwīsh, 3rd edn, Beirut: Al-Maktab al-Islāmī; Laoust, H. (2003a), ‘Ibn Taymiyya’, in: *EI*, vol. III, pp. 951–955.

195 Ibn Taymiyya (n.d.), vol. 8, pp. 81–158.

196 Hoover, Jon (2002).

197 Hoover, Jon (2007), *Ibn Taymiyya's Theodicy of Perpetual Optimism*, Leiden: Brill.
198 Ibn al-Qayyim (1398/1977), *Shifā' al-'alīl fī masā'il al-qaḍā' wa al-qadar wa al-ḥikma wa al-ta'līl*, ed. Muḥammad Badr al-Dīn Abū Firās al-Na'sānī al-Ḥalabī, Beirut: Dār al-Fikr.
199 Ibn 'Abd al-Salām, al-'Izz (1992), *Al-Fitan wa al-balāya wa al- miḥan wa al-razāyā*, ed. Iyād Khālid al-Ṭabbā', 1st edn, Damascus and Beirut: Dār al-Fikr/Dār al-Fikr al-Mu'āṣir; Qāsimī, Jamāl al-Dīn al- (1424/2003), *Tafsīr al-Qāsimī al-musammā maḥāsin al-ta'wīl*, Cairo: Dār al-Ḥadīth, pp. 490–494.
200 See Ibn 'Abd al-Salām, al-'Izz (n.d.), *Qawā'id al-aḥkām fī maṣāliḥ al-anām*, Beirut: Dār al-Kutub al-'Ilmiyya, pp. 73–77.
201 Ibn al-Wazīr, Muḥammad b. Ibrāhīm (1987), vol. 1, pp. 108–204.
202 Ibid., vol. 1, p. 188.
203 Jackson, Sherman A. (1996), *Islamic Law and the State: The Constitutional Jurisprudence of Shihāb al-Dīn al-Qarāfī*, Leiden: Brill, Leiden, pp. 32–33.
204 Julaynid, Muhammad al-Sayyid al- (1981), pp. 198–220.
205 Hoover, Jon (2002), pp. 117–118.
206 Frank, Richard (1994), p. 16.
207 Ghazālī, Abū Ḥāmid al- (1327/1909), 'Al-Ḥikma fī makhlūqāt Allāh 'azz wa jall', in: Ghazālī, Abū Ḥāmid al- (1327/1909), *Al-Rasā'il al-farā'id min taṣānīf al-imām al-Ghazālī*, Cairo: Maktabat al-Jundī, pp. 15–96.
208 See Sharabāṣī, Aḥmad al- (1375/1956), vol. 1, pp. 260–285.
209 Madkhalī, Muḥammad Rabī' Hadī al- (1409/1988), *Al-Ḥikma wa al-ta'līl fī af'āl Allāh ta'ālā*, Damanhūr, Egypt: Maktabat Līna li al-Nashr wa al-Twazī'.
210 Zamīlī, Zuhayr Muḥammad al- (1409/1988), *Limādhā ja'al Allāh al-amrāḍ*, 1st edn, Amman: Dār al-Furqān.
211 Qaraḍāwī, Yūsuf al- (1421/2000), *Al-Īmān bi al-qadar*, 1st edn, Cairo: Maktabat Wahba, pp. 82–87.
212 Būṭī, Muḥammed Sa'īd Ramaḍān al- (2001), pp. 188–206.
213 See Sha'rawi, Mohammad M. al- (1995), *Good and Evil*, London: Dar al-Taqwa, esp. pp. 58–59.
214 For some of those who expressed such statements, see Watt, W. Montgomery (1979), 'Suffering in Sunnite Islam', in: *SI*, vol. 50, p. 5; Ormsby, Eric L. (1984), p. 54.
215 Ibn al-Qayyim (1398/1977), pp. 3–4.
216 Qur'ān 26:9, 68, 104, 122, 140, 159, 175, 191, 30:5, 32:6, 44:42.
217 See Qur'ān 2:129, 209, 220, 228, 240, 260, 3:6, 18, 62, 126; 4:56, 158, 165; 5:38, 118, 8:49, 63, 67; 9:40, 71, 14:4, 16:60, 27:9, 29:26, 42, 30:27, 31:9, 27, 34:27, 35:2, 39:1, 40:8, 42:3, 45:37, 46:2, 57:1, 59:1, 24, 60:5, 61:1, 62:1, 3; 64:18.
218 See Ibn Taymiyya (1404/1983), *Daqā'iq al-tafsīr al-jāmi' li tafsīr Ibn Taymiyya*, ed. Muḥammad al-Sayyid al-Julaynid, 2nd edn, Damascus: Mu'assasat 'Ulūm al-Qur'ān, vol. 2, p. 54.
219 See Wahhāb, Sulaymān b. 'Abd al- (n.d.), *Taysīr al-'Azīz al-Ḥamīd fī sharḥ kitāb al-tawḥīd*, Riyadh: Maktabat al-Riyāḍ al-Ḥadītha.
220 For an overview of the arguments advanced against both Mu'tazilites and Ash'arites concerning divine justice, see Hoover, Jon (2002), pp. 270–284. For wise purposiveness, see ibid., pp. 86–113.
221 Ibn Taymiyya (1389/1969), 'Qā'ida fī ma'nā kawn al-Rabb 'ādil wa fī tanazzuhih 'an al-ẓulm', in: *Jāmi' al-rasā'il*, ed. Muḥammad Rashād Rafīq Sālim, Cairo: Maṭba'at al-Madanī, vol. 1, p. 123. Cf. Hoover, Jon (2002), p. 282.
222 Ibn Taymiyya (1406/1985), 3, p. 195; Hoover, Jon (2002), p. 109.
223 Hoover, Jon (2002), p. 110.
224 Ibn al-Qayyim (1398/1977), vol. 1, pp. 51–52; Qaraḍāwī, Yūsuf al- (1421/2000), pp. 35–36.
225 See Ibn al-Qayyim (1398/1977), vol. 1, pp. 51–52; Qaraḍāwī, Yūsuf al- (1421/2000), pp. 47–48.

226 Qurṭubī, Abū ʻAbd Allāh Muḥammad b. Aḥmad al- (1372/1952), *Al-Jāmiʻ li aḥkām al-Qur'ān*, ed. Aḥmad ʻAbd al-ʻAlīm al-Bardūnī, 2nd edn, Cairo: Dār al-Shaʻb, vol. 7, p. 315.

227 Ibn al-Wazīr, Muḥammad b. Ibrāhīm (1987), vol. 1, pp. 211–215.

228 Ibn al-Qayyim (1398/1977), vol. 1, pp. 78, 184, 190–192, 239; Ormsby, Eric L. (1984), p. 245.

229 Ibn al-Wazīr, Muḥammad b. Ibrāhīm (1987), vol. 1, pp. 211; Ibn al-Qayyim (1348/1929), vol. 2, p. 430.

230 See Ibn al-Qayyim (1398/1977), vol. 1, p. 187.

231 Ghazālī, Abū Ḥāmid al- (1407/1987), p. 65.

232 Ghazālī, Abū Ḥāmid al- (1992), pp. 55–57.

233 Diyāb, Adīb al-Nāyif (2000), p. 34

234 Ridgeon, Lloyd (1998), 'A Sufi Perspective of Evil', in: *Iran: Journal of the British Institute of Persian Studies*, vol. XXXVI, p. 114.

235 Ansari, M. Abdul Haq (2003), 'Mawdūdi's Contribution to Theology', in: *MS*, vol. 93, pp. 521–531, pp. 529, 530.

236 On him, see Weismann, Itzchak (1997), 'Saʻid Hawwa and Islamic Revivalism in Baʻthist Syria', in: *SI*, vol. 85, no. 1, pp. 131–154.

237 Ḥawwā, Saʻīd (1424/2004), *Allāh jall jalāluh*, 4th edn, Cairo: Dār al-Salām, pp. 89–90.

238 Qaraḍāwī, Yūsuf al- (1421/2000), p. 82. In a personal discussion with him about that opinion, al-Qaraḍāwī told me that he did not mean that God's actions are unjustifiable. However, he added that maintaining that all God's actions can be justified and their wise purposes understood could be misconceived as conducive to endorsing the Muʻtazilī principle that God's actions are to be evaluated by the same criterion as human actions. This discussion took place in January 2003 in Dublin during the proceedings of 10th session of the European Council for Fatwa and Research.

239 Ibn al-Wazīr, Muḥammad b. Ibrāhīm (1987), vol. 1, p. 210.

240 Ibn al-Qayyim (1398/1977), vol. 1, p. 302.

241 Ibn al-Qayyim (1973), *Iʻlām al-muwaqqiʻīn ʻan Rabb al-ʻĀlamīn*, ed. Ṭāhā ʻAbd al-Ra'ūf Saʻd, Beirut: Dār al-Jīl, vol. 2, p. 334–335. It is, however, believed that the straightforward reason (ʻ*aql ṣarīḥ*) can never disagree with the authentic text of revelation (*naṣṣ ṣarīḥ*). *Imam* Ibn Taymiyya wrote a famous book on this topic: see Ibn Taymiyya (1409/1988), *Dar' taʻāruḍ al-ʻaql wa al-naql*, ed. Muḥammad al-Sayyid al-Julaynid and ʻAbd al-Ṣabūr Shahīn, 1st edn, Cairo: Markaz al-Ahrām li al-Tarjama wa al-Nashr.

242 Rispler-Chaim, Vardit (2007), *Disability in Islamic Law*, Dordrecht, The Netherlands: Springer, p. 7.

243 See Ibn Taymiyya (n.d.), vol. 1, p. 42 and Ibn al-Qayyim (1348/1929), vol. 1, pp. 324, 327, 37.

244 Sharabāṣī, Aḥmad al- (1375/1956), vol. 1, p. 264.

245 Būṭī, Muḥammad Saʻīd Ramaḍān, al- (2001), pp. 199–204.

246 Zaydān, ʻAbd al-Karīm (1414/1994), *Al-Sunan al-ilāhiyya fī al-umam wa al-jamāʻāt wa al-afrād fī al-sharīʻa al-islāmiyya*, 3rd edn, Beirut: Mu'assasat al-Risāla, p. 212.

247 Ṭabarī, Muḥammad b. Jarīr al- (1405/1984), *Jāmiʻ al-bayān fī ta'wīl al-Qur'ān: tafsīr al-Tabarī*, Beirut: Dār al-Fikr, vol. 25, p. 32.

248 Bayḍāwī, ʻAbd Allāh b. ʻUmar al- (1416/1996), *Ṭawāliʻ al-anwār bi sharḥ al-mar'ashī*, Cairo, vol. 5, p. 131.

249 Ṭabarī, Muḥammad b. Jarīr al- (1405/1984), vol. 5, p. 175.

250 Qurṭubī, Abū ʻAbd Allāh Muḥammad b. Aḥmad al- (1372/1952), vol. 5, p. 285.

251 Ṭabarī, Muḥammad b. Jarīr al- (1405/1984), vol. 5, p. 175.

252 Qurṭubī, Abū ʻAbd Allāh Muḥammad b. Aḥmad al- (1372/1952), vol. 5, p. 285.

253 Ibid., p. 397.

254 On him, see Dhahabī, Muḥammad b. Aḥmad b. 'Uthmān al- (1413/1992), vol. 2, pp. 508–512.
255 Suyūṭī, Jalāl al-Dīn al- (1993), *Al-Durr al-manthūr fī al-tafsīr bi al-ma'thūr*, Beirut: Dār al-Fikr, vol. 7, p. 355.
256 On him, see Hinds, M. (2003), 'Mu'āwiya b. Abī Sufyān', in: *EI*, vol. VII, pp. 263–268.
257 Aṣbahānī, Abū Nu'aym al- (1405/1984), vol. 9, p. 154.
258 Ibn al-'Imād (n.d.), vol. 1, p. 86.
259 Qurṭubī, Abū 'Abd Allāh Muḥammad b. Aḥmad al- (1372/1952), vol. 16, p. 31.
260 Ghazālī, Abū Ḥāmid, al- (n.d.), vol. 2, p. 387.
261 'Asqalānī, Ibn Ḥajar al- (1412/1992), *Al-Iṣāba fī tamyīz al-ṣaḥāba*, ed. 'Alī Muḥammad al-Bījāwī, 1st edn, Beirut: Dār al-Jīl, vol. 6, p. 649.
262 Ibid., vol. 1, p. 291.
263 Ibn al-Jawzī (n.d.), *Talqīḥ fuhūm ahl al-athar fī 'uyūn al-tārīkh wa al-siyar*, Delhi, p. 310.
264 Dhahabī, Muḥammad b. Aḥmad b. 'Uthmān al- (n.d.), pp. 113, 144.
265 'Asqalānī, Ibn Ḥajar al- (1379/1959), *Fatḥ al-Bārī*, ed. Muḥammad Fu'ād 'Abd al-Bāqī and Muḥibb al-Dīn al-Khaṭīb, Beirut: Dār al-Ma'rifa, vol. 2, pp. 240–241, vol. 5, pp. 104–105.
266 Aṣbahānī, Abū Nu'aym al- (1405/1984), vol. 9, p. 154.
267 See for instance Ibn al-Jawzī (1987), pp. 21, 30, 31, 197–199, 203, 204, 290, 291, 310, 311, 390, 391, Ibn al-Qayyim (n.d.b), *Al-Jawāb al-kāfī li man sa'al 'an al-dawā' al-shāfī: al-dā' wa al-dawā'*, Beirut: Dār al-Kutub al-'Ilmiyya, pp. 39–86, 80–81.
268 *Imam* al-Bukhārī (194–256 A.H.) mentioned in his *Al-Adab al-mufrad* a number of prophetic traditions under a separate section entitled '*Bāb kaffārat al-marīḍ*' or 'Section of the Expiation of the Sick'. See Bukhārī Abū 'Abd Allāh al- (1407/1989), *Al-Adab al-mufrad*, ed. Muḥammad Fu'ād 'Abd al-Bāgī, 3rd edn, Beirut: Dār al-Bashā'ir al-Islāmiyya, vol. 1, p. 173. Imam Ḍiyā al-Dīn al-Maqdisī did the same in his *Kitāb al-amrāḍ wa al-kaffarāt wa al-ṭibb wa al-ruqyāt*. See Maqdisī, Abū 'Abd Allāh Ḍiyā' al-Dīn al- (1420/1999), *Kitāb amrāḍ al-kaffarāt wa al-ṭibb wa al-ruqyāt*, 2nd edn, Cairo: Dār Ibn 'Affān, pp. 40–41.
269 Muslim, Abū al-Ḥusayn b. al-Ḥajjāj (n.d.), *Ṣaḥīḥ Muslim*, ed. Muḥammad Fu'ād 'Abd al-Bāqī, Beirut: Dār Iḥyā' al-Turāth al-'Arabī, ḥadīth no. 2572, vol. 4, p. 1992.
270 Ibn Abī Shayba (1409/1988), *Muṣannaf Ibn Abī Shayba*, ed. Kamāl Yūsuf al-Ḥūt, 1st edn, Riyadh: Maktabat al-Rushd, vol. 2, pp. 440, 442.
271 'Asqalānī, Ibn Ḥajar al- (1379/1959), vol. 10, p. 112.
272 Ibn al-Qayyim (1407/1986), *Zād al-ma'ād fī Hady' khayr al-'ibād*, ed. Shu'ayb al-Arna'ūṭ and 'Abd al-Qādir al-Arna'ūṭ, 14th edn, Beirut/Kuwait: Mu'assasat al-Risāla/Maktabat al-Manār al-Islāmiyya, vol. 4, p. 192.
273 Haythamī, Abū al-Ḥasan 'Alī b. Abī Bakr al- (1407/1986), *Majma' al-zawā'id wa manba' al-fawā'id*, Cairo and Beirut: Dār al-Rayyān li al-Turāth-Dār al-Kitāb al-'Arabī, vol. 7, pp. 104–105; ḥadīth no. 1694, vol. 8, pp. 161–163.
274 Zamīlī, Zuhayr Muḥammad al- (1409/1988), p. 56.
275 See for instance Ibn Abī Usāma, al-Ḥārith (1412/1992), *Musnad al-Ḥārith*, ed. Ḥusayn Aḥmad Ṣāliḥ al-Bakrī, 1st edn, Al-Madīna al-Munawwara: Markaz Khidmat al-Sunna wa al-Sīra al-Nabawiyya, vol. 1, p. 250.
276 Maqdisī, Abū 'Abd Allāh Ḍiyā' al-Dīn al- (1420/1999), ḥadīth no. 26, pp. 63–64.
277 For just examples, see Qurṭubī, Abū 'Abd Allāh Muḥammad b. Aḥmad al- (1372/1952), vol. 3, p. 430, vol. 7, pp. 156–158.
278 Ibid, vol. 7, p. 157.
279 Ibn al-Qayyim (1395/1975), *Al-Rūḥ*, Beirut: Dār al-Kutub al-'Ilmiyya, vol. 1, p. 88.
280 See Ibn Yūsuf, Mar'ī (1410/1989), vol. 1, p. 57.
281 On him, see Bell, Joseph Norment (1979), *Love Theory in Later Ḥanbalite Islam*, New York: State University of New York Press, pp. 185–186.

282 Ibn Yūsuf, Mar'ī (1410/1989), p. 57.
283 Rispler-Chaim, Vardit (2007), p. 11, quoting from Hijazi, Qudsiyah (n.d.), *Islam va aftal 'aqab uftadeh*, Iran: Markaz Tahqiqat wa Intisharat Huquqi Qudsi, p. 422.
284 Rispler-Chaim, Vardit (2007), p. 10, quoting from Hijazi, Qudsiyah (n.d.), pp. 398, 403.
285 Sharabāṣī, Aḥmad al- (1375/1956), vol. 1, p. 265.
286 Ibid., p. 237.
287 See Zaydān, 'Abd al-Karīm (1414/1994), pp. 212–213.
288 Tirmidhī, Abū 'Īsā al- (n.d.), *Sunan al-Tirmidhī*, ed. Aḥmad Muḥammad Shākir *et al.*, Beirut: Dār Iḥyā' al-Turāth al-'Arabī, ḥadīth no. 2396, vol. 4, p. 601.
289 Muslim, Abū al-Ḥusayn b. al-Ḥajjāj (n.d.), ḥadīth no. 2572, vol. 4, p. 1992; Abū Zakariyya Yaḥyā b. Sharaf al- (1392/1972) *Sharḥ al-Nawawī 'alā ṣaḥīḥ Muslim*, 2nd edn, Beirut: Dār Iḥyā' al-Turāth al-'Arabī, vol. 16, p. 128.
290 See Haythamī, Abū al-Ḥasan 'Alī b. Abī Bakr al- (1407/1986), vol. 2, p. 292.
291 See Maqdisī, Abū 'Abd Allāh Ḍiyā' al-Dīn al- (1420/1999), pp. 42–43.
292 Robson, J. (2003), vol. I, p. 1129.
293 Bayḍāwī, 'Abd Allāh b. 'Umar al- (1416/1996), vol. 5, p. 131.
294 Suyūṭī, Jalāl al-Dīn al- and Jalāl al-Dīn al-Maḥallī (n.d.), *Tafsīr al-Jalālayn*, 1st edn, Cairo: Dār al Ḥadīth, p. 643.
295 'Asqalānī, Ibn Ḥajar al- (1379/1959), vol. 10, p. 108.
296 On him, see Ibn al-'Imād (n.d.), vol. 1, p. 470.
297 Nawawī, Yaḥyā b. Sharaf al- (1392/1972), vol. 16, pp. 128–129.
298 'Asqalānī, Ibn Ḥajar al- (1379/1959), vol.10, p. 110.
299 Zaydān, 'Abd al-Karīm (1414/1994), p. 213.
300 According to some scholars, prophets are infallible and thus exempted from committing either major or minor sins: see Ibn Ḥazm, Abū Muḥammad 'Alī (n.d.), vol. 4, p. 136.
301 Ibn Yūsuf, Mar'ī (1410/1989), vol. 1, p. 57.
302 See, for instance, their disagreements on whether a prophet can be blind: Ṣafadī, Ṣalāḥ al-Dīn Khalīl b. Aybak al- (1329/1911), *Nakt al-himyān fī nukat al-'umyān*, ed. A. Zakī, Cairo, pp. 43–44; Sharabāṣī, Aḥmad al- (1375/1956), vol. 1, p. 193.
303 Kan'ān, Aḥmad Muḥammad (1420/2000), *Al-Mawsū'a al-ṭibbiyya al-fiqhiyya: mawsū'a jāmi'a li al-aḥkām al-fiqhiyya fī al-ṣiḥḥa wa al-Maraḍ wa al-mumārasāt al-ṭibbiyya*, 1st edn, Beirut: Dār al-Nafā'is, p. 81.
304 Qurṭubī, Abū 'Abd Allāh Muḥammad b. Aḥmad al- (1372/1952), vol. 9, p. 248.
305 Shawkānī, Muḥammad ibn 'Alī ibn Muḥammad al- (n.d.), vol. 2, p. 522.
306 'Asqalānī, Ibn Ḥajar al- (1379/1959), vol. 6, p. 421.
307 Ṭabarī, Muḥammad b. Jarīr al- (1405/1984), vol. 16, p. 159.
308 Ayoub, Mahmoud M. (1977), p. 277.
309 See Rāzī, Muḥammad b. Abī Bakr b. 'Abd al-Qādir al- (1415/1995), *Mukhtār al-ṣiḥāḥ*, ed. Maḥmūd Khāṭir, Beirut: Maktabat Lubnān Nāshirūn, vol. 1, pp. 291, 257.
310 Munāwī, 'Abd al-Ra'ūf al- (1356/1937), *Fayḍ al-qadīr sharḥ al-jāmi' al-ṣaghīr*, 1st edn, Cairo: Al-Maktaba al-Tijāriyya al-Kubrā, vol. 2, p. 459.
311 Mundhirī, Abū Muḥammad 'Abd al-'Aẓīm b. 'Abd al-Qawī al- (1417/1996), *Al-Targhīb wa al-tarhīb*, ed. Ibrāhīm Shams al-Dīn, 1st edn, Beirut: Dār al-Kutub al-'Ilmiyya, ḥadīth no. 5169, vol. 4, p. 143.
312 See Būṭī, Muḥammad Sa'īd Ramaḍān, al- (2001), pp. 193–196.
313 'Asqalānī, Aḥmad b. 'Alī b. Ḥajar al- (1379/1959), vol. 10, p. 112.
314 Ibn Kathīr (1401/1980), *Tafsīr Ibn Kathīr*, Beirut: Dār al-Fikr, vol. 2, p. 239.
315 Sharabāṣī, Aḥmad al- (1375/1956), vol. 1, pp. 261–262.
316 Zamīlī, Zuhayr Muḥammad al- (1409/1988), pp. 52–70.
317 Būṭī, Muḥammad Sa'īd Ramaḍān, al- (2001), pp. 193–196.
318 Zamīlī, Zuhayr Muḥammad al- (1409/1988), pp. 70–72.

319 See Ibn Yūsuf, Mar'ī (1410/1989), vol. 1, pp. 57–58.
320 Māturīdī, Abū Manṣūr al- (n.d.), p. xxxv.
321 Ibid., p. 17; Pessagno, J. Meric (1984), pp. 72–73.
322 See Pessagno, J. Meric (1984), pp. 73–74.
323 Ibid., p. 74.
324 Māturīdī, Abū Manṣūr al- (n.d.), p. 22; Pessagno, J. Meric (1984), pp. 74–75.
325 Māturīdī, Abū Manṣūr al- (n.d.), p. 109; Pessagno, J. Meric (1984), p. 75.
326 Pessagno, J. Meric (1984), pp. 72, 73, 80–81.
327 Qāsimī, Jamāl al-Dīn al- (1424/2003), vol. 1, p. 490.
328 Sharabāṣī, Aḥmad al- (1375/1956), vol. 1, p. 274.
329 Sha'rawi, Muḥammad M. al- (1995), p. 59.
330 Būṭī, Muḥammad Sa'īd Ramaḍān, al- (2001), pp. 190–193.
331 Zamīlī, Zuhayr Muḥammad al- (1409/1988), pp. 83–84.
332 Ibn al-Qayyim (1348/1929), p. 326.
333 Ibid.
334 Ibid., pp. 364.
335 Būṭī, Muḥammad Sa'īd Ramaḍān, al- (2001), pp. 196–199.

3 Practical theology

1 On him, see Qushayrī, 'Abd al-Karīm al- (1968), *Al-Taḥbīr fī al-Tadhkīr*, ed. Ibrāhīm Basyūnī, Cairo: Dār al-Kitāb al-'Arabī li al-Ṭibā'a wa al-Nashr, pp. 4–8; Qushayri, al- (1990), *Principles of Sufism*, trans. B.R. von Schlegell, Berkeley, Calif.: Mizan Press, pp. i–xvii, esp. iv.

2 Ḥusayn, 'Abd al-Razzāq (1420/1999), *Al-I'āqa fī al-adab al-'arabī*, 1st edn, al-Shāriqa, UAE: Manshurāt Madīnat al-Shāriqa li al-Khadamāt al-Insāniyya, p. 19. On the author, see Dhahabī, Muḥammad b. Aḥmad b. 'Uthmān al- (1413/1992), *Siyar a'lām al-nubalā'*, ed. Shu'ayb al-Arna'ūṭ and Muḥammad Nu'aym al-'Arqasūsī, 9th edn, Beirut: Mu'assasat al-Risāla, vol. 20, pp. 151–156.

3 See, for instance, Ibn al-Qayyim (1407/1986), *Zād al-ma'ād fī Hady' khayr al-'ibād*, ed. Shu'ayb al-Arna'ūṭ and 'Abd al-Qādir al-Arna'ūṭ, 14th edn, Beirut and Kuwait: Mu'assasat al-Risāla/Maktabat al-Manār al-Islāmiyya, vol. 4, pp. 188–196.

4 Manbijī, Muḥammad b. Muḥammad al- (1347/1929), *Tasliyat ahl al-maṣā'ib*, 1st edn, Cairo: Maktabat al-Khanjī.

5 See, for instance, Ibn Nāṣir al-Dīn, Muḥammad b. 'Abd Allāh (1420/1999), *Bard al-akbād 'ind faqd al-awlād*, Riyadh: Dār Ibn Khuzayma li al-Nashr wa al-Tawzī'; Suyūṭī, Jalāl al-Dīn al- (1304/1880), *Bard al-akbād 'ind faqd al-awlād*, Cairo. For a Shī'ī source on the same topic, see 'Alamī, Zayn al-Dīn Jabā'ī al- (1923), *Musakkin al-fu'ād 'ind faqd al-aḥibba wa al-awlād*, Al-Najaf.

6 Ibn Fahd (d. 954/1547), 'Al-Nukat al-ẓirāf fī al-maw'iẓa bi dhawī al-'āhāt min al-ashrāf', MS 383, Chester Beatty Library, Dublin, folio 15a; Ghaly, Mohammed (2005–2006), 'Writings on Disability in Islam: The 16th Century Polemic on Ibn Fahd's al-Nukat al-Ẓirāf', in: *ASJ*, vol. XIII, no. 2, vol. XIV, no. 1, p. 21.

7 There are two editions available: Qārī, 'Alī b. Sulṭān b. Muḥammad al-Harawī al- (1993), *Tasliyat al-a'mā 'an baliyyat al-'amā*, ed. 'Abd al-Karīm b. Ṣunaytān al-Madīna al-Munawwara: Dār al-Bukhārī li al-Nashr wa al-Tawzī'; Qārī, 'Alī b. Sulṭān b. Muḥammad al-Harawī al- (1994), *Tasliyat al-a'mā 'an baliyyat al-'amā: wa ma yata'allaq bi al-a'mā min nawādir wa aḥkām fī al-sharī'at al-islām*, ed. Mabrūk Ismā'īl Mabrūk, Cairo: Maktabat al-Qur'ān.

8 Ibn Fahd (d. 954/1547), folios 56b–61a.

9 Snir, Reuven (1999), '*Bāb al Maḥabba* (The Chapter on Love) in *Al-Risāla al-Qushayriyya*: Rhetorical and Thematic Structure', in: *Israel Oriental Studies*, vol. XIX, p. 132.

10 Ibid., p. 137.
11 Ibid., p. 136.
12 Ibn Taymiyya (1401/1981), *Al-'Ubūdiyya*, Beirut: Dār al-Kutub al-'Ilmiyya.
13 Ibn al-Qayyim (1393/1973), *Madārij al-sālikīn*, ed. Muḥammad Ḥāmid al-Fiqī, 2nd edn, Beirut: Dār al-Kitāb al-'Arabī, vol. 1, pp. 97–110, 123.
14 Lory, P. (2003), 'Shādhilliyya', in: *EI*, vol. IX, pp. 172–175.
15 See, for instance, Rājiḥī, 'Abd al-'Azīz al- (1420/199), *Sharḥ al-'ubūdiyya li shaykh al-islām Ibn Taymiyya*, Riyadh: Dār al-Faḍīla.
16 See Qushayri, al- (1990), pp. 131–139, 147–156.
17 See, for instance, Ghazālī, Abū Ḥāmid, al- (n.d.), *Iḥyā' 'ulūm al-dīn*, Beirut: Dār al-Ma'rifa, vol. 4, pp. 60–141.
18 Ibn al-Qayyim (n.d.), *'Uddat al-ṣābirīn wa dhakhīrat al-shākirīn*, ed. Zakariyya 'Alī Yūsuf, Beirut: Dār al-Kutub al-'Ilmiyya. This book was recently abridged and translated by Nasiruddin al-Khattab: see Ibn al-Qayyim (1998), *Patience and Gratitude: An Abridged Translation of 'Uddat as-Sabirin wa Dhakhirat ash-Shakirin*, trans. Nasiruddin al-Khattab, London: Ta-Ha Publishers.
19 See, for instance, Khālid, 'Amr (2002), *Al-Ṣabr wa al-dhawq*, Cairo: Arīj li al-Nashr wa al-Tawzī'.
20 Qaraḍāwī, Yūsuf al- (1410/1989), *Al-Ṣabr fī al-Qur'ān*, Cairo: Maktabat Wahba.
21 Qāsimī, Jamāl al-Dīn al- (1424/2003), *Tafsīr al-Qasimī al-musammā maḥāsin al-ta'wīl*, Cairo: Dār al-Ḥadīth, vol. 1, p. 490.
22 Qushayri, al- (1990), p. 173.
23 Ibn al-Qayyim (n.d.a), *Miftāḥ dār al-sa'āda*, Beirut: Dār al-Kutub al-'Ilmiyya, vol. 1, p. 273.
24 Būṭī, Muḥammad Sa'īd Ramaḍān, al- (2001), *Al-Insān musayyar am mukhayyar*, 2nd edn, Beirut: Dār al-Fikr al-Mu'āṣir and Damascus: Dār al-Fikr, pp. 193–196.
25 Qushayri, al- (1990), p. 170.
26 Ibid.
27 Ibn al-Jawzī (1399/1979), *Ṣifat al-ṣafwa*, ed. Maḥmūd Fakhūrī and Muḥammad Ruwās Qal'ajī, 2nd edn, Beirut: Dār al-Ma'rifa, vol. 4, p. 229.
28 He is Abū al-Ḥasan 'Alī b. Ibrāhīm b. Salama al-Qazwīnī al-Qaṭṭān. On him, see Dhahabī, Muḥammad b. Aḥmad b. 'Uthmān al- (1413/1992), vol. 15, pp. 463–466.
29 'Speaking too much' in this context could mean being over-proud with one's knowledge.
30 Dhahabī, Muḥammad b. Aḥmad b. 'Uthmān al- (1413/1992), vol. 15, p. 464.
31 See Ibn Taymiyya (n.d.), *Kutub wa rasā'il wa fatāwā Ibn Taymiyya fī al-'aqīda*, ed. 'Abd al-Raḥmān Muhammad Qāsim al-Najdī, Maktabat Ibn Taymiyya, vol. 2, p. 109.
32 On him, see Bencheneb, M. and Somogyi, J. de (2003), 'Al-Dhahabī', in: *EI*, vol. II, pp. 215–216.
33 Dhahabī, Muḥammad b. Aḥmad b. 'Uthmān al- (n.d.), pp. 113, 144.
34 Ibn Taymiyya (1401/1981), p. 12.
35 See Būṭī, Muḥammad Sa'īd Ramaḍān, al- (2001), pp. 207–215.
36 Qaraḍāwī, Yūsuf al- (1421/2000), pp. 99–101.
37 Ibn Ḥamza, Muṣṭafā (1414/1993), *Ḥuqūq al-mu'awwaqīn fī al-islām*, Casablanca: Maṭba'at al-Najāḥ al-Jadīda, p. 54.
38 Abū Jayb, Sa'dī (1402/1982), *Al-Muw'awwaq wa al-mujtama' fī al-sharī'a al-islāmiyya*, Damascus and Beirut: Dār al-Fikr al-Mu'āṣir/Dār al-Fikr, p. 33, note 4.
39 Ḥusayn, 'Abd al-Razzāq (1420/1999), p. 16–29.
40 See, for instance, Sharabāṣī, Aḥmad al- (n.d.), *Fī 'ālam al-makfūfīn*, Cairo: Maṭba'at Lajnat al-Bayān al-'Arabī, vol. 2, pp. 130–265; Jamjūm, Zuhayr (1410/1990), *Ashhar al-muw'awwaqīn fī al-'ālam*, Amman: Dār 'Ammār li al-Nashr wa al-Tawzī'; Qubaysī, Muḥammad (1996), *'Uẓamā' mashāhīr wa 'abāqira mu'awwaqūn*, Cairo: Mu'assasat al-Riḥāb al-Ḥadītha; Ḥusayn, 'Abd al-Razzāq (1420/1999), esp. pp. 169–306.

41 Wensinck, A.J. (2003), 'Ṣabr', in: *EI*, vol. VIII, p. 685.
42 Ibn al-Qayyim (1998), p. 7. For further information on the linguistic denotation of *ṣabr* in Arabic, see Wensinck, A.J. (2003).
43 Ibn al-Qayyim (1998), pp. 11, 16, 19.
44 Manbijī, Muḥammad b. Muḥammad al- (1347/1929), pp. 116–118.
45 Ibn al-Qayyim (1998), p. 26.
46 Ibid., p. 10.
47 Bukhārī, Abū 'Abd Allāh al- (1407/1987), *Ṣaḥīḥ al-Bukhārī*, ed. Muṣṭafā Dīb al-Baghā, 3rd edn, Beirut: Dār Ibn Kathīr/al-Yamāma, ḥadīth No. 1400, vol. 2, p. 534, and ḥadīth no. 6105, vol. 5, p. 2375.
48 Ibn al-Qayyim (1998), pp. 21–22.
49 Ibid., pp. 58–59.
50 Ibid., p. 18.
51 See ibid., pp. 39–42. Cf. Qaraḍāwī, Yūsuf al- (1410/1989), pp. 7–8.
52 Ibn al-Qayyim (n.d.), vol. 1, pp. 44–47.
53 Bukhārī, Abū 'Abd Allāh al- (1407/1987), ḥadīth no. 5328, vol. 5, p. 2140.
54 Ibid., vol. 5, p. 2140, *Bāb faḍl man dhahaba baṣaruh* (section on the merit of one who lost his eyesight); Ibn Abī Usāma, al-Ḥārith (1412/1992), *Musnad al-Ḥārith*, ed. Ḥusayn Aḥmad Ṣāliḥ al-Bakrī, 1st edn, Al-Madīna al-Munawwara: Markaz Khidmat al-Sunna wa al-Sīra al-Nabawiyya, vol. 1, p. 351, *Bāb fī man ibtuliya bi baṣarih* (section on one who has been afflicted with losing his eyesight).
55 Bukhārī, Abū 'Abd Allāh al- (1407/1987), ḥadīth no. 5329, vol. 5, p. 2140.
56 Qaraḍāwī, Yūsuf al- (1410/1989), p. 34.
57 Ibn al-Qayyim (1998), p. 24.
58 Ibid., p. 24.
59 Ibid.
60 Ibid., pp. 8, 23.
61 Ibn Hishām (1411/1990), *Al-Sīra al-nabawiyya*, ed. Ṭāhā 'Abd al-Ra'ūf Sa'd, 1st edn, Beirut: Dār al-Jīl, vol. 2, p. 268.
62 Ibn al-Qayyim (1998), p. 8.
63 Ibid.
64 Tirmidhī, Abū 'Īsā al- (n.d.), *Sunan al-Tirmidhī*, ed. Aḥmad Muḥammad Shākir *et al.*, Beirut: Dār Iḥyā' al-Turāth al-'Arabī, ḥadīth no. 3487, vol. 5, p. 521.
65 Muslim, Abū al-Ḥusayn b. al-Ḥajjāj (n.d.), *Ṣaḥīḥ Muslim*, ed. Muḥammad Fu'ād 'Abd al-Bāqī, Beirut: Dār Iḥyā' al-Turāth al-'Arabī, ḥadīth no. 2688.
66 On him, see Dhahabī, Muḥammad b. Aḥmad b. 'Uthmān al- (1413/1992), vol. 4, pp. 421–437.
67 Qaraḍāwī, Yūsuf al- (1416/1996), p. 189.
68 Aṣfahānī, Rāghib al- (n.d.), *Al-Mufradāt fī gharīb al-Qur'ān*, ed. Muḥammad Sayyid Kīlānī, Beirut: Dār al-Ma'rifa, vol. 1, p. 256.
69 Ibid.
70 On him, see Dhahabī, Muḥammad b. Aḥmad b. 'Uthmān al- (1413/1992), vol. 9, pp. 313–316.
71 On him, see ibid., vol. 7, pp. 387–396.
72 A city in Khurasan at that time. On this city, see Ḥamawī, Abū 'Abd Allāh Yaqūt b. 'Abd Allāh al- (n.d.), *Mu'jam al-buldān*, Beirut: Dār al-Fikr, vol. 1, pp. 479–480.
73 Ghazālī, Abū Ḥāmid, al- (n.d.), vol. 4, p. 215. Cf. Schimmel, Annemarie (1975), *Mystical Dimensions of Islam*, Chapel Hill: University of North Carolina Press, p. 125.
74 He is one of the Companions of the Prophet of Islam. On him, see Dhahabī, Muḥammad b. Aḥmad b. 'Uthmān al- (1413/1992), vol. 1, pp. 505–557.
75 Ibn al-Qayyim (1998), p. 67.
76 Ibid., pp. 67–68.

77 Schimmel, Annemarie (1975), p. 126.
78 On him see Dhahabī, Muḥammad b. Aḥmad b. 'Uthmān al- (1413/1992), vol. 7, pp. 229–279.
79 Ibn al-Qayyim (1998), p. 68.
80 Usually rendered in English as 'acquiescence', 'contentment' or 'approval' but in the general sense the significance of this conception can hardly be conveyed completely or precisely in English by a single word. See Watt, W. Montgomery (1979), 'Suffering in Sunnite Islam', in: *SI*, vol. 50, pp. 17–18.
81 On him, see Dhahabī, Muḥammad b. Aḥmad b. 'Uthmān al- (1413/1992), vol. 1, pp. 532–536.
82 Schimmel, Annemarie (1975), p. 126.
83 Ibid.
84 For further elaborations on these two types of love, see Ibn al-Qayyim (1375/1956), pp. 18–52, esp. pp. 45–47, 51–52; Bell, Joseph Norment (1979), pp. 148–149.
85 Ibn al-Qayyim (1358/1939), *Ṭarīq al-hijratayn wa bāb al-sa'ādatayn*, Cairo: Idārat al-Ṭibā'a al-Munīriyya, pp. 410, 411; Bell, Joseph Norment (1979), p. 120.
86 Bell, Joseph Norment (1979), p. 120.
87 Ibid.
88 Ibid.
89 Ibid., p. 84.
90 Ibn al-Qayyim (1393/1973), vol. 2, p. 227.

4 Human dignity of people with disabilities: influence of physiognomy?

1 Office of the High Commissioner of Human Rights (1975), *Declaration on the Rights of Disabled Persons*, available at http://www.unhchr.ch/html/menu3/b/72.htm (accessed 18 April 2009).
2 United Nations (2006), *Draft Resolution: Convention on the Rights of Persons with Disabilities*, United Nations, General Assembly, 6 December 2006, available at http://www.un.org (accessed 3 August 2007).
3 Alūsī, Abū al-Faḍl Maḥmūd al- (n.d.), *Rūḥ al-ma'ānī fī tafsīr al-Qur'ān al-'Aẓīm wa al-sab' al-mathānī*, Beirut: Dār Iḥyā' al-Turāth al-'Arabī, vol. 15, p. 117, quoted by Kamali, Muhammad Hashim (2002), *The Dignity of Man: An Islamic Perspective*, Cambridge: The Islamic Texts Society, p. 2.
4 See Kamali, Muhammad Hashim (2002), pp. 2–9.
5 On him, see 'Adiyy, 'Abd al-Karīm (1982–1983), 'Al-Firāsa 'ind al-'Arab', in: *MMLAD*, vol. 57, issue 4, pp. 707, 708, 722–724.
6 He was a member of the Academy of the Arabic Language in Damascus during the period 1979–1985. For more information, see Naffākh, Aḥmad Rātib al- (1985) 'Faqīd al-majma': al-ustādh 'Abd al-Karīm Zahūr 'Adiyy', in: *MMLAD*, vol. 60, no. 3, pp. 625–626.
7 Mourad, Youssef (1939), *La Physiognomonie arabe et le Kitāb al-Firāsa de Fakhr Al-Dīn Al-Rāzi*, Paris: P. Geuthner; 'Adiyy, 'Abd al-Karīm (1982–1983), vol. 57, no. 4, pp. 707–728, vol. 58, no. 1, pp. 343–365, vol. 58, no. 2, pp. 161–193, vol. 58, no. 3, pp. 570–631; Ghersetti, Antonella (1996), 'Firāsa and Intelligence: The Silly and the Intelligent in Arab Physiognomy', in: *The Arabist: Budapest Studies in Arabic*, vol. 17, pp. 121–131; Ghersetti, Antonella (1999), *Il kitāb Arisṭāṭalīs al-faylasūf fī l-firāsa: nella traduzione di Ḥunayn b. Isḥāq*, Rome: Herder for Università Ca' Foscari di Venezia, Dipartimento di Scienze dell'Antichità e del Vicino Oriente, Rome; Ghersetti, Antonella and Swain, Simon (2007), 'The Semiotic Paradigm: Physiognomy and Medicine in Islamic Culture', in: Swain, Simon, *Seeing the Face, Seeing the Soul: Polemon's Physiognomy from Classical Antiquity to Medieval Islam*, Oxford: Oxford

University Press, pp. 281–308.; Hoyland, Robert (2005), 'Physiognomy in Islam', in: *Jerusalem Studies in Arabic and Islam*, 30, pp. 361–402; Hoyland, Robert (2007), 'A New Edition of the Leiden Polemon' in: Swain, Simon, *Seeing the Face, Seeing the Soul: Polemon's Physiognomy from Classical Antiquity to Medieval Islam*, Oxford: Oxford University Press, pp. 329–342; Hoyland, Robert (2007a), 'The Islamic Background to Polemon's Treatise' in: Swain, Simon, *Seeing the Face, Seeing the Soul: Polemon's Physiognomy from Classical Antiquity to Medieval Islam*, Oxford: Oxford University Press, pp. 227–280.

8 Swain, Simon (ed.) (2007), *Seeing the Face, Seeing the Soul: Polemon's Physiognomy from Classical Antiquity to Medieval Islam*, Oxford: Oxford University Press.

9 For a detailed presentation of these argumentations, see Rāzī, Fakhr al-Dīn al- (1939), *Kitāb al-firāsa*, ed. Youssef Mourad, Paris: P. Geuthner, pp. 5–6; Anṣārī, Abū Ṭālib al- (1332/1914), *Kitāb al-siyāsa fī 'ilm al-firāsa*, Cairo: Al-Maṭba'a al-Kulliyya bi al-Sikka al-Jadīda, pp. 2–3; Ghumrī, Zayn al-'Ābidīn al- (d. 970/1562a), 'Al-Bahja al-insiyya fī al-firāsa al-insāniyya', MS 4485, Chester Beatty Library, Dublin, fol. 2a–4b; Hoyland, Robert (2005), pp. 363–365.

10 Ghazālī, Abū Ḥāmid, al- (n.d.), *Iḥyā' 'ulūm al-dīn*, Beirut: Dār al-Ma'rifa, vol. 4, p. 105. A slightly different English translation of this passage appears in Hoyland, Robert (2005), p. 362.

11 Ghazālī, Abū Ḥāmid al- (n.d.a), pp. 134–140; Mourad, Youssef (1939), p. 24; 'Adiyy, 'Abd al-Karīm (1982–1983), vol. 57, issue, 4, pp. 713, 725.

12 Ghazālī, Abū Ḥāmid al- (1958), *Qawā'id al-'aqā'id*, ed. Mūsā b. Naḍr, 1st edn, Beirut: 'Ālam al-Kutub, p. 180.

13 Ibid.

14 Rāzī, Fakhr al-Dīn al- (1939).

15 Khalīfa, Ḥājjī (1412/1992), *Kashf al-ẓunūn 'an asāmī al-kutub wa al-funūn*, Beirut: Dār al-Kutub al-'Ilmiyya, vol. 2, p. 997.

16 Ghumrī, Zayn al-'Ābidīn al- (d. 970/1562a); Ghumrī, Zayn al-'Ābidīn al- (d. 970/1562), 'Al-Bahja al-saniyya fī al-firāsa al-insāniyya wa al-bahja al-murḍiyya fī al-firāsa al-īmāniyya', MS 335954, Makhṭūṭāt al-Azhar al-Sharīf, available online at www.alazharonline.org (accessed 3 June 2006).

17 On him, see Laoust, H. (2003c), 'Ibn al-Jawzī', in: *EI*, vol. III, pp. 751–752.

18 Laoust, H. (2003), 'Ibn Qayyim al-Jawziyya', in: *EI*, vol. III, pp. 821–822.

19 On him, see Laoust, H. (2003a), 'Ibn Taymiyya', in: *EI*, vol. III, pp. 951–955.

20 He is known to be the last great representative of medieval Ḥanablism: see Laoust, H. (2003), vol. III, p. 822.

21 Hoyland, Robert (2005), p. 361.

22 See, for instance, Ibn Sayyidih (1316/1898–1321/1903), *Kitāb al-mukhaṣṣaṣ*, 1st edn, Cairo: al-Maṭba'a al-Amīriyya al-Kubrā bi Bulāq, p. 26; Ibn al-'Arabī (n.d.), *Aḥkām al-Qur'ān*, 1st edn, Beirut: Dār al-Kutub al-'Ilmiyya, vol. 3, p. 107.

23 See Farāhīdī, al-Khalīl b. Aḥmad al- (1980–1985), *Kitāb al-'ayn*, ed. Mahdī al-Makhzūmī and Ibrāhīm al-Samarrā'ī, Baghdad: Manshurāt Wizārat al-Thaqāfa wa al-I'lām, vol. 7, p. 245; Ibn Sayyidih (1316–1321/1898–1903), p. 26; Rāzī, Muḥammad b. Abī Bakr b. 'Abd al-Qādir al- (1415/1995), *Mukhtār al-ṣiḥāḥ*, ed. Maḥmūd Khāṭir, Beirut: Maktabat Lubnān Nāshirūn, vol. 1, p. 208; see Ibn Qutayba Abū Muḥammad 'Abd Allāh b. Muslim (1406/1986), *'Uyūn al-akhbār*, ed. Mufīd Muḥammad Qamīḥa, 1st edn, Beirut: Dār al-Kutub al-'Ilmiyya, vol. 1, p. 107, vol. 2, p. 237, 240.

24 Ibn Manẓūr, Muḥammad b. Makram (n.d.), *Lisān al-'Arab*, 1st edn, Beirut: Dār Ṣādir, vol. 6, p. 160; Wizārat al-Awqāf wa al-Shu'ūn al-Islāmiyya bi al-Kuwayt (n.d.), *Al-Mawsū'a al-fiqhiyya*, Kuwait, vol. 32, p. 77.

25 Hoyland, Robert (2005), p. 373.

26 Pellat, Ch. (2003b), 'Iyās b. Mu'āwiya', in: *EI*, vol. IV, p. 291.

27 See Fahd, T. (2003), 'Ḳiyāfa', in: *EI*, vol. V, p. 235.

28 Hoyland, Robert (2005), p. 362–363.
29 See for instance, Jāḥiẓ, Abū 'Uthmān 'Amr b. Baḥr al- (1356/1938–1364/1945), *Al-Ḥayawān*, ed. 'Abd al-Salām Muḥammad Harūn, Cairo, vol. 1, p. 123, quoted by Hoyland, Robert (2005), p. 363.
30 Khalīfa, Ḥājjī (1412/1992), vol. 2, p. 346.
31 Anṣārī, Abū Ṭālib al- (1332/1914), p. 3.
32 Hoyland, Robert (2005), p. 368.
33 Munāwī, 'Abd al-Ra'ūf al- (1356/1937), *Fayḍ al-qadīr sharḥ al-jāmi' al-ṣaghīr*, 1st edn, Cairo: Al-Maktaba al-Tijāriyya al-Kubrā, vol. 2, pp. 414–415, quoted by Hoyland, Robert (2005), p. 386–387.
34 Hoyland, Robert (2005), p. 368.
35 Ibid., p. 387.
36 Ghumrī, Zayn al-'Ābidīn al- (d. 970/1562a), fol. 1b.; Ghumrī, Zayn al-'Ābidīn al- (d. 970/1562), fol. 1b.
37 Hoyland, Robert (2005), p. 368.
38 Ghumrī, Zayn al-'Ābidīn al- (d. 970/1562a), fol. 2b, 3a; Ghumrī, Zayn al-'Ābidīn al- (d. 970/1562), fol. 2a. For the technical meaning of this term, especially in Sufi literature, see Gardet, L. (2003d), 'Kashf', in: *EI*, vol. IV, pp. 696–698.
39 Tirmidhī, Abū 'Īsā al (n.d.), *Sunan al-Tirmidhī*, ed. Aḥmad Muḥammad Shākir *et al.*, Beirut: Dār Iḥyā' al-Turāth al-'Arabī, ḥadīth no. 3127, vol. 5, p. 298; Hoyland, Robert (2005), pp. 364–365.
40 Hoyland, Robert (2005), pp. 364–365.
41 See for instance, Ibn Sayyidih (1316/1898–1321/1903), p. 26.
42 Hoyland, Robert (2005), p. 365.
43 Ibn al-Qayyim (1412/1992), *Rawḍat al-muḥibbīn wa nuzhat al-mushtāqīn*, Beirut: Dār al-Kitāb al-'Arabī, vol. 1, pp. 101–102.
44 A. Oommen and T. Oommen (2003), 'Physiognomy: A Critical Review', in: *Journal of the Anatomical Society of India*, vol. 52, no. 2, p. 189.
45 Hoyland, Robert (2005), p. 361.
46 Ibid., p. 368.
47 Ghumrī, Zayn al-'Ābidīn al- (d. 970/1562a), fol. 1b; Ghumrī, Zayn al-'Ābidīn al- (d. 970/1562), fol. 1b.
48 Ghumrī, Zayn al-'Ābidīn al- (d. 970/1562a), fol. 2a, 41a; Ghumrī, Zayn al-'Ābidīn al- (d. 970/1562), fol. 1b, 8b.
49 Hoyland, Robert (2005), p. 368.
50 Fahd, T. (2003a), vol. II, p. 916.
51 'Adiyy, 'Abd al-Karīm (1982–1983), vol. 58, no. 2, pp. 181–183
52 Ibid., vol. 58, no. 1, p. 355.
53 For Arabic lexicons, see Farāhīdī, al-Khalīl b. Aḥmad al- (1980–1985), vol. 7, p. 245; Ibn Sayyidih (1316/1898–1321/1903), p. 26.
54 See Mourad, Youssef (1939), p. 1; Ghersetti, Antonella (1996), p. 121.
55 Ibn Qutayba Abū Muḥammad 'Abd Allāh b. Muslim (1406/1986), vol. 1, p. 326.
56 Inostrantsev, K. (1907–1908), 'Materialy iz arabskikh istochnikov dlia kulturnoy istorii sasanidskoy Persii', in: *Zapiski Vostochnogo otdeleniia Rossiiskogo arkheologicheskogo obshchestva*, vol. 18, p. 120.
57 On him, see Stegemann, Willy (1952), 'Polemon', in: *Pauly-Wissowa*, xxi, 2, cols 1320–1357; Witkam, J.J. (1980), 'Aflimūn', in: *EI*, Leiden: Brill, Supplement Fascicules 1–2, pp. 44–45. There are many variations of this name. In English it is usually Polemon (see Hoyland, Robert (2005), p. 361 ff.; Fahd, T. (2003a), vol. II, pp. 916–917) but sometimes Polemo (see for instance Rosenthal, F. (1965), *The Classical Heritage in Islam*, Berkeley and Los Angeles: University of California Press, pp. 37, 43, 126). In Arabic, there are at least four variations, viz., *Aflimūn* (see Rosenthal, F. (1965), pp. 37, 43, 126; Hoyland, Robert (2005), p. 361, note 3),

Iflīmūn, Fulaymūn (Witkam, J.J. (1980), p. 45) and *Flīmūn* (Fahd, T. (2003a), vol. II, p. 916).

58 It was edited by ‘Abd al-Raḥmān Badawi: Badawī, ‘Abd al-Raḥmān (1954), *Al-Uṣūl al-yūnāniyya li al-naẓariyyāt al-siyāsiyya fī al-islām*, Cairo: Maṭba‘at Dār al-Kutub al-Miṣriyya, pp. 67–171. The text was also translated into English by a certain Ismail Ali, an Egyptian who worked on it as a student at the University of London under the supervision of A.S. Fulton: see Steele, Robert (1920), *Secretum Secretorum*, Oxford: Clarendon, pp. 176–266; Manzalaoui, Mahmoud (1974), ‘The Pseudo-Aristotelian *Kitāb Sirr al-Asrār*: Facts and Problems’, in: *Oriens*, vol. 23, p. 141.

59 It was edited and translated into Italian by Antonella Ghersetti: Ghersetti, Antonella (1999), pp. 3–50.

60 Hoyland, Robert (2005), p. 368.

61 See Steele, Robert (1920), pp. ix–lxiii; Badawī, ‘Abd al-Raḥmān (1954), pp. 32–75; Manzalaoui, Mahmoud (1974), pp. 141–257; Koningsveld, P.S. van (1998), ‘Greek Manuscripts in the Early Abbasid Empire: Fiction and Facts about their Origin, Translation and Destruction’, in: *Bibliotheca Orientalis*, vol. 55, no. iv, pp. 347–349.

62 Hoyland, Robert (2005), pp. 368–369. It is to be noted that this chapter is sometimes omitted and at other times reproduced on its own: see Manzalaoui, Mahmoud (1974), p. 142, 155–156.

63 Manzalaoui, Mahmoud (1974), pp. 163–164;

64 See Steele, Robert (1920), p. xv.

65 Manzalaoui, Mahmoud (1974), p. 157.

66 For an overall view of this question and the proposed answers, see Steele, Robert (1920), pp. xv–xvi; Badawī, ‘Abd al-Rahmān (1954), pp. 36–45; Manzalaoui, Mahmoud (1974), pp. 157–166.

67 Ghersetti, Antonella (1999), pp. xvii–xxvii.

68 A main witness of this book is the Leiden manuscript Or. 198 (I). The manuscript has been re-edited by Robert Hoyland: see Hoyland, Robert (2007), pp. 329–342.

69 See Stegemann, Willy (1952), col 1320–1357; Witkam, J.J. (1980), p. 44.

70 On him, see Zaman, Muhammad Qasim (2003), ‘Al-Ya‘qūbī’, in: *EI*, vol. XI, pp. 257–258.

71 Ya‘qūbī, Aḥmad b. Ya‘qūb al- (1883), *Tārīkh*, ed. T. Houtsma, Leiden: Brill, vol. 1, p. 135, quoted by Hoyland, Robert (2005), p. 361, note 3.

72 Jāḥiẓ, Abū ‘Uthmān ‘Amr b. Baḥr al- (1356/1938–1364/1945), vol. 3, p. 146, 269–275, 284.

73 Polemon was later also quoted by other well-known scholars such as Ibn al-Nadīm (d. 377/987), Ibn Ḥazm (d. 413/1022), Ibn al-Qiftī (d. 646/1248) and Ibn Abī Uṣaybi‘a (d. 668/1270): see Witkam, J.J. (1980), p. 45.

74 See Hoyland, Robert (2005), p. 361.

75 See Mourad, Youssef (1939), pp. 384–86; Witkam, J.J. (1980), p. 45.

76 Rāzī, Fakhr al-Dīn al- (1939), pp. 6–7.

77 Qanwajī, Ṣiddīq b. Ḥasan al- (1978), *Abjad al-‘ulūm: al-washy al-marqūm fī bayān aḥwāl al-‘ulūm*, ed. ‘Abd al-Jabbār Zakkār, Beirut: Dār al-Kutub al-‘Ilmiyya, vol. 2, p. 396. For an example on women, see Anṣārī, Abū Ṭālib al- (1332/1914), p. 18.

78 Qanwajī, Ṣiddīq b. Ḥasan al- (1978), vol. 2, p. 396.

79 Rāzī, Fakhr al-Dīn al- (1939), pp. 83–84; Qanwajī, Ṣiddīq b. Ḥasan al- (1978), vol. 2, p. 396; Anṣārī, Abū Ṭālib al- (1332/1914), p. 17.

80 Records of manuscripts written on this science provide us with a title dedicated to this specific issue, viz., *Darj al-siyāsa fī ‘ilm al-firāsa wa mā yadull ‘ala al-khayl min malaḥa wa qabāḥa*: see Bābānī, Ismā‘īl Bashā al- (1364/1945), *Īḍāḥ al-maknūn fī al-dhayl ‘alā kashf al-ẓunūn*, Istanbul: Millī Eĝitim Basimevi, vol. 1, p. 463.

81 Zamakhsharī, al- (1976), *Rabī‘ al-abrār*, Baghdad: Dār al-Shu‘ūn al-Thaqāfiyya al-‘Āmma, vol. 1, p. 866.

82 Ibn Ḥamdūn (1996), *Al-Tadhkira al-Ḥamadūniyya*, ed. Iḥsān 'Abbās & Bakr 'Abbās, Beirut: Dār Ṣādir, vol. 8, p. 32.
83 Tawḥīdī, Abū Ḥayyān al- and Ibn Miskawayh (1370/1951), *Al-Hawāmil wa al-Shawāmil*, ed. Aḥmad Amīn and al-Sayyid Aḥmad Ṣaqr, Cairo: Maṭba'at Lajnat al-Ta'līf wa al-Tarjama wa al-Nashr, pp. 166–172; Hoyland, Robert (2005), p. 391–392.
84 See Ibn Sīnā (1406/1986), *Tis' rasā'il fī al-ḥikma wa al-ṭabī'iyyāt*, ed. Ḥasan 'Āṣī, Beirut: Dār Qābis, p. 88.
85 Ibn al-Athīr, Majd al-Dīn (1963), *Al-Nihāya fī gharīb al-ḥadīth wa al-athar*, ed. Ṭāhir Aḥmad al-Zāwī and Maḥmūd Muḥammad al-Ṭanāḥī, Cairo, vol. 3, p. 428.
86 Ibn Manẓūr, Muḥammad b. Makram (n.d.), vol. 6, p. 160.
87 To mention the best known, see Rāzī, Fakhr al-Dīn al- (1939); Anṣārī, Abū Ṭālib al- (1332/1914); Zaydān, Jurjī (1423/2003), *'Ilm al-firāsa al-ḥadīth*, Cairo: Maktabat al-Thaqāfa al-Dīniyya; Witkam, J.J. (1980), p. 45.
88 Aṣbahānī, Abū Nu'aym al- (1405/1984), *Ḥilyat al-awliyā'*, 4th edn, Beirut: Dār al-Kitāb al-'Arabī, vol. 10, p. 237, quoted by Hoyland, Robert (2005), p. 387.
89 To mention just some examples, see Ghazālī, Abū Ḥāmid, al- (n.d.), vol. 4, pp. 348, 349; Aṣbahānī, Abū Nu'aym al- (1405/1984), vol. 2, p. 319, vol. 4, pp. 68, 214, vol. 6, pp. 156, 286; Ibn al-Jawzī (1399/1979), *Ṣifat al-ṣafwa*, ed. Maḥmūd Fakhūrī and Muḥammad Ruwās Qal'ajī, 2nd edn, Beirut: Dār al-Ma'rifa, vol. 2, pp. 193–196, 463–466, 501, 502, vol. 4, pp. 9, 18, 19, 60, 86, 272, 282, 283, 383, 401, 402.
90 For the other positive side in the Greek literature on people with disabilities, see Garland, Robert (1995), *The Eye of the Beholder: Deformity and Disability in the Graeco-Roman World*, London: Duckworth, pp. 89, 96–104.
91 See Ghersetti, Antonella (1999), p. 29.
92 Badawī, 'Abd al-Raḥmān (1954), p. 118; Steele, Robert (1920), pp. 219–200.
93 Ghersetti, Antonella (1999), pp. 20–21. For similar Aristotelian quotations, see Garland, Robert (1995), p. 90.
94 See Hoyland, Robert (2007), pp. 444–454.
95 Iṣfahānī, al-Rāghib al- (1420/1999), *Muḥaḍarāt al-udabā'*, ed. 'Umar al-Ṭabbā', Beirut: Dār al-Qalam, vol. 2, p. 314.
96 Hoyland, Robert (2005), p. 367.
97 Iṣfahānī, al-Rāghib al- (1420/1999), vol. 2, p. 311.
98 Ghumrī, Zayn al-'Ābidīn al- (d. 970/1562a), fol. 41.
99 Rāzī, Fakhr al-Dīn al- (1939).
100 Khalīfa, Ḥājjī (1412/1992), vol. 2, p. 997.
101 Ghumrī, Zayn al-'Ābidīn al- (d. 970/1562a); Ghumrī, Zayn al-'Ābidīn al- (d. 970/1562).
102 Anṣārī, Abū Ṭālib al- (1332/1914), p. 2.
103 Hoyland, Robert (2005), p. 367.
104 For discussions on the other six authorities and their names, see Anṣārī, Abū Ṭālib al- (1332/1914), p. 2.
105 This category includes *Ādāb al-Shāf'ī wa Manāqibih* by Ibn Abī Ḥātim al-Rāzī (d. 327 A.H), *Manāqib al-Shāf'ī* by Fakhr al-Dīn al-Rāzī (d. 606 A.H.), *Manāqib al-Shāf'ī* by Ibn Kathīr (d. 774 A.H.) and *Tawālī al-ta'sīs li ma'ālī Muḥammad b. Idrīs* by Ibn Ḥajar al-'Asqalāni (d. 852 A.H.).
106 See for instance the biographical notes on al-Shāfi'ī in Aṣbahānī, Abū Nu'aym al- (1405/1984), vol. 9, pp. 63–161.
107 See Hoyland, Robert (2005), p. 367.
108 'Adiyy, 'Abd al-Karīm (1982–1983), vol. 58, no. 1, pp. 353–354.
109 Ghaly, Mohammed (2005–2006), p. 10, note 9.
110 Anṣārī, Abū Ṭālib al- (1332/1914), p. 34.
111 Ghumrī, Zayn al-'Ābidīn al- (d. 970/1562a), fol. 41.
112 Ibid., fol. 36.
113 Ibid., fol. 34.

114 Anṣārī, Abū Ṭālib al- (1332/1914), p. 26.
115 Rāzī, Fakhr al-Dīn al- (1413/1993), *Manāqib al-imām al-Shāfiʿī*, ed. Aḥmad Ḥijāzī al-Saqqā, Beirut: Dār al-Jīl, p. 291.
116 Subkī, Abū Naṣr ʿAbd al-Wahhāb b. ʿAlī b. ʿAbd al-Kāfī al- (1992), *Ṭabaqāt al-shāfiʿiyya al-kubrā*, ed. ʿAbd al-Fattāḥ Muḥammad al-Ḥilw and Maḥmūd Muḥammad al-Ṭanāḥī, 2nd edn, Cairo: Hajar li al-Ṭibāʿa wa al-Nashr wa al-Tawzīʿ wa al-Iʿlān, vol. 2, p. 129.
117 Bayhaqī, Abū Bakr Aḥmad b. al-Ḥusayn al- (1390/1970), *Manāqib al-Shāfiʿī*, ed. Al-Sayyid Aḥmad Ṣaqr, Cairo: Maktabat Dār al-Turāth, vol. 2, p. 133.
118 Rāzī, Ibn Abī Ḥātim al- (1372/1953), *Ādāb al-Shāfiʿī wa manāqibuh*, ed. ʿAbd al-Ghanī ʿAbd al-Khāliq, Cairo: Maktab Nashr al-Thaqāfa al-Islāmiyya, p. 131.
119 Dhahabī, Muḥammad b. Aḥmad b. ʿUthmān al- (1413/1992), *Siyar aʿlām al-nubalāʾ*, ed. Shuʿayb al-Arnaʾūṭ and Muḥammad Nuʿaym al-ʿArqasūsī, 9th edn, Beirut: Muʾassasat al-Risāla, vol. 10, p. 40.
120 Rāzī, Ibn Abī Ḥātim al- (1372/1953), pp. 131–132.
121 Ibn al-Qayyim (n.d.a), *Miftāḥ dār al-saʿāda*, Beirut: Dār al-Kutub al-ʿIlmiyya, vol. 2, p. 222.
122 See Ibn Fahd (d. 954/1547), ʻAl-Nukat al-ẓirāf fī al-mawʿiẓa bi dhawī al-ʿāhāt min al-ashrāfʼ, MS 383, Chester Beatty Library, Dublin, fol. 6b.
123 This book retells the tales and anecdotes of the caliphs in Islamic history with special focus on those in the Abbasid period. Part of the book was translated into English by Godfrey Clerk: see Clerk, Godfrey (1873), *Iʿlām-en-Nās: Historical Tales and Anecdotes of the Early Khalīfahs*, London: Henry S. King.
124 The lame instead of the one-eyed, the yellow person (*aṣfar*) instead of one who is fair and ruddy in complexion (*ashqar*), and one with sunk temples (*ghāʾir al-ṣudghayn*) instead of sunk eyes (*ghāʾir al-ʿAynayn*): see Itlīdī, Muḥammad Diyāb al- (1998), *Iʿlām al-nās bimā waqaʿa li al-barāmika maʿa banī al-ʿAbbās*, ed. Ayman ʿAbd al-Jābir al-Biḥīrī, Cairo: Dār al-Āfāq al-ʿArabiyya, p. 137.
125 Itlīdī, Muḥammad Diyāb al- (1998), p. 137.
126 See Itlīdī, Muḥammad Diyāb al- (d. after 1100/1688), ʻIʿlām al-nās bimā waqaʿa li al-Barāmika maʿa Banī al-ʿAbbāsʼ, MS 335954, Makhṭūṭāt al-Azhar al-Sharīf, available online at www.alazharonline.org (accessed 16 June 2006).
127 Daylamī, Shīrawayh al- (1407/1987), *Al-Firdaws bi maʾthūr al-khiṭāb*, Beirut: Dār al-Kitāb al-ʿArabī, ed. Fawwāz Aḥmad al-Zamarlī and Muḥammad al-Muʿtaṣim bi Allāh al-Baghdādī, vol. 1, p. 473.
128 See, for instance, Sakhāwī Muḥammad b. ʿAbd al-Raḥmān al- (1399/1979), *Al-Maqāṣid al-ḥasana*, ed. ʿAbd Allāh Muḥammad al-Ṣiddīq, Beirut: Dār al-Kutub al-ʿIlmiyya, p. 18; ʿAjlūnī, Muḥammad b. Ismāʿīl al- (1405/1984), *Kashf al-khafāʾ*, ed. Aḥmad al-Qallāsh, 4th edn, Beirut: Muʾassasat al-Risāla, vol. 1, pp. 40–41.
129 Sakhāwī, Muḥammad b. ʿAbd al-Raḥmān al- (1399/1979), p. 18; ʿAjlūnī, Muḥammad b. Ismāʿīl al- (1405/1984), vol. 1, pp. 40–41.
130 See, for instance, Sakhāwī, Muḥammad b. ʿAbd al-Raḥmān al- (1399/1979), pp. 18, 136–137; ʿAjlūnī, Muḥammad b. Ismāʿīl al- (1405/1984), vol. 1, pp. 40–41.
131 On him, see ʿAdiyy, ʿAbd al-Karīm (1982–1983), vol. 57, no. 4, pp. 707, 708, 722–724.
132 Mourad, Youssef (1939), p. 61; ʿAdiyy, ʿAbd al-Karīm (1982–1983), vol. 58, issue 1, pp. 343–355.
133 Hoyland, Robert (2005), p. 367.
134 Rāzī, Ibn Abī Ḥātim al- (1372/1953), pp. 129–132.
135 Ibid., p. 129.
136 Rāzī, Fakhr al-Dīn al- (1413/1993), p. 291.
137 Ibn al-Qayyim (n.d.a), vol. 2, p. 223.
138 Zaydān, Jurjī (1423/2003), p. 5.
139 ʿAdiyy, ʿAbd al-Karīm (1982–1983), vol. 58, no. 1, pp. 343–355.
140 See, for instance, Rāzī, Fakhr al-Dīn al- (1413/1993), p. 323.

141 See, for instance, Bayhaqī, Abū Bakr Aḥmad b. al-Ḥusayn al- (1390/1970), vol. 2, pp. 185–219.
142 Ibid, vol. 2, p. 135.
143 Shāfi'ī, Muḥammad b. Idrīs al- (1410/1990), *Al-Umm*, Beirut: Dār al-Ma'rifa, vol. 5, p. 23, vol. 8, p. 426ff; Hilālī, Sa'd al-Dīn al- (1421/2001), *Al-Baṣma al-wirāthiyya wa 'alā'iquhā al-shar'iyya: dirāsa fiqhiyya muqārana*, Kuwait: Majlis al-Nashr al-'Ilmī, pp. 197ff.
144 Khalīfa, Ḥājjī (1412–1992), vol. 1, p. 500, vol. 2, p. 1367; Brockelmann, Carl (1937–1942), *Geschichte der arabischen Litteratur*, 2nd edn, 2 vols, and *Supplement* (to 1st edn), 3 vols, Leiden: Brill, Supplement. I, p. 305.
145 Bayhaqī, Abū Bakr Aḥmad b. al-Ḥusayn al- (1390/1970), vol. 2, p. 136.
146 Rāzī, Fakhr al-Dīn al- (1413/1993), pp. 73–74.
147 Ghersetti, Antonella (1999), pp. xiv, vi.
148 See Hoyland, Robert (2005), p. 367.
149 Pellat, Ch. (2003a), vol. VI, p. 349.
150 Ibid., p. 352.
151 See ibid., vol. VI, p. 353.
152 See Ibn al-Qayyim (n.d.a), vol. 2, pp. 219–221.
153 See Abū Zahra, Muḥammad (1948), *Al-Shāfi'ī: ḥayātuh wa 'aṣruh: ārā'uh al-fiqhiyya*, 2nd edn, Beirut: Dār al-Fikr al-'Arabī, pp. 46–48.
154 Hoyland, Robert (2005), p. 362.
155 Witkam, J.J. (1980), p. 44
156 Fahd, T. (1966), p. 385.
157 Ghersetti, Antonella and Swain, Simon (2007), p. 309 and note 2.
158 More than one researcher are inclined that it is apocryphal, see Brockelmann, Carl (1937–1942), vol. I, p. 152; Mourad, Youssef (1939), p. 36; Ghersetti, Antonella (1996), p. 126.
159 Inostrantsev, K. (1907–1908), p. 136.
160 Ibn Qutayba Abū Muḥammad 'Abd Allāh b. Muslim (1406/1986), vol. 1, p. 326.
161 Rāzī, Ibn Abī Ḥātim al- (1372/1953), p. 35.
162 For an overview of other legends in this regard, see Koningsveld, P.S. van (1998).
163 See Shāfi'ī, Muḥammad b. Idrīs al- (1988), *Dīwān al-imām al-Shāfi'ī*, ed. Muḥammad Ibrāhīm Silīm, Cairo: Maktabat Ibn Sīnā; Bayhaqī, Abū Bakr Aḥmad b. al-Ḥusayn al- (1390/1970), vol. 2, pp. 60–113.
164 The content of this work is expressive of the opinions adopted by al-Shāfi'ī during his last years in Egypt besides numerous other texts, some of which, according to J. Schacht, date from the 'Iraqī period. Additionally, many other works compiled by al-Shāfi'ī are also included in *Al-Umm*: see Schacht, J. (1950), *The Origins of Muhammadan Jurisprudence*, Oxford: Clarendon Press, p. 330; Chaumont, E. (2003), 'Al-Shāfi'ī', in: EI, vol. IX, p. 184.
165 See Shāfi'ī, Muḥammad b. Idrīs al- (1410/1990), vol. 5, pp. 18, 23, 32, 249, 250, 256, vol. 6, pp. 36, 213, 265–268, vol. 7, pp. 138, 187, 242, vol. 8, pp. 64, 213, 237, 324, 329, 330, 334, 426, 436.
166 Ibid., vol. 2, pp. 196, 237, vol. 4, pp. 104, 114, 117, vol. 5, p. 186, vol. 6, p. 194, vol. 7, pp. 1, 167, 177, vol. 8, pp. 276, 639.
167 Ibid., vol. 1, pp. 19, 26, 31, 38, 39, 65, 68, 91, 109, 128, 131, 133, 142, 152, 162, 172, 179, 180, 187, 188, 189, 217, 233, 240, vol. 2, 47, 65, 169, 170, 209, 220, 221, 229, 233, 283, vol. 3, p. 94, vol. 4, pp. 50, 147, 150, 171, 173, vol. 5, pp. 41, 109, 153, 161, 174, vol. 6, pp. 34, 77, 86, vol. 7, pp. 25, 74, 175, 202, 204, 212, 221, 232, 244, vol. 8, pp. 112, 180, 169, 205, 352, 376, 608, 611, 615, 628, 629, 650, 656, 665.
168 Ibid., vol. 2, pp. 189, 221, 227, vol. 3, p. 254, vol. 7, pp. 14, 153, vol. 5, pp. 67, 108, 221, 300, vol. 6, pp. 70, 132, vol. 7, pp. 259, 332, 333, vol. 8, pp. 168, 292, 352.
169 Ibid., vol. 2, pp. 196, 237, vol. 4, pp. 104, 114, 117, vol. 5, p. 186, vol. 6, p. 194, vol. 7, pp. 1, 167, 177, vol. 8, pp. 276, 639.

170 Ibid., vol. 1, pp. 19, 26, 31, 38, 39, 65, 68, 91, 109, 128, 131, 133, 142, 152, 162, 172, 179, 180, 187, 188, 189, 217, 233, 240, vol. 2, 47, 65, 169, 170, 209, 229, 233, vol. 3, p. 94, vol. 4, pp. 50, 147, 150, vol. 5, pp. 41, 109, 153, 161, 174, vol. 6, pp. 34, vol. 7, pp. 25, 175, 202, 204, 212, 221, 232, 244, vol. 8, pp. 112, 180, 205, 608, 611, 615, 628, 629, 650, 656, 665.

171 Ibid., vol. 2, p. 189, vol. 7, p. 14.

172 It is to be noted that it is a well-known phenomenon in Islamic history that some scholars were known for their disabilities and the disability of each was the epithet he was known as. For more examples in this respect, see Abū Jayb, Sa‘dī (1402/1982), *Al-Muw‘awwaq wa al-mujtama‘ fī al-sharī‘a al-islāmiyya*, Damascus and Beirut: Dār al-Fikr al-Mu‘āṣir/Dār al-Fikr, pp. 32–33.

173 Ibn al-Qayyim (n.d.a), vol. 2, p. 489.

174 Ibn al-Nadīm (1398/1978), *Al-Fihrist*, Beirut: Dār al-Ma‘rifa, vol. 1, pp. 295–296.

175 Brockelmann, Carl (1937–1942), Supplement I, p. 305.

176 Khalīfa, Ḥājjī (1412–1992), vol. 1, p. 500, vol. 2, p. 1367.

177 Ibid., vol. 2, p. 346.

178 Shāfi‘ī, Muḥammad b. Idrīs al- (1410/1990), vol. 5, p. 23, vol. 8, p. 426 ff.; Hilālī, Sa‘d al-Dīn al- (1421/2001), pp. 197 ff.

179 Brockelmann, Carl (1937–1942), Supplement. I, p. 305. Youssef Mourad opined that this manuscript is available in *Maktbat al-madrasa al-islāmiyya* (Library of the Islamic School) in *al-Jāmi‘ al-kabīr* (The Grand Mosque). It is highly possible, Mourad added, that it is not written by al-Shāfi‘ī and that some of his disciples collected his sayings: see Mourad, Youssef (1939), pp. 57–58. Mourad was unable to get a photocopy of the manuscript. Now, under current circumstances in Iraq, it seems impossible to have access to the manuscript.

180 On him, see Dhahabī, Muḥammad b. Aḥmad b. ‘Uthmān al- (1413/1992), vol. 9, pp. 175–191.

181 Ibid., vol. 9, p. 180.

182 Aṣbahānī, Abū Nu‘aym al- (1405/1984), vol. 9, p. 78.

183 On him, see Dhahabī, Muḥammad b. Aḥmad b. ‘Uthmān al- (1413/1992), vol. 7, pp. 456–466.

184 Bāsalāma, Ḥusayn b. ‘Abd Allāh (1326/1908), *Al-Jawhar al-lammā‘ fīmā thabat bi al-samā‘ min ḥikam al-imām al-shāfi‘ī al-manẓūma wa al-manthūra al-thābita bi al-asānīd al-ma’thūra*, Cairo: Maṭba‘at Kurdistān al-‘Ilmiyya, p. 28.

185 Dhahabī, Muḥammad b. Aḥmad b. ‘Uthmān al- (1413/1992), vol. 12, pp. 591–592.

186 Subkī, Abū Naṣr ‘Abd al-Wahhāb b. ‘Alī b. ‘Abd al-Kāfī al- (1992), vol. 2, p. 131.

187 Shāfi‘ī, Muḥammad b. Idrīs al- (1410/1990), vol. 6, p. 197.

188 Ibid., vol. 4, p. 171; Shāfi‘ī, Muḥammad b. Idrīs al- (1412/1991), vol. 2, pp. 23–24.

189 ‘Asqalānī, Ibn Ḥajar al- (1301/1883), p. 68.

190 Rāzī, Ibn Abī Ḥātim al- (1372/1953), pp. 129–132.

191 Rāzī, Fakhr al-Dīn al- (1413/1993), pp. 73–74.

192 Ibid., pp. 131–132; Aṣbahānī, Abū Nu‘aym al- (1405/1984), vol. 9, p. 144.

193 Rāzī, Ibn Abī Ḥātim al- (1372/1953), p. 132.

194 Garland, Robert (1995), p. 2.

195 Sakhāwī, Muḥammad b. ‘Abd al-Raḥmān al- (1399/1979), p. 18.

196 Ibid.

197 Ibn Fahd (d. 954/1547), fol. 6b.

198 Ibid., fol. 7a–8b.

199 Subkī, Abū Naṣr ‘Abd al-Wahhāb b. ‘Alī b. ‘Abd al-Kāfī al- (1992), vol. 3, p. 295–297, vol. 3, pp. 478–483, vol. 4, pp. 83, 84, vol. 7, pp. 82, 99, 301, 338, 339, vol. 8, pp. 148, 151, 152, 294, 345, 346, 354, 371, 372, vol. 10, pp. 95–96; Ibn Qāḍī Shuhba, Abū Bakr b. Muḥammad (1407/1986), *Ṭabaqāt al-Shāfi‘iyya*, ed. Al-Hāfiz ‘Abd al-‘Alīm Khān, 1st edn, Beirut: ‘Ālam al-Kutub, vol. 2, pp. 35, 36, 93, 94, 103, 104, 206, 224.

200 Subkī, Abū Naṣr 'Abd al-Wahhāb b. 'Alī b. 'Abd al-Kāfī al- (1992), vol. 5, 300–301.
201 Ibid., vol. 7, pp. 166–167.
202 Ibid., vol. 2, pp. 270, 271, 286, 287, 288, vol. 3, p. 222.
203 This has been stated by those who quoted him and elaborated this chapter such as al-Nawawī: see Nawawī, Yaḥyā b. Sharaf al- (n.d.), *Al-Majmū' sharḥ al-muhadhdhab*, Cairo: Maṭba'at al-Munīriyya, vol. 9, p. 368 and al-Suyūṭī, see Suyūṭī, Jalāl al-Dīn al- (1403/1983), *Al-Ashbāh wa al-naẓā'ir*, 1st edn, Beirut: Dār al-Kutub al-'Ilmiyya, p. 251.
204 On him, see Subkī, Abū Naṣr 'Abd al-Wahhāb b. 'Alī b. 'Abd al-Kāfī al- (1992), vol. 6, pp. 70–78.
205 Ibn al-'Arabī (n.d.), vol. 3, pp. 106–107; Shāṭibī, Abū Isḥāq al- (n.d.), *Al-Muwāfaqāt fī uṣūl al-sharī'a*, Cairo: Al-Maktaba al-Tawfīqiyya, vol. 2, p. 229.
206 Bujayramī, Sulaymān b. Muḥammad al- (1415/1995), *Ḥāshiyat al-Bujayramī 'alā al-khaṭīb*, Beirut: Dār al-Fikr, vol. 6, p. 439.
207 Ibid., vol. 4, p. 443.
208 Ibn Mufliḥ, Ibrāhīm b. Muḥammad (n.d.), vol. 3, p. 574.
209 Qanwajī, Ṣiddīq b. Ḥasan al- (1978), vol. 2, p. 396.
210 He is known to be the last great representative of medieval Ḥanablism, see Laoust, H. (2003b), 'Ḥanābila', in: *EI*, vol. III, p. 161.
211 Ibn al-Jawzī (n.d.a), *Ṣayd al-khāṭir*, Cairo: al-Maktaba al-Tawfīqiyya, ed. 'Imād Zakī al-Bārūdī, p. 227.
212 Ibid., p. 228.
213 On this term, see Radtke, B. *et al.* (2003), 'Walī', in: *EI*, vol. IX, pp. 109–124.
214 Ibn al-Jawzī (n.d.a), p. 311.
215 Ibid., pp. 308–309.
216 Ibn al-Jawzī (n.d.), *Talqīḥ fuhūm ahl al-athar fī 'uyūn al-tārīkh wa al-siyar*, Delhi, p. 11.
217 Ibn al-Jawzī (n.d.a), p. 211.
218 Observations of a physiognomic nature are also to be found in another book by Ibn al-Jawzī: see Ibn al-Jawzī (1987a), *Mukhtaṣar luqaṭ al-manāfi'*, ed. Aḥmad Yūsuf al-Daqqāq, 1st edn, Damascus: Dār al-Ma'mūn li al-Turāth; Ghersetti, Antonella (2007), p. 292.
219 Ghersetti, Antonella (1996), p. 123.
220 Badawī, 'Abd al-Raḥmān (1954), pp. 182–186.
221 Ibn al-Jawzī (1990), *Akhbār al-ḥamqā wa al-mughaffalīn*, ed. Muḥammad Amīn Farshūkh, Beirut: Dār al-Fikr al-'Arabī, p. 23.
222 Ibn al-Jawzī (1399/1979), vol. 1, pp. 20–32.
223 See, for instance, Ibn al Jawzī (1399/1979), vol. 1, pp. 350, 501, 502, 583, 645, vol. 2, pp. 193–196, vol. 4, pp. 383, 401–402.
224 Ibn al-Qayyim (1416/1996), *Badā'i' al-Fawā'id*, ed. Hishām 'Abd al-'Azīz 'Aṭā *et al.*, 1st edn, Mecca: Maktabat Nazār Muṣṭafā al-Bāz, vol. 3, pp. 634–636.
225 Ibn al-Qayyim (n.d.d), *Al-Ṭuruq al-ḥukmiyya*, Damascus: Maktabat Dār al-Bayān, pp. 3–76.
226 Johansen, Baber (2002), 'Signs as Evidence: The Doctrine of Ibn Taymiyya (1263–1328) and Ibn Qayyim al-Jawziyya (d. 1351) on Proof', in: *ILS*, vol. 9, no. 2, pp. 169–170
227 Ibn al-Qayyim (n.d.d), p. 3; Johansen, Baber (2002), p. 188.
228 Ibn al-Qayyim (n.d.d), p. 3.
229 Ibn al-Qayyim (n.d.d), p. 33; Johansen, Baber (2002), p. 188.
230 Ibn al-Qayyim (n.d.d), pp. 3, 13.
231 Ibid., pp. 3, 10; Johansen, Baber (2002), p. 189.
232 Ibn al-Qayyim (n.d.d), pp. 3, 12. Ibn al-Qayyim's theory did not die out but rather was adopted by later scholars: see, for instance, Zuḥaylī, Wahba al- (1414/1994),

Wasā'il al-ithbāt fī al-sharī'a al-islāmiyya fī al-mu'āmalāt al-madaniyya wa al-aḥwāl al-shakhṣiyya, Riyadh and Damascus: Maktabat al-Mu'ayyad/Maktabat Dār al-Bayān, vol. 2, pp. 553–557; Haven, E.C. van der (2006), 'The Bey, the Mufti and the Scattered Pearls', unpublished PhD dissertation submitted to Leiden University, The Netherlands, pp. 146–155.

233 Ibn al-Qayyim (1412/1992), vol. 1, pp. 101, 102.

234 Laoust, H. (2003), vol. III, p. 822.

235 Ibn al-Qayyim (1393/1973), *Madārij al-sālikīn*, ed. Muḥammad Ḥāmid al-Fiqī, 2nd edn, Beirut: Dār al-Kitāb al-'Arabī, vol. 1, pp. 482–495.

236 Harawī, 'Abd Allāh Al-Anṣārī al- (1408/1988), *Kitāb manāzil al-sā'irīn*, Beirut: Dār al-Kutub al-'Ilmiyya, vol. 1, pp. 80–81.

237 Ibn al-Qayyim (1393/1973), vol. 1, p. 131.

238 Ibid., vol. 2, p. 486.

239 Ibn al-Qayyim (1393/1973), vol. 2, pp. 487–488.

240 Ibn al-Qayyim (1395/1975), *Al-Rūḥ*, Beirut: Dār al-Kutub al-'Ilmiyya, vol. 1, p. 40.

241 Ibid., vol. 1, p. 40.

242 Ibn al-Qayyim (1393/1973), vol. 2, p. 488.

243 Ibn al-Qayyim (1395/1975), vol. 1, p. 40.

244 Ibn al-Qayyim (1393/1973), vol. 2, p. 43.

245 Ibn al-Qayyim (n.d.a), vol. 2, pp. 221–223.

246 Michot, Yahya J. (2000), 'Ibn Taymiyya on Astrology: Annotated Translation of Three Fatwas', in: *JIS*, vol. 11, no. 2, p. 152.

247 Ibn al-Qayyim (n.d.a), vol. 2, pp. 219–221.

248 Goldziher, I. (1981), 'The Attitude of Orthodox Islam toward the Ancient Sciences', in: Swartz, Merlin L., *Studies on Islam*, Oxford: Oxford University Press, p. 185; Livingston, John (1971), 'Ibn Qayyim al-Jawziyya: A Fourteenth Century Defense against Astrological Divination and Alchemical Transmutation', in: *JAOS*, vol. 91, no. 1, pp. 96, notes 1, 97; Livingston, John (1992), 'Science and the Occult in the Thinking of Ibn Qayyim al-Jawziyya' in: *JAOS*, vol. 112, no. 4, p. 598.

249 Livingston, John (1992), p. 598.

250 See Hoyland, Robert (2005), p. 391, note 84; Ghersetti, Antonella (2007), p. 285.

251 Ghazālī, Abū Ḥāmid al- (1958), p. 181; Mourad, Youssef (1939), p. 24.

252 Ibn Rushd (1965), *Tahāfut al-tahāfut*, ed. Sulaymān Dunyā, Cairo: Dār al-Ma'ārif, pp. 767–769; Mourad, Youssef (1939), p. 24.

253 Ghumrī, Zayn al-'Ābidīn al- (d. 970/1562a), fol. 14a–15b; Livingston, John (1992), p. 599.

254 Rāzī, Fakhr al-Dīn al- (1939), pp. 6–7; Anṣārī, Abū Ṭālib al- (1332/1914), pp. 3–4.

255 Michot, Yahya J. (2000), p. 149.

256 Ibn Taymiyya (n.d.b), *Al-Siyāsa al-shar'iyya fī iṣlāḥ al-rā'ī wa al-ra'iyya*, n.p.: Maktabat Ibn Taymiyya; Johansen, Baber (2002), esp. pp. 168, 181, 186, 187, 192.

257 Ibn Taymiyya (n.d.a), *Majmū' al-fatāwā*, ed. 'Abd al-Raḥmān b. Qāsim and Muḥammad b. 'Abd al-Raḥmān b. Qāsim, Riyadh: Mujamma' al-Malik Fahd, vol. 10, p. 473.

258 See Michot, Yahya J. (2000).

259 Ibn Taymiyya (n.d.a), vol. 7, p. 199.

260 Ibid., vol. 5, p. 82.

261 Rāzī, Fakhr al-Dīn al- (1939), pp. 10–11.

262 Ibn Taymiyya (n.d.a), vol. 5, p. 82.

263 Ibid., vol. 11, p. 125. The italics are mine.

264 Ibid., vol. 15, p. 416, vol. 22, p. 126.

265 Ibid., vol. 22, p. 126.

266 Ḥanbalī, Ibn Rajab al- (1408/1987), *Jāmi' al-'ulūm wa al-ḥikam*, 1st edn, Beirut: Dār al-Ma'rifa, vol. 1, pp. 333–334.

267 Ibid., vol. 1, p 334.

268 Wizārat al-Awqāf wa al-Shu'ūn al-Islāmiyya bi al-Kuwayt (n.d.), vol. 32, p. 78. For the Shī'ī Zaydī School, see Murtaḍā, Aḥmad b. Yaḥyā al- (n.d.), *Al-Baḥr al-zakhkhār al-jāmi' li madhāhib 'ulamā' al-amṣār*, Beirut: Dār al-Kitāb al-Islāmī, vol. 2, pp. 39–40.

269 Ibn al-'Arabī (n.d.), vol. 3, p. 107; Ibn Farḥūn, Ibrāhīm b. 'Alī b. Muḥammad al-Ya'murī (1406/1986), *Tabṣirat al-Ḥukkām,* 1st edn, Beirut: Dār al-Kutub al-'Ilmiyya, vol. 2, p. 235; Shāṭibī, Abū Isḥāq al- (n.d.), vol. 2, p. 229.

270 Ibn Farḥūn, Ibrāhīm b. 'Alī b. Muḥammad al-Ya'murī (1406/1986), vol. 2, p. 235.

271 Ibn al-'Arabī (n.d.), vol. 3, pp. 106–107.

272 Ibn 'Arabī, Muhyī al-Dīn (1418/1997), *Al-Tadbīrāt al-ilāhiyya fī iṣlāḥ al-mamlaka al-insāniyya*, Cairo: Maktabat 'Ālam al-Fikr li al-Ṭibā'a wa al-Nashr, p. 148.

273 Shāṭibī, Abū Isḥāq al- (n.d.), vol. 2, pp. 225–232.

274 Ibn al-'Arabī (n.d.), vol. 3, p. 107; Shāṭibī, Abū Isḥāq al- (n.d.), vol. 2, p. 229.

275 Aṭfīsh, Muḥammad b. Yūsuf (1405/1985), *Sharḥ al-Nīl wa shifā' al-'alīl*, 3rd edn, Maktabat al-Irshād, vol. 14, p. 608.

5 The ethics of writing on people with disabilities

1 There is no agreement on the year of his death. Opinions are divided between 821, 822 and 824 CE. See Dhahabī, Muḥammad b. Aḥmad b. 'Uthmān al- (1413/1992), *Siyar a'lām al-nubalā'*, ed. Shu'ayb al-Arna'ūṭ and Muḥammad Nu'aym al-'Arqasūsī, 9th edn, Beirut: Mu'assasat al-Risāla, vol. 10, pp. 103–104; Ibn al-Nadīm (1398/1978), Al-Fihrist, Beirut: Dār al-Ma'rifa, vol. 1 pp. 145–46; Pellat, Ch. (2003d), 'Al-Haytham B. 'Adī', in: *EI*, vol., III p. 328.

2 For instance, on defects he wrote *Kitāb al-mathālib al-kabīr, Kitāb al-mathālib al-ṣaghīr* and *Kitāb mathālib rabī'a*. As for exploits, he wrote *Kitāb tārīkh al-ashrāf al-kabīr* and *Kitāb tārīkh al-ashrāf al-ṣaghīr*. For a list of more than fifty books attributed to him, see Ibn al-Nadīm (1398/1978), vol. 1, p. 154.

3 Jāḥiẓ, Abū 'Uthmān 'Amr b. Baḥr al- (1407/1987), *Kitāb al-burṣān wa al-'urjān wa al-'umyān wa al-ḥulān*, ed. Muḥammad Mursī al-Khūlī, 4th edn, Beirut: Mu'assasat al-Risāla, p. *yā'*.

4 Ibid., p. 6.

5 Ibid., pp. 7–8.

6 Pellat, Ch. (2003d), 'Al-Haytham B. 'Adī' in: *EI*, vol. III, p. 328. Pellat said that none of his works survived. However, his aforementioned booklet on luminaries with disabilities is available.

7 See Pellat, Ch. (2003e), 'Nādira', in: *EI*, vol. VII (2003), pp. 856–858.

8 For an extended list of such sources, see Sadān, Yūsuf (1983), *Al-Adab al-'arabī al-hāzil wa nawādir al-thuqalā'*, Tel Aviv: Tel Aviv University, p. 13, note 5.

9 Ibid., pp. 26–28, note 36.

10 Ibid., pp. 56–71.

11 Ibid., pp. 19, 25–36.

12 Haytamī, Ibn Ḥajar al- (1403/1983), *Al-Fatāwā al-fiqhiyya al-kubrā: fatāwā Ibn Ḥajar*, n.p.: Al-Maktaba al-Islāmiyya, vol. 4, pp. 82–83.

13 Haytamī, Ibn Ḥajar al- (1994), *Al-Zawājir 'an iqtirāf al-kabā'ir*, 1st edn, Beirut: Dār al-Fikr, pp. 8–33.

14 Ibn Fahd (1420/2000), *Kitāb nayl al-muna bi dhayl bulūgh al-qirā li takmilat itḥāf al-warā*, London: Mu'assasat al-Furqān li al-Turāth al-Islāmī, p. 5.

15 The book is *Ḥifẓ al-'uhūd 'alā ḥukm waqf dār al-fuhūd*. See ibid., vol. 1, pp. 6, 12, vol. 2, pp. 713–714.

16 Ibid., vol. 1, pp. 7–8.

17 A well-known juristic book in the Shafi'ī school. It is to be noted that Ibn Ḥajar al-Haytamī wrote a commentary on this book which later became one of the authoritative

textbooks of the Shafiʻī school. See Schacht, J. and Arendonk, C. van (2003), 'Ibn Ḥajar al-Haytamī', in: *EI*, vol. III, p. 779.

18 ʻAydarūsī Muḥyī al-Dīn ʻAbd al-Qādir al- (1934), *Tārīkh al-nūr al-musāfir ʻan akhbār al-qarn al-ʻāshir*, Baghdad: Al-Maktaba al-ʻArabiyya, pp. 241–242.

19 For a full list of these works, see Hīla, Muḥammad Ḥabīb al- (1994), *Al-Tārīkh wa al-mu'arrikhūn bi Makka: min al-qarn al-thālith al-hijrī ilā al-thālith ʻashar*, 1st edn, Beirut: Dār al-Gharb al-Islāmī, pp. 197–213.

20 Ibid., pp. 198, 201–204, 207–208.

21 Ibid., pp. 210–213.

22 Sanjarī, ʻAlī b. Tāj al-Dīn al- (1998), *Manā'iḥ al-karam fī akhbār Makka wa al-bayt wa wulāt al-ḥaram*, Mecca: Jāmiʻat Umm al-Qurā, vol. 1, p. 19.

23 *Jawālī* is a tax imposed on the *dhimmis* and émigrés living in the Islamic *umma*. Sanjarī, ʻAlī b. Tāj al-Dīn al- (1998), vol. 1, p. 22, note 3.

24 Sanjarī, ʻAlī b. Tāj al-Dīn al- (1998), vol. 1, p. 22.

25 Hīla, Muḥammad Ḥabīb al- (1994), pp. 226–227.

26 Schacht, J. and Arendonk, C. van (2003), vol. III, p. 779.

27 For details on these five points, see Ibn Fahd (1420/2000), vol. 2, pp. 664, 668, 717, 722, 771–772.

28 Ibid., vol. 2, pp. 664–669.

29 Ibid., vol. 2, p. 717.

30 Ibid., vol. 1, p. 20.

31 Ibn Fahd (d. 954/1547), 'Al-Nukat al-ẓirāf fī al-mawʻiẓa bi dhawī al-ʻāhāt min al-ashrāf', MS 383, Chester Beatty Library, Dublin, fol. 51b.

32 Ibn Fahd (d. 954/1547), fol. 16a–16b.

33 Ibn Hajar al-Haytamī, Haytamī, Ibn Ḥajar al- (1403/1983), vol. 4, p. 83.

34 Ibid.

35 Ibn Fahd (d. 954/1547), fol. 15b–16a.

36 Ibid., fol. 59b.

37 Ibid., fol. 15b.

38 Ibid., fol. 15b–16b.

39 Ibid., fol. 16a.

40 Ibid., fol. 11a.

41 An autograph of this work is preserved in the Chester Beatty Library in Ireland, MS 3838. As stated by Arberry, no other copy appears to be recorded. I am currently in the final stages of making a critical Arabic edition of this text.

42 Ibn Fahd (d. 954/1547), fol. 59b.

43 He is well known as a Muslim mystic. On him, see Arnaldez, R. (2003b), 'Al-Muḥāsibī', in: *EI*, vol. VII, pp. 466–467.

44 On him, see Munajjid, Ṣalāḥ al-Dīn al- (1965), *Al-Mu'arrikhūn al-dimashqiyyūn wa āthāruhum al-makhṭūṭa min al-qarn al-thālith al-hijrī ilā nihāyat al-qarn al-ʻāshir*, Cairo: Maṭbaʻat Miṣr, pp. 79–81.

45 Ibn Fahd (d. 954/1547), fol. 9b.

46 Haytamī, Ibn Ḥajar al- (1403/1983), vol. 4, p. 82.

47 For further details on the traditional costume worn in Islamic lands and the position of ʻ*imāma* there, see Stillman, Y.K. *et al.* (2003), 'Libās', in: *EI*, vol. V, pp. 732–750.

48 Haytamī, Ibn Ḥajar al- (n.d.a), *Darr al-ghamāma fī dharr al-Ṭaylaṣān wa al-ʻadhba wa al-ʻimāma*, Cairo: Maṭbaʻat al-Saʻāda, p. 2.

49 *Bulugh al-arab fī ḥukm tijān al-ʻarab*; see Hīla, Muḥammad Ḥabīb al- (1994), p. 198.

50 See Ibn Fahd (1420/2000), vol. 1, pp. 321, 489.

51 This is the case for instance with ʻAli b. Taj al-Dīn al-Sanjarī (d. 1713) in his voluminous work on the history of Mecca *Manā'iḥ al-karam* although he made eighteen references to Ibn Hajar: see Sanjarī, ʻAlī b. Tāj al-Dīn al- (1998), vol. 1, pp. 68, 91, 92, 99, 100, 230, 250, 295, 382, 441, 500, vol. 2, pp. 80, 81, 196; vol. 3,

pp. 313, 338, 340, vol. 4, p. 72; Snouck Hurgronje, C. (1888), *Mekka: Die Stadt und ihre Heren*, Maritnus Nijnhoff, vol. 1, pp. 104–108.

52 Ibn Fahd (d. 954/1547), fol. 42b.

53 Ibid., fol. 15b.

54 Ibn Fahd (d. 954/1547), fol. 42b; Ibn Manẓūr, Muḥammad b. Makram (n.d.), *Lisān al-'Arab*, 1st edn, Beirut: Dār Ṣādir, vol. 8, p. 262, item q-r-'.

55 For further details on this legal norm in the Ḥanafī school, see Sarakhsī, Muḥammad b. Aḥmad b. Abī Sahl al- (1409/1989), *Al-Mabsūṭ*, Beirut: Dār al-Ma'rifa, vol., 1, p. 101. For the Mālikī school, see Bāji, Sulaymān b. Khalaf al- (n.d.), *Al-Muntaqā sharḥ al-muwaṭṭa'*, 2nd edn, Beirut: Dār al-Kitāb al-Islāmī, vol. 1, pp. 75–76.

56 Ibn Qudāma (1405/1985), *Al-Mughnī*, Beirut: Dār Iḥyā' al-Turāth al-'Arabī, vol. 1, pp. 184–185.

57 Nawawī, Yaḥyā b. Sharaf al- (n.d.), *Al-Majmū' sharḥ al-muhadhdhab*, Cairo: Maṭba'at al-Munīriyya, vol. 1, p. 438.

58 Contents of this letter are elaborated below.

59 Ibn Fahd (d. 954/1547), fol. 15a.

60 This book is one of the missing works of al-Muḥāsibī: see Muḥāsibī, al-Ḥārith b. Asad al- (1986), *Al-Waṣāyā*, Beirut: Dār al-Kutub al-'Ilmiyya, p. 39; Smith, Margaret (1935), *An Early Mystic of Baghdad: A Study of the Life and Teachings of Harith b. Asad al-Muhasibi*, London: The Sheldon Press, pp. 31, 147. However, Smith suggests that the book of al-Muḥāsibī treats this concept in the mystic sense, i.e. absence from creation and the presence with God, rather than the juristic one. The extensive quotation made by Ibn Fahd here suggests that al-Muḥāsibī used *ghība* (backbiting) in its juristic sense in this book.

61 He is a credible jurist, especially within the Shāfi'ī school. On him, see Watt, W. Montgomery (2003a), 'Al-Ghazālī', in: *EI*, vol. II, pp. 1038–1041, vol. II, pp. 1038–1041.

62 Haytamī, Ibn Ḥajar al- (1403/1983), vol. 1, p. 4.

63 Ibid., vol. 4, p. 82; Ibn Fahd (d. 954/1547), fol. 10a.

64 Haytamī, Ibn Ḥajar al- (1403/1983), vol. 4, p. 82.

65 Ibn Fahd (d. 954/1547), fol. 13a, 13b; Haytamī, Ibn Ḥajar al- (1403/1983), vol. 4, p. 82; Haytamī, Ibn Ḥajar al- (1994), vol. 2, pp. 23–24.

66 Haytamī, Ibn Ḥajar al- (1403/1983), vol. 4, p. 82.

67 Ibn Fahd (d. 954/1547), fol. 13b.

68 Haytamī, Ibn Ḥajar al- (1403/1983), vol. 4, p. 82.

69 Ibid.

70 Ibid., vol. 4, p. 83.

71 Ibn Fahd (d. 954/1547), fol. 11b.

72 Ibid., fol. 12b–14a.

73 Ibn Fahd (d. 954/1547), fol. 11a–13b.

74 Haytamī, Ibn Ḥajar al- (1403/1983), vol. 4, p. 83.

75 Ibid., vol. 4, p. 83.

76 On him, see Chaumont, E. (2003), 'Al-Shāfi'ī', in: *EI*, vol. IX, vol. IX, pp. 181–185.

77 Haytamī, Ibn Ḥajar al- (1403/1983), vol. 4, p. 83.

78 Haytamī, Ibn Ḥajar al- (1994), vol. 2, p. 19.

79 Ibid.

80 Ibn Fahd (d. 954/1547), in the margin of fol. 3a.

81 Ibid., fol. 3a.

82 Ibid., fol. 3a, 3b.

83 This is according to the Islamic calendar. According to the Gregorian calendar, it is the tenth century.

84 Ibn Fahd (d. 954/1547), fol. 3a. It is to be noted that the notion of this honorific title is based on a prophetic tradition stating that every century would have a renewer of religion. This title was always reserved for those with very high scholarly prestige such

as al-Shāfi'ī who was recognized as the *mujaddid* of the second century. On further elaboration of the purport of this title and the responsibility of its holder, see Ābādī, Abū al-Ṭayyib Muḥammad Shams al-Ḥaqq (1415/1994), *'Awn al-ma'būd sharḥ sunan Abū Dawūd*, 2nd edn, Beirut: Dār al-Kutub al-'Ilmiyya, vol. 11, pp. 259–267.

85 He is one of the most venerated personalities in Islamic history and the founder of the Ḥanbalī school. On him, see Laoust, H. (2003b), 'Ḥanābila', in: *EI*, vol. III, pp. 157–162.

86 An eminent traditionist, and authorities like Aḥmad b. Ḥanbal are reported to be among his pupils. On him, see Dhahabī, Muḥammad b. Aḥmad b. 'Uthmān al- (1413/1992), vol. 11, pp. 71–96.

87 He is also a very well-known traditionist. On him, see ibid., vol. 13, pp. 65–85.

88 Haytamī, Ibn Ḥajar al- (1403/1983), vol. 4, p. 82.

89 Ibid., vol. 4, p. 83.

90 On him, see Dhahabī, Muḥammad b. Aḥmad b. 'Uthmān al- (1413/1992), vol. 22, pp. 352–357.

91 Ibn al-Jawzī (n.d.), *Talqīḥ fuhūm ahl al-athar fī 'uyūn al-tārīkh wa al-siyar*, Delhi, pp. 229–231.

92 See, for instance, Haytamī, Ibn Ḥajar al- (1403/1983), vol. 2, p. 31, 84, 116, 135, vol. 4, p. 259; Haytamī, Ibn Ḥajar al- (1994), vol. 1, pp. 20, 28, 127.

93 Haytamī, Ibn Ḥajar al- (1403/1983), vol. 4, p. 82.

94 For the full text of the fatwa and its context, see Suyūṭī, Jalāl al-Dīn al- (1995), *Al-Ḥāwī li al-fatāwī*, Cairo: Maktabat al-Qudsī, vol. 1, pp. 152–165.

95 Ibn Fahd (d. 954/1547), fol. 14a.

96 See Ibn Ṭulūn (1962–1964), *Mufākahat al-khillān fī ḥawādith al-zamān*, Cairo: al-Mu'assasa al-Miṣriyya al-'Āmma li al-Ta'līf wa al-Tarjama wa al-Ṭibā'a wa al-Nashr, p. 14, note 16; Hīla, Muḥammad Ḥabīb al- (1994), p. 196.

97 Ibn Fahd (d. 954/1547), fol. 15a.

98 See Ḥamawī, Aḥmad b. Muḥammad al- (1405/1985), *Ghamz 'uyūn al-baṣā'ir fī sharḥ al-ashbāh wa al-naẓā'ir*, Beirut: Dār al-Kutub al-'Ilmiyya, pp. 334–335.

99 Qārī, 'Alī b. Sulṭān b. Muḥammad al-Harawī al- (1993), *Tasliyat al-a'mā 'an baliyyat al-'amā*, ed. 'Abd al-Karīm b. Ṣunaytān, al-Madīna al-Munawwara: Dār al-Bukhārī li al-Nashr wa al-Tawzī'.

100 See, for instance, Ḥusayn, 'Abd al-Razzāq (1420/1999), *Al-I'āqa fī al-adab al-'arabī*, 1st edn, al-Shāriqa, UAE: Manshurāt Madīnat al-Shāriqa li al-Khadamāt al-Insāniyya.

6 Employability of people with disabilities

1 http://www.ilo.org/global/Themes/Skills__Knowledge_and_Employability/Disability andWork/lang—en/index.htm (accessed 15 June 2007).

2 Convention on the Rights of Persons with Disabilities (2006), *Some Facts about Persons with Disabilities, United Nations*, a report published 14–16 August 2006, available at http://www.un.org (accessed 15 July 2007), p. 2.

3 International Labour Organization (2006), *ILO Welcomes New UN Convention on Rights of People With Disabilities*, press release ILO/06/58, available at http://www.ilo.org (accessed 3 August 2007).

4 http://www.ilo.org/global/Themes/Skills__Knowledge_and_Employability/Disabilityand Work/lang—en/index.htm (accessed 15 June 2007).

5 United Nations (2006), *Draft Resolution: Convention on the Rights of Persons with Disabilities*, United Nations, General Assembly, 6 December 2006, available at http://www.un.org (accessed 3 August 2007).

6 For a full list of the signatory states and regional integration organizations, see http://www.un.org/esa/socdev/enable/conventionsign.htm (accessed 15 June 2007).

7 Bannā, Jamāl al- (1985), *Ta'mīq ḥāssat al-'amal fī al-mujtama' al-islāmī*, Al-Ittiḥād al-Islāmī al-Dawlī li al-'Amal, available at http://islamiccall.org/TaamiqInd.htm (accessed 3 August 2007).

8 See, for instance, Qurashī, Bāqir, Sharīf al- (1402/1982), *Al-'Amal wa ḥuqūq al-'āmil fī al-islām*, 2nd edn, Tehran: Dār Iḥyā' Turāth Ahl al-Bayt; 'Awaḍ, al-Sayyid Ḥanafī (1998), *Al-'Amal wa qaḍāya al-ṣinā'a fī al-islām*, Cairo: Al-Maktab al-'Ilmī li al-Kumbyūtar.

9 Sarakhsī, Muḥammad b. Aḥmad b. Abī Sahl al- (1409/1989), *Al-Mabsūṭ*, Beirut: Dār al-Ma'rifa, vol. 15, p. 56; Ibn 'Abd al-Salām, al-'Izz (n.d.), *Qawā'id al-aḥkām fī maṣāliḥ al-anām*, Beirut: Dār al-Kutub al-'Ilmiyya, vol. 2, p. 81.

10 Tyan, E. (2003), 'Īdjār, Īdjāra', in: *EI*, vol. III, p. 1107.

11 Anṣārī, Abū Yaḥyā Zakariyya al- (n.d.a), *Al-Ghurar al-bahiyya sharḥ al-bahja al-wardiyya*, Cairo: Al-Maṭba'a al-Maymaniyya, vol. 3, pp. 344–345; Wizārat al-Awqāf wa al-Shu'ūn al-Islāmiyya bi al-Kuwayt (n.d.), *Al-Mawsū'a al-fiqhiyya*, Kuwait, vol. 15, p. 208.

12 Wizārat al-Awqāf wa al-Shu'ūn al-Islāmiyya bi al-Kuwayt (n.d.), vol. 15, p. 208.

13 Khaṭīb, Muḥammad b. Aḥmad Shirbīnī al- (1415/1994), *Mughnī al-muḥtāj ilā ma'rifat alfāẓ al-minhāj*, Beirut: Dār al-Kutub al-'Ilmiyya, vol. 3, pp. 619–620.

14 Nawawī, Yaḥyā b. Sharaf al- (n.d.), *Al-Majmū' sharḥ al-muhadhdhab*, Cairo: Maṭba'at al-Munīriyya, vol. 9, p. 169; Tyan, E. (2003), vol. III, p. 1107.

15 See Khaṭīb, Muḥammad b. Aḥmad Shirbīnī al- (1415/1994), vol. 3, pp. 619–620.

16 Abū Ghudda, 'Abd al-Sattār (1411/1991), 'Ri'āyat al-mu'awwaqīn fī al-islām', in: *Buḥūth fī al-fiqh al-ṭibbī wa al-ṣiḥḥa al-nafsiyya min manẓūr islāmī*, Cairo: Dār al-Aqṣā/Maṭba'at al-Ḥaramyn, p. 325.

17 Nawawī, Yaḥyā b. Sharaf al- (n.d.), vol. 9, p. 366.

18 Ibn Ḥazm, Abū Muḥammad 'Alī (n.d.), *Al-Muḥallā bi al-āthār*, Beirut: Dār al-Fikr, vol. 7, p. 554.

19 See, for instance, Nawawī, Yaḥyā b. Sharaf al- (n.d.), vol. 9, p. 366.

20 Ḥamawī, Aḥmad b. Muḥammad al- (1405/1985), *Ghamz 'uyūn al-baṣā'ir fī sharḥ al-ashbāh wa al-naẓā'ir*, Beirut: Dār al-Kutub al-'Ilmiyya, vol. 3, p. 454.

21 Pedersen, J. *et al.* (2003), 'Masdjid', in: *EI*, vol. VI, pp. 675–677.

22 Wizārat al-Awqāf wa al-Shu'ūn al-Islāmiyya bi al-Kuwayt (n.d.), vol. 1, pp. 291–292.

23 Pedersen, J. *et al.* (2003), vol. VI, p. 677.

24 Nawawī, Yaḥyā b. Sharaf al- (n.d.), vol. 3, p. 107; Wizārat al-Awqāf wa al-Shu'ūn al-Islāmiyya bi al-Kuwayt (n.d.), vol. 1, pp. 364, 367.

25 Nawawī, Yaḥyā b. Sharaf al- (n.d.), vol. 3, pp. 80–81; Wizārat al-Awqāf wa al-Shu'ūn al-Islāmiyya bi al-Kuwayt (n.d.), vol. 2, p. 357.

26 See, for instance, Qurashī, Muḥammad b. Muḥammad al- (n.d.), *Ma'ālim al-qurba fī ma'ālim al-ḥisba*, Cambridge: Dār al-Funūn, p. 177.

27 Ibn Qudāma (1405/1985), *Al-Mughnī*, Beirut: Dār Iḥyā' al-Turāth al-'Arabī, vol. 1, pp. 248–249.

28 Zayn al-Dīn, 'Abd al-Raḥīm b. al-Ḥusayn al-'Irāqī (n.d.), *Ṭarḥ al-tathrīb fī sharḥ al-taqrīb*, Dār Iḥyā' al-Kutub al-'Arabiyya, vol. 2, p. 211.

29 For a full account of these traditions, see Shawkānī, Muḥammad b. 'Alī b. Muḥammad al- (1413/1993), *Nayl Al-awṭār*, Cairo: Dār al-Hadīth, 1st edn, vol. 2, pp. 53–54.

30 Kāsānī, Abū Bakr Mas'ūd b. Aḥmad al- (1406/1986), *Badā'i' al-sanā'i' fī tartīb al-sharā'i'*, 2nd edn, Beirut: Dār al-Kutub al-'Ilmiyya, vol. 1, p. 149.

31 Nawawī, Yaḥyā b. Sharaf al- (n.d.), vol. 3, p. 114.

32 See Ibn Nujaym, Zayn al-Dīn b. Ibrāhīm (n.d.), *Al-Baḥr al-rā'iq sharḥ kanz al-daqā'iq*, 2nd edn, Beirut: Dār al-Kitāb al-Islāmī, vol. 1, p. 272.

33 Ṣan'ānī, Muḥammad b. Ismā'īl al-Kaḥlānī al- (n.d.), *Subul al-salām*, Cairo: Dār al-Ḥadīth, vol. 2, pp. 380–381.

34 Ibn al-Ḥājj (n.d.), *Al-Madkhal*, Beirut: Dār al-Turāth, vol. 1, p. 250.
35 Ḥattāb, Abū ‘Abd Allāh al- (1412/1992), *Mawāhib al-Jalīl fī sharḥ mukhtaṣar al-Khalīl*, 3rd edn, Beirut: Dār al-Fikr, vol. 1, p. 440.
36 Qurashī, Muḥammad b. Muḥammad al- (n.d.), pp. 176–177.
37 Haytamī, Ibn Ḥajar al- (1994), *Al-Zawājir ‘an iqtirāf al-kabā’ir*, 1st edn, Beirut: Dār al-Fikr, vol. 1, p. 147.
38 See Clouston, W.A. (2003), *Flowers from a Persian Garden and Other Papers*, London: Kessinger Publishing, p. 33; Dobbins, Frank S. (2003), *Error's Chains: How Forged and Broken, Part 2*, London: Kessinger Publishing, p. 753; Pedersen, J. *et al.* (2003), vol. VI, p. 676; Hearn, Lafcadio (2004), *Karma and Other Stories and Essays*, London: Kessinger Publishing, p. 79; Gordon-Cumming, Constance Frederica (2006), *Via Cornwall to Egypt*, Boston: Adamant Media Corporation, p. 106.
39 Iliffe, John (1987), *The African Poor: A History*, Cambridge: Cambridge University Press, p. 43.
40 Crecelius, Daniel (1991), ‘Incidences of *Waqf* Cases in Three Cairo Courts: 1640–1802’, in: *JESHO*, vol. 29, p. 66.
41 Ripley, George (1858), *The New American Cyclopaedia: A Popular Dictionary of General Knowledge*, New York and London: D. Appelton, p. 11.
42 Wensinck, A.J. and D.A. King (2003), ‘Mīḳāt’, in: *EI*, vol. VII, p. 29.
43 Ibid., vol. VI, pp. 674–675.
44 Wizārat al-Awqāf wa al-Shu’ūn al-Islāmiyya bi al-Kuwayt (n.d.), vol. 1, pp. 291–292.
45 Pedersen, J. *et al.* (2003), vol. VI, p. 674.
46 Wizārat al-Awqāf wa al-Shu’ūn al-Islāmiyya bi al-Kuwayt (n.d.), vol. 6, p. 19.
47 Ibn Qudāma (1405/1985), vol. 2, p. 13; Ibn al-Murtaḍā, Aḥmad b. Yaḥyā (n.d.), *Al-Baḥr al-zakhkhār al-jāmi‘ li madhāhib ‘ulamā’ al-amṣār*, Beirut: Dār al-Kitāb al-Islāmī, vol. 2, p. 310.
48 Shāfi‘ī, Muḥammad b. Idrīs al- (1410/1990), *Al-Umm*, Beirut: Dār al-Ma‘rifa, vol. 1, pp. 191–192.
49 Ibn Nujaym, Zayn al-Dīn b. Ibrāhīm (n.d.), *Al-Baḥr al-rā’iq sharḥ kanz al-daqā’iq*, 2nd edn, Beirut: Dār al-Kitāb al-Islāmī, vol. 1, pp. 369–370.
50 Ibn Qudāma (1405/1985), vol. 2, p. 13.
51 Wizārat al-Awqāf wa al-Shu’ūn al-Islāmiyya bi al-Kuwayt (n.d.), vol. 6, p. 212.
52 Ibid., vol. 6, p. 212, vol. 29, p. 249.
53 The fatwa is available on http://www.al-eman.com/Ask/ask3.asp?id=11672 (accessed 20 May 2007).
54 On him, see Arnaldez, R. (2003a), vol. III, pp. 790–799.
55 Ibn Ḥazm, Abū Muḥammad ‘Alī (n.d.), vol. 3, p. 127.
56 Scalenghe, Sara (2004–2005), ‘The Deaf in Ottoman Syria, 16th–18th Centuries’, in: *ASJ*, vol. XII no. 2, vol. XIII no. 1, p. 15.
57 Tyan, E. and Káldy Nagy, Gy (2003), ‘Ḳāḍī’, in: *EI*, vol. IV, p. 373.
58 Wizārat al-Awqāf wa al-Shu’ūn al-Islāmiyya bi al-Kuwayt (n.d.), vol. 33, p. 303; Tyan, E. and Káldy Nagy, Gy (2003), vol. IV, p. 374.
59 Tyan, E. and Káldy Nagy, Gy (2003), vol. IV, p. 375.
60 Ibid., vol. IV, p. 373.
61 Ibn Qudāma (1405/1985), vol. 10, pp. 90–91.
62 For the full list of these conditions, see Māwardī, Ibn Ḥabīb al- (n.d.a), *Al-Aḥkām al-sulṭāniyya*, Beirut: Dār al-Kutub al-‘Ilmiyya, pp. 82–83.
63 Māwardī, Ibn Ḥabīb al- (n.d.a), p. 82.
64 Wizārat al-Awqāf wa al-Shu’ūn al-Islāmiyya bi al-Kuwayt (n.d.), vol. 33, pp. 291–293.
65 Ibid.
66 Quḍāt, Muṣṭafa al- (1406/1985), ‘Aḥkām al-mu‘awwaqīn fī al-sharī‘a al-islāmiyya: aḥkām al-‘umyān’, unpublished MA thesis presented to Dār al-Ḥadīth al-Ḥasaniyya, Rabat, Morocco, pp. 229–232.

67 On him, see Schacht, J. (2003), 'Ibn Suraydj', in: *EI*, vol. III, pp. 949–950.
68 See 'Abd Allāh, Laylā Muḥammad (1418/1997), *Aḥkām al-akhras fī al-fiqh al-islāmī*, Cairo: Maktabat al-Zahrā', p. 292.
69 Quḍāt, Muṣṭafa al- (1406/1985), p. 228.
70 Anṣārī, Abū Yaḥyā Zakariyya al- (n.d.a), vol. 5, p. 218.
71 On him, see Brockelmann, Carl (2003a), 'Al-Māwardī', in: *EI*, vol. IV, p. 969.
72 Māwardī, Ibn Ḥabīb al- (n.d.a), p. 84.
73 Kīlānī, Sarī Zayd al- (n.d.), 'Aḥkām al-mu'awwaqīn fī al-fiqh al-islāmī', unpublished PhD dissertation presented to the Faculty of Islamic Sharia and Law, al-Azhar University, Cairo, p. 397–399.
74 Quḍāt, Muṣṭafa al- (1406/1985), pp. 230–231.
75 On him, see Rosenthal, F. (2003), 'Al-Ṣafadī', in: *EI*, vol. VIII, pp. 758–760.
76 See Ṣafadī, Ṣalāḥ al-Dīn Khalīl b. Aybak al- (1997), *Nakt al-himyān fī nukat al-'umyān*, ed. Ṭāriq Ṭanaṭāwī, Cairo: Dār al-Ṭalā'i', pp. 156, 226; Quḍat, Muṣṭafa al- (1406/1985), pp. 229–230.
77 Scalenghe, Sara (2004–2005), p. 15.
78 Quḍāt, Muṣṭafa al- (1406/1985), pp. 230–231.
79 Wizārat al-Awqāf wa al-Shu'ūn al-Islāmiyya bi al-Kuwayt (n.d.), vol. 6, pp. 217–218.
80 See, for instance, Shāfi'ī, Muḥammad b. Idrīs al- (1410/1990), vol. 1, p. 188; Kāsānī, Abū Bakr Mas'ūd b. Aḥmad al- (1406/1986), vol. 1, p. 224.
81 Māwardī, Ibn Ḥabīb al- (n.d.a), pp. 5, 18–19.
82 Ibid., p. 6.
83 Ibid., pp. 20–21.
84 Ibid.
85 Ibid.
86 Haytamī, Ibn Ḥajar al- (1403/1983), *Tuḥfat al-muḥtāj fī sharḥ al-minhāj*, Beirut: Dār Iḥyā' al-Turāth al-'Arabī, vol. 9, p. 75.
87 Ibn Ḥazm, Abū Muḥammad 'Alī (n.d.), vol. 4, p. 129.
88 Kīlānī, Sarī Zayd al- (n.d.), p. 379, 380, 385–387, 388–389.
89 'Abd Allāh, Laylā Muḥammad (1418/1997), p. 278.
90 On this term, see Kamali, Muhammad Hashim (2003), *Principles of Islamic Jurisprudence*, 3rd edn, Cambridge: The Islamic Texts Society, pp. 468–499.
91 Wizārat al-Awqāf wa al-Shu'ūn al-Islāmiyya bi al-Kuwayt (n.d.), vol. 33, pp. 292 293.
92 See, for instance, Najjār, 'Abd al-Majīd al- (1428/2007), 'Tajdīd fiqh al-siyāsa al-shar'iyya', in: *SRECFR* (May), vol. 10–11, no. 1, pp. 295–330.

7 Medical treatment of people with disabilities

1 For a general overview, see Hamarneh, Sami (1964), *Bibliography on Medicine and Pharmacy in Medieval Islam*, Stuttgart: Wissenschaftliche Verlagsgesellschaft; Agha, Zouhir M. (1983), *Bibliography of Islamic Medicine and Pharmacy*, London, distributed by Brill; Savage-Smith, Emilie *et al.* (2003), 'Ṭibb', in: *EI*, vol. X, pp. 459–461.
2 See 'Ajūba, Mukhtār Ibrāhīm *et al.* (1417/1996), *Al-I'āqa fī al-turāth al-'arabī al-islāmī*, Riyadh: Maṭābi' Jāmi'at al-Malik Su'ūd.
3 See, for instance, Dols, Michael W. (1987), 'Insanity and its Treatment in Islamic Society', in: *Medical History*, 31, pp. 1–14; Dols, Michael W. (1992), *Majnūn: Madman in Medieval Islamic Society*, ed. Diana E. Immisch, Oxford: Clarendon Press.
4 See, for instance, Quḍāt, Muṣṭafa al- (1406/1985), 'Aḥkām al-mu'awwaqīn fī al-sharī'a al-islāmiyya: aḥkām al-'umyān', unpublished MA thesis presented to Dār al-Ḥadīth al-Ḥasaniyya, Rabat, Morocco; Kīlānī, Sarī Zayd al- (n.d.), 'Aḥkām

al-mu'awwaqīn fī al-fiqh al-islāmī', unpublished PhD dissertation presented to the Faculty of Islamic Sharia and Law, al-Azhar University, Cairo; Rispler-Chaim, Vardit (2007), *Disability in Islamic Law*, Dordrecht, The Netherlands: Springer.

5 Quḍāt, Muṣṭafa al- (1412/1992), 'Ḥuqūq al-mu'awwaqīn bayn al-sharī'a al-islāmiyya wa al-qānūn', PhD dissertation presented to Dār al-Ḥadīth al-Ḥasaniyya, Rabat, Morocco, pp. 45ff, 67–71.

6 Rispler-Chaim, Vardit (1993), *Islamic Medical Ethics in the Twentieth Century*, Leiden: Brill, pp. 7–18, 28–43. As the title indicates, its topic is limited to the twentieth century, also the few discussions with relevance to disability.

7 See, for instance, Ibn Taymiyya (1408/1971), *Al-Fatāwā al-kubrā*, 1st edn, Beirut: Dār al-Kutub al-'Ilmiyya, vol. 3, p. 7.

8 On this term, see Radtke, B. *et al.* (2003), 'Walī', in: *EI*, vol. IX, pp. 109–124.

9 Ḥalabī, Badr al-Dīn Ibn Ḥabīb al- (d. 779/1377), 'Al-Najm al-thāqib fī ashraf al-manāqib', MS 309826, Makhṭūṭāt al-Azhar al-Sharīf, available online www.alazharonline.org (accessed 5 May 2006), fol. 33b–35b; Ibn Fahd (d. 954/1547), 'Al-Nukat al-ẓirāf fī al-maw'iẓa bi dhawī al-'āhāt min al-ashrāf', MS 383, Chester Beatty Library, Dublin, fol. 27b–36b.

10 Dols, Michael W. (1992), p. 229, note 79.

11 Ispahany, Batool (trans.) and Newman, Andrew J. (ed.) (1991), *Islamic Medical Wisdom: The Ṭibb al-A'imma*, London: The Muhammadi Trust, p. xxx.

12 Wizārat al-Awqāf wa al-Shu'ūn al-Islāmiyya bi al-Kuwayt (n.d.), *Al-Mawsū'a al-fiqhiyya*, Kuwait, vol. 11, p. 115.

13 Ibid.

14 Meyerhof, M. and T. Sarnelli (2003), 'Djarrāḥ', in: *EI*, vol. III, p. 481.

15 Ibn Mufliḥ, Ibrāhīm b. Muḥammad (1400/1979), *Al-Mubdi' fī sharḥ al-muqni'*, Beirut: Al-Maktab al-Islāmī, vol. 2, p. 454.

16 Ibn al-Ḥājj (n.d.), *Al-Madkhal*, Beirut: Dār al-Turāth, vol. 4, pp. 121–124.

17 Ibn al-Qayyim (1998a), *Medicine of the Prophet*, trans. Penelope Johnstone, Oxford: The Islamic Texts Society, pp. 3–7.

18 Ibn al-Qayyim (n.d.b), *Al-Jawāb al-kāfī li man sa'al 'an al-dawā' al-shāfī: al-dā' wa al-dawā'*, Beirut: Dār al-Kutub al-'Ilmiyya.

19 Meyerhof, M. and T. Sarnelli (2003), vol. III, p. 481.

20 Wizārat al-Awqāf wa al-Shu'ūn al-Islāmiyya bi al-Kuwayt (n.d.), vol. 11, p. 124.

21 Ibn Abī Uṣaybi'a (n.d.), *'Uyūn al-anbā' fī ṭabqāt al-aṭibbā'*, ed. Nazār Riḍā, Beirut: Dār Maktabat al-Ḥayāt, p. 438.

22 Qaraḍāwī, Yūsuf al- (1424/2003), Fatāwā mu'āṣira, 3rd edn, Kuwait: Dār al-Qalam li al-Nashr wa al-Twazī', vol. 3, pp. 58–59.

23 Ibn Abī Uṣaybi'a (n.d.), p. 530, 532. On him, see Arnaldez, R. (2003), vol. III, pp. 909–920.

24 Ibn Qāḍī Shuhba, Abū Bakr b. Muḥammad (1407/1986), *Ṭabaqāt al-Shāfi'iyya*, ed. Al-Hāfiz 'Abd al-'Alīm Khān, 1st edn, Beirut: 'Ālam al-Kutub, vol. 2, p. 187; Savage-Smith, Emilie *et al.* (2003), vol. X, p. 455. For a list of other physicians who were also known as noted jurists, see Ibn Abī Uṣaybi'a (n.d.), pp. 408, 412, 462, 470, 648, 650, 683, 684, 685, 752, 761.

25 On him, see Bar, Mohammed Ali al- (1995), *Contemporary Topics in Islamic Medicine*, Jeddah: Saudi Publications and Distributing House, pp. 1–2.

26 On him, see http://www.islamonline.net/livedialogue/arabic/Guestcv.asp?hGuestID=kl0M7j (accessed 16 June 2007).

27 Rāzī, Fakhr al-Dīn al- (1413/1993), *Manāqib al-imām al-Shāfi'ī*, ed. Aḥmad Ḥijāzī al-Saqqā, Beirut: Dār al-Jīl, pp. 73–74.

28 Ibn al-Qayyim (n.d.a), *Miftāḥ dār al-sa'āda*, Beirut: Dār al-Kutub al-'Ilmiyya, vol. 2, p. 220.

29 For some names among the Ḥanafī jurists, see Ibn Abī al-Wafā' (n.d.), *Al-Jawāhir al-muḍī'a fī ṭabaqāt al-Ḥanafiyya*, Karachi: Mīr Muḥammad Kutub Khāna, pp. 103,

216. For the Shāfi'ī jurists, see Subkī, Abū Naṣr 'Abd al-Wahhāb b. 'Alī b. 'Abd al-Kāfī al- (1992), *Ṭabaqāt al-shāfi'iyya al-kubrā*, ed. 'Abd al-Fattāḥ Muḥammad al-Ḥilw and Maḥmūd Muḥammad al-Ṭanāḥī, 2nd edn, Cairo: Hajar li al-Ṭibā'a wa al-Nashr wa al-Tawzī' wa al-I'lān, vol. 4, p. 387, vol. 8, p. 397. For the Ḥanbalī jurists, see Ibn Abī Ya'lā (n.d.), *Ṭabaqāt al-Ḥanābila*, ed. Muḥammad Ḥāmid al-Fiqī, Beirut: Dār al-Ma'rifa, vol. 2, p. 205.

30 Wizārat al-Awqāf wa al-Shu'ūn al-Islāmiyya bi al-Kuwayt (n.d.), vol. 12, p. 135.

31 Ibn al-Ḥājj (n.d.), vol. 4, p. 140.

32 Rāzī, Fakhr al-Dīn al- (1413/1993), p. 287.

33 Rahman, Fazlur (1982), 'Islam and Health: Some Theological, Historical and Sociological Perspectives', in: *HI*, vol. V, p. 79.

34 Ibid.

35 Ibid., p. 83.

36 Qaraḍāwī, Yūsuf al- (2006), 'Preventing Child Vaccination: Permissible?', a fatwa published on 1 January 2006, available at http://www.islamonline.net (accessed 5 July 2007).

37 Sharaf al-Dīn, 'Alī al-Ṭāhir (2007), 'Al-Baḥth al-'ilmī fī al-'ulūm al-ṭabī'iyya fī ḍaw' al-maqāṣid al-shar'iyya', in: *Majallat majma' al-fiqh al-islāmī*, no. 4, 1428/2007, pp. 261–263.

38 Rahman, Fazlur (1982), p. 83; Rahman, Fazlur (1989), *Health and Medicine in the Islamic Tradition: Change and Identity*, New York: Crossroad, p. 37, quoting from Naysabūrī, 'Abd Allāh b. Bisṭām (1965), *Ṭibb al-a'imma*, Najaf: Al-Maktaba al-Ḥaydariyya, pp. 3–4.

39 Rahman, Fazlur (1982), 84.

40 Ispahany, Batool (trans.) and Newman, Andrew J. (ed.) (1991), *Islamic Medical Wisdom: The Ṭibb al-A'imma*, London: The Muhammadi Trust, p. xvi.

41 Ibid., p. xiii.

42 Rahman, Fazlur (1984), p. 589; Ispahany, Batool (trans.) and Newman, Andrew J. (ed.) (1991), pp. xiv, xv, xxxiv–xxxvii.

43 Ghazālī, Abū Ḥāmid, al- (n.d.), *Iḥyā' 'ulūm al-dīn*, Beirut: Dār al-Ma'rifa, vol. 4, p. 283.

44 Wizārat al-Awqāf wa al-Shu'ūn al-Islāmiyya bi al-Kuwayt (n.d.), vol. 11, p. 117.

45 Ibid., vol. 11, p. 117; Murtaḍā, Aḥmad b. Yaḥyā al- (n.d.), *Al-Baḥr al-zakhkhār al-jāmi' li madhāhib 'ulamā' al-amṣār* , Beirut: Dār al-Kitāb al-Islāmī, vol. 3, p. 85.

46 On this term, see Gülen, Fethullah M. (1999), *Key Concepts in the Practice of Sufism*, Fairfax, Va.: Fountain, pp. 67–71; Lewisohn, L. (2003), 'Tawakkul', in: *EI*, vol. X, pp. 376–378.

47 Wizārat al-Awqāf wa al-Shu'ūn al-Islāmiyya bi al-Kuwayt (n.d.), vol. 11, p. 117.

48 Ibn al-Ḥājj (n.d.), vol. 4, p. 115; Wizārat al-Awqāf wa al-Shu'ūn al-Islāmiyya bi al-Kuwayt (n.d.), vol. 14, p. 20.

49 Ibn Mufliḥ, Ibrāhīm b. Muḥammad (n.d.), vol. 2, p. 348.

50 Rahman, Fazlur (1989), pp. 48–49.

51 Ibn al-Qayyim (1998a), pp. 9–13.

52 Dhahabī, Muḥammad b. Aḥmad b. 'Uthmān al- (1349/1930), *Al-Ṭibb al-nabawī*, Cairo: Muṣṭafā al-Bābī al-Ḥalabī wa Awladuh bi Miṣr, pp. 40–41.

53 Buhūtī, Manṣūr b. Yūnus al- (1402/1982), *Kashshāf al-qinā' 'an matn al-iqnā'*, Beirut: Dār al-Kutub al-'Ilmiyya, vol. 2, p. 76.

54 Ghazālī, Abū Ḥāmid, al- (n.d.), vol. 4, p. 283.

55 Qasṭallānī, Aḥmad b. Muḥammad al- (1326/1908), *Al-Mawāhib al-ladunniyya bi al-minaḥ al-Muḥammadiyya*, Cairo: Al-Maṭba'a al-Sharafiyya, vol. 2, p. 140. On him, see Brockelmann, Carl (2003), 'Al-Ḳasṭalānī', in: *EI*, vol. IV, p. 736.

56 Qasṭallānī, Aḥmad b. Muḥammad al- (1326/1908), vol. 2, p. 140.

57 Rahman, Fazlur (1989), p. 49.

58 Ghazālī, Abū Ḥāmid, al- (n.d.), vol. 4, p. 283.

59 This Fiqh Academy, founded in June 1983, is affiliated to the Organization of the Islamic Conference. Each Muslim country nominates an expert in Islamic disciplines as its representative. While governments nominate the representatives, once nominated, only the Academy can revoke their membership. The academy has currently fifty-seven members. For more information on this academy, see http://www.fiqhacademy.org.sa/ (accessed 18 May 2008).
60 Ibn al-Khodja, Mohamed Habib (ed.) (2000), *Resolutions and Recommendations of the Council of the Islamic Fiqh Academy*, Jeddah, pp. 139–140.
61 See: Ashqar, ʻUmar Sulaymān al- (2003), ʻAl-Tadāwī bayn al-akhdh bi al-asbāb wa al-tawakkul ʻalā Allāhʼ, a fatwa published on 8 July 2003, http://www.islamonline.net (accessed 18 June 2007); Qaradāghī, ʻAlī al- (2004), ʻAl-Tadāwī: ḥukmuh wa aqwāl al-fuqahāʼ fīhʼ, a fatwa published on 7 December 2004, http://www.islamonline.net (accessed 18 June 2007).
62 Ashqar, ʻUmar Sulaymān al- (2003).
63 See Ghaly, Mohammed (2007), ʻIslam en handicap: praktijkthemaʼs en islamitische ethische opvattingenʼ, in: *Tijdschrift voor gezondheidszorg en ethiek*, jaargang 17, no. 2, pp. 42–43.
64 Ibn al-Qayyim (1998a), p. 137.
65 See for instance, Rohé, George H. (1885), *A Text-Book of Hygiene: A Comprehensive Treatise on the Principles and Practice of Preventive Medicine from an American Standpoint*, Baltimore, Md.
66 Givens, Benjamin P. and Hirschman, Charles (1994), ʻModernization and Consanguineous Marriage in Iranʼ, in: *Journal of Marriage and the Family*, vol. 56, no. 4, p. 821.
67 Bittles, A.H. (2001), p. 89.
68 Ibid., p. 90. For case-studies, see Hoodfar E. and Teebi, A.S. (1996), ʻGenetic Referrals of Middle Eastern Origin in a Western City: Inbreeding and Disease Profileʼ, *Journal of Medical* Genetic, 33, pp. 212–215; Teebi A.S. and Farag, T.I. (1997); Nelson J. *et al.* (1997), pp. 142–146.
69 Bittles, A.H. (2001), ʻConsanguinity and its Relevance to Clinical Geneticsʼ, in: *Clinical Genetics*, 60, p. 93.
70 Ibid., p. 90.
71 Ibid., p. 92.
72 Ibid.
73 Ibid., p. 89.
74 Idrissi I. al- *et al.* (1992), ʻCumulative Incidence of Retinoblastoma in Riyadh, Saudi Arabiaʼ, in: *Ophthalamic Paediat. Genet.*, vol. 13, pp. 9–12; Willems, P.J. (2000), ʻGenetic Causes of Hearing Lossʼ, in: *The New England Journal of Medicine*, vol. 342, pp. 1101–1109; Bittles, A.H. (2001), p. 93.
75 Bittles, A.H. (2001), p. 92.
76 Māwardī, Ibn Ḥabīb al- (n.d.), *Adab al-Dunyā wa al-Dīn*, Beirut: Dār Maktabat al-Ḥayāt, pp. 159–160; Murtaḍā, Aḥmad b. Yaḥyā al- (n.d.), vol. 4, p. 84.
77 ʻAsqalānī, Ibn Ḥajar al- (1384/1964), *Talkhīṣ al-ḥabīr*, ed. Al-Sayyid ʻAbd Allāh Hāshim al-Yamānī al-Madanī, Ṭabʻat al-Madīna al-Munawwara, vol. 3, p. 146.
78 Bujayramī, Sulaymān b. Muḥammad al- (1415/1995), *Ḥāshiyat al-Bujayramī ʻalā al-khaṭīb*, Beirut: Dār al-Fikr, vol. 3, p. 363.
79 ʻAsqalānī, Ibn Ḥajar al- (1384/1964), vol. 3, p. 146.
80 Shubīr, Muḥammad ʻUthmān (1421/2001a), ʻMawqif al-islām min al-amrāḍ al-wirāthiyyaʼ, in: Ashqar, ʻUmar Sulaymān al- *et al.* (1421/2001) *Dirāsāt fiqhiyya fī qaḍāyā ṭibbiyya muʻāṣira*, Amman: Dār al-Nafāʼis, vol. 1, pp. 337–338.
81 This opinion is shared by another Saudi Mufti, Ṣāliḥ al-Fawzān, who said that the scientistʼs attribution of congenital disorders to consanguineous marriage is false: see ʻUlamāʼ al-Ḥijāz wa al-Lajna al-Dāʼima li al-Buḥūth al-ʻIlmiyya wa al-Iftāʼ (2004), *Fatāwā al-ṭibb wa al-tadāwī*, Alexandria: Dār al-Īmān, pp. 96–97, quoted by Rispler-Chaim, Vardit (2007), p. 145, note 426.

82 Shāyi', 'Abd al-Ilāh b. 'Uthmān b. 'Abd Allāh (1418/1997), *Al-Lu'lu' al-thamīn min fatāwā al-mu'awwaqīn*, Riyadh: Dār al-Ṣumay'ī li al-Nashr wa al-Tawzī', vol. 1, pp. 21–22. A full translation of the fatwa is available in Rispler-Chaim, Vardit (2007), p. 97. However, I have used my own translation, believing that it is closer to the Arabic text.
83 'Ārif, 'Alī 'Ārif (1421/2001), 'Qaḍāyā fiqhiyya fī al-jīnāt al-bashariyya', in: Ashqar, 'Umar Sulaymān al- *et al.* (1421/2001), vol. 2, pp. 735–803, vol. 2, p. 684, note 4.
84 See, for instance, the resolution of the council of the Islamic Fiqh Academy, no. 82/13/08, Ibn al-Khodja, Mohamed Habib (ed.) (2000), p.183; the resolution of the European Council for Fatwa and Research no. 14/2, *Scientific Review of the European Council for Fatwa and Research*, July 2005, vol. 7, pp. 413–414.
85 'Ārif, 'Alī 'Ārif (1421/2001), vol. 2, pp. 794–795.
86 Ibid., pp. 786–788.
87 Rispler-Chaim, Vardit (1999), 'The Right not to be Born: Abortion of the Disadvantaged Fetus in Contemporary Fatwas', in: *MW*, vol. LXXXIX, no. 2, p. 136.
88 Rispler-Chaim, Vardit (2007), p. 60.
89 Wizārat al-Awqāf wa al-Shu'ūn al-Islāmiyya bi al-Kuwayt (n.d.), vol. 2, p. 56.
90 Kyriakides-Yeldham, Anthony (2005), 'Islamic Medical Ethics and the Straight Path of God', in: *Islam and Christian–Muslim Relations*, July 2005, vol. 16, no. 3, pp. 215–216; Rispler-Chaim, Vardit (1993), p. 7.
91 Wizārat al-Awqāf wa al-Shu'ūn al-Islāmiyya bi al-Kuwayt (n.d.), vol. 2, p. 57.
92 Ibid., vol. 2, p. 58.
93 See, for instance, Rispler-Chaim, Vardit (1993), pp. 7–16.
94 Ibid., pp. 14–15; Rispler-Chaim, Vardit (1999), pp. 134–136.
95 Rispler-Chaim, Vardit (1999), pp. 134–135.
96 Ibid., pp. 135–136.
97 Qaraḍāwī, Yūsuf al- (1415/1994), vol. 2, p. 549.
98 Rispler-Chaim, Vardit (2007), p. 59.
99 Rispler-Chaim, Vardit (1999), p. 136.
100 Qaraḍāwī, Yūsuf al- (1415/1994), vol. 2, p. 549.
101 www.who.int/gpv-dvacc/history/history.htm (accessed 20 March 2006).
102 National Immunization Program, Centers for Disease Control and Prevention (2007), *Epidemiology and Prevention of Vaccine Preventable Diseases*, 10th edn, Atlanta, Ga.: the Pink Book, p. 101.
103 Stern, Alexandra Minna and Howard Markel (2005), 'The History of Vaccines and Immunization: Familiar Patterns, New Challenges', in: *Health Affairs*, vol. 24, no. 3, p. 617.
104 Ibid.
105 Ibid.
106 Ibid.
107 Ibid., pp. 617–618.
108 Ibid., p. 617.
109 For a full text of the fatwa in Arabic with a list of the names of the twelve scholars who signed it, see Qaraḍāwī, Yūsuf al- (2007), 'Hal yaḥrum al-taṭ'īm li iḥtimāl ḍararih?', a fatwa pubslished on 2 April 2007 available at http://www.islamonline.net (accessed 5 July 2007). For an English translation, see Qaradawi, Yusuf al- (2006), 'Preventing Child Vaccination: Permissible?', a fatwa published on 1 January 2006, available at http://www.islamonline.net (accessed 5 July 2007).
110 Ashqar, 'Umar Sulaymān al- (1421/2001), vol. 1, p. 246.
111 Rispler-Chaim, Vardit (1993), p. 28.
112 Ashqar, 'Umar Sulaymān al- (1421/2001), pp. 247–248.
113 Daigeler, A. *et al.* (2003), 'Orthotropic and Heterotopic Lower Leg Reimplantation: Evaluation of Seven Patients', in: *The Journal of Bone & Joint Surgery*, 85-B, p. 554.
114 Ashqar, 'Umar Sulaymān al- (1421/2001), p. 277.

115 Ashqar, 'Umar Sulaymān al- (1421/2001), pp. 254–266.
116 Ibid., p. 265.
117 Ibn Nujaym, Zayn al-Dīn b. Ibrāhīm (n.d.), *Al-Baḥr al-rā'iq sharḥ kanz al-daqā'iq*, 2nd edn, Beirut: Dār al-Kitāb al-Islāmī, vol. 1, p. 115.
118 Ibn al-Khodja, Mohamed Habib (ed.) (2000), p. 53.
119 On him, see Jād al-Ḥaqq, 'Alī Jād al-Ḥaqq (2005), vol. 1, pp. 5–6.
120 Ibid., pp. 242–257.
121 See, for instance, Kyriakides-Yeldham, Anthony (2005), p. 221.
122 For an elaboration of these ethical concepts, see Rispler-Chaim, Vardit (1993), p. 28.
123 Wiegers, Gerard (2002), 'Muslim Discussions on Organ Donations to Adherents of other Religions', in: Shadid, W.A.R. and Koningsveld, P.S. van (2002) *Intercultural Relations and Religious Authorities: Muslims in the European Union*, Leuven: Peeters, p. 218; Qaraḍāwī, Yūsuf al- (1415/1994), vol. 2, p. 530–533.
124 Qaraḍāwī, Yūsuf al- (1415/1994), vol. 2, pp. 534–535.
125 Rispler-Chaim, Vardit (1993), p. 39, quoting from Ghanem, Isam (1982), *Islamic Medical Jurisprudence*, London: A. Probsthain, p. 276.
126 See Makdisi, George (2003), 'Ibn Ḳudāma al-Maḳdisī', vol. III, pp. 842–843.
127 Ibn Qudāma (1405/1985), *Al-Mughnī*, Beirut: Dār Iḥyā' al-Turāth al-'Arabī, vol. 4, p. 177.
128 Rispler-Chaim, Vardit (1993), p. 35.
129 Ibid., p. 36.
130 Qaraḍāwī, Yūsuf al- (1415/1994), vol. 2, p. 533.
131 Ibid.
132 Ibid.
133 Ibid., pp. 539–540.
134 Ibid., vol. 2, pp. 535–537.
135 Ibid., pp. 537.
136 Rispler-Chaim, Vardit (1993), pp. 36–37.
137 Qaraḍāwī, Yūsuf al- (1424/2003), vol. 3, pp. 666–667; Wiegers, Gerard (2002), pp. 220–221.
138 Qaraḍāwī, Yūsuf al- (1415/1994), vol. 2, pp. 538–539.
139 Jamīlī, Khālid Rashīd al- (1410/1990), 'Aḥkām naql al-khiṣyatayn wa al-mibyaḍayn wa aḥkām naql a'ḍā' al-janīn al-nāqiṣ al-khilqa fī al-sharī'a al-islāmiyya', in: *Majallat majma' al-fiqh al-islāmī* (1410/1990), vol. 6, no. 3, pp. 1985–1987.
140 Quḍāt, Muṣṭafa al- (1412/1992), p. 70.
141 Australian Academy of Science (1999), *On Human Cloning: A Position Statement*, 4 February 1999, Canberra, p. 4.
142 Kyriakides-Yeldham, Anthony (2005), p. 218.
143 Australian Academy of Science (1999), p. 4.
144 Qaraḍāwī, Yūsuf al- (1424/2003), vol. 3, pp. 528–529.
145 Savage-Smith, Emilie (1996), pp. 927–928.
146 Ibn al-Qayyim (1998a), p. 5.
147 Ibid., p. 8.
148 For instance, Ibn al-Jawzī's *Al-Ṭibb al-ruḥānī* falls into this category. See Ibn al-Jawzī (1348/1929).
149 Ibn al-Qayyim (1998a), p. 109.
150 Wizārat al-Awqāf wa al-Shu'ūn al-Islāmiyya bi al-Kuwayt (n.d.), vol. 13, pp. 27–28.
151 Shawkānī, Muḥammad b. 'Alī b. Muḥammad al- (1413/1993), *Nayl Al-awṭār*, Cairo: Dār al-Ḥadīth, 1st edn, vol. 8, p. 232.
152 Qasṭallānī, Aḥmad b. Muḥammad al- (1326/1908), vol. 2, p. 144.
153 Ibn al-Qayyim (1998a), p. 9.
154 Shawkānī, Muḥammad b. 'Alī b. Muḥammad al- (1413/1993), vol. 8, p. 246.
155 Wizārat al-Awqāf wa al-Shu'ūn al-Islāmiyya bi al-Kuwayt (n.d.), vol. 13, p. 28.

156 Ibn Taymiyya (1408/1971), vol. 3, p. 7.
157 Ibn al-Qayyim (1998a), p. 109.
158 Qasṭallānī, Aḥmad b. Muḥammad al- (1326/1908), vol. 2, p. 141.
159 Munāwī, ʻAbd al-Ra'ūf al- (1356/1937), *Fayḍ al-qadīr sharḥ al-jāmi' al-ṣaghīr*, 1st edn, Cairo: Al-Maktaba al-Tijāriyya al-Kubrā, vol. 3, p. 515. On him, see Hamdan, A. Saleh (2003), 'al-munāwī', in: *EI*, vol. VII, p. 565.
160 Shawkānī, Muḥammad b. ʻAlī b. Muḥammad al- (1413/1993), vol. 8, p. 233. On him, see Haykel, Bernard (2003), *Revival and Reform in Islam: The Legacy of Muhammad al-Shawkānī*, Cambridge: Cambridge University Press.
161 Qasṭallānī, Aḥmad b. Muḥammad al- (1326/1908), vol. 2, p. 142.
162 Ispahany, Batool (trans.) and Newman, Andrew J. (ed.) (1991), pp. xxx–xxxi.
163 Ashqar, ʻUmar Sulaymān al- *et al.* (1421/2001), vol. 1, pp. 14–17.
164 Ibn Bāz ʻAbd Allah (1416/1995), ''Ilāj al-amrāḍ al-ʻuḍwiya bi al-Qur'ān', in: *Majallat al-Da'wa*, no. 1497, 1/2/1416, available at http://www.alifta.com (accessed 18 June 2007); Ibn Bāz ʻAbd Allāh (1418/1997), ''Ilāj al-saraṭān bi al-Qur'ān', in: Majallat al-Da'wa, no. 1637, 19/12/1418, available at http://www.alifta.com (accessed 18 June 2007).
165 Ṣiddīq, ʻAbd Allāh al- (1392/1972), *Kamāl al-īmān fī al-tadāwī bi al-Qur'ān*, Tiṭwān, Morocco: al-Maṭba'a al-Mahdiyya.
166 Ibid., pp. 1 (note 1), 4, 33.
167 On him, see Ende, W. (2003a), 'Rashīd Riḍā', in: *EI*, vol. III, pp. 445–448.
168 On him, see Ende, W. (2003), 'Shaltūt', in: *EI* vol. IX, pp. 260–261.
169 Riḍā, Rashīd (1315/1898–1354/1935), *Al-Manār*, Cairo: Maṭba'at al-Manār, vol. 7, issue 10, p. 390.
170 Shaltūt, Maḥmūd (1408/1988), *Al-Fatāwā: dirāsa li mushkilāt al-muslim al-mu'āṣir fī ḥayātih al-yawmiyya wa al-'āmma*, Cairo: Dār al-Shurūq, 15th edn, pp. 206–208.
171 Riḍā, Rashīd (1315/1898–1354/1935), vol. 7, issue 10, p. 391.
172 Ibid., pp. 391–392.
173 Qaraḍāwī, Yūsuf al- (1415/1994a), *Mawqif al-islām min al-ilhām wa al-kashf wa al-ru'ā wa al-kahāna wa al-ruqā*, 1st edn, Cairo: Maktabat Wahba, p. 154.
174 Shubīr, Muḥammad ʻUthmān (1421/2001), 'Ḍawābiṭ al-tadāwī bi al-ruqā wa al-tamā'im fī al-fiqh al-islāmī', in: Ashqar, ʻUmar Sulaymān al- *et al.* (1421/2001), vol. 2, pp. 460–461.
175 Munāwī, ʻAbd al-Ra'ūf al- (1356/1937), vol. 3, p. 515.
176 Ibn ʻAbd al-Barr, Abū ʻAmr Yūsuf (1387/1967), *Al-Tamhīd limā fī al-muwaṭṭa' min al-ma'ānī wa al-asānīd*, ed. Muṣṭafā b. Aḥmad al-ʻAlawī and Muḥammad ʻAbd al-Kabīr al-Bakrī, Rabat: Wizārat ʻUmūm al-Awqāf wa al-Shu'ūn al-Islāmiyya, vol. 23, pp. 174–175.
177 Munāwī, ʻAbd al-Ra'ūf al- (1356/1937), vol. 3, p. 515, vol. 4, pp. 236–237.
178 Ibid., vol. 3, p. 515.
179 Ibid., vol. 4, p. 236.
180 See Bayhaqī, Abū Bakr Aḥmad b. al-Ḥusayn al- (1410/1989), *Shu'ab al-īmān*, ed. Muḥammad al-Sa'īd Basyūnī Zaghlūl, Beirut: Dār al-Kutub al-ʻIlmiyya, vol. 3, pp. 29, 282–283; ʻAjlūnī, Muḥammad b. Ismā'īl al- (1405/1984), *Kashf al-khafā'*, ed. Aḥmad al-Qallāsh, 4th edn, Beirut: Mu'assasat al-Risāla, vol. 1, pp. 329, 330, 432, 482, vol. 2, pp. 28–29.
181 Lane, E.W. (1968), *Arabic–English Lexicon*, Beirut: Librairie du Liban, part 5, p. 2192; Wizārat al-Awqāf wa al-Shu'ūn al-Islāmiyya bi al-Kuwayt (n.d.), vol. 13, p. 121.
182 Lane, E.W. (1968), part 5, p. 1140; Wizārat al-Awqāf wa al-Shu'ūn al-Islāmiyya bi al-Kuwayt (n.d.), vol. 23, p. 96.
183 Ibn al-Qayyim (1998a), p. 132ff.
184 Wizārat al-Awqāf wa al-Shu'ūn al-Islāmiyya bi al-Kuwayt (n.d.), vol. 13, p. 22.
185 Lane, E.W. (1968), part 1, p. 316; Wizārat al-Awqāf wa al-Shu'ūn al-Islāmiyya bi al-Kuwayt (n.d.), vol. 14, p. 30.

186 Wizārat al-Awqāf wa al-Shu'ūn al-Islāmiyya bi al-Kuwayt (n.d.), vol. 14, p. 30.
187 Lane, E.W. (1968), vol. 8, p. 2795; Wizārat al-Awqāf wa al-Shu'ūn al-Islāmiyya bi al-Kuwayt (n.d.), vol. 13, p. 23.
188 Wizārat al-Awqāf wa al-Shu'ūn al-Islāmiyya bi al-Kuwayt (n.d.), vol. 13, p. 23.
189 Ibn al-Qayyim (1998a), p. 132; 'Asqalānī, Ibn Ḥajar al- (1379/1959), Fatḥ al-Bārī, ed. Muḥammad Fu'ād 'Abd al-Bāqī and Muḥibb al-Dīn al-Khaṭīb, Beirut: Dār al-Ma'rifa, vol. 10, p. 196.
190 See, for instance, Wizārat al-Awqāf wa al-Shu'ūn al-Islāmiyya bi al-Kuwayt (n.d.), vol. 23, p. 96–97.
191 Ibid., vol. 13, p. 24.
192 Ibid., vol. 13, p. 21.
193 Ibid., vol. 2, p. 13.
194 Ibn al-Qayyim (1998a), pp. 46–50.
195 'Asqalānī, Ibn Ḥajar al- (1379/1959), vol. 10, p. 196.
196 Ibid.
197 Ispahany, Batool (trans.) and Newman, Andrew J. (ed.) (1991), pp. 36, 37, 41, 92.
198 Ibid., p. 14.
199 Ibid., pp. 112–113.
200 Ibid., p. 139.
201 Ibid., pp. 146–147.
202 For an overview of such unlawful practices, see Shubīr, Muḥammad 'Uthmān (1421/2001), vol. 2, pp. 470–475, and the standpoint of Islam, pp. 498–506.
203 Suyūṭī, Jalāl al-Dīn al- (1387/1967), *Al-Itqān fī 'ulūm al-Qur'ān*, 1st edn, Cairo: Maktabat wa Maṭba'at al-Mashhad al-Ḥusaynī, vol. 4, pp. 137–143.
204 Ibid., vol. 4, p. 142. For other parts of Qur'ān used for the same medical purpose, see vol. 4, pp. 138–139.
205 Zarkashī, Abū 'Abd Allāh al- (1391/1971), *Al-Burhān fī 'ulūm al-Qur'ān*, ed. Muḥammad Abū al-Faḍl Ibrāhīm, Beirut: Dār al-Ma'rifa, vol. 1, pp. 434–437; Suyūṭī, Jalāl al-Dīn al- (1387/1967), vol. 4, p. 137.
206 See, for instance, Samāḥa, Riyāḍ Muḥammad (1996), *Dalīl al-mu'ālijīn bi al-Qur'ān*, Cairo: Al-Maktaba al-Tawfīqiyya; 'Abd Allāh, Muḥammad Maḥmūd (1996), *I'jāz al-Qur'ān fī 'ilāj al-siḥr wa al-ḥasad wa mass al-shayṭān*, Beirut: Mu'assasat al-Īmān and Dār al-Rashīd; Mināwī, Naṣīf 'Awaḍ al- (2000), *Al-Bayān fī al-'ilāj bi al-Qur'ān*, Cairo: Markaz al-Kitāb li al-Nashr.
207 Fahd, T. (2003b), 'Khawāṣṣ al-Ḳur'ān', in: *EI*, vol. IV, p. 1134. For examples of this literature, see Ghazālī, Abū Ḥāmid al- (pseudo) (1970), *Al-Ṭibbal -Rūḥānī li al-jism al-insānī fī 'ilm al-ḥarf,* Beirut: Al-Maktaba al-Thagāfiyya, Būnī, Abū al-'Abbās Aḥmad al- (1951), esp. p. 198 ff.
208 Fahd, T. (2003b), vol. IV, p. 1134.
209 Marrākushī, Ibn 'Abd al-Salām al- (d. 660/1262), *'Khawāṣṣ al-Burda fī bur' al-dā''*, Or. 11752:2, Leiden, fol. 8b, 12a.
210 Shubīr, Muḥammad 'Uthmān (1421/2001), vol. 2, pp. 513–514.
211 Shawkānī, Muḥammad b. 'Alī b. Muḥammad al- (1413/1993), vol. 8, pp. 232, 233, 245; Shubīr, Muḥammad 'Uthmān (1421/2001), vol. 2, pp. 501–503. For the Shī'ī tradition, see Ispahany, Batool (trans.) and Newman, Andrew J. (ed.) (1991), pp. 54–56.
212 'Asqalānī, Ibn Ḥajar al- (1379/1959), vol. 10, p. 195.
213 Fahd, T. (2003c), 'Ruḳiya', in: *EI*, vol. VIII, pp. 600–601.
214 Ispahany, Batool (trans.) and Newman, Andrew J. (ed.) (1991), pp. 54–56.
215 Hoffer, Cor (1992), 'The Practice of Islamic Healing', in: Shadid W.A.R. and P.S. van Koningsveld (eds). *Islam in Dutch Society: Current Developments and Future Prospects*, The Netherlands: Kok Pharos, pp. 40–41; Hoffer, Cor (2000), 'Volksgeloof en religieuze geneeswijzen onder moslims in Nederland', a PhD dissertation submitted to Leiden University.

8 Financial aid for people with disabilities

1 Wizārat al-Awqāf wa al-Shu'ūn al-Islāmiyya bi al-Kuwayt (n.d.), *Al-Mawsū'a al-fiqhiyya*, Kuwait, vol. 4, pp. 223–224.
2 Mahmood, Tahir (1989), 'Law and the Elderly in the Islamic Tradition–Classical Precepts and Modern Legislation', in: *Islamic and Comparative Law Quarterly*, vol. IX, p. 33; Wizārat al-Awqāf wa al-Shu'ūn al-Islāmiyya bi al-Kuwayt (n.d.), vol. 4, p. 223.
3 Mahmood, Tahir (1989), p. 33.
4 Quṭb, Sayyid (1349/1974), *Al-'Adāla al-ijtimā'iyya fī al-islām*, Beirut and Cairo: Dār al-Shurūq, p. 65.
5 Zayla'ī, 'Uthmān b. 'Alī al- (n.d.), *Tabyīn al-ḥaqā'iq sharḥ kanz al-daqā'iq*, 2nd edn, Beirut: Dār al-Kitāb al-Islāmī, vol. 3, pp. 50–51.
6 Doi, 'Abdur Rahmān I. (1404/1984), *Sharī'ah: The Islamic Law,* London: Ta Ha Publishers, p. 204.
7 Majlis al-A'lā li al-Shu'ūn al-Islāmiyya, al- (1386–1411/1966–1990), *Mawsū'at al-fiqh al-islāmī al-muqāran*, compiled by a group of specialists in Islamic law, Cairo, vol. 18, part 16, p. 318.
8 Ibid., p. 322.
9 Ibid.
10 Ibid., p. 324.
11 Ibid.
12 Ibid., p. 325.
13 Jazīrī, 'Abd al-Raḥmān al- (1420/1999), *Al-Fiqh 'alā al-madhāhib al-arba'a*, 1st edn, Cairo: Dār al-Manār, vol. 4, pp. 454–460.
14 Abyānī, Muḥammad Zayd al- (1342/1924), *Mukhtaṣar sharḥ al-aḥkām al-shar'iyya fī al-aḥwāl al-shakhṣiyya*, Cairo, p. 352.
15 'Abd al-Ḥakīm, Ibn Muḥammad (1332/1914), *Ḥuqūq al-usra*, Cairo: Maṭba'at al-Jamāliyya, pp. 231–232.
16 Sarakhsī, Muḥammad b. Aḥmad b. Abī Sahl al- (1409/1989), *Al-Mabsūṭ,* Beirut: Dār al-Ma'rifa, vol. 5, p. 223. Cf. Bakhtiar, Laleh (1996), *Encyclopaedia of Islamic Law: A Compendium of the Views of the Major Schools*, Chicago: ABC International Group, p. 490.
17 Bakhtiar, Laleh (1996), p. 490.
18 Ibn Qudāma (n.d.), *Al-Muqni' fī fiqh imām al-sunna Aḥmad Ibn Ḥanbal*, Cairo: Al-Maṭba'a al-Salafiyya wa Maktabatuhā, vol. 2, p. 320.
19 Fityān, Farīd (1986), *Sharḥ qānūn al-aḥwāl al-shakhṣiyya ma'a ta'dīlāt al-qanūn wa aḥkām maḥkamat al-tamyīz*, London: Dār Wāṣit, p. 212.
20 Ibn Qudāma (1408/1998), vol. 3, pp. 373–374.
21 See Ābādī, Abū al-Ṭayyib Muḥammad Shams al-Ḥaqq (1415/1994), *'Awn al-ma'būd sharḥ sunan Abū Dawūd*, 2nd edn, Beirut: Dār al-Kutub al-'Ilmiyya, vol. 9, p. 323.
22 Ibn Qudāma (1405/1985), *Al-Mughnī*, Beirut: Dār Iḥyā' al-Turāth al-'Arabī, vol. 8, p. 172.
23 Abū Zahra, Muḥammad (ed.) (1963), *Usbū' al-fiqh al-islāmī*, Cairo: Al-Majlis al-A'lā li Ri'āyat al-Funūn, pp. 319, 322.
24 'Abd al-Ḥakīm, Ibn Muḥammad (1332/1914), p. 344. Cf. Ibn Qudāma (1405/1985), vol. 8, p. 186.
25 Nasir, Jamal J. (1990), *The Islamic Law of Personal Status*, 2nd edn, London: Graham & Trotman, p. 193.
26 Ibid.
27 Jazīrī, 'Abd al-Raḥmān al- (1420/1999), vol. 4, pp. 478–481.
28 Nasir, Jamal J. (1990), p. 194.
29 Jazīrī, 'Abd al-Raḥmān al- (1420/1999), vol. 4, p. 481.

30 Quḍāt, Muṣṭafa al- (1406/1985), 'Aḥkām al-mu'awwaqīn fī al-sharī'a al-islāmiyya: aḥkām al-'umyān', unpublished MA thesis presented to Dār al-Ḥadīth al-Ḥasaniyya, Rabat, Morocco, pp. 180–183; Kīlānī, Sarī Zayd al- (n.d.), 'Aḥkām al-mu'awwaqīn fī al-fiqh al-islāmī', unpublished PhD dissertation presented to the Faculty of Islamic Sharia and Law, al-Azhar University, Cairo, pp. 251–292; Quḍāt, Muṣṭafa al- (1412/1992), 'Ḥuqūq al-mu'awwaqīn bayn al-sharī'a al-islāmiyya wa al-qānūn', PhD dissertation presented to Dār al-Ḥadīth al-Ḥasaniyya, Rabat, Morocco, pp. 148–151; 'Abd Allāh, Laylā Muḥammad (1418/1997), 'Abd Allāh, Laylā Muḥammad (1418/1997), *Aḥkām al-akhras fī al-fiqh al-islāmī*, Cairo: Maktabat al-Zahrā', pp. 153–168.

31 Rispler-Chaim, Vardit (2007), *Disability in Islamic Law*, Dordrecht, The Netherlands: Springer, 47–65.

32 Ibid., p. 47.

33 Bakhtiar, Laleh (1996), p. 424.

34 Ibn Qudāma (1405/1985), vol. 7, pp. 37–38.

35 Ibn Ḥamza, Muṣṭafā (1414/1993), *Ḥuqūq al-mu'awwaqīn fī al-islām*, Casablanca: Maṭba'at al-Najāḥ al-Jadīda, p. 31.

36 Rispler-Chaim, Vardit (2007), p. 52.

37 Ibn Qudāma (1405/1985), vol. 7, p. 5.

38 Nawawī, Yaḥyā b. Sharaf al- (n.d.), *Al-Majmū' sharḥ al-muhadhdhab*, Cairo: Maṭba'at al-Munīriyya, vol. 9, p. 367.

39 Wizārat al-Awqāf wa al-Shu'ūn al-Islāmiyya bi al-Kuwayt (n.d.), vol. 29, p. 68.

40 Kīlānī, Sarī Zayd al- (n.d.), pp. 278–279, note 2; Quḍāt, Muṣṭafa al- (1406/1985), pp. 180–182.

41 Kīlānī, Sarī Zayd al- (n.d.), pp. 280–287; Quḍāt, Muṣṭafa al- (1406/1985), pp. 183.

42 Qāsimī, Jamāl al-Dīn al- (1424/2003), *Tafsīr al-Qāsimī al-musammā maḥāsin al-ta'wīl*, Cairo: Dār al-Ḥadīth, vol. 3, pp. 24–26.

43 On him, see Rispler-Chaim, Vardit (2007), p. 143.

44 Ibid., pp. 51–52.

45 Rispler-Chaim, Vardit (1996), 'Islamic Law of Marriage and Divorce and the Disabled Person: The Case of the Epileptic Wife', in: *Die Welt des Islams*, vol. 36, no. 1, p. 101.

46 'Abd al-Ḥamīd, Muḥammad Muḥyī al-Dīn (1966), *Al-Aḥwāl al-shakṣiyya fī al-sharī'a al-islāmiyya*, Cairo: Maktabat 'Alī Ṣubayḥ wa-Awlāduh, pp. 314–315.

47 Rispler-Chaim, Vardit (1996), p. 101.

48 Ibid., p. 104.

49 Ibid., pp. 92–93.

50 Mirdāwī, 'Alī b. Sulaymān al- (n.d.), *Al-Inṣāf fī masā'il al-khilāf*, ed. Muḥammad Ḥāmid al-Fiqī, Beirut: Dār Iḥyā' al-Turāth al-'Arabī, vol. 8, p. 203.

51 Ibid.

52 Alami, Dawoud S. al- (1992), *The Marriage Contract in Islamic Law*, London: Graham & Trotman, p. 74.

53 Wizārat al-Awqāf wa al-Shu'ūn al-Islāmiyya bi al-Kuwayt (n.d.), vol. 29, p. 67. Translations of the terms is based on Rispler-Chaim, Vardit (2007), p. 55.

54 Ibid., p. 68.

55 Ibid.

56 Rispler-Chaim, Vardit (2007), p. 54.

57 Wizārat al-Awqāf wa al-Shu'ūn al-Islāmiyya bi al-Kuwayt (n.d.), vol. 29, pp. 67–68.

58 Kīlānī, Sarī Zayd al- (n.d.), p. 282.

59 Dols, Michael W. (1992), *Majnūn: Madman in Medieval Islamic Society*, ed. Diana E. Immisch, Oxford: Clarendon Press, p. 4.

60 Rispler-Chaim, Vardit (2007), pp. 64–65.

61 Wizārat al-Awqāf wa al-Shu'ūn al-Islāmiyya bi al-Kuwayt (n.d.), vol. 16, p. 108.

62 Kīlānī, Sarī Zayd al- (n.d.), p. 278.

63 Ibn Mufliḥ, Ibrāhīm b. Muḥammad (1400/1979), *Al-Mubdi' fī sharḥ al-muqni'*, Beirut: Al-Maktab al-Islāmī, vol. 7, p. 109.
64 Wizārat al-Awqāf wa al-Shu'ūn al-Islāmiyya bi al-Kuwayt (n.d.), vol. 31, p. 40.
65 Kīlānī, Sarī Zayd al- (n.d.), pp. 280–287.
66 Rispler-Chaim, Vardit (2007), p. 50.
67 Ibid., p. 51.
68 Ibid., pp. 54–55.
69 For the Arabic text of the fatwa, see Jād al-Ḥaqq, 'Alī Jād al-Ḥaqq (2005), *Al-Fatāwā al-islāmiyya*, 1st edn, Cairo: Dār al-Fārūq li al-Nashr wa al-Tawzī', vol. 3, pp. 246–247. The fatwa has been quoted and partially translated by Rispler-Chaim: Rispler-Chaim, Vardit (1996), pp. 90–106.
70 Ibid., pp. 96–97.
71 Rispler-Chaim, Vardit (2007), p. 55.
72 See Bakhtiar, Laleh (1996), pp. 475–476.
73 Ibid., p. 476.
74 Ibid., p. 476.
75 Jazīrī, 'Abd al-Raḥmān al- (1420/1999), vol. 4, p. 472.
76 Bakhtiar, Laleh (1996), p. 476.
77 Ibid.
78 Jazīrī, 'Abd al-Raḥmān al- (1420/1999), vol. 4, pp. 470–471.
79 Ibid., vol. 4, pp. 471–472.
80 The opinions expressed by the Shafi'īs and the Ḥanbalīs are based on Jazīrī, 'Abd al-Raḥmān al- (1420/1999), vol. 4, pp. 470–472. The opinion of the Ja'farī schools is quoted from Bakhtiar, Laleh (1996), p. 477.
81 Bakhtiar, Laleh (1996), p. 477.
82 Sarakhsī, Muḥammad b. Aḥmad b. Abī Sahl al- (1409/1989), vol. 5, p. 192; Bakhtiar, Laleh (1996), p. 486.
83 Bakhtiar, Laleh (1996), p. 486.
84 Ibid.
85 Ibid., p. 487.
86 Ibid.
87 Ibn Qudāma (1405/1985), vol. 8, p. 156.
88 Ibid.
89 Jazīrī, 'Abd al-Raḥmān al- (1420/1999), vol. 4, pp. 461–462.
90 Ibn Qudāma (1405/1985), vol. 8, p. 156.
91 Ibid.
92 Ibn Taymiyya (1949), *Mukhtaṣar al-fatāwā*, Cairo: Maṭba'at Ibn 'Alī al-Ba'lī, p. 454.
93 Ibn Rushd (2000), *Bidāyat al-Mujtahid wa Nihāyat al-Muqtaṣid: The Distinguished Jurist's Primer*, trans. Imran Ahsan Khan Nyazee and Muhammad Abdul Rauf, Qatar: Centre for Muslim Contribution to Civilization, Garnet Publishing Limited, vol. 2, p. 590.
94 Bakhtiar, Laleh (1996), p. 478.
95 See Ibn Nujaym, Zayn al-Dīn b. Ibrāhīm (n.d.a), *Al-Baḥr al-rā'iq sharḥ kanz al-daqā'iq*, Beirut: Dār al-Ma'rifa, vol. 4, p. 198.
96 'Abd al'Aṭī, Hammūda (1977), *The Family Structure in Islam*, Indianapolis: The American Trust Publications, p. 152. For further details see Kāsānī, Abū Bakr Mas'ūd b. Aḥmad al- (1406/1986), *Badā'i' al-sanā'i' fī tartīb al-sharā'i'*, 2nd edn, Beirut: Dār al-Kutub al-'Ilmiyya, vol. 4, p. 15.
97 'Abd Allāh, 'Umar (1968), *Aḥkām al-sharī'a al-islāmiyya fī al-aḥwāl al-shakhṣiyya*, Alexandria: Dār al-Ma'ārif, p. 250.
98 Bakhtiar, Laleh (1996), p. 484.
99 Ibid.
100 See, for example, Sarakhsī, Muḥammad b. Aḥmad b. Abī Sahl al- (1409/1989), vol. 21, p. 105; Ibn Qudāma (1405/1985), vol. 8, p. 159.

101 Jazīrī, 'Abd al-Raḥmān al- (1420/1999), vol. 4, p. 456; 'Abd al'Aṭī, Hammūda (1977), p. 153.
102 Jazīrī, 'Abd al-Raḥmān al- (1420/1999), vol. 4, p. 456.
103 See, for example, Abū Zahra, Muḥammad (ed.) (1963), p. 335.
104 'Abd al'Aṭī, Hammūda (1977), pp. 153–154.
105 Doi, 'Abdur Rahmān I. (1404/1984), p. 204.
106 'Abd al'Aṭī, Hammūda (1977), p. 153.
107 Nasir, Jamal J. (1990), p. 102.
108 Doi, 'Abdur Rahmān I. (1404/1984), p. 328.
109 Ibn Rushd (2000), vol. II, p. 406.
110 Coulson, N.J. (1971), *Succession in the Muslim Family*, Cambridge: Cambridge University Press, pp. 31–34, 41–42, 243.
111 Quṭb, Sayyid (1349/1974), p. 67.
112 Nasir, Jamal J. (1990), pp. 266–267.
113 Ibn Qudāma (1405/1985), vol. 5, p. 348.
114 Kubaysī, Muḥammad 'Ubayd al- (1397/1977), *Aḥkām al-waqf fī al-sharī'a al-islāmiyya*, Baghdad: Maṭba'at al-Irshād, vol. 1, p. 91.
115 Shāfi'ī, Muḥammad b. Idrīs al- (1410/1990), *Al-Umm*, Beirut: Dār al-Ma'rifa, vol. 1, pp. 274, 257.
116 Sarakhsī, Muḥammad b. Aḥmad b. Abī Sahl al- (n.d.), *Al-Mabsūṭ*, 1st edn, Cairo: Maṭba'at al-Sa'āda, vol. 12, p. 27.
117 Ibn Ḥazm, Abū Muḥammad 'Alī (1347–1352/1928–1933), *Al-Muḥallā bi al-āthār*, ed. Muḥammad Munīr al-Dimashqī, Cairo: Idārat al-Maṭba'a al-Munīriyya, vol. 9, p. 157.
118 Murtaḍā, Aḥmad b. Yaḥyā al- (1368/1949), *Al-Baḥr al-zakhkhār al-jāmi' li madhāhib 'ulamā' al-amṣār*, 1st edn, Cairo: Maṭba'at Anṣār al-Sunna al-Muḥammadiyya, vol. 4, p. 146.
119 Ḥillī, Ja'far b. al-Ḥasan al- (n.d.), *Sharā'i' al-islām fī masā'il al-ḥalāl wa al-ḥarām*, Beirut: Maṭba'at Dār Maktabat al-Ḥayāt, vol. 1, p. 246.
120 Ibid.
121 Sarakhsī, Muḥammad b. Aḥmad b. Abī Sahl al- (n.d.), vol. 12, p. 29.
122 See Kubaysī, Muḥammad 'Ubayd al- (1397/1977), vol. 1, pp. 311–348.
123 Haytamī, Ibn Ḥajar al- (1403/1983), *Tuḥfat al-muḥtāj fī sharḥ al-minhāj*, Beirut: Dār Iḥyā' al-Turāth al-'Arabī, vol. 6, pp. 237–238.
124 Ibn Nujaym, Zayn al-Dīn b. Ibrāhīm (n.d.a), vol. 5, p. 204.
125 Haytamī, Ibn Ḥajar al- (1403/1983), vol. 3, p. 226.
126 Haytamī, Ibn Ḥajar al- (n.d.), *Tuḥfat al-muḥtāj fī sharḥ al-minhāj*, Beirut: Dār Iḥyā' al-Turāth al-'Arabī, vol. 6, pp. 237–238.
127 Khaṭīb, Muḥammad b. Aḥmad Shirbīnī al- (n.d.), *Mughnī al-muḥtāj ilā ma'rifat alfāẓ al-minhāj*, Beirut: Dār al-Fikr, vol. 2, p. 377.
128 Haytamī, Ibn Ḥajar al- (n.d.), vol. 6, pp. 235ff.
129 Hoexter, M. (1995), 'Ḥuqūq Allāh and Ḥuqūq al-'Ibād as Reflected in the Waqf Institution', in: *Jerusalem Studies in Arabic and Islam*, no. 19, p. 141.
130 Kubaysī, Muḥammad 'Ubayd al- (1397/1977), vol. 1, p. 42.
131 Ghānim, Ibrāhīm al-Bayyūmī (1419/1998), *Al-Awqāf wa al-siyāsa fī Miṣr*, 1st edn, Cairo: Dār al-Shurūq, p. 47.
132 Baer, Gabriel (1997), 'The Waqf as a Prop for the Social System (Sixteenth–Twentieth Centuries)', in: *ILS*, vol. 4, no. 3, p. 265.
133 Doi, 'Abdur Rahmān I. (1404/1984), pp. 338, 340.
134 Ibn Qudāma (1405/1985), vol. 5, p. 322.
135 Baer, Gabriel (1997), p. 265.
136 Ibid.
137 Kubaysī, Muḥammad 'Ubayd al- (1397/1977), vol. 1, pp. 34–35.

138 For a detailed discussion of this issue, see Layish, Aharon (1997), 'The Family Waqf and the *Shar'ī* Law of Succession', in: *ILS*, vol. 4, no. 3, pp. 352–388.
139 Shawkānī, Muḥammad b. 'Alī b. Muḥammad al- (1347/1928), vol. 2, p. 141.
140 For further details about the opinions of those opponents, see Kubaysī, Muḥammad 'Ubayd al- (1397/1977), vol. 1, pp. 42–50.
141 Ibid., p. 35.
142 Ibn Qudāma (1405/1985), vol. 5, p. 388.
143 See Azmi, S.H. (1991), 'Traditional Islamic Social Welfare: Its Meaning, History and Contemporary Relevance', part II, in: *IQ*, London, vol. 35, no. 4, p. 221.
144 Summers, Della (1992), *Longman Dictionary of English Language and Culture*, London: Longman, p. 253.
145 Ibid., p. 1259.
146 Giddens, Anthony (1997), *Sociology*, 3rd edn, Cambridge: Polity Press, p. 585.
147 Kazi, M.U. (1996), *Family and Social Obligations in Islam*, Karachi: Ferozsons, p. 75.
148 Muslim, Abū al-Ḥusayn b. al-Ḥajjāj (n.d.), *Ṣaḥīḥ Muslim*, ed. Muḥammad Fu'ād 'Abd al-Bāqī, Beirut: Dār Iḥyā' al-Turāth al-'Arabī, p. 1354.
149 Baer, Gabriel (1997), p. 291.
150 Othman, Moh. Zain b. Haji (1983), 'Origin of the Institution of *Waqf*', in: *HI*, vol. VI, no. 2, p. 3.
151 Hoexter, M. (1995), p. 138.
152 Kubaysī, Muḥammad 'Ubayd al- (1397/1977), vol. 1, p. 33.
153 Othman, Moh. Zain b. Haji (1983), p. 9.
154 'Abd al-Qādir, 'Alī (1959), 'Land Property and Land Tenure in Islam', in *IQ*, vol. 5, p. 7.
155 Othman, Moh. Zain b. Haji (1983), p. 9.
156 Kubaysī, Muḥammad 'Ubayd al- (1397/1977), vol. 1, p. 100.
157 Othman, Moh. Zain b. Haji (1983), p. 9.
158 Ibid.
159 Ibid., p. 3.
160 Ibid., p. 4.
161 Qaraḍāwī, Yūsuf al- (2001), 'Al-Mu'awwaqūn wa dawruhum fī al-mujtama'', an episode of *Al-Sharī'a wa al-Ḥayāt* (*Sharī'a and Life*), a programme broadcast by al-Jazeera on 21 July 2001, available at http://www.qaradawi.net (accessed 25 June 2007).
162 Qarār'a, Jamīl 'Ubayd al- (1420/1999), 'Riy'āyat al-mu'āqīn fī al-islām', in: *Majallat al-sharī'a wa al-dirāsāt al-islāmiyya*, Kuwait, no. 39, p. 303–304.
163 Nowsheravi, A.R. (1983), 'Muslim Hospitals in the Medieval Period', in: *IS*, vol. 22, no. 2, p. 57.
164 Dunlop, M. *et al.* (2003), 'Bīmāristān', in: *EI*, vol. I, p. 1224.
165 Nowsheravi, A.R. (1983), p. 57.
166 Ibid.
167 Sibā'ī, Muṣṭafā al- (1381/1962), *Akhlāqunā al-ijtimā'iyya*, Damascus: Maktabat al-Shabāb al-Muslim, p. 334.
168 Ibid, p. 48.
169 Qaraḍāwī, Yūsuf al- (2001).
170 Sābiq, al-Sayyid (n.d.), *Fiqhu us-Sunna*, trans. Muhammad Sa'eed Dabas and Jamal al-Din Zarabozo, Cairo: Dar al-Fatch for Arab Information, vol. 2, p. 1.
171 Ibid., p. 2.
172 Ibid., vol. 3, p. 75.
173 Townsend, Peter and Dorothy Wedderburn (1965), *The Aged and the Welfare State*, London: G. Bell, p. 15.
174 Sābiq, al-Sayyid (n.d.), vol. 2, p. 1.

175 Walī Allāh, Shāh (1996), *Ḥujjat Allāh al-Bāligha: The Conclusive Argument from God*, trans. Marcia K. Hermansen, Leiden: Brill, p. 221.
176 Bahiyy, Muḥammad al- (1971), *Al-Fikr al-islāmī wa al-mujtama' al-mu'āṣir: mushkilāt al-usra wa al-takāful*, Tripoli, Libya: Dār al-Fikr, p. 363.
177 Qaraḍāwī, Yūsuf al- (1422/2001), *Malāmiḥ al-mujtama' al-muslim alladhī nanshuduh*, 3rd edn, Cairo: Maktabat Wahba, p. 154.
178 Ibid., pp. 226–227.
179 Qaraḍāwī, Yūsuf al- (1414/1994), *Fiqh al-zakāt*, 21st edn, Cairo: Maktabat Wahba, pp. 934–936.
180 Ibn Ḥamza, Muṣṭafā (1414/1993), *Ḥuqūq al-mu'awwaqīn fī al-islām*, Casablanca, p. 51.
181 Ṭabarī, Muḥammad b. Jarīr al- (1405/1984), *Jāmi' al-bayān fī ta'wīl al-Qur'ān: tafsīr al-Ṭabarī*, Beirut: Dār al-Fikr, vol. 10, p. 110.
182 Ibid., p. 111.
183 Ibn Salām, Abū 'Ubayd al-Qāsim (1388/1968), *Kitāb al-amwāl*, ed. Muḥammad Khalīl Harrās, 1st edn, Cairo: Maktabat al-Kulliyyāt al-Azhariyya, p. 764.
184 Ibid.
185 Bahiyy, Muḥammad al- (1971), p. 371.
186 Qaraḍāwī, Yūsuf al- (2001).
187 Ibn Bāz, 'Abd Allāh (1413/1992), 'Jawāz ṣarf al-zakāt 'alā ḥajāt al-mu'awwaqīn al-fuqarā'', in: *Al-I'āqa wa al-ta'hīl*, Riyadh, no. 1, p. 17.
188 Labbān, Ibrāhīm al- (1383/1964), 'Ḥaqq al-fuqarā' fī amwāl al-aghnyā'', in: *Al-Mu'tamar al-awwal li majma' al-buḥūth al-islāmiyya*, Cairo: Majma' al-Buḥūth al-Islāmiyya, Al-Azhar, pp. 247–248.
189 Ibn Ḥazm, Abū Muḥammad 'Alī (1347/1928–1352/1933), vol. 6, p. 156.
190 Ibid., vol. 6, pp. 156–159.
191 Sābiq, al-Sayyid (n.d.), vol. 2, pp. 91–92.
192 Ibid., vol. 2, p. 92.
193 See for instance the opinion of Shaykh Ibrāhīm al-Labbān, the former dean of Dār al-'Ulūm Faculty, Cairo University, and the member of the Islamic Researches Complex, Labbān, Ibrāhīm al- (1383/1964).

9 Conclusion

1 Scalenghe, Sara (2007), 'Disability', in: Meri, Josef W. (ed.) (2006) *Medieval Islamic Civilization: An Encylopedia*, vol. 1, p. 209.
2 Rispler-Chaim, Vardit (2007), *Disability in Islamic Law*, Dordrecht, The Netherlands: Springer, p. 95.

Bibliography

1 Works published in Arabic

Ābādī, Abū al-Ṭayyib Muḥammad Shams al-Ḥaqq (1415/1994) *'Awn al-ma'būd sharḥ sunan Abū Dawūd*, 2nd edn, Beirut: Dār al-Kutub al-'Ilmiyya, 9 volumes.

'Abd al-Ḥakīm, Ibn Muḥammad (1332/1914) *Ḥuqūq al-usra*, Cairo: Maṭba'at al-Jamāliyya.

'Abd al-Ḥamīd, al-Sayyid Muḥammad (1418/1998) *Al-Ta'wīq 'al-i'āqa'*, Cairo: Al-Maktaba al-Azhariyya li al-Turāth.

'Abd al-Ḥamīd, Muḥammad Muḥyī al-Dīn (1966) *Al-Aḥwāl al-shakṣiyya fī al-sharī'a al-islāmiyya*, Cairo: Maktabat 'Alī Ṣubayḥ wa-Awlāduh.

'Abd al-Jabbār, al-Qāḍī Abū al-Ḥasan (1380–1389/1960–1969) *Al-Mughnī fī abwāb al-tawḥīd wa al-'adl*, Cairo, 20 volumes.

—— (1384/1965) *Sharḥ al-uṣūl al-khamsa*, 1st edn, Cairo: Maktabat Wahba.

'Abd Allāh, Muḥammad 'Abd Allāh (1422/2001) 'Ḥuqūq al-mu'āqīn nafsiyyan wa 'aqliyyan fī al-islām wa al-qawānīn al-ma'mūl bihā', in: 'Awaḍī, 'Abd al-Raḥmān 'Abd Allāh al- and Aḥmad Rajā'ī al-Jundī (eds), *Al-Mushāwara al-buldāniyya ḥawl tashrī'āt al-ṣiḥḥa al-nafsiyya fī mukhtalaf al-sharā'i' bimā fī dhālik al-sharī'a al-islāmiyya*, Kuwait: Islamic Organization for Medical Sciences, vol. 2, pp. 665–721.

'Abd Allāh, Muḥammad Maḥmūd (1996) *I'jāz al-Qur'ān fī 'ilāj al-siḥr wa al-ḥasad wa mass al-shaytān*, Beirut: Mu'assasat al-Īmān and Dār al-Rashīd.

'Abd Allāh, Laylā Muḥammad (1418/1997) *Aḥkām al-akhras fī al-fiqh al-islāmī*, Cairo: Maktabat al-Zahrā'.

'Abd Allāh, 'Umar (1968) *Aḥkām al-sharī'a al-islāmiyya fī al-aḥwāl al-shakhṣiyya*, Alexandria: Dār al-Ma'ārif.

Abū Ghudda, 'Abd al-Sattār (1411/1991) 'Ri'āyat al-mu'awwaqīn fī al-islām', in: *Buḥūth fī al-fiqh al-ṭibbī wa al-ṣiḥḥa al-nafsiyya min manẓūr islāmī*, Cairo: Dār al-Aqṣā and Maṭba'at al-Ḥaramyn, pp. 215–239.

—— (2001) 'Mas'ūliyyāt wa ḥuqūq al-mu'āqīn 'aqliyyan wa nafsiyyan', in: 'Awaḍī, 'Abd al-Raḥmān 'Abd Allāh al- and Aḥmad Rajā'ī al-Jundī (eds) *Al-Mushāwara al-buldāniyya*, Kuwait, vol. 2, pp. 734–775.

Abū Jayb, Sa'dī (1402/1982) *Al-Muw'awwaq wa al-mujtama' fī al-sharī'a al-islāmiyya*, Damascus and Beirut: Dār al-Fikr al-Mu'āṣir and Dār al-Fikr.

Abū Ya'lā, Ibn al-Farrā' (1974) *Al-Mu'tamad fī uṣūl al-dīn*, Beirut.

Abū Zahra, Muḥammad (1948) *Al-Shāfi'ī: ḥayātuh wa 'aṣruh: ārā'uh al-fiqhiyya*, 2nd edn, Beirut: Dār al-Fikr al-'Arabī.

—— (ed.) (1963) *Usbū' al-fiqh al-islāmī*, Cairo: Al-Majlis al-A'lā li Ri'āyat al-Funūn.

—— (1970) *Al-Wilāyā 'alā al-nafs*, Beirut: Dār al-Rā'id al-'Arabī.

Abyānī, Muḥammad Zayd al- (1342/1924) *Mukhtaṣar sharḥ al-aḥkām al-shar'iyya fī al-aḥwāl al-shakhṣiyya*, Cairo.

'Adiyy, 'Abd al-Karīm (1982–1983) 'Al-Firāsa 'ind al-'Arab', *MMLAD*, vol. 57, no. 4, pp. 707–728, vol. 58, no. 1, pp. 343–365, vol. 58, no. 2, pp. 161–193, vol. 58, no. 3, pp. 570–631.

'Ajlūnī, Muḥammad b. Ismā'īl al- (1405/1984) *Kashf al-khafā'*, ed. Aḥmad al-Qallāsh, 4th edn, Beirut: Mu'assasat al-Risāla.

'Ajūba, Mukhtār Ibrāhīm *et al.* (1417/1996) *Al-I'āqa fī al-turāth al-'arabī al-islāmī*, Riyadh: Maṭābi' Jāmi'at al-Malik Su'ūd.

'Alamī, Zayn al-Dīn Jabā'ī al- (1923) *Musakkin al-fu'ād 'ind faqd al-aḥibba wa al-awlād*, Al-Najaf.

Alūsī, Abū al-Faḍl Maḥmūd al- (n.d.) *Rūḥ al-ma'ānī fī tafsīr al-Qur'ān al-'Aẓīm wa al-sab' al-mathānī*, Beirut: Dār Iḥyā' al-Turāth al-'Arabī, 30 volumes.

Anṣārī, Abū Ṭālib al- (1332/1914) *Kitāb al-siyāsa fī 'ilm al-firāsa*, Cairo: Al-Maṭba'a al-Kulliyya bi al-Sikka al-Jadīda.

Anṣārī, Abū Yaḥyā Zakariyya al- (1418/1997) *Fatḥ al-Wahhāb bi sharḥ manhaj al-ṭullāb*, 1st edn, Beirut: Dār al-Kutub al-'Ilmiyya, 2 volumes.

—— (n.d.) *Tuḥfat al-ṭullāb bi sharḥ taḥrīr tanqīḥ al-lubāb*, Pekalongan, Indonesia: Maktabat wa Maṭba'at Rājāmūra Vkālūghān.

—— (n.d.a) *Al-Ghurar al-bahiyya sharḥ al-bahja al-wardiyya*, Cairo: Al-Maṭba'a al-Maymaniyya, 5 volumes.

'Ārif, 'Alī 'Ārif (1421/2001) 'Qaḍāyā fiqhiyya fī al-jīnāt al-bashariyya', in: Ashqar, 'Umar Sulaymān al- *et al.* (1421/2001), *Dirāsāt fiqhiyya fī qaḍāyā ṭibbiyya Mu'āṣira*, Amman: Dār al-Nafā'is, vol. 2, pp. 735–803.

Aṣbahānī, Abū Nu'aym al- (1405/1984) *Ḥilyat al-awliyā'*, 4th edn, Beirut: Dār al-Kitāb al-'Arabī, 10 volumes.

Aṣfahānī, Rāghib al- (n.d.) *Al-Mufradāt fī gharīb al-Qur'ān*, ed. Muḥammad Sayyid Kīlānī, Beirut: Dār al-Ma'rifa.

Ash'arī, Abū al-Ḥasan 'Alī b. Ismā'īl al- (1397/1977) *Al-Ibāna 'an uṣūl al-diyāna*, ed. Fawqiyya Ḥusayn Maḥmūd, 1st edn, Cairo: Dār al-Anṣār.

—— (1988) *Risāla ilā ahl al-thaghr*, ed. 'Abd Allāh Shākir Muḥammad al-Junaydī, Damascus: Maktabat al-'Ulūm wa al-Ḥikam.

—— (n.d.) *Maqālāt al-islāmiyyīn wa ikhtilāf al-muṣallīn*, ed. Hellmut Ritter, 3rd edn, Beirut: Dār Iḥyā' al-Turāth al-'Arabī.

Ashqar, 'Umar Sulaymān al- (1413/1991) *Tārīkh al-fiqh al-islāmī*, Jordan: Dār al-Nafā'is and Kuwait: Maktabat al-Falāḥ.

—— (1421/2001) 'I'ādat waṣl mā quṭi' min jasad al-insān', in: Ashqar, 'Umar Sulaymān al- *et al.* (1413/1991), *Dirāsāt fiqhiyya fī qaḍāyā ṭibbiyya Mu'āṣira*, Amman: Dār al-Nafā'is, vol. 1, pp. 243–303.

—— (2003) 'Al-Tadāwī bayn al-akhdh bi al-asbāb wa al-tawakkul 'alā Allāh', a fatwa published on 8 July 2003, http://www.islamonline.net (accessed 18 June 2007).

—— *et al.* (1421/2001) *Dirāsāt fiqhiyya fī qaḍāyā ṭibbiyya mu'āṣira*, Amman: Dār al-Nafā'is.

'Asqalānī, Ibn Ḥajar al- (1301/1883) *Tawālī al-ta'sīs bi ma'ālī Muḥammad Ibn Idrīs*, 1st edn, Cairo: Bulāq.

—— (1379/1959) *Fatḥ al-Bārī*, ed. Muḥammad Fu'ād 'Abd al-Bāqī and Muḥibb al-Dīn al-Khaṭīb, Beirut: Dār al-Ma'rifa, 13 volumes.

—— (1384/1964) *Talkhīṣ al-ḥabīr*, ed. Al-Sayyid 'Abd Allāh Hāshim al-Yamānī al-Madanī, Ṭab'at al-Madīna al-Munawwara, 2 volumes.

—— (1972) *Al-Durar al-kāmina fī a'yān al-mi'a al-thāmina*, ed. Muḥammad 'Abd al-Mu'īd Khān, 2nd edn, Hayderabad, India: Ṭab'at Majlis Dā'irat al-Ma'ārif al-'Uthmāniyya, 4 volumes.

—— (1404/1984) *Tahdhīb al-tahdhīb*, 1st edn, Beirut: Dār al-Fikr, 12 volumes.

—— (1406/1986) *Lisān al-mizān*, 3rd edn, Beirut: Mu'assasat al-A'lamī li al-Maṭbū'āt, 7 volumes.

—— (1412/1992) *Al-Iṣāba fī tamyīz al-ṣaḥāba*, ed. 'Alī Muḥammad al-Bījāwī, 1st edn, Beirut: Dār al-Jīl, 8 volumes.

Aṭfīsh, Muḥammad b. Yūsuf (1405/1985) *Sharḥ al-Nīl wa shifā' al-'alīl*, 3rd edn, Maktabat al-Irshād, 17 volumes.

'Awaḍ, al-Sayyid Ḥanafī (1998) *Al-'Amal wa qaḍāya al-ṣinā'a fī al-islām*, Cairo: Al-Maktab al-'Ilmī li al-Kumbyūtar.

'Awaḍī, 'Abd al-Raḥmān 'Abd Allāh al- and Aḥmad Rajā'ī al-Jundī (eds) (1422–2001) *Al-Mushāwara al-buldāniyya ḥawl tashrī'āt al-ṣiḥḥa al-nafsiyya fī mukhtalaf al-sharā'i' bimā fī dhālik al-sharī'a al-islāmiyya*, Kuwait: Islamic Organization for Medical Sciences, 2 volumes.

'Aydarūsī Muḥyī al-Dīn 'Abd al-Qādir al- (1934) *Tārīkh al-nūr al-musāfir 'an akhbār al-qarn al-'āshir*, Baghdad: Al-Maktaba al-'Arabiyya, 2 volumes.

Bābānī, Ismā'īl Bashā al- (1364/1945) *Īḍāḥ al-maknūn fī al-dhayl 'ala kashf al-ẓunūn*, Istanbul: Millī Eğitim Basimevi.

Badawī, 'Abd al-Raḥmān (1954) *Al-Uṣūl al-yūnāniyya li al-naẓariyyāt al-siyāsiyya fī al-islām*, Cairo: Maṭba'at Dār al-Kutub al-Miṣriyya.

Badrān, Abū al-'Aynayn Badrān (1988) *Ḥuqūq al-awlād fī al-sharī'a al-islāmiyya wa al-qānūn*, Alexandria: Mu'assasat Shabāb al-Jāmi'a.

Badrī, Mālik al- (2001) 'Tashrī'āt al-ṣiḥḥa al-nafsiyya min manẓūr islāmī', in: 'Awaḍī, 'Abd al-Raḥmān 'Abd Allāh al- and Aḥmad Rajā'ī al-Jundī (eds) (1422–2001) *Al-Mushāwara al-buldāniyya*, Kuwait, vol. 1, pp. 345–372.

Baghdādī, Abū Bakr Aḥmad 'Alī b. Thābit al-Khaṭīb al- (n.d.) *Tārīkh Baghdād*, Beirut: Dār al-Kutub al-'Ilmiyya, 14 volumes.

Baghdādī, Abū Manṣūr 'Abd al-Qāhir al- (1346/1928) *Uṣūl al-dīn*, Istanbul.

—— (1977) *Al-Farq bayn al-firaq*, 2nd edn, Beirut: Dār al-Āfāq al-Jadīda.

Bahiyy, Muḥammad al- (1971) *Al-Fikr al-islāmī wa al-mujtama 'al-mu'āṣir: mushkilāt al-usra wa al-takāful*, Tripoli, Libya: Dār al-Fikr.

Bāji, Sulaymān b. Khalaf al- (n.d.) *Al-Muntaqā sharḥ al-muwaṭṭa'*, 2nd edn, Beirut: Dār al-Kitāb al-Islāmī, 7 volumes.

Bannā, Jamāl al- (1985) *Ta'mīq ḥāssat al-'amal fī al-mujtama 'al-islāmī*, Al-Ittiḥād al-Islāmī al-Dawlī li al-'Amal, available at http://islamiccall.org/TaamiqInd.htm (accessed 3 August 2007).

Baqmī, Ṣāliḥ al-Marzūqī al- (2006) *Al-Ta'rīf bi al-Majma' al-Fiqhī al-Islāmī bi Makka al-Mukarrama*, 3rd edn, Mecca: Rābitat al-'Ālam al-Islāmī.

Barnāmaj wa al-mulakhkhaṣāt al-'ilmiyya, al-: al-mu'tamar al-dawlī al-thānī li al-i'āqa wa al-ta'hīl (2000) Riyadh: Prince Salman Center for Disability Research and Disabled Children's Association.

Basalāma, Ḥusayn b. 'Abd Allāh (1326/1908) *Al-Jawhar al-lammā' fīmā thabat bi al-samā' min ḥikam al-imām al-shāfi'ī al-manẓūma wa al-manthura al-thābita bi al asānīd al-ma'thūra*, Cairo: Maṭba'at Kurdistān al-'Ilmiyya.

Bayāḍī, Kamāl al-Dīn Aḥmad al- (1949) *Ishārāt al-marām min 'ibarāt al-imām*, Cairo: Maṭba'at Al-Ḥalabī.

Bayḍāwī, 'Abd Allāh b. 'Umar al- (1323/1905) *Ṭawāli' al-anwār bi sharḥ al-mar'ashī*, Cairo.

—— (1416/1996) *Tafsīr al- Bayḍāwī*, ed. 'Abd al-Qādir 'Arafāt Ḥassūna, Beirut: Dār al-Fikr, 5 volumes.

Bayhaqī, Abū Bakr Aḥmad b. al-Ḥusayn al- (1390/1970) *Manāqib al-Shāfi'ī*, ed. Al-Sayyid Aḥmad Ṣaqr, Cairo: Maktabat Dār al-Turāth, 2 volumes.

—— (1410/1989) *Shu'ab al-īmān*, ed. Muḥammad al-Sa'īd Basyūnī Zaghlūl, Beirut: Dār al-Kutub al-'Ilmiyya, 6 volumes.

Bayyūmī, Muḥammad Rajab al- (1420/1999) *Al-Nahḍa al-islāmiyya fī siyar a'lāmihā al-mu'āṣirīn*, Damascus: Dār al-Qalam.

Bazdawī, Abū al-Yusr al- (1307/1889) *Uṣūl al-dīn*, Istanbul.

Bazzār, Abū Hafṣ 'Umar b. 'Alī b. Mūsā al- (1400/1979) *Al-A'lām al-'aliyya fī manāqib Ibn Taymiyya*, ed. Zuhayr al-Shāwīsh, 3rd edn, Beirut: Al-Maktab al-Islāmī.

Buhūtī, Manṣūr b. Yūnus al- (1402/1982) *Kashshāf al-qinā' 'an matn al-iqnā'*, Beirut: Dār al-Kutub al-'Ilmiyya.

Bujayramī, Sulaymān b. Muḥammad al- (1415/1995) *Ḥāshiyat al-Bujayramī 'alā al-khaṭīb*, Beirut: Dār al-Fikr, 4 volumes.

Bukhārī, 'Abd al-'Azīz b. Aḥmad b. Muḥammad al- (n.d.) *Kashf al-asrār sharḥ uṣūl al-Bazdawī*, Beirut: Dār al-Kitāb al-Islāmī, 4 volumes.

Bukhārī, Abū 'Abd Allāh al- (1407/1987) *Ṣaḥīḥ al-Bukhārī*, ed. Muṣṭafā Dīb al-Baghā, 3rd edn, Beirut: Dār Ibn Kathīr/al-Yamāma, 6 volumes.

—— (1409/1989) *Al-Adab al-mufrad*, ed. Muḥammad Fu'ād 'Abd al-Bāqī, 3rd edn, Beirut: Dār al-Bashā'ir al-Islāmiyya.

Būnī, Abū al-'Abbās Aḥmad al- (1951) *Manba' uṣūl al-ḥikma*, Cairo: Muṣṭafā al-Bābī al-Ḥalabī.

Būṭī, Muḥammad Sa'īd Ramaḍān, al- (2001) *Al-Insān musayyar am mukhayyar*, 2nd edn, Beirut: Dār al-Fikr al-Mu'āṣir and Damascus: Dār al-Fikr.

Dāraqutnī, 'Alī b. 'Umar al- (1310/1892) *Sunan al-Dāraquṭnī*, Delhi: Matba'at al-Anṣār, 4 volumes.

—— (1402/1981) *Kitāb al-ṣifāt*, ed. 'Abd Allāh al-Ghunaymān, 1st edn, Al-Madīna al-Munawwara, Saudi Arabia: Maktabat al-Dār.

Dawūd, 'Abd al-Bārī Muḥammad (1417/1997) *Al-Fanā' 'ind al-ṣūfiyya al-muslimīn wa al-'aqā'id al-ukhrā*, 1st edn, Cairo: Al-Dār al-Miṣriyya al-Lubnāniyya.

Daylamī, Shīrawayh al- (1407/1987) *Al-Firdaws bi ma'thūr al-khiṭāb*, Beirut: Dār al-Kitāb al-'Arabī, ed. Fawwāz Aḥmad al-Zamarlī and Muḥammad al-Mu'taṣim bi Allāh al-Baghdādī, 5 volumes.

Dhahabī, Muḥammad b. Aḥmad b. 'Uthmān al- (1349/1930) *Al-Ṭibb al-nabawī*, Cairo: Muṣṭafā al-Bābī al-Ḥalabī wa Awladuh bi Miṣr.

—— (1413/1992) *Siyar a'lām al-nubalā'*, ed. Shu'ayb al-Arna'ūṭ and Muḥammad Nu'aym al-'Arqasūsī, 9th edn, Beirut: Mu'assasat al-Risāla, 23 volumes.

—— (1419/1998) *Tārīkh al-islām*, ed. 'Umar b. 'Abd al-Salām al-Tadmurī, 3rd edn, Beirut: Dār al-Kitāb al-'Arabī, 49 volumes.

—— (n.d.) *Al-Kabā'ir*, Beirut: Dār al-Nadwa al-Jadīda.

Farāhīdī, al-Khalīl b. Aḥmad al- (1980–1985) *Kitāb al-'ayn*, ed. Mahdī al-Makhzūmī and Ibrāhīm al-Samarrā'ī, Baghdad: Manshurāt Wizārat al-Thaqāfa wa al-I'lām, 8 volumes.

Fayyūmī, Aḥmad b. Muḥammad b. 'Alī al- (n.d.) *Al-Miṣbāḥ al-munīr fī gharīb al-sharḥ al-kabīr*, Beirut: Al-Maktaba al-'Ilmiyya.

Fityān, Farīd (1986) *Sharḥ qānūn al-aḥwāl al-shakhṣiyya ma'a ta'dīlāt al-qanūn wa aḥkām maḥkamat al-tamyīz*, London: Dār Wāṣit.

Ghānim, Ibrāhīm al-Bayyūmī (1419/1998) *Al-Awqāf wa al-siyāsa fī Miṣr*, 1st edn, Cairo: Dār al-Shurūq.

Ghazālī, Abū Ḥāmid al- (1327/1909) 'Al-Ḥikma fī makhlūqāt Allāh 'azz wa jall', in: Ghazālī, Abū Ḥāmid al- *Al-Rasā'il al-farā'id min taṣānīf al-imām al-Ghazālī*, Cairo: Maktabat al-Jundī, pp. 15–96.

—— (1985) *Qawā'id al-'aqā'id*, ed. Mūsā b. Naḍr, 1st edn, Beirut: 'Ālam al-Kutub.

—— (1407/1987) *Al-Maqṣad al-asnā fī sharḥ ma'ānī asmā' Allāh al-ḥusnā*, ed. Bassām 'Abd al-Wahhāb al-Jābī, 1st edn, Limassol, Cyprus: Al-Jaffān wa al-Jābī.

—— (n.d.) *Iḥyā' 'ulūm al-dīn*, Beirut: Dār al-Ma'rifa, 4 volumes.

—— (n.d.a) *Maqāṣid al-falāsifa*, ed. Sulaymān Dunyā, 2nd edn, Cairo: Dār al-Ma'ārif.

—— (pseudo) (1970) *Al-Ṭibb al-Rūḥānī li al-jism al-insānī fī 'ilm al-ḥarf*, Beirut: Al-Maktaba al-Thaqāfiyya.

Grīsha, 'Alī (1987) *Ḥurumāt lā ḥuqūq: ḥuqūq al-insān fī ẓill al-islām dirāsa muqārana*, Cairo: Dar al-I'tiṣām.

Ḥamawī, Abū 'Abd Allāh Yaqūt b. 'Abd Allāh al- (n.d.) *Mu'jam al-buldān*, Beirut: Dār al-Fikr, 5 volumes.

Ḥamawī, Aḥmad b. Muḥammad al- (1405/1985) *Ghamz 'uyūn al-baṣā'ir fī sharḥ al-ashbāh wa al-naẓā'ir*, Beirut: Dār al-Kutub al-'Ilmiyya, 4 volumes.

Ḥanbalī, Ibn Rajab al- (1408/1987) *Jāmi' al-'ulūm wa al-ḥikam*, 1st edn, Beirut: Dār al-Ma'rifa.

Harawī, 'Abd Allāh Al-Anṣārī al- (1408/1988) *Kitāb manāzil al-sā'irīn*, Beirut: Dār al-Kutub al-'Ilmiyya.

Ḥaṭṭāb, Abū 'Abd Allāh al- (1412/1992) *Mawāhib al-Jalīl fī sharḥ mukhtaṣar al-Khalīl*, 3rd edn, Beirut: Dār al-Fikr, 6 volumes.

Ḥawwā, Sa'īd (1424/2004) *Allāh jall jalāluh*, 4th edn, Cairo: Dār al-Salām.

Haytamī, Ibn Ḥajar al- (1403/1983) *Al-Fatāwā al-fiqhiyya al-kubrā: fatāwā Ibn Ḥajar*, n.p.: Al-Maktaba al-Islāmiyya, 4 volumes.

—— (1994) *Al-Zawājir 'an iqtirāf al-kabā'ir*, 1st edn, Beirut: Dār al-Fikr, 2 volumes.

—— (n.d.) *Tuḥfat al-muḥtāj fī sharḥ al-minhāj*, Beirut: Dār Iḥyā' al-Turāth al-'Arabī, 10 volumes.

—— (n.d.a) *Darr al-ghamāma fī dharr al-Ṭaylaṣān wa al-'adhba wa al-'imāma*, Cairo: Maṭba'at al Sa'āda.

Haythamī, Abū al-Ḥasan 'Alī b. Abī Bakr al- (1407/1986) *Majma' al-zawā'id wa manba ' al-fawā'id*, Cairo and Beirut: Dār al-Rayyān li al-Turāth-Dār al-Kitāb al-'Arabī, 10 volumes.

—— (n.d.) *Mawārid al-ẓam'ān ilā zawā'id Ibn Ḥibbān*, ed. Muḥammad 'Abd al-Rāziq Ḥamza, Beirut: Dār al-Kutub al-'Arabiyya.

Hīla, Muḥammad Ḥabīb al- (1994) *Al-Tārīkh wa al-mu'arrikhūn bi Makka: min al-qarn al-thālith al-hijrī ilā al-thālith 'ashar*, 1st edn, Beirut: Dār al-Gharb al-Islāmī.

Hilālī, Sa'd al-Dīn al- (1421/2001) *Al-Baṣma al-wirāthiyya wa 'alā'iquhā al-shar'iyya: dirāsa fiqhiyya muqārana*, Kuwait: Majlis al-Nashr al-'Ilmī.

Hilālī, Salīm b. 'Īd al- (1413/1992) *Madārij al-'ubūdiyya min hady khayr al-bariyya*, Riyadh: Dār al-Ṣumay'ī.

Ḥillī, Ja'far b. al-Ḥasan al- (1408/1987) *Sharā'i' al-islām fī masā'il al-ḥalāl wa al-ḥarām*, 2nd edn, Mu'assasat Maṭbū'āt Ismā'ilyān, n.p., 4 volumes, reprint without date, Ḥillī, Ja'far b. al-Ḥasan al- (n.d.) Beirut: Maṭba'at Dār Maktabat al-Ḥayāt.

Ḥusayn, 'Abd al-Razzāq (1420/1999) *Al-I'āqa fī al-adab al-'arabī*, 1st edn, al-Shāriqa, UAE: Manshurāt Madīnat al-Shāriqa li al-Khadamāt al-Insāniyya.

Ibn 'Abd al-Barr, Abū 'Amr Yūsuf (1387/1967) *Al-Tamhīd limā fī al-muwaṭṭa' min al-ma'ānī wa al-asānīd*, ed. Muṣṭafā b. Aḥmad al-'Alawī and Muḥammad 'Abd al-Kabīr al-Bakrī, Rabat: Wizārat 'Umūm al-Awqāf wa al-Shu'ūn al-Islāmiyya, 24 volumes.

Ibn 'Abd al-Salām, al-'Izz (1992) *Al-Fitan wa al-balāya wa al- miḥan wa al-razāyā*, ed. Iyād Khālid al-Ṭabbā', 1st edn, Damascus and Beirut: Dār al-Fikr and Dār al-Fikr al-Mu'āṣir.

—— (n.d.) *Qawā'id al-aḥkām fī maṣāliḥ al-anām*, Beirut: Dār al-Kutub al-'Ilmiyya, 2 volumes.

Ibn 'Abd al-Wahhāb, Muḥammad (n.d.) *Mu'allafāt al-Shaykh Muḥammad Ibn 'Abd al-Wahhāb*, ed. 'Abd al-'Azīz Zayd al-Rūmī *et al.*, Riyadh: Jāmi'at al-Imām Muḥammad b. Sa'ūd.

Ibn Abī al-Dunyā (1410/1989) *Al-Riḍā 'an Allāh bi qaḍā'ih*, ed. Ḍiyā' al-Ḥasan al-Salafī, 1st edn, Bombay: Al-Dār al-Salafiyya.

Ibn Abī al-Wafā' (n.d.) *Al-Jawāhir al-muḍī'a fī ṭabaqāt al-Ḥanafiyya*, Karachi: Mīr Muḥammad Kutub Khāna.

Ibn 'Ābidīn, Muḥammad Amīn b. 'Umar (n.d.) *Al-'Uqūd al-durriyya fī tanqīḥ al-fatāwā al-ḥāmidiyya*, Beirut: Dār al-Ma'rifa.

Ibn Abī Shayba (1409/1988) *Muṣannaf Ibn Abī Shayba*, ed. Kamāl Yūsuf al-Ḥūt, 1st edn, Riyadh: Maktabat al-Rushd, 16 volumes.

Ibn Abī Usāma, al-Ḥārith (1412/1992) *Musnad al-Ḥārith*, ed. Ḥusayn Aḥmad Ṣāliḥ al-Bakrī, 1st edn, Al-Madīna al-Munawwara: Markaz Khidmat al-Sunna wa al-Sīra al-Nabawiyya.

Ibn Abī Uṣaybi'a (n.d.) *'Uyūn al-anbā' fī ṭabqāt al-aṭibbā'*, ed. Nazār Riḍā, Beirut: Dār Maktabat al-Ḥayāt.

Ibn Abī Ya'lā (n.d.) *Ṭabaqāt al-Ḥanābila*, ed. Muḥammad Ḥāmid al-Fiqī, Beirut: Dār al-Ma'rifa, 2 volumes.

Ibn al-'Arabī (n.d.) *Aḥkām al-Qur'ān*, 1st edn, Beirut: Dār al-Kutub al-'Ilmiyya, 4 volumes.

Ibn al-Akfānī (1989) *Kitāb irshād al-qāṣid ilā asnā al-maqāṣid*, ed. J. Witkam, Leiden: Ter Lugt Pers.

Ibn al-Athīr, Majd al-Dīn (1963) *Al-Nihāya fī gharīb al-ḥadīth wa al-athar*, ed. Ṭāhir Aḥmad al-Zāwī and Maḥmūd Muḥammad al-Ṭanāḥī, Cairo, 5 volumes.

Ibn al-Ḥājj (n.d.) *Al-Madkhal*, Beirut: Dār al-Turāth, 4 volumes.

Ibn al-'Imād (n.d.) *Shadharāt al-dhahab fī tārīkh man dhahab*, Beirut: Dār al-Kutub al-'Ilmiyya, 4 volumes.

Ibn al-Jawzī (1348/1929) *Al-Ṭibb al-rūḥānī*, Damascus: Maktabat al-Qudsī wa al-Budayr.

—— (1399/1979) *Ṣifat al-ṣafwa*, ed. Maḥmūd Fakhūrī and Muḥammad Ruwās Qal'ajī, 2nd edn, Beirut: Dār al-Ma'rifa, 4 volumes.

—— (1987) *Ṣayd al-khāṭir*, ed. Ādam Abū Snīna, Amman: Dār al-Fikr, reprint without date, Ibn al-Jawzī (n.d.a) Cairo: al-Maktaba al-Tawfīqiyya, ed. 'Imād Zakī al-Bārūdī.

—— (1987a) *Mukhtaṣar luqaṭ al-manāfi'*, ed. Aḥmad Yūsuf al-Daqqāq, 1st edn, Damascus: Dār al-Ma'mūn li al-Turāth.

—— (1990) *Akhbār al-ḥamqā wa al-mughaffalīn*, ed. Muḥammad Amīn Farshūkh, Beirut: Dār al-Fikr al-'Arabī.

—— (1990a) *Akhbār al-ẓirāf wa al-mutamājinīn*, Beirut: Dār al-Fikr.

—— (n.d.) *Talqīḥ fuhūm ahl al-athar fī 'uyūn al-tārīkh wa al-siyar*, Delhi.

Ibn al-Malāḥimī (1991) *Al-Mu'tamad fī uṣūl al-dīn*, ed. Martin J. McDermott and Wilfred Madelung, London: Dār al-Hudā.

Ibn al-Murtaḍā, Aḥmad b. Yaḥyā (n.d.) *Al-Baḥr al-zakhkhār al-jāmi' li madhāhib 'ulamā' al-amṣār*, Beirut: Dār al-Kitāb al-Islāmī, 6 volumes.

Ibn al-Nadīm (1398/1978) *Al-Fihrist*, Beirut: Dār al-Ma'rifa.

Ibn al-Qayyim (1348/1929) *Mukhtaṣar al-ṣawā'iq al-mursala 'ala al-Jahmiyya wa al-Mu'aṭṭila*, ed. Muḥammad Ḥāmid al-Fiqī, Mecca: Al-Maṭba'a al-Salafiyya, 2 volumes.

—— (1358/1939) *Ṭarīq al-hijratayn wa bāb al-sa'ādatayn*, Cairo: Idārat al-Ṭibā'a al-Munīriyya.

—— (1375/1956) *Rawḍat al-muḥibbīn wa nuzhat al-mushtāqīn*, ed. Aḥmad 'Ubayd, Cairo: Maṭba'at al-Sa'āda, reprint, Ibn al-Qayyim (1412/1992) Beirut: Dār al-Kitāb al-'Arabī.

—— (1393/1973) *Madārij al-sālikīn*, ed. Muḥammad Ḥāmid al-Fiqī, 2nd edn, Beirut: Dār al-Kitāb al-'Arabī, 3 volumes.

—— (1973) *I'lām al-muwaqqi'īn 'an Rabb al-'Ālamīn*, ed. Ṭāhā 'Abd al-Ra'ūf Sa'd, Beirut: Dār al-Jīl, 4 volumes.

—— (1395/1975) *Al-Rūḥ*, Beirut: Dār al-Kutub al-'Ilmiyya.

—— (1398/1977) *Shifā' al-'alīl fī masā'il al-qaḍā' wa al-qadar wa al-ḥikma wa al-ta'līl*, ed. Muḥammad Badr al-Dīn Abū Firās al-Na'sānī al-Ḥalabī, Beirut: Dār al-Fikr.

—— (1407/1986) *Zād al ma'ād fī Hady khayr al-'ibād*, ed. Shu'ayb al-Arna'ūṭ and 'Abd al-Qādir al-Arna'ūṭ, 14th edn, Beirut/Kuwait: Mu'assasat al-Risāla/Maktabat al-Manār al-Islāmiyya, 5 volumes.

—— (1416/1996) *Badā'i' al-Fawā'id*, ed. Hishām 'Abd al-'Azīz 'Aṭā *et al.*, 1st edn, Mecca: Maktabat Nazār Muṣṭafā al-Bāz.

—— (n.d.) *'Uddat al-ṣābirīn wa dhakhīrat al-shākirīn*, ed. Zakariyya 'Alī Yūsuf, Beirut: Dār al-Kutub al-'Ilmiyya.

—— (n.d.a) *Miftāḥ dār al-sa'āda*, Beirut: Dār al-Kutub al-'Ilmiyya, 2 volumes.

—— (n.d.b) *Al-Jawāb al-kāfī li man sa'al 'an al-dawā' al-shāfī: al-dā' wa al-dawā'*, Beirut: Dār al-Kutub al-'Ilmiyya.

—— (n.d.d) *Al-Ṭuruq al-ḥukmiyya*, Damascus: Maktabat Dār al-Bayān.

—— (n.d.e) *Al-Ṭibb al-nabawī*, ed. 'Abd al-Ghanī 'Abd al-Khāliq, Beirut: Dār al-Fikr.

Ibn al-Wazīr, Muḥammad b. Ibrāhīm (1987) *Īthār al-ḥaqq 'alā al-khalq fī radd al-khilāfāt ilā al-madhhab al-ḥaqq min uṣūl al-tawḥīd*, 2nd edn, Beirut: Dār al-Kutub al-'Ilmiyya.

Ibn 'Arabī, Muḥyī al-Dīn (1328/1910) 'Tāj al-Rasā'il', in: *Majmū' al-Rasā'il*, Cairo.

—— (1418/1997) *Al-Tadbīrāt al-ilāhiyya fī iṣlāḥ al-mamlaka al-insāniyya*, Cairo: Maktabat 'Ālam al-Fikr li al-Ṭibā'a wa al-Nashr.

Ibn 'Ashūr, Muḥammad al-Ṭāhir (1997) *Tafsīr al-taḥrīr wa al-tanwīr*, Tunisia: Dār Saḥnūn li al-Nashr wa al-Twazī', 12 volumes.

Ibn Bāz, 'Abd Allāh (1413/1992) 'Jawāz ṣarf al-zakāt 'ala ḥajāt al-mu'awwaqīn al-fuqarā', *Al-I'āqa wa al-ta'hīl*, Riyadh, Saudi Arabia, no. 1, p. 17.

—— (1416/1995) ''Ilāj al-amrāḍ al-'uḍwiya bi al-Qur'ān', in: *Majallat al-Da'wa*, no. 1497, 1/2/1416, available at http://www.alifta.com (accessed 18 June 2007).

—— (1418/1997) ''Ilāj al-saraṭān bi al-Qur'an', in: *Majallat al-Da'wa*, no. 1637, 19/12/1418, available at http://www.alifta.com (accessed 18 June 2007).

Ibn Fahd (1420/2000) *Kitāb nayl al-munā bi dhayl bulūgh al-qirā li takmilat itḥāf al-warā*, London: Mu'assasat al-Furqān li al-Turāth al-Islāmī, 2 volumes.

Ibn Farḥūn, Ibrāhīm b. 'Alī b. Muḥammad al-Ya'murī (1406/1986) *Tabṣirat al-Ḥukkām*, 1st edn, Beirut: Dār al-Kutub al-'Ilmiyya.

Ibn Ḥabīb, Abū al-Qāsim al-Ḥasan b. Muḥammad (1418/1998) *'Uqalā' al-majānīn*, Beirut: Dār al-Nafā'is.

Ibn Ḥabīb, Muḥammad (1361/1942) *Kitāb al-muḥabbar*, ed. Elza Lichten Stitter, Hyderabad.

Ibn Ḥamdūn (1996) *Al-Tadhkira al-Ḥamadūniyya*, ed. Iḥsān 'Abbās and Bakr 'Abbās, Beirut: Dār Ṣādir, 10 volumes.

Ibn Ḥamza, Muṣṭafā (1414/1993) *Ḥuqūq al-mu'awwaqīn fī al-islām*, Casablanca: Maṭba'at al-Najāḥ al-Jadīda.

Ibn Ḥanbal, Aḥmad (n.d.) *Musnad Aḥmad*, Cairo: Mu'assasat Qurṭuba, 6 volumes.

Ibn Ḥazm, Abū Muḥammad ʻAlī (1347–1352/1928–1933) *Al-Muḥallā bi al-āthār*, ed. Muḥammad Munīr al-Dimashqī, Cairo: Idārat al-Maṭbaʻa al-Munīriyya, two reprints without date, Beirut: Dār al-Fikr, 12 volumes, and Beirut: Dār al-Āfāq al-Jadīda, 11 volumes.

—— (n.d.) *Al-Fiṣal fī al-milal wa al-ahwā' wa al-niḥal*, Cairo: Maktabat al-Khanjī, 5 volumes.

Ibn Ḥibbān (1395/1975) *Kitāb al-thiqāt*, ed. Al-Sayyid Sharaf al-Dīn Aḥmad, 1st edn, Beirut: Dār al-Fikr, 9 volumes.

—— (1414/1993) *Ṣaḥīḥ Ibn Ḥibbān*, ed. Shuʻayb al-Arna'ūṭ, 2nd edn, Beirut: Mu'assasat al-Risāla, 16 volumes.

Ibn Hishām (1411/1990) *Al-Sīra al-nabawiyya*, ed. Ṭāhā ʻAbd al-Ra'ūf Saʻd, 1st edn, Beirut: Dār al-Jīl, 6 volumes.

Ibn Kathīr (1401/1980) *Tafsīr Ibn Kathīr*, Beirut: Dār al-Fikr, 4 volumes.

—— (n.d.) *Al-Bidāya wa al-nihāya*, Beirut: Maktabat al-Maʻārif, 12 volumes.

Ibn Khayyāṭ, Khalīfa (1386/1967) *Tārīkh khalīfa Ibn Khayyāṭ*, ed. Akram Ḍiyā' al-ʻUmarī, Baghdad: Al-Majmaʻ al-ʻIlmī li al-ʻIrāq.

Ibn Khuzayma (1387/1968) *Kitāb al-tawḥīd wa ithbāt ṣifāt al-Rabb ʻazz wa jall*, ed. Muḥammad Khalīl Harrās, Cairo: Maktabat al-Kulliyyāt al-Azhariyya.

Ibn Manẓūr, Muḥammad b. Makram (n.d.) *Lisān al-ʻArab*, 1st edn, Beirut: Dār Ṣādir, 15 volumes.

Ibn Mufliḥ, Ibrāhīm b. Muḥammad (1400/1979) *Al-Mubdiʻ fī sharḥ al-muqniʻ*, Beirut: Al-Maktab al-Islāmī, 10 volumes.

—— (1418/1997) *Kitāb al-furūʻ fī fiqh al-imām Aḥmad Ibn Ḥanbal*, ed. Abū al-Zahrā' Ḥāzim al-Qāḍī, 1st edn, Beirut: Dār al-Kutub al-ʻIlmiyya, 6 volumes.

—— (n.d.) *Al-Ādāb al-sharʻiyya wa al-minaḥ al-marʻiyya*, Beirut: ʻĀlam al-Kutub, 3 volumes.

Ibn Nāṣir al-Dīn, Muḥammad b. ʻAbd Allāh (1420/1999) *Bard al-akbād ʻind faqd al-awlād*, Riyadh: Dār Ibn Khuzayma li al-Nashr wa al-Tawzīʻ.

Ibn Nujaym, Zayn al-Dīn b. Ibrāhīm (n.d.) *Al-Baḥr al-rā'iq sharḥ kanz al-daqā'iq*, 2nd edn, Beirut: Dār al-Kitāb al-Islāmī, 8 volumes, reprint without date, Beirut: Dār al-Maʻrifa, 7 volumes.

Ibn Qāḍī Shuhba, Abū Bakr b. Muḥammad (1407/1986) *Ṭabaqāt al-Shāfiʻiyya*, ed. Al-Ḥāfiẓ ʻAbd al-ʻAlīm Khān, 1st edn, Beirut: ʻĀlam al-Kutub, 4 volumes.

Ibn Qudāma (1405/1985) *Al-Mughnī*, Beirut: Dār Iḥyā' al-Turāth al-ʻArabī, 10 volumes.

—— (1408/1998) *Al-Kāfī fī fiqh al-imām Aḥmad Ibn Ḥanbal*, ed. Zuhayr al-Shāwīsh, 5th edn, Beirut: Al-Maktab al-Islāmī, 4 volumes.

—— (n.d.) *Al-Muqniʻ fī fiqh imām al-sunna Aḥmad Ibn Ḥanbal*, Cairo: Al-Maṭbaʻa al-Salafiyya wa Maktabatuhā.

Ibn Qutayba Abū Muḥammad ʻAbd Allāh b. Muslim (1388/1969) *Al-Maʻārif*, ed. Tharwat ʻUkāsha, 2nd edn, Cairo: Dār al-Maʻārif.

—— (1406/1986) *ʻUyūn al-akhbār*, ed. Mufīd Muḥammad Qamīḥa, 1st edn, Beirut: Dār al-Kutub al-ʻIlmiyya, 4 volumes.

Ibn Rushd (1965) *Tahāfut al-tahāfut*, ed. Sulaymān Dunyā, Cairo: Dār al-Maʻārif, 2 volumes.

Ibn Rusta, Abū ʻAlī Aḥmad b. ʻUmar (1419/1998) *Al-Aʻlāq al-nafīsa*, ed. Khalīl al-Manṣūr, Beirut: Dār al-Kutub al-ʻIlmiyya.

Ibn Salām, Abū ʻUbayd al-Qāsim (1388/1968) *Kitāb al-amwāl*, ed. Muḥammad Khalīl Harrās, 1st edn, Cairo: Maktabat al-Kulliyyāt al-Azhariyya.

Ibn Sayyidih (1316/1898–1321/1903) *Kitāb al-mukhaṣṣaṣ*, 1st edn, Cairo: al-Maṭbaʻa al-Amīriyya al-Kubrā bi Bulāq, 17 volumes.

Ibn Sīnā (1406/1986) *Tis' rasā'il fī al-ḥikma wa al-ṭabī'iyyāt*, ed. Ḥasan 'Āṣī, Beirut: Dār Qābis.

Ibn Taymiyya (1949) *Mukhtaṣar al-fatāwā*, Cairo: Maṭba'at Ibn 'Alī al-Ba'lī.

—— (1389/1969) 'Qā'ida fī ma'nā kawn al-Rabb 'ādil wa fī tanazzuhih 'an al-ẓulm', in: *Jāmi' al-rasā'il*, ed. Muḥammad Rashād Rafīq Sālim, Cairo: Maṭba'at al-Madanī, vol. 1, pp. 121–142.

—— (1973) *Al-Muntaqā min minhāj al-i'tidāl fī naqḍ kalām ahl al-rafḍ wa al-i'tizāl: mukhtaṣar minhāj al-sunna*, abridged by Abū 'Abd Allāh Muḥammad b. 'Uthmān al-Dhahabī, ed. Muḥibb al-Dīn al-Khaṭīb, Cairo: Al-Maṭba'a Al-Salafiyya wa Maktabatuhā.

—— (1401/1981) *Al-'Ubūdiyya*, Beirut: Dār al-Kutub al-'Ilmiyya.

—— (1404/1983) *Daqā'iq al-tafsīr al-jāmi' li tafsīr Ibn Taymiyya*, ed. Muḥammad al-Sayyid al-Julaynid, 2nd edn, Damascus: Mu'assasat 'Ulūm al-Qur'ān, 6 volumes.

—— (1406/1985) *Minhāj al-sunna al-nabawiyya fī naqḍ kalām al-Shī'a wa al-Qadariyya*, ed. Muḥammad Rashād Sālim, Mu'assasat Qurṭuba, 8 volumes.

—— (1408/1987) *Al-Fatāwā al-kubrā*, 1st edn, Beirut: Dār al-Kutub al-'Ilmiyya, 6 volumes.

—— (1409/1988) *Dar' ta'āruḍ al-'aql wa al-naql*, ed. Muḥammad al-Sayyid al-Julaynid and 'Abd al-Ṣabūr Shahīn, 1st edn, Cairo: Markaz al-Ahrām li al-Tarjama wa al-Nashr, 10 volumes.

—— (n.d.) *Kutub wa rasā'il wa fatāwā Ibn Taymiyya fī al-'aqīda*, ed. 'Abd al-Raḥmān Muḥammad Qāsim al-Najdī, Maktabat Ibn Taymiyya, 7 volumes.

—— (n.d.a) *Majmū' al-fatāwā*, ed. 'Abd al-Raḥmān b. Qāsim and Muḥammad b. 'Abd al-Raḥmān b. Qāsim, Riyadh: Mujamma' al-Malik Fahd, 37 volumes.

—— (n.d.b) *Al-Siyāsa al-shar'iyya fī iṣlāḥ al-rā'ī wa al-ra'iyya*, n.p.: Maktabat Ibn Taymiyya.

Ibn Ṭulūn (1962-1964) *Mufākahat al-khillān fī ḥawādith al-zamān*, Cairo: al-Mu'assasa al-Miṣriyya al-'Āmma li al-Ta'līf wa al-Tarjama wa al-Ṭibā'a wa al-Nashr, 2 volumes.

Ibn Yūsuf, Mar'ī (1410/1989) *Raf' al-shubha wa al-gharar 'amman yaḥtajj 'ala fi'l al-ma'āṣī bi al-qadar*, ed. As'ad Muḥammad al-Maghribī, 1st edn, Mecca: Dār Ḥirā'.

Ījī, 'Aḍud al-Dīn 'Abd al-Raḥmān b. Aḥmad al- (1997) *Kitāb al-mawāqif*, ed. 'Abd al-Raḥmān 'Imīra, 1st edn, Beirut: Dār al-Jīl, 3 volumes.

'Illaysh, Muḥammad b. Aḥmad b. Muḥammad (n.d.) *Fatḥ al-'aliyy al-mālik fī al-fatwā 'alā madhhab al-imām Mālik*, Beirut: Dār al-Ma'rifa, 2 volumes.

Iṣfahānī, al-Rāghib al- (1420/1999) *Muḥaḍarāt al-udabā'*, ed. 'Umar al-Ṭabbā', Beirut: Dār al-Qalam, 2 volumes.

Itlīdī, Muḥammad Diyāb al- (1998) *I'lām al-nās bimā waqa'a li al-barāmika ma'a banī al-'Abbās*, ed. Ayman 'Abd al-Jābir al-Biḥīrī, Cairo: Dār al-Āfāq al-'Arabiyya.

Jād al-Ḥaqq, 'Alī Jād al-Ḥaqq (1979) 'Dawr al-sharī'a al-islāmiyya fī taḥqīq ahdāf al-mujtama'': A fatwa issued on 1 April 1979, no. 1321', *Barnāmaj fatāwā Dār al-Iftā' al-Miṣriyya mundh 'ām 1312* A.H. (a software version), Cairo: Al-Majlis al-A'lā li al-Shu'ūn al-Islāmiyya.

—— (2005) *Al-Fatāwā al-islāmiyya*, 1st edn, Cairo: Dār al-Fārūq li al-Nashr wa al-Tawzī', 5 volumes.

Jāḥiẓ, Abū 'Uthmān 'Amr b. Baḥr al- (1356–1364/1938–1945) *Al-Ḥayawān*, ed. 'Abd al-Salām Muḥammad Harūn, Cairo, 8 volumes.

—— (1407/1987) *Kitāb al-burṣān wa al-'urjān wa al-'umyān wa al-ḥulān*, ed. Muḥammad Mursī al-Khūlī, 4th edn, Beirut: Mu'assasat al-Risāla.

Jamīlī, Khālid Rashīd al- (1410/1990) 'Aḥkām naql al-khiṣyatayn wa al-mibyaḍayn wa aḥkām naql a'ḍā' al-janīn al-nāqiṣ al-khilqa fī al-sharī'a al-islāmiyya', *Majallat majma' al-fiqh al-islāmī* (1410/1990), vol. 6, no. 3, pp. 1985–1997.

Jamjūm, Zuhayr (1410/1990) *Ashhar al-muw'awwaqīn fī al-'ālam*, Amman: Dār 'Ammār li al-Nashr wa al-Tawzī'.

Jaṣṣāṣ, Aḥmad b. 'Alī al-Rāzī al- (1405/1984) *Aḥkām al-Qur'ān*, ed. Muḥammad al-Ṣādiq Qamḥāwī, Beirut: Dār Iḥyā' al-Turāth al-'Arabī, 5 volumes.

Jazīrī, 'Abd al-Raḥmān al- (1420/1999) *Al-Fiqh 'alā al-madhāhib al-arba'a*, 1st edn, Cairo: Dār al-Manār, 5 volumes.

Julaynid, Muḥammad al-Sayyid al- (1981) *Qaḍiyyat al-khayr wa al-sharr fī al-fikr al-islāmī: uṣūluhā al-naẓariyya, jawānibuhā al-taṭbīqiyya: dirāsa 'ilmiyya li mas'ūliyyat al-insān fī al-islām*, 2nd edn, Cairo: Matba'at al-Ḥalabī.

Jurjānī, 'Alī b. Muḥammad b. 'Alī al- (1405/1984) *Al-Ta'rīfāt*, ed. Ibrāhīm al-Ibyārī, 1st edn, Beirut: Dār al-Kitāb al-'Arabī.

Juwaynī, Abū al-Ma'ālī, al- (1969) *Al-Shāmil fī uṣūl al-dīn*, ed. 'Alī al-Nashshār *et al.*, Alexandria.

Kalabādī, Abū Bakr Muḥammad al- (1412/1992) *Al-Ta'arruf li madhhab ahl al-taṣawwuf*, ed. Maḥmūd Amīn al-Nawāwī, 3rd edn, Cairo: Al-Maktaba al-Azhariyya li al-Turāth.

Kan'ān, Aḥmad Muḥammad (1420/2000) *Al-Mawsū'a al-ṭibbiyya al-fiqhiyya: mawsū'a jāmi'a li al-aḥkām al-fiqhiyya fī al-ṣiḥḥa wa al-Maraḍ wa al-mumārasāt al-ṭibbiyya*, 1st edn, Beirut: Dār al-Nafā'is.

Kāsānī, Abū Bakr Mas'ūd b. Aḥmad al- (1406/1986) *Badā'i' al-sanā'i' fī tartīb al-sharā'i'*, 2nd edn, Beirut: Dār al-Kutub al-'Ilmiyya, 7 volumes.

Khālid, 'Amr (2002) *Al-Ṣabr wa al-dhawq*, Cairo: Arīj li al-Nashr wa al-Tawzī'.

Khalīfa, Ḥājjī (1412/1992) *Kashf al-ẓunūn 'an asāmī al-kutub wa al-funūn*, Beirut: Dār al-Kutub al-'Ilmiyya, 2 volumes.

Khaṣṣāf, al- (1904) *Kitāb aḥkām al-waqf*, Cairo: Maṭba'at Dīwān 'Umūm al-Awqāf al-Miṣriyya.

Khaṭīb, Muḥammad b. Aḥmad Shirbīnī al- (n.d.) *Mughnī al-muḥtāj ilā ma'rifat alfāẓ al-minhāj*, Beirut: Dār al-Fikr, 4 volumes.

Khuwārizmī, Jamāl al-Dīn Abū Bakr al- (1327/1909) *Mufīd al-'ulūm wa mubīd al-humūm*, Cairo: Al-Maṭba'a al-Sharqiyya.

Kīlānī, Sarī Zayd al- (n.d.) 'Aḥkām al-mu'awwaqīn fī al-fiqh al-islāmī', unpublished PhD dissertation presented to the Faculty of Islamic Sharia and Law, al-Azhar University, Cairo.

Kubaysī, Muḥammad 'Ubayd al- (1397/1977) *Aḥkām al-waqf fī al-sharī'a al-islāmiyya*, Baghdad: Maṭba'at al-Irshād.

Labbān, Ibrāhīm al- (1383/1964) 'Ḥaqq al-fuqarā' fī amwāl al-aghnyā'', in: *Al-Mu'tamar al-awwal li majma' al-buḥūth al-islāmiyya*, Cairo: Majma' al-Buḥūth al-Islāmiyya, Al-Azhar, pp. 241–256.

Madkhalī, Muḥammad Rabī' Hadī al- (1409/1988) *Al-Ḥikma wa al-ta'līl fī af'āl Allāh ta'ālā*, Damanhūr, Egypt: Maktabat Līna li al-Nashr wa al-Twazī'.

Majlis al-A'lā li al-Shu'ūn al-Islāmiyya, al- (1386/1960–1411/1990) *Mawsū'at al- fiqh al-islāmī al-muqāran*, compiled by a group of specialists in Islamic Law, Cairo, 20 volumes.

Māliḥ, Haytham al- (2001) 'Al-Mu'āq aw al-mu'awwaq bayn al-islām wa madāris ukhrā', in: 'Awaḍī, 'Abd al-Raḥmān 'Abd Allāh al- and Aḥmad Rajā'ī al-Jundī (eds), *Al-Mushāwara al-buldāniyya*, Kuwait, vol. 2, pp. 481–517.

Manbijī, Muḥammad b. Muḥammad al- (1347/1929) *Tasliyat ahl al-maṣā'ib*, 1st edn, Cairo: Maktabat al-Khanjī.

Mānkdīm, Aḥmad b. al-Ḥusayn b. Abū Hāshim al-Ḥusaynī Shashdīw (1965) *Kitāb sharḥ al-uṣūl al-khamsa li qāḍī al-quḍāt 'Abd al-Jabbār Ibn Aḥmad al-Hamadhānī al-Asadābādī*, ed. 'Abd al-Karīm 'Uthmān, Cairo: Maktabat Wahba.

Maqdisī, Abū 'Abd Allāh Ḍiyā' al-Dīn al- (1420/1999) *Kitāb amrāḍ al-kaffarāt wa al-ṭibb wa al-ruqyāt*, 2nd edn, Cairo: Dār Ibn 'Affān.

Māturīdī, Abū Manṣūr al- (n.d.) *Kitāb al-tawḥīd*, ed. Fatḥalla Khulayf, Alexandria: Dār al-Jāmi'āt al-Miṣriyya.

Māwardī, Ibn Ḥabīb al- (n.d.) *Adab al-Dunyā wa al-Dīn*, Beirut: Dār Maktabat al-Ḥayāt.

—— (n.d.a) *Al-Aḥkām al-sulṭāniyya*, Beirut: Dār al-Kutub al-'Ilmiyya.

Mināwī, Naṣīf 'Awaḍ al- (2000) *Al-Bayān fī al-'ilāj bi al-Qur'ān*, Cairo: Markaz al-Kitāb li al-Nashr.

Minyāwī, Muḥammad Badr al- (2001) 'Al-Mu'āqūn 'aqliyyan aw nafsiyyan bayn al-islām wa al-qawānīn al-waḍ'iyya wa ḥuqūquhum qibal al-usra wa al-mujtama'', in: 'Awaḍī, 'Abd al-Raḥmān 'Abd Allāh al- and Aḥmad Rajā'ī al-Jundī (eds), *Al-Mushāwara al-buldāniyya*, Kuwait, vol. 1, pp. 395–443.

Mirdāwī, 'Alī b. Sulaymān al- (n.d.) *Al-Inṣāf fī masā'il al-khilāf*, ed. Muḥammad Ḥāmid al-Fiqī, Beirut: Dār Iḥyā' al-Turāth al-'Arabī, 12 volumes.

Mit'āl, Ṣalāḥ 'Abd al- (2001) 'Al-Wathīqa al-asāsiyya al-ijtimā'iyya 'an ri'āyat al-marīḍ 'aqliyyan fī al-islām: al-iṭār al-wiqā'ī fī al-mujtama' al-islāmī', in: 'Awaḍī, 'Abd al-Raḥmān 'Abd Allāh al- and Aḥmad Rajā'ī al-Jundī (eds), *Al-Mushāwara al-buldāniyya*, Kuwait, vol. 2, pp. 523–538.

Mizzī, Abū al-Ḥajjāj al- (1400/1980) *Tahdhīb al-kamāl*, ed. Bashshā 'Awwād Ma'rūf, 1st edn, Beirut: Mu'assasat al-Risāla, 35 volumes.

Mudhārī, Ibrāhīm b. Muṣṭafā al-Ḥalabī al- (1358/1939) *Al-Lum'ah fī taḥqīq mabāḥith al-wujūd wa al-ḥudūth wa al-qadar wa af'āl al-'ibād*, ed. Muḥammad Zāhid b. al-Ḥasan al-Kawtharī, 1st edn, Cairo: Maktab Nashr al-Thaqāfa al-Islāmiyya.

Muḥāsibī, al-Ḥārith b. Asad al- (1986) *Al-Waṣāyā*, Beirut: Dār al-Kutub al-'Ilmiyya.

Munajjid, Ṣalāḥ al-Dīn al- (1965) *Al-Mu'arrikhūn al-dimashqiyyūn wa āthāruhum al-makhṭūṭa min al-qarn al-thālith al-hijrī ilā nihāyat al-qarn al-'āshir*, Cairo: Maṭba'at Miṣr.

Munāwī, 'Abd al-Ra'ūf al- (1356/1937) *Fayḍ al-qadīr sharḥ al-jāmi' al-ṣaghīr*, 1st edn, Cairo: Al-Maktaba al-Tijāriyya al-Kubrā, 6 volumes.

Munaẓẓamat al Ṣiḥḥa al-'Ālamiyya (2001) *Al-Taṣnīf al-dawlī li ta'diyat al-waẓā'if wa al-'ajz wa al-ṣiḥḥa (ICF)*, an electronic version.

Mundhirī, Abū Muḥammad 'Abd al-'Aẓīm b. 'Abd al-Qawī al- (1417/1996) *Al-Targhīb wa al-tarhīb*, ed. Ibrāhīm Shams al-Dīn, 1st edn, Beirut: Dār al-Kutub al-'Ilmiyya, 3 volumes.

Murtaḍā, Aḥmad b. Yaḥyā al- (1368/1949) *Al-Baḥr al-zakhkhār al-jāmi' li madhāhib 'ulamā' al-amṣār*, 1st edn, Cairo: Maṭba'at Anṣār al-Sunna al-Muḥammadiyya, reprint without date, Beirut: Dār al-Kitāb al-Islāmī, 6 volumes.

Mūsā, Nāṣir b. 'Alī al- (2001) 'Muṣṭalaḥāt fī al-Tarbiyya al-Khāṣṣa bayn al-Tawḍīḥ wa al-Taṣḥīḥ', *Al-Tarbiyya al-khāṣṣa* (April), no. 2, pp. 20–21.

Muslim, Abū al-Ḥusayn b. al-Ḥajjāj (n.d.) *Ṣaḥīḥ Muslim*, ed. Muḥammad Fu'ād 'Abd al-Bāqī, Beirut: Dār Iḥyā' al-Turāth al-'Arabī, 5 volumes.

Muṭahharī, Murtaḍā al- (1424/2003) *Al-'Adl al-ilāhī*, trans. Muḥammad 'Abd al-Mun'im al-Khaqānī, Tehran: Dār al-Fiqh li al-Ṭibā'a wa al-Nashr.

Muṭarrizī, Nāṣir b. 'Abd al-Sayyid Abū al-Makārim al- (n.d.) *Al-Mughrib fī tartīb al-mu'rib*, Beirut: Dār al-Kitāb al-'Arabī.

Muṭawwa', Munīra Khālid al- (1422/2001) 'Waraqat 'amal ḥawl al-'amal al-ijtimā'ī wa dawrih fī ḥimāyat al-mu'āqīn wa al-ḥusūl 'alā ḥuqūqihim muqaddama ilā nadwat ḥuqūq al-mu'āqīn nafsiyyan wa 'aqliyyan fī al-islām', in: 'Awaḍī, 'Abd al-Raḥmān 'Abd Allāh al- and Aḥmad Rajā'ī al-Jundī (eds), *Al-Mushāwara al-buldāniyya*, Kuwait, vol. 2, pp. 641–657.

Naffākh, Aḥmad Rātib al- (1985) 'Faqīd al-majma': al-ustādh 'Abd al-Karīm Zahūr 'Adiyy', *MMLAD*, vol. 60, no. 3, pp. 625, 626.

Najjār, 'Abd al-Majīd al- (1428/2007) 'Tajdīd fiqh al-siyāsa al-shar'iyya', *SRECFR* (May), vol. 10–11, no. 1, pp. 295–330.

Nasafī, Abū al-Barakāt al- (n.d.) *Tafsīr al-Nasafī*, n.p., 4 volumes.

Nasafī, Maymūn b. Muḥammad al- (1990) *Tabṣirat al-adilla fī uṣūl al-dīn 'alā ṭarīqat al-imām Abī Manṣūr al-Māturīdī*, Damascus: Al-Ma'had al-'Ilmī al-Faransī li al-Dirāsāt al-'Arabiyya, 2 volumes.

Nashmī, 'Ajīl Jāsim al- (1423/2002) 'Al-Ḥuqūq al-ma'nawiyya li al-barāmij wa ahkām naskhihā', *SRECFR* (Rabī' Thānī/June), no. 1, pp. 129–211.

Nawawī, Yaḥyā b. Sharaf al- (1392/1972) *Sharḥ al-Nawawī 'alā ṣaḥīḥ Muslim*, 2nd edn, Beirut: Dār Iḥyā' al-Turāth al-'Arabī, 18 volumes.

—— (n.d.) *Al-Majmū' sharḥ al-muhadhdhab*, Cairo: Maṭba'at al-Munīriyya, 11 volumes.

Naysabūrī, 'Abd Allāh b. Bisṭām (1965) *Ṭibb al-a'imma*, Najaf: Al-Maktaba al-Ḥaydariyya.

Qanwajī, Ṣiddīq b. Ḥasan al- (1978) *Abjad al-'ulūm: al-washy al-marqūm fī bayān aḥwāl al-'ulūm*, ed. 'Abd al-Jabbār Zakkār, Beirut: Dār al-Kutub al-'Ilmiyya, 3 volumes.

Qaradāghī, 'Alī al- (1426/2005) 'Al-Faḥṣ al-ṭibbī qabl al-zawāj min manẓūr islāmī: dirāsa 'ilmiyya fiqhiyya', *SRECFR* (July), vol. 7, pp. 273–320.

Qaraḍāwī, Yūsuf al- (1410/1989) *Al-Ṣabr fī al-Qur'ān*, Cairo: Maktabat Wahba.

—— (1414/1994) *Fiqh al-zakāt*, 21st edn, Cairo: Maktabat Wahba.

—— (1415/1994) *Fatāwā mu'āṣira*, Kuwait: Dār al-Qalam li al-Nashr wa al-Twazī', vol. 2.

—— (1415/1994a) *Mawqif al-islām min al-ilhām wa al-kashf wa al-ru'ā wa al-kahāna wa al-ruqā*, 1st edn, Cairo: Maktabat Wahba.

—— (1416/1996) *Al-Īmān wa al-ḥayāt*, 10th edn, Cairo: Maktabat Wahba.

—— (1417/1997) *Min fiqh al-dawla fī al-islām*, Cairo: Dār al-Shurūq.

—— (1420/2000) *Fatāwā mu'āṣira*, Kuwait: Dār al-Qalam li al-Nashr wa al-Twazī', vol. 1.

—— (1421/2000) *Al-Īmān bi al-qadar*, 1st edn, Cairo: Maktabat Wahba.

—— (1422/2001) *Malāmiḥ al-mujtama' al-muslim alladhī nanshuduh*, 3rd edn, Cairo: Maktabat Wahba.

—— (2001) 'Al-Mu'awwaqūn wa dawruhum fī al-mujtama'', an episode of *Al-Sharī'a wa al-Hayāt* (*Sharī'a and Life*), programme broadcast by al-Jazeera on 21 July 2001, available at http://www.qaradawi.net (accessed 25 June 2007).

—— (1423/2002) *Al-Sunna maṣdar li al-ma'rifa wa al-ḥadāra*, 3rd edn, Cairo: Dār al-Shurūq.

—— (1424/2003) *Fatāwā mu'āṣira*, 3rd edn, Kuwait: Dār al-Qalam li al-Nashr wa al-Twazī', vol. 3.

—— (1426/2005) *Fuṣūl fī al-'aqīda bayn al-salaf wa al-khalaf*, Cairo: Maktabat Wahba.

—— (2007) 'Hal yaḥrum al-taṭ'īm li iḥtimāl ḍararih?', a fatwa published on April 2007, available at http://www.islamonline.net (accessed 5 July 2007).

Qarāfī, Aḥmad b. Idrīs al- (1402/1982) *Anwār al-burūq fī anwā' al-furūq*, 2nd edn, Beirut: 'Ālam al-Kutub, 2 volumes.

Qarār'a, Jamīl 'Ubayd al- (1420/1999) 'Riy'āyat al-mu'āqīn fī al-islām', in: *Majallat al-sharī'a wa al-dirāsāt al-islāmiyya*, Kuwait, no. 39, pp. 257–321.

Qārī, 'Alī b. Sulṭān b. Muḥammad al-Harawī al- (1404/1983) *Al-Maṣnū' fī ma'rifat al-ḥadīth al-mawḍū'*, ed. 'Abd al-Fattāḥ Abū Ghudda, Riyadh: Maktabat al-Rushd.

—— (1993) *Tasliyat al-a'mā 'an baliyyat al-'amā*, ed. 'Abd al-Karīm b. Ṣunaytān al-Munawwara: Dār al-Bukhārī li al-Nashr wa al-Tawzī'.

—— (1994) *Tasliyat al-a'mā 'an baliyyat al-'amā: wa ma yata'allaq bi al-a'mā min nawādir wa aḥkām fī al-sharī'at al-islām*, ed. Mabrūk Ismā'īl Mabrūk, Cairo: Maktabat al-Qur'ān.

Qāsimī, Jamāl al-Dīn al- (1424/2003) *Tafsīr al-Qāsimī al-musammā maḥāsin al-ta'wīl*, Cairo: Dār al-Ḥadīth, 9 volumes.

Qasṭallānī, Aḥmad b. Muḥammad al- (1326/1908) *Al-Mawāhib al-ladunniyya bi al-minaḥ al-Muḥammadiyya*, Cairo: Al-Maṭba'a al-Sharafiyya, 2 volumes.

Qayrawānī, Abū Bakr Muḥammad b. al-Labbād (1986) *Kitāb al-radd 'alā al-shāfi'ī*, Tunis.

Qaysarānī, Muḥammad b. Ṭāhir al- (1415/1994) *Tadhkirat al-ḥuffāẓ*, ed. Ḥamdī 'Abd al-Majīd Ismā'īl al-Salafī, 1st edn, Riyadh: Dār al-Ṣumay'ī, 4 volumes.

Qazwīnī, Zakariyya b. Muḥammad b. Maḥmūd al- (1405/1985) *Mufīd al-'ulūm wa mubīd al-humūm*, ed. Muḥammad 'Abd al-Qādir 'Aṭā, Beirut: Dār al-Kutub al-'Ilmiyya.

Qubaysī, Muḥammad (1996) *'Uẓamā' mashāhīr wa 'abāqira mu'awwaqūn*, Cairo: Mu'assasat al-Riḥāb al-Ḥadītha.

Quḍāt, Muṣṭafa al- (1406/1985) 'Aḥkām al-mu'awwaqīn fī al-sharī'a al-islāmiyya: aḥkām al-'umyān', unpublished MA thesis presented to Dār al-Ḥadīth al-Ḥasaniyya, Rabat, Morocco.

—— (1412/1992) 'Ḥuqūq al-mu'awwaqın bayn al-sharī'a al islāmiyya wa al-qānūn', PhD dissertation presented to Dār al-Ḥadīth al-Ḥasaniyya, Rabat, Morocco.

Qurashī, Bāqir Sharīf al- (1402/1982) *Al-'Amal wa ḥuqūq al-'āmil fī al-islām*, 2nd edn, Tehran: Dār Iḥyā' Turāth Ahl al-Bayt.

Qurashī, Muḥammad b. Muḥammad al- (n.d.) *Ma'ālim al-qurba fī ma'ālim al-ḥisba*, Cambridge: Dār al-Funūn.

Qurṭubī, Abū 'Abd Allāh Muḥammad b. Aḥmad al- (1372/1952) *Al-Jāmi' li aḥkām al-Qur'ān*, ed. Aḥmad 'Abd al-'Alīm al-Bardūnī, 2nd edn, Cairo: Dār al-Sha'b, 20 volumes.

Qushayrī, 'Abd al-Karīm al- (1968) *Al-Taḥbīr fī al-tadhkīr*, ed. Ibrāhīm Basyūnī, Cairo: Dār al-Kitāb al-'Arabī li al-Ṭibā'a wa al-Nashr.

Quṭb, Sayyid (1349/1974) *Al-'Adāla al-ijtimā'iyya fī al-islām*, Beirut and Cairo: Dār al-Shurūq.

Rājiḥī, 'Abd al-'Azīz al- (1420/1990) *Sharḥ al-'ubūdiyya li shaykh al-islām Ibn Taymiyya*, Riyadh: Dār al-Faḍīla.

Ramlī, Muḥammad b. Aḥmad al- (n.d.) *Sharḥ Zubad Ibn Raslān: ghāyat al-bayān fī sharḥ Ibn Raslān*, Beirut: Dār al-Ma'rifa.

Razı, Fakhr al-Dīn al- (1343/1924) *Kitāb al-mabāḥith al-mashriqiyya fī 'ilm al-ilāhiyyāt wa al-ṭabī'iyyāt*, 1st edn, Hyderabad: Majlis Dā'irat al-Ma'ārif al-Niẓāmiyya, 2 volumes.

—— (1939) *Kitāb al-firāsa*, ed. Youssef Mourad, Paris: P. Geuthner.

—— (1400/1980) *Sharḥ asmā' Allāh al-ḥusnā*, ed. Ṭāhā 'Abd al-Ra'ūf Sa'd, Cairo: Maktabat al-Kulliyyāt al-Azhariyya.

—— (1413/1993) *Manāqib al-imām al-Shāfi'ī*, ed. Aḥmad Ḥijāzī al-Saqqā, Beirut: Dār al-Jīl.

Rāzī, Ibn Abī Ḥātim al- (1372/1953) *Ādāb al-Shāfi'ī wa manāqibuh*, ed. 'Abd al-Ghanī 'Abd al-Khāliq, Cairo: Maktab Nashr al-Thaqāfa al-Islāmiyya.

Rāzī, Muḥammad b. Abī Bakr b. 'Abd al-Qādir al- (1415/1995) *Mukhtār al-ṣiḥāḥ*, ed. Maḥmūd Khāṭir, Beirut: Maktabat Lubnān Nāshirūn.

Riḍā, Rashīd (1315/1898–1354/1935) *Al-Manār*, Cairo: Maṭba'at al-Manār, 35 volumes.

Sadān, Yūsuf (1983) *Al-Adab al-'arabī al-hāzil wa nawādir al-thuqalā'*, Tel Aviv: Tel Aviv University.

Ṣafadī, Ṣalāḥ al-Dīn Khalīl b. Aybak al- (1329/1911) *Nakt al-himyān fī nukat al-'umyān*, ed. A. Zakī, Cairo, reprint (1997), ed. Ṭāriq Ṭanaṭāwī, Cairo: Dār al-Ṭalā'i'.

—— (1409/1988) *Al-Shu'ūr bi al-'ūr*, ed. 'Abd al-Razzāq Ḥusayn, Amman.

Sa'īd, Nadyā Muḥammad al- (1425/2004) 'Ri'āyat dhawī al-iḥtiyājāt al-khāṣṣa min manẓūr islāmī', *Al-Jundī al-muslim*, 33, no. 114, pp. 90–93.

Ṣa'īdī, 'Abd al-Mit'āl al- (1357/1939) *Al-Mirāth fī al-sharā'i' al-samāwiyya wa al-waḍ'iyya*, Cairo: Maṭba'at al-Sharq al-Islāmiyya.

Sakhāwī, Muḥammad b. 'Abd al-Raḥmān al- (1399/1979) *Al-Maqāṣid al-ḥasana*, ed. 'Abd Allāh Muḥammad al-Ṣiddīq, Beirut: Dār al-Kutub al-'Ilmiyya.

Samāḥa, Riyāḍ Muḥammad (1996) *Dalīl al-mu'ālijīn bi al-Qur'ān*, Cairo: Al-Maktaba al-Tawfīqiyya.

Ṣan'ānī, Muḥammad b. Ismā'īl al-Kaḥlānī al- (n.d.) *Subul al-salām*, Cairo: Dār al-Ḥadīth, 2 volumes.

Sanjarī, 'Alī b. Tāj al-Dīn al- (1998) *Manā'iḥ al-karam fī akhbār Makka wa al-bayt wa wulāt al-ḥaram*, Mecca: Jāmi'at Umm al-Qurā, 6 volumes.

Sarakhsī, Muḥammad b. Aḥmad b. Abī Sahl al- (1409/1989) *Al-Mabsūṭ*, Beirut: Dār al-Ma'rifa, 30 volumes, reprint (n.d.) 1st edn, Cairo: Maṭba'at al-Sa'āda.

Shāfi'ī, Ḥasan Maḥmūd al- (1411/1991) *Al-Madkhal ilā dirāsat 'ilm al-kalām*, 2nd edn, Cairo: Maktabat Wahba.

Shāfi'ī, Muḥammad b. Idrīs al- (1988) *Dīwān al-imām al-Shāfi'ī*, ed. Muḥammad Ibrāhīm Silīm, Cairo: Maktabat Ibn Sīnā.

—— (1410/1990) *Al-Umm*, Beirut: Dār al-Ma'rifa, 8 volumes.

—— (1412/1991) *Aḥkām al-Qur'ān*, Beirut: Dār al-Kutub al-'Ilmiyya, 2 volumes.

Shahrastānī, Muḥammad b. 'Abd al-Karīm al- (1416/1996) *Al-Milal wa al-niḥal*, ed. Amīr 'Alī Mihannā and 'Alī Ḥasan Fa'ūd, 5th edn, Beirut: Dār al-Ma'rifa, 2 volumes.

Shaltūt, Maḥmūd (1408/1988) *Al-Fatāwā: dirāsa li mushkilāt al-muslim al-mu'āṣir fī ḥayātih al-yawmiyya wa al-'āmma*, Cairo: Dār al-Shurūq, 15th edn.

Shanqīṭī, Muḥammad al-Amīn al- (1404/1983) *Manāhij wa dirāsāt li āyāt al-asmā' wa al-ṣifāt*, ed. 'Atiyya Muḥammad Sālim, 4th edn, Kuwait: Al-Dār al-Salafiyya.

Sharabāṣī, Aḥmad al- (1375/1956) *Fī 'ālam al-makfūfīn*, Cairo: Maṭba'at Nahḍat Miṣr, vol. 1.

—— (n.d.) *Fī 'ālam al-makfūfīn*, Cairo: Maṭba'at Lajnat al-Bayān al-'Arabī, vol. 2.

Sharaf al-Dīn, 'Alī al-Ṭāhir (2007) 'Al-Baḥth al-'ilmī fī al-'ulūm al-ṭabī'iyya fī ḍaw' al-maqāṣid al-shar'iyya', *Majallat majma' al-fiqh al-islāmī*, no. 4, pp. 253–270.

Sharḥ al-'aqīda al-Ṭaḥāwiyya (1391/1971) compiled by a group of scholars, 4th edn, Beirut: Al-Maktab al-Islāmī.

Sharqāwī, 'Iffat al- (1980) *Qaḍāya insāniyya fī a'māl al-mufassirīn*, Beirut: Dār al-Nahḍa al-'Arabiyya.

Shāṭibī, Abū Isḥāq al- (n.d.) *Al-Muwāfaqāt fī uṣūl al-sharī'a*, Cairo: Al-Maktaba al-Tawfīqiyya, 4 volumes.

Shawkānī, Muḥammad b. 'Alī b. Muḥammad al- (1347/1928) *Al-Darārī al-muḍiyya sharḥ al-ḍurar al-bahiyya*, 1st edn, Cairo: Maṭba'at Miṣr al-Ḥurra, 2 volumes.

—— (1973) *Nayl Al-awṭār*, Beirut: Dār al-Jīl, 9 volumes, reprint (1413/1993) Cairo: Dār al-Hadīth, 1st edn, 8 volumes.

—— (n.d.) *Fatḥ al-qadīr al-jāmi' bayn fannay al-riwāya wa al-dirāya min 'ilm al-tafsīr*, Beirut: Dār al-Fikr, 5 volumes.

Shaybānī, Aḥmad b. 'Amr b. Abī 'Āṣim al- (1407/1987) *Al-Diyāt*, Karachi: Idārat al-Qur'ān wa al-'Ulūm al-Islāmiyya.

Shāyi', 'Abd al-Ilāh b. 'Uthmān b. 'Abd Allāh (1418/1997) *Al-Lu'lu' al-thamīn min fatāwā al-mu'awwaqīn*, Riyadh: Dār al-Ṣumay'ī li al-Nashr wa al-Tawzī', vol. 1.

—— (1420/1999) *Ārā' Ibn Taymiyya ḥawl al-i'āqa*, Riyadh: Dār al-Ṣumay'ī li al-Nashr wa al-Tawzī'.

Shubīr, Muḥammad 'Uthmān (1421/2001) 'Ḍawābiṭ al-tadāwī bi al-ruqā wa al-tamā'im fī al-fiqh al-islāmī', in: Ashqar, 'Umar Sulaymān al- *et al.*, *Dirāsāt fiqhiyya fī qaḍāyā ṭibbiyya Mu'āṣira*, Amman: Dār al-Nafā'is, vol. 2, pp. 461–525.

—— (1421/2001a) 'Mawqif al-islām min al-amrāḍ al-wirāthiyya' in: Ashqar, 'Umar Sulaymān al- *et al.*, *Dirāsāt fiqhiyya fī qaḍāyā ṭibbiyya mu'āṣira*, Amman: Dār al-Nafā'is, vol. 1, pp. 333–347.

Sibā'ī, Muṣṭafā al- (1955) *Akhlāqunā al-ijtimā'iyya*, Damascus: Maktabat al-Shabāb al-Muslim.

—— (1381/1962) *Ishtirākiyyat al-islām*, Cairo: Dār wa Maṭābi' al-Sha'b.

Ṣiddīq, 'Abd Allāh al- (1392/1972) *Kamāl al-īmān fī al-tadāwī bi al-Qur'ān*, Tiṭwān, Morocco: al-Maṭba'a al-Mahdiyya.

Ṣu'aylīk, Muḥammad Abū (1420/1999) *Fiqh al-ibtilā'*, 1st edn, Beirut: Dār al-Bayāriq.

Subkī, Abū Naṣr 'Abd al-Wahhāb b. 'Alī b. 'Abd al-Kāfī al- (1992) *Ṭabaqāt al-shāfi'iyya al-kubrā*, ed. 'Abd al-Fattāḥ Muḥammad al-Ḥilw and Maḥmūd Muḥammad al-Ṭanāḥī, 2nd edn, Cairo: Hajar li al-Ṭibā'a wa al-Nashr wa al-Tawzī' wa al-I'lān, 10 volumes.

Suyūṭī, Jalāl al-Dīn al- (1304/1880) *Bard al-akbād 'ind faqd al-awlād*, Cairo.

—— (1387/1967) *Al-Itqān fī 'ulūm al-Qur'ān*, 1st edn, Cairo: Maktabat wa Maṭba'at al-Mashhad al-Ḥusaynī, 2 volumes.

—— (1389/1969) *Tanwīr al-ḥawālik*, Cairo: Al-Maktaba al-Tijāriyya al-Kubrā.

—— (1403/1983) *Al-Ashbāh wa al-naẓā'ir*, 1st edn, Beirut: Dār al-Kutub al-'Ilmiyya.

—— (1993) *Al-Durr al-manthūr fī al-tafsīr bi al-ma'thūr*, Beirut: Dār al-Fikr, 8 volumes.

—— (1995) *Al-Ḥāwī li al-fatāwī*, Cairo: Maktabat al-Qudsī, 2 volumes.

Suyūṭī, Jalāl al-Dīn al- and Jalāl al-Dīn al-Maḥallī (n.d.) *Tafsīr al-Jalālayn*, 1st edn, Cairo: Dār al-Ḥadīth.

Ṭabarī, Muḥammad b. Jarīr al- (1405/1984) *Jāmi' al-bayān fī ta'wīl al-Qur'ān: tafsīr al-Ṭabarī*, Beirut: Dār al-Fikr, 20 volumes.

—— (1407/1986) *Tārīkh al-umam wa al-mulūk: tārīkh al-Ṭabarī*, 1st edn, Beirut: Dār al-Kutub al-'Ilmiyya, 5 volumes.

Ṭabbāra, 'Afīf 'Abd al-Fattāḥ (1999) *Al-Khaṭāyā fī naẓar al-islām*, Beirut: Dār al-'Ilm li al-Malāyīn.

Taftazanı, Sa'd al-Dīn Mas'ūd b. 'Umar al- (n.d.) *Sharḥ al-'aqā'id al-nasafiyya*, Karachi, Pakistan: Nashr Nūr Muḥammad.

Ṭaḥāwī, Aḥmad b. Muḥammad b. Salāma al- (1399/1979) *Sharḥ ma'ānī al-āthār*, 1st edn, Beirut: Dār al-Ma'rifa, 4 volumes.

Tawḥīdī, Abū Ḥayyān al- and Ibn Miskawayh (1370/1951) *Al-Hawāmil wa al-Shawāmil*, ed. Aḥmad Amīn and al-Sayyid Aḥmad Ṣaqr, Cairo: Maṭba'at Lajnat al-Ta'līf wa al-Tarjama wa al-Nashr.

Tirmidhī, Abū 'Īsā al- (n.d.) *Sunan al-Tirmidhī*, ed. Aḥmad Muḥammad Shākir *et al.*, Beirut: Dār Ihyā' al-Turāth al-'Arabī, 5 volumes.

'Ukbarī, Muḥammad b. Muḥammad b. al-Nu'mān al- (known as al-Shaykh al-Mufīd) (1371/1951) *Awā'il al-maqālāt fī al-madhāhib wa al-mukhtārāt*, 2nd edn, Tabriz: Maṭba'at al-Riḍā'ī.

Ulamā' al-Ḥijāz wa al-Lajna al-Dā'ima li al-Buḥūth al-'Ilmiyya wa al-Iftā' (2004) *Fatāwā al-ṭibb wa al-tadāwī*, Alexandria: Dār al-Īmān.

'Uthaymīn, Muḥammad b. Ṣāliḥ al- (1421/2000) *Sharḥ al-'aqīda al-wāsiṭiyya*, ed. Fahd b. Nāṣir b. Ibrāhīm b. al-Sulaymān, 1st edn, Riyadh: Dār al-Thurayya li al-Nashr.

'Uthmān, 'Abd al-Karīm (1971) *Naẓariyyat al-taklīf: ārā' al-qāḍī 'Abd al-Jabbār al-kalāmiyya*, Beirut: Mu'assasat al-Risāla.

Wahhāb, Sulaymān b. 'Abd al- (n.d.) *Taysīr al-'Azīz al-Ḥamīd fī sharḥ kitāb al-tawḥīd*, Riyadh: Maktabat al-Riyāḍ al-Ḥadītha.

Wālī, Ḥusayn (1909) *Kitāb al-tawḥīd*, Cairo: Maṭba'at al-Wā'iẓ.

Wazna, Ṭal'at b. Ḥamza al- (1412/2000) *Al-I'āqa wa al-ta'hīl: usus wa mabādi'*, paper presented to the 2nd International Conference on Disability and Rehabilitation, Markaz al-Amīr Salmān li Abḥāth al-I'āqa, Riyadh.

Wizārat al-Awqāf wa al-Shu'ūn al-Islāmiyya bi al-Kuwayt (n.d.) *Al-Mawsū'a al-fiqhiyya*, Kuwait, 34 volumes.

Ya'qūbī, Aḥmad b. Ya'qūb al- (1883) *Tārīkh*, ed. T. Houtsma, Leiden: Brill, 2 volumes.

Zāda, 'Abd al-Raḥmān b. Muḥammad Shaykhī (n.d.) *Majma' al-anhur fī sharḥ multaqā al-abḥur*, Beirut: Dār Iḥyā' al-Turāth al-'Arabī, 2 volumes.

Zajjāj, Abū Isḥāq Ibrāhīm al- (1974) *Tafsīr asmā' Allāh al-ḥusnā*, ed. Aḥmad Yūsuf al-Daqqāq, Damascus: Dār al-Thaqāfa al-'Arabiyya.

Zamakhsharī, al- (1976) *Rabī' al-abrār*, Baghdad: Dār al-Shu'ūn al-Thaqāfiyya al-'Āmma, 4 volumes.

Zamīlī, Zuhayr Muḥammad al- (1409/1988) *Limādhā ja'al Allāh al-amrāḍ*, 1st edn, Amman: Dār al-Furqān.

Zarkashī, Abū 'Abd Allāh al- (1391/1971) *Al-Burhān fī 'ulūm al-Qur'ān*, ed. Muḥammad Abū al-Faḍl Ibrāhīm, Beirut: Dār al-Ma'rifa, 4 volumes.

Zaydān, 'Abd al-Karīm (1414/1994) *Al-Sunan al-ilāhiyya fī al-umam wa al-jamā'āt wa al-afrād fī al-sharī'a al-islāmiyya*, 3rd edn, Beirut: Mu'assasat al-Risāla.

Zaydān, Jurjī (1423/2003) *'Ilm al-firāsa al-ḥadīth*, Cairo: Maktabat al-Thaqāfa al-Dīniyya.

Zayla'ī, 'Uthmān b. 'Alī al- (n.d.) *Tabyīn al-ḥaqā'iq sharḥ kanz al-daqā'iq*, 2nd edn, Beirut: Dār al-Kitāb al-Islāmī, 6 volumes.

Zayn al-Dīn, 'Abd al-Raḥīm b. al-Ḥusayn al-'Irāqī (n.d.) *Ṭarḥ al-tathrīb fī sharḥ al-taqrīb*, Dār Iḥyā' al-Kutub al-'Arabiyya, 8 volumes.

Ziriklī, Khayr al-Dīn al- (2002) *Al-A'lām*, 15th edn, Beirut: Dār al-'Ilm li al-Malāyīn, 8 volumes.

Zuḥaylī, Wahba al- (1414/1994) *Wasā'il al-ithbāt fī al-sharī'a al-islāmiyya fī al-mu'āmalāt al-madaniyya wa al-aḥwāl al-shakhṣiyya*, Riyadh and Damascus: Maktabat al-Mu'ayyad/Maktabat Dār al-Bayān, 2 volumes.

—— (1418/1997) *Naẓariyyat al-ḍarūra al-shar'iyya: muqārana ma'a al-qanūn al-waḍ'ī*, 4th edn, Damascus and Beirut: Dār al-Fikr/Dār al-Fikr al-Mu'āṣir.

1.1 Manuscripts

Ghumrī, Zayn al-'Ābidīn al- (d. 970/1562) 'Al-Bahja al-saniyya fī al-firāsa al-insāniyya wa al-bahja al-murḍiyya fī al-firāsa al-īmāniyya', MS 335954, Makhṭūṭāt al-Azhar al-Sharīf, available online at www.alazharonline.org (accessed 3 June 2006).

—— (d. 970/1562a) 'Al-Bahja al-insiyya fī al-firāsa al-insāniyya', MS 4485, Chester Beatty Library, Dublin.

Ḥalabī, Badr al-Dīn Ibn Ḥabīb al- (d. 779/1377) 'Al-Najm al-thāqib fī ashraf al-manāqib', MS 309826, Makhṭūṭāt al-Azhar al-Sharīf, available online at www.alazharonline.org (accessed 5 May 2006).

Ibn Fahd (d. 954/1547) 'Al-Nukat al-ẓirāf fī al-maw'iẓa bi dhawī al-'āhāt min al-ashrāf', MS 383, Chester Beatty Library, Dublin.

Itlīdī, Muḥammad Diyāb al- (d. after 1100/1688) 'I'lām al-nās bimā waqa'a li al-Barāmika ma'a Banī al-'Abbās', MS 335954, Makhṭūṭāt al-Azhar al-Sharīf, available online at www.alazharonline.org (accessed 16 June 2006).

Marrākushī, Ibn 'Abd al-Salām al- (d. 660-1262) 'Khawāṣṣ al-Burda fī bur' al-dā'', Or. 11752:2, Leiden.

2 Works published in other languages

'Abd al'Aṭī, Hammūda (1977) *The Family Structure in Islam*, Indianapolis: The American Trust Publications.

Abrahamov, Binyamin (1993) ''Abd al-Jabbār's Theory of Divine Assistance (*luṭf*)', *Jerusalem Studies in Arabic and Islam*, vol. 16, pp. 7–38.

—— (1998) *Islamic Theology: Traditionalism and Nationalism*, Edinburgh: Edinburgh University Press.

Agha, Zouhir M. (1983) *Bibliography of Islamic Medicine and Pharmacy*, London: distributed by Brill.

Ahlwardt, W. (1895) *Verzeichniss der Arabischen Handschriften der Königlichen Bibliothek zu Berlin*, vol. 7, Berlin: A. Asher & Co.

Alami, Dawoud S. al- (1992) *The Marriage Contract in Islamic Law*, London: Graham & Trotman.

Amedroz, H.F. (1911) 'The *Mazalim* Jurisdiction in the *Ahkam Sultaniyya* of Māwardī', *JRAS*, vol. 31, pp. 640–641.

Ansari, M. Abdul Haq (2003) 'Mawdūdi's Contribution to Theology', *MS*, vol. 93, pp. 521–531.

Ansari, Zafar Ishaq (1969) 'Taftazānī's Views on Taklīf, *Jabr* and *Qadar*: A Note of the Development of Islamic Theological Doctrines', *Arabica: Revue d'Études Arabes*, Leiden, vol. XVI, pp. 65–78.

Arberry, Arthur J. (1959) *The Chester Beatty Library: A Handlist of the Arabic Manuscripts*, Dublin: Hodges Figgis.

Arnaldez, R. (2003) 'Ibn Rushd', *EI*, vol. III, pp. 909–920.

—— (2003a) 'Ibn Ḥazm', *EI*, vol. III, pp. 790–799.

—— (2003b) 'Al-Muḥāsibī', *EI*, vol. VII, pp. 466–467.

Ash'arī, Abū al-Ḥasan 'Alī b. Ismā'īl al- (1940) *Al-Ibāna 'an Uṣūl al-Diyāna: The Elucidiation of Islam's Foundation*, trans Walter C. Klein, New Haven, Conno.: American Oriental Society.

Australian Academy of Science (1999) *On Human Cloning: A Position Statement*, 4 February 1999, Canberra.

Autuori, A. (1983) 'Antecedenti greci e arabi del Kitāb al-firāsa di Fakhr al-Dīn al-Rāzī', *Annali, Istituto Universitario Orientale di Napoli*, no. 43, pp. 43–60.

Awa, Mohamed S. el- (1982) *Punishment in Islamic Law: A Comparative Study*, Indianapolis: American Trust Publications.

Ayoub, Mahmoud M. (1977) 'The Problem of Suffering in Islam', *Journal of Dharma*, vol. 2, pp. 267–294.

Azmi, S.H. (1991) 'Traditional Islamic Social Welfare: Its Meaning, History and Contemporary Relevance', part II, *IQ*, vol. 35, no. 4, pp. 209–224.

Babu Sahib, Maulavi M.H. (1987) 'Legal Issues in Human Organ Transplant: Indian Perspective', *Islam and Comparative Law Quarterly*, vol. 7, pp. 144–164.

Baer, Gabriel (1997) 'The Waqf as a Prop for the Social System (Sixteenth-Twentieth Centuries)', *ILS*, vol. 4, no. 3, pp. 264–297.

Baghdādī, Abū Manṣūr ʻAbd al-Qāhir al- (1920) *Muslim Schisms and Sects: Al-Farq bayn al-Firaq*, trans. Abraham S. Halkin, New York: Columbia University Press.
Bakhtiar, Laleh (1996) *Encyclopaedia of Islamic Law: A Compendium of the Views of the Major Schools*, Chicago: ABC International Group.
Bar, Mohammed Ali al- (1995) *Contemporary Topics in Islamic Medicine*, Jeddah: Saudi Publications and Distributing House.
Bazna, Maysaa S. and Hatab, Tarek A. (2005) 'Disability in the Qur'an: The Islamic Alternative to Defining, Viewing, and Relating to Disability', *JRDH*, vol. 9, no. 1, pp. 5–27.
Beaurecueil, S. de (2003) 'Al-Anṣārī al-Harawī', *EI*, vol. I, pp. 515–516.
Bell, Joseph Norment (1979) *Love Theory in Later Ḥanbalite Islam*, New York: State University of New York Press.
Bencheneb, M. and Somogyi, J. de (2003) 'Al-Dhahabī', *EI*, vol. II, pp. 215–216.
Beneken, M.M. *et al.*, (1997) *Social Integration of People with Disabilities in 12 South-Mediterranean Countries*, Utrecht: sDG, Netherlands Foundation for Rehabilitation.
Bernand, M. (2003) 'Muʻamalāt', *EI*, vol. II, pp. 255–257.
Berry, Donald L. (2003) *Islam and Modernity through the Writings of Islamic Modernist Fazlur Rahman*, Lewiston, NY: Edwin Mellen Press.
Bittles, A.H. (2001) 'Consanguinity and its Relevance to Clinical Genetics', *Clinical Genetics*, 60, pp. 89–98.
Bousquet, G.H. (2003) 'ʻIbādāt', *EI*, vol. III, pp. 647–648.
Bowker, John (1969) 'The Problem of Suffering in the Qur'an', *Religious Studies*, vol. 4, pp. 183–202.
—— (1970) *Problems of Suffering in Religions of the World*, Cambridge: Cambridge University Press.
Brockelmann, Carl (1937–1942) *Geschichte der arabischen Litteratur*, 2nd edn, 2 volumes and *supplement* (to 1st edn), 3 vols, Leiden: Brill.
—— (2003) 'Al-Ḳasṭalānī', *EI*, vol. IV, p. 736.
—— (2003a) 'Al-Māwardī', *EI*, vol. IV, p. 969.
—— (2003b) 'Al-Sharīf al-Murtaḍā', *EI*, vol. VII, p. 634.
Chaumont, E. (2003) 'Al-Shāfiʻī', *EI*, vol. IX, pp. 181–185.
—— (2003a) 'Al-Shāfiʻiyya', *EI*, vol. IX, pp. 185–189.
Clerk, Godfrey (1873) *I'lām-en-Nās: Historical Tales and Anecdotes of the Early Khalīfahs*, London: Henry S. King.
Clouston, W.A. (2003) *Flowers from a Persian Garden and Other Papers*, London: Kessinger Publishing.
Conrad, Lawrance I. (1999) 'Medicine and Martyrdom: Some Discussions of Suffering and Divine Justice in Early Islamic Society', in: John R. Hinnells and Roy Porter, *Religion, Health and Suffering*, London and New York: Kegan Paul International, pp. 212–236.
Coulson, N.J. (1964, 1971) *Succession in the Muslim Family*, Cambridge: Cambridge University Press.
Crecelius, Daniel (1986) 'Incidences of *Waqf* Cases in Three Cairo Courts: 1640–1802', *JESHO*, vol. 29, pp. 176–189.
—— (1991) 'The Waqf of Muhammad Bey Abu al-Dhahab in Historical Perspective', *International Journal of Middle East Studies*, vol. 23, no. 1, pp. 57–81.
Daigeler A. *et al.* (2003) 'Orthotropic and Heterotopic Lower Leg Reimplantation: Evaluation of Seven Patients', *The Journal of Bone & Joint Surgery*, 85-B, pp. 554–558.

Declaration on the Rights of Disabled Persons (1975) *Declaration on the Rights of Disabled Persons Proclaimed by General Assembly Resolution 3447 (XXX) of 9 December 1975*, available at http://www.unhchr.ch (accessed 3 August 2007).

Devlieger, Patrick J. (1999) 'From Handicap to Disability: Language Use and Cultural Meaning in the United States', *Disability and Rehabilitation*, vol. 21, no. 7, pp. 346–354.

Diyāb, Adīb al-Nāyif (2000) 'Ibn 'Arabī on Human Freedom, Destiny and the Problem of Evil', *Al-Shajara: Journal of the International Institute of Islamic Thought and Civilization (ISTAC)*, vol. 5, no. 1, pp. 25–43.

Dobbins, Frank S. (2003) *Error's Chains: How Forged and Broken, Part 2*, London: Kessinger Publishing.

Doi, 'Abdur Rahmān I. (1404/1984) *Sharī'ah: The Islamic Law*, London: Ta Ha Publishers.

Dols, Michael W. (1979) 'Leprosy in Medieval Arabic Medicine', *Journal of the History of Medicine and Allied Sciences*, 36, pp. 314–333.

—— (1983) 'The Leper in Medieval Islamic Society', *Speculum*, 58, pp. 891–916.

—— (1987) 'Insanity and its Treatment in Islamic Society', *Medical History*, 31, pp. 1–14.

—— (1992) *Majnūn: Madman in Medieval Islamic Society*, ed. Diana E. Immisch, Oxford: Clarendon Press.

Dunlop, M. *et al.* (2003) 'Bīmāristān', *EI*, vol. I, pp. 1222–1226.

Eiesland, Nancy (1994) *The Disabled God: Toward a Liberatory Theology of Disability*, Nashville, Tenn.: Abingdon Press.

Eliade, Mercea (1987) *The Encyclopaedia of Religion*, New York: Macmillan Publishing Company.

Ende, W. (2003) 'Shaltūt', *EI*, vol. IX, pp. 260–261.

—— (2003a) 'Rashīd Riḍā', *EI*, vol. III, pp. 445–448.

English, R.W. (1977) 'Correlates of Stigmas towards Physically Disabled Persons', in: R.P. Marinelli, and A.E. Dell Orto (eds) *The Psychological and Social Impact of Physical Disability*, New York: Springer Publishing Company.

Ess, Josef van (1971) *Frühe Mu'tazilitische Häresiographie, Zwei Werke des Nāshi' al-Akbar (gest. 293 A.H.)*, Wiesbaden [Beiruter Texte und Studien, 11].

—— (2003) 'Naẓẓām, Abū Isḥāq Ibrāhīm', *EI*, vol. VII, p. 1057, vol. VIII, p. 1.

Fahd, T. (1966) *La Divination arabe*, Leiden: Brill.

—— (2003) 'Ḳiyāfa', *EI*, vol. V, p. 235.

—— (2003a) 'Firāsa', *EI*, vol. II, pp. 916–917.

—— (2003b) 'Khawāṣṣ al-Ḳur'ān', *EI*, vol. IV, pp. 1133–1134.

—— (2003c) 'Ruḳiya', *EI*, vol. VIII, pp. 600–601.

Foerster, R. (1893) *Scriptores Physiognomonici Graeci et Latini*, Leipzig: Teubner.

Frank, Richard (1965) 'The Neoplatonism of Ǧahm Ibn Ṣafwān', *Le Muséon*, vol. LXXVIII, 3–4, pp. 395–424.

—— (1992) 'The Science of *Kalām*', *Arabic Sciences and Philosophy*, vol. 2, pp. 27–37.

—— (1994) *Creation and the Cosmic System: Al-Ghazālī and Avicenna*, Heidelberg: Carl Winter Universtätsverlag.

Fyzee, Asaf A.A. (1942) *A Shi'ite Creed: A Translation of Risālatu'l-I'tiqādāt of Muḥammad b. 'Alī Ibn Bābawayhi al-Qummī Known as Shaykh Ṣadūq*, Oxford: Oxford University Press.

—— (2003) 'Ibn Bābawayh', *EI*, vol. III, pp. 226–227.

Gardet, L. (2003) 'al-Ḳaḍā wa'l Ḳadar', *EI*, vol. IV, pp. 365–367.

—— (2003a) ''Ilm al-Kalām', *EI*, vol. III, pp. 1141–1150.

—— (2003b) ''Aḳliyyāt', *EI*, vol. I, pp. 342–343.

—— (2003c) 'al-Asmā' al-Ḥusnā', *EI*, vol. I, pp. 714–717.

—— (2003d) 'Kashf', *EI*, vol. IV, pp. 696–698.

—— (2003e) 'Fitna', *EI*, vol. II, pp. 930–932.

Garland, Robert (1995) *The Eye of the Beholder: Deformity and Disability in the Graeco-Roman World*, London: Duckworth.

Gaventa, William C. and Coulter, David L. (eds) (2001) *Spirituality and Intellectual Disability: International Perspectives on the Effect of Culture and Religion on Healing Body, Mind and Soul*, New York: The Haworth Pastoral Press. Co-published simultaneously in: *JRDH*, vol. 5, no. 2/3.

Ghaly, Mohammed (2001) 'Citizenship in Islam', unpublished paper submitted to Leiden University as a partial fulfilment of the requirements for obtaining an MA in Islamic Studies, Leiden.

—— (2005–2006) 'Writings on Disability in Islam: The 16th Century Polemic on Ibn Fahd's al-Nukat al-Ẓirāf', *ASJ*, vol. XIII, no. 2, vol. XIV, no. 1, pp. 9–38.

—— (2007) 'Islam en handicap: praktijkthema's en islamitische ethische opvattingen', *Tijdschrift voor gezondheidszorg en ethiek*, jaargang 17, no. 2, pp. 40–45.

—— (2008) 'Physical and Spiritual Treatment of Disability in Islam: Perspectives of Early and Modern Jurists', vol. 12, no. 2, pp. 105–143.

—— (2008b) 'Visies op mensen met verstandelijke beperkingen binnen de islamitische traiditie', *Nederlands Tijdschrift voor de Zorg aan mensen met verstandelijke beperkingen (NTZ)*, vol. 34, no. 2, pp. 115–126.

—— (2008c) 'Islam and Disability: Perspectives in Islamic Theology and Jurisprudence', Leiden University, PhD dissertation.

Ghanem, Isam (1982) *Islamic Medical Jurisprudence*, London: A. Probsthain.

Ghazālī, Abū Ḥāmid al- (1958) *Tahafut al-Falasifa [Incoherence of the Philosophers]*, trans. Sabih Ahmad Kamali, Lahore: The Pakistan Philosophical Congress.

—— (1992) *Al-Ghazālī: The Ninety-Nine Beautiful Names of God: Al-Maqṣad al-Asnā fī Sharḥ Maʿānī Asmā' Allāh al-Ḥusnā*, trans. David B. Burrell and Nazih Daher, Cambridge: The Islamic Texts Society.

Ghersetti, Antonella (1996) 'Firāsa and Intelligence: The Silly and the Intelligent in Arab Physiognomy', *The Arabist: Budapest Studies in Arabic*, vol. 17, pp. 121–131.

—— (1999) *Il kitāb Arisṭāṭalīs al-faylasūf fī l-firāsa: nella traduzione di Ḥunayn b. Isḥāq*, Rome: Herder for Università Ca' Foscari di Venezia and Dipartimento di Scienze dell'Antichità e del Vicino Oriente, Rome.

—— (2007) 'The Semiotic Paradigm: Physiognomy and Medicine in Islamic Culture', in: Simon Swain, *Seeing the Face, Seeing the Soul: Polemon's Physiognomy from Classical Antiquity to Medieval Islam*, Oxford: Oxford University Press, pp. 281–308.

Ghersetti, Antonella and Simon Swain (2007) 'Polemon's Physiognomy in the Arabic Tradition' in: Simon Swain, *Seeing the Face, Seeing the Soul: Polemon's Physiognomy from Classical Antiquity to Medieval Islam*, Oxford University Press, pp. 309–322.

Giddens, Anthony (1997) *Sociology*, 3rd edn, Cambridge: Polity Press.

Gimaret, D. (1990) *La Doctrine d'al-Ashʿarī*, Paris.

—— (2003) 'Uṣūl al-Dīn', *EI*, vol. X, pp. 930–931.

—— (2003a) 'Taklīf', *EI*, vol. X, pp. 138–139.

Givens, Benjamin P. and Hirschman, Charles (1994) 'Modernization and Consanguineous Marriage in Iran', *Journal of Marriage and the Family*, vol. 56, no. 4, pp. 820–834.

Goldziher, I. (1981) 'The Attitude of Orthodox Islam toward the Ancient Sciences', in: Merlin L. Swartz, *Studies on Islam*, Oxford: Oxford University Press, pp. 185–215.

Goldziher, I. and Schacht, Joseph (2003) 'Fiḳh', *EI*, vol. II, pp. 886–887.

Gordon-Cumming, Constance Frederica (2006) *Via Cornwall to Egypt*, Boston: Adamant Media Corporation.

Gülen, Fethullah M. (1999) *Key Concepts in the Practice of Sufism*, Fairfax V.: Fountain.

Haj, Fareed (1970) *Disability in Antiquity*, New York: Philosophical Library.

Hallaq, Wael B. (1997) *A History of Islamic Legal Theories: An Introduction to Sunnī Uṣūl al-Fiqh*, Cambridge: Cambridge University Press.

Hamarneh, Sami (1964) *Bibliography on Medicine and Pharmacy in Medieval Islam*, Stuttgart: Wissenschaftliche Verlagsgesellschaft.

Hamdan, A. Saleh (2003) 'al-Munāwī', *EI*, vol. VII, p. 565.

Ḥasan, Ahmed (1974) 'Rationality of Islamic Legal Injunctions', *IS*, no. 13, pp. 95–109.

Hastings, James (1974) *The Encyclopaedia of Religion and Ethics*, Edinburgh and New York: Clark.

Haven, E.C. van der (2006) 'The Bey, the Mufti and the Scattered Pearls', unpublished PhD dissertation submitted to Leiden University, The Netherlands.

Haykel, Bernard (2003) *Revival and Reform in Islam: The Legacy of Muhammad al-Shawkānī*, Cambridge: Cambridge University Press.

Hearn, Lafcadio (2004) *Karma and Other Stories and Essays*, London: Kessinger Publishing.

Heemskerk, Margaretha T. (1995) *Pain and Compensation in Mu'tazilite Doctrine: 'Abd al-Jabbār's Teaching and its Adoption by Mānkdīm and Ibn Mattawayh*, Nijmegen, The Netherlands: Quikprint.

—— (2000) *Suffering in the Mu'tazilite Theology: 'Abd al-Jabbār's Teaching on Pain and Divine Justice*, Leiden: Brill.

—— (2006) 'Suffering', *EI*, vol. 5, pp. 132–136.

Hijazi, Qudsiyah (n.d.) *Islam va aftal 'aqab uftadeh*, Iran: Markaz Tahqiqat wa Intisharat Huquqi Qudsi.

Ḥillī, Ḥasan b. Yūsuf b. 'Alī b. al-Muṭahhar al- (1958) *Al-Bābu 'l-ḥādī 'ashar*, trans. William Mcellwee Miller, commentary by Miqdād-i-Fāḍil al-Ḥillī, London: The Royal Asiatic Society of Great Britain and Ireland.

Hinds, M. (2003) 'Mu'āwiya b. Abī Sufyān', *EI*, vol. VII, pp. 263–268.

Hodgson, Peter Crafts (1994) *Winds of the Spirit: A Constructive Christian Theology*, Louisville, Ky.: Westminster John Knox Press.

Hoexter, M. (1984) 'Le contrat de quasi-aliénation des *awqāf* à Alger à la fin de la domination turque: étude de deux documents d' *'anā'*, *BSOAS*, vol. 47, pp. 243–259.

—— (1995) 'Ḥuqūq Allāh and Ḥuqūq al-'Ibād as Reflected in the Waqf Institution', *Jerusalem Studies in Arabic and Islam*, no. 19, pp. 133–156.

Hoffer, Cor (1992) 'The Practice of Islamic Healing', in: W.A.R. Shadid and P.S. van Koningsveld (eds) *Islam in Dutch Society: Current Developments and Future Prospects*, Kampen, The Netherlands: Kok Pharos.

—— (2000) 'Volksgeloof en religieuze geneeswijzen onder moslims in Nederland', PhD dissertation submitted to Leiden University.

Hoodfar, E. and Teebi, A.S. (1996) 'Genetic Referrals of Middle Eastern Origin in a Western City: Inbreeding and Disease Profile', *Journal of Medical Genetics*, 33, pp. 212–215.

Hoover, Jon (2002) 'An Islamic Theodicy: Ibn Taymiyya on the Wise Purpose of God, Human Agency and Problems of Evil and Justice', a thesis submitted to the University of Birmingham for the degree of the Doctor of Philosophy.

—— (2007) *Ibn Taymiyya's Theodicy of Perpetual Optimism*, Leiden: Brill.

Hoyland, Robert (2005) 'Physiognomy in Islam', *Jerusalem Studies in Arabic and Islam*, 30, pp. 361–402.

—— (2007) 'A New Edition of the Leiden Polemon', in: Swain, Simon, *Seeing the Face, Seeing the Soul: Polemon's Physiognomy from Classical Antiquity to Medieval Islam*, Oxford: Oxford University Press, pp. 329–342.

—— (2007a) 'The Islamic Background to Polemon's Treatise', in: Swain, Simon, *Seeing the Face, Seeing the Soul: Polemon's Physiognomy from Classical Antiquity to Medieval Islam*, Oxford: Oxford University Press, pp. 227–280.

Hujwīrī, 'Alī b. 'Uthmān al- (1911, 1959) *The 'Kashf al-Maḥjūb', the Oldest Persian Treatise on Sufism by al Hujwiri*, trans. Reynold A. Nicholson, Gibb Memorial series no. 1911, reprinted in London, 1959.

Ibn al-Khodja, Mohamed Habib (ed.) (2000) *Resolutions and Recommendations of the Council of the Islamic Fiqh Academy*, Jeddah.

Ibn al-Qayyim (1998) *Patience and Gratitude: An Abridged Translation of 'Uddat as-Sabirin wa Dhakhirat ash-Shakirin*, trans. Nasiruddin al-Khattab, London: Ta-Ha Publishers.

—— (1998a) *Medicine of the Prophet*, trans. Penelope Johnstone, Oxford: The Islamic Texts Society.

Ibn Rushd (2000) *Bidāyat al-Mujtahid wa Nihāyat al-Muqtaṣid: The Distinguished Jurist's Primer*, trans. Imran Ahsan Khan Nyazee and Muhammad Abdul Rauf, Qatar: Centre for Muslim Contribution to Civilization, Garnet Publishing Limited, 2 volumes.

Idrissi I. al- *et al.* (1992) 'Cumulative Incidence of Retinoblastoma in Riyadh, Saudi Arabia', *Ophthalamic Paediat. Genet.*, vol. 13, pp. 9–12.

Iliffe, John (1987) *The African Poor: A History*, Cambridge: Cambridge University Press.

Inati, Shams C. (2000) *The Problem of Evil: Ibn Sīnā's Theodicy*, New York: Global Publications, Institute of Global Cultural Studies, Binghamton University.

Inostrantsev, K. (1907–1908) 'Materialy iz arabskikh istochnikov dlia kulturnoy istorii sasanidskoy Persii', *Zapiski Vostochnogo otdeleniia Rossiiskogo arkheologicheskogo obshchestva*, vol. 18, pp. 113–232.

International Labour Organization (2006) *ILO Welcomes New UN Convention on Rights of People With Disabilities, press release ILO/06/58*, available at http://www.ilo.org (accessed 3 August 2007).

Ispahany, Batool (trans.) and Andrew J. Newman (ed.) (1991) *Islamic Medical Wisdom: The Ṭibb al-A'imma*, London: The Muhammadi Trust.

Jackson, Sherman A. (1996) *Islamic Law and the State: The Constitutional Jurisprudence of Shihāb al-Dīn al-Qarāfī*, Leiden: Brill.

—— (2000) 'Setting the Record Straight: Ibn al-Labbād's Refutation of al-Shāfi'ī', *JIS*, 11:2, pp. 121–146.

Jafri, S.H.M. (2003) 'Al-Ḥillī', *EI*, vol. III, p. 390.

Johansen, Baber (2002) 'Signs as Evidence: The Doctrine of Ibn Taymiyya (1263–1328) and Ibn Qayyim al-Jawziyya (d. 1351) on Proof', *ILS*, vol. 9, no. 2, pp. 168–193.

Kader, Abdel (1954) 'Al-Junayd's Theory of Fanā'', *IC*, vol. 1, no. 4, pp. 219–228.

Kamali, Muhammad Hashim (1993) 'Fundamental Rights of the Individual: An Analysis of Haqq (Right) in Islamic Law', *American Journal of Islamic Sciences*, 1993b, vol. 10, no. 3, pp. 340–366.

—— (2002) *The Dignity of Man: An Islamic Perspective*, Cambridge: The Islamic Texts Society.

—— (2003) *Principles of Islamic Jurisprudence*, 3rd edn, Cambridge: The Islamic Texts Society.

Kazi, M.U. (1996) *Family and Social Obligations in Islam*, Karachi: Ferozsons.
Khadduri, Majid (1961) *Islamic Jurisprudence: Shāfiʿī's Risāla*, Baltimore, Md.: The Johns Hopkins Press.
—— (1984) *The Islamic Conception of Justice*, Baltimore, Md.: The Johns Hopkins Press.
Koningsveld, P.S. van (1998) 'Greek Manuscripts in the Early Abbasid Empire: Fiction and Facts about their Origin, Translation and Destruction', *Bibliotheca Orientalis*, vol. 55, no. iv, pp. 346–372.
Kraus, P. and Vajda, G. (2003) 'Ibn al-Rāwandī', *EI*, vol. III, pp. 904–906.
Kyriakides-Yeldham, Anthony (2005) 'Islamic Medical Ethics and the Straight Path of God', *Islam and Christian–Muslim Relations* (July), vol. 16, no. 3, pp. 213–225.
Lane, E.W. (1968) *Arabic–English Lexicon*, Beirut: Librairie du Liban, Beirut, 8 volumes.
Laoust, H. (2003) 'Ibn Qayyim al-Jawziyya', *EI*, vol. III, pp. 821–822.
—— (2003a) 'Ibn Taymiyya', *EI*, vol. III, pp. 951–955.
—— (2003b) 'Ḥanābila', *EI*, vol. III, pp. 157–162.
—— (2003c) 'Ibn al-Jawzī', *EI*, vol. III, pp. 751–752.
Lari, Sayyid Mujtaba Musavi (2003) *God and His Attributes: Lessons on Islamic Doctrine Book One*, trans. Ḥamid Algar, Qom, Iran: Al-Hadi.
Layish, Aharon (1997) 'The Family Waqf and the *Sharʿī* Law of Succession', *ILS*, vol. 4, no. 3, pp. 352–388.
Legenhausen, G. (1988) 'Notes towards an Ash'arite Theodicy', *Religious Studies*, vol. 24, pp. 257–266.
Levi, D. (1941) 'The Evil Eye and the Lucky Hunchback', in: R. Stilwell (ed.) *Antioch-on-the-Orontes. III The Excavations 1937–1939*. Oxford.
Lewisohn L. (2003) 'Tawakkul', *EI*, vol. X, pp. 376–378.
Livingston, John (1971) 'Ibn Qayyim al-Jawziyya: A Fourteenth Century Defense against Astrological Divination and Alchemical Transmutation', *JAOS*, vol. 91, no. 1, pp. 96–103.
—— (1992) 'Science and the Occult in the Thinking of Ibn Qayyim al-Jawziyya', *JAOS*, vol. 112, no. 4, pp. 598–610.
Lory, P. (2003) 'Shādhilliyya', *EI*, vol. IX, pp. 172–175.
Madelung, Wilfred (2003) 'Al-Mufīd', *EI*, vol. VII, pp. 312–313.
—— (2003a) 'Al-Māturīdī', *EI*, vol. VI, pp. 846–847.
Mahmood, Tahir (1989) 'Law and the Elderly in the Islamic Tradition–Classical Precepts and Modern Legislation', *Islamic and Comparative Law Quarterly*, vol. IX, pp. 33–44.
Mairs, Nancy (1986) *Plaintext*, Tucson: University of Arizona.
Makdisi, George (1962–1963) 'Ash'arī and the Ash'arites in Islamic Religious History', *SI*, vol. 17 (1962), pp. 37–80, vol. 18 (1963), pp. 19–39.
—— (2003) 'Ibn Ḳudāma al-Maḳdisī', *EI*, vol. III, pp. 842–843.
Manzalaoui, Mahmoud (1974) 'The Pseudo-Aristotelian *Kitāb Sirr al-Asrār*: Facts and Problems', *Oriens*, vol. 23, pp. 141–257.
Maqsood, Ruqaiyyah Waris (2000) *The Problem of Evil: A Study of Evil, Fate, Freewill and Predestination, Forgiveness and Love*, Delhi: Adam Publishers & Distributors.
Marghinānī, Alī b. Abī Bakr al- (1963) *The Hedaya or Guide: A Commentary on the Mussulman Laws*, trans. Charles Hamelton, London: T. Bensley.
May, Rollo (1981) *Freedom and Destiny*, New York and London: W.W. Norton.
McGrath, Alister E. (1998) *Historical Theology: An Introduction to the History of Christian Thought*, Oxford: Blackwell Publishing.
Meier, F. (2003) 'Bishr al-Ḥāfī', *EI*, vol. I, pp. 1243–1246.
Meyerhof, M. and T. Sarnelli (2003) 'Djarrāḥ', *EI*, vol. III, pp. 481–482.

Michot, Yahya J. (2000) 'Ibn Taymiyya on Astrology: Annotated Translation of Three Fatwas', *JIS*, vol. 11, no. 2, pp. 147–208.

Miles, M. (1981) 'Some Historical Notes on Religions, Ideologies and the Handicapped', *Al-Mushir*, vol. XXIII, no. 4, pp. 125–134.

Mourad, Youssef (1939) *La Physiognomie arabe et le Kitāb al-Firāsa de Fakhr Al-Dīn Al-Rāzi*, Paris: P. Geuthner.

Mutahhari, Murtada (2002) *Understanding Islamic Sciences: Philosophy, Theology, Mysticism, Morality, Jurisprudence*, London: Islamic College for Advanced Studies (ICAS) Press.

Muzaffar, Allama Muhammad Riza (1985) *The Beliefs of the Shi'ite School*, Accra: Islamic Seminary Publications.

Nash, Melissa C. (1997) 'Disability, Religion, and Ritual: Experiences of People Who have Learning Difficulties in a "Treetop Community" in Scotland', *The Scottish Journal of Religious Studies*, vol. 18, no. 1, pp. 181–197.

Nasir, Jamal J. (1990) *The Islamic Law of Personal Status*, 2nd edn, London: Graham & Trotman.

National Immunization Program, Centers for Disease Control and Prevention (2007) *Epidemiology and Prevention of Vaccine Preventable Diseases*, 10th edn, Atlanta, Ga.: The Pink Book.

Navar, Iraj and Chelkowski, Peter J. (1994) 'If You Are Merciful, O Bounteous, Full of Compassion, Why Make Hell, Punishment, and the Need to Account for each Action', in: Alma Giese and Christoph Bürgel (eds) *God Is Beautiful and He Loves Beauty*, Berlin: Peter Lang, pp. 111–129.

Nelson J. *et al.* (1997) 'Consanguineous Marriage and its Clinical Consequences in Migrants to Australia', *Clinical Genetics*, 52, pp. 142–146.

Nosek, M.A. (1995) 'Conference on Spirituality and Disability Held by NIH', *Disability Studies Quarterly*, 15, pp. 34–37.

Nowsheravi, A.R. (1983) 'Muslim Hospitals in the Medieval Period', *IS*, vol. 22, no. 2, pp. 51–62.

Obermann, Julian (1935) 'Political Theology in Early Islam: Ḥasan al-Baṣrī's Treatise on Qadar', *JAOS*, vol. 55, pp. 138–162.

Office of the High Commissioner of Human Rights (1971) *Declaration on the Rights of Mentally Retarded Persons*, available at http://www.unhchr.ch/html/menu3/b/m_mental.htm (accessed 18 April 2009).

—— (1975) *Declaration on the Rights of Disabled Persons*, available at http://www.unhchr.ch/html/menu3/b/72.htm (accessed 18 April 2009).

Oommen, A. and T. Oommen (2003) 'Physiognomy: A Critical Review', *Journal of the Anatomical Society of India*, vol. 52, no. 2, pp. 189–191.

Ormsby, Eric L. (1984) *Theodicy in Islamic Thought: The Dispute Over al-Ghazālī's 'Best of all Possible Worlds'*, Princeton, NJ: Princeton University Press.

Othman, Moh. Zain b. Haji (1983) 'Origin of the Institution of *Waqf*', *HI*, vol. VI, no. 2, pp. 3–23.

Otten, Henry J. (1985) 'The Problem of Evil in Islam', *The Bulletin of Christian Institutes of Islamic Studies*. vol. 1, pp. 1–23.

Pedersen, J. *et al.* (2003) 'Masdjid', *EI*, vol. VI, pp. 644–707.

Pellat, Ch. (2003a) 'Manāḳib', *EI*, vol. VI, pp. 349–357.

—— (2003b) 'Iyās b. Mu'āwiya', *EI*, vol. IV, p. 291.

—— (2003c) 'Al-Djāḥiẓ', *EI*, vol. II, pp. 385–387.

—— (2003d) 'Al-Haytham B. 'Adī', *EI*, vol. III, p. 328.

—— (2003e) 'Nādira', *EI*, vol. VII, pp. 856–858.

Pessagno, J. Meric (1984) 'The Uses of Evil in the Maturidian Thought', *SI*, vol. LIX, pp. 59–82.

Peters, R. *et al.* (2003) 'Waḳf', *EI*, vol. XI, pp. 59–99.

Qaradawi, Yusuf al- (2006) 'Preventing Child Vaccination: Permissible?' a fatwa published on 1 January 2006, available at http://www.islamonline.net (accessed 5 July 2007).

Qushayri, al- (1990) *Principles of Sufism*, trans. B.R. von Schlegell, Berkeley, Califo: Mizan Press.

Radtke, B. *et al.* (2003) 'Walī', *EI*, vol. XI, pp. 109–124.

Rahbar, Daud (1960) *God of Justice: A Study in the Ethical Doctrine of the Qur'ān*, Leiden: Brill.

Rahman, Fazlur (1982) 'Islam and Health: Some Theological, Historical and Sociological Perspectives', *HI*, vol. V, no. 4, pp. 75–88.

—— (1984) 'Islam and Medicine: A General Overview', *Perspectives in Biology and Medicine*, vol. 27, no. 4, pp. 585–597.

—— (1989) *Health and Medicine in the Islamic Tradition: Change and Identity*, New York: Crossroad.

—— (2000) *Revival and Reform in Islam: A Study of Islamic Fundamentalism*, ed. Ebrahim Moosa, Oxford: Oneworld.

—— (2003) 'Baḳā' wa Fanā'', *EI*, vol. I, pp. 950–951.

Rashed, R. and Jolivet, J. (2003) 'Al-Kindī', *EI*, vol. V, pp. 122–123.

Rehman, Mutazid Wali-ur (1939) 'Iqbāl's Doctrine of Destiny', *IC*, vol. 13, pp. 150–175.

Ridgeon, Lloyd (1998) 'A Sufi Perspective of Evil', *Iran: Journal of the British Institute of Persian Studies*, vol. XXXVI, pp. 113–122.

Ripley, George (1858) *The New American Cyclopaedia: A Popular Dictionary of General Knowledge*, New York and London: D. Appelton.

Rispler-Chaim, Vardit (1993) *Islamic Medical Ethics in the Twentieth Century*, Leiden: Brill.

—— (1996) 'Islamic Law of Marriage and Divorce and the Disabled Person: The Case of the Epileptic Wife', *Die Welt des Islams*, vol. 36, no. 1, pp. 90–106.

—— (1999) 'The Right not to be Born: Abortion of the Disadvantaged Fetus in Contemporary Fatwas', *MW*, vol. LXXXIX, no. 2, pp. 130–143.

—— (2007) *Disability in Islamic Law*, Dordrecht, The Netherlands: Springer.

Ritter, Hellmut (1950) 'Risālat Ibn Sīnā fī al-Rizq', *Revue de l'Académie Arabe de Domas (Majallat al-majma' al-'ilmī al-'arabī)*, vol. 25, pp. 199–209.

—— (1952) 'Muslim Mystics' Strife with God', *Oriens*, vol. 5, pp. 1–15.

—— (1959) *Das Meer der Seele*, Leiden: Brill.

Robinson, Mary (1998) 'Human Rights and Disabled Persons', in: Rachel Hurst (ed.) *Are Disabled People Included?*, Disability Awareness in Action, Freeways Print, UK.

Robson, J. (2003) 'Al-Bayḍāwī', *EI*, vol. I, p. 1129.

Rohé, George H. (1885) *A Text-Book of Hygiene: A Comprehensive Treatise on the Principles and Practice of Preventive Medicine from an American Standpoint*, Baltimore, Md.

Rosenthal, F. (1965) *The Classical Heritage in Islam*. Berkeley and Los Angeles: University of California Press.

—— (2003) 'Al-Ṣafadī', *EI*, vol. VIII, pp. 758–760.

—— (2003a) 'Ibn Hadjar al-'Asḳalānī', *EI*, vol. III, pp. 776–778.

Sābiq, al-Sayyid (1410/1991) *Fiqhu us-Sunna*, trans. 'Abdul-Majīd Khokhar *et al.*, Indianapolis: American Trust Publications.

—— (n.d.) *Fiqhu us-Sunna*, trans. Muhammad Sa`eed Dabas and Jamal al-Din Zarabozo, Cairo: Dar al-Fateh for Arab Information.

Sachedina, Abdulaziz (1999) 'Can God Inflict Unrequited Pain on His Creatures? Muslim Perspectives on Health and Suffering', in: John R. Hinnells and Roy Porter, *Religion, Health and Suffering*, London and New York: Kegan Paul International, pp. 65–84.

Savage-Smith, Emilie (1996) 'Medicine', in: Roshdi Rashed (ed.) *Encyclopedia of the History of Arabic Science*, London and New York: Routledge, vol. 3, pp. 903–962.

Savage-Smith, Emilie *et al.* (2003) 'Ṭibb', *EI*, vol. X, pp. 452–461.

Scalenghe, Sara (2004–2005) 'The Deaf in Ottoman Syria, 16th–18th Centuries', *ASJ*, vol. XII no. 2, and vol. XIII no. 1, pp. 10–25.

—— (2007) 'Disability', in: Josef W. Meri (ed.) *Medieval Islamic Civilization: An Encylopedia*, vol. 1, pp. 208–209.

Schacht, J. (1950) *The Origins of Muhammadan Jurisprudence*, Oxford: Clarendon Press.

—— (2003) 'Ibn Suraydj', *EI*, vol. III, pp. 949–950.

Schacht, J. and Arendonk, C. van (2003) 'Ibn Ḥajar al-Haytamī', *EI*, vol. III, pp. 778–779.

Schimmel, Annemarie (1975) *Mystical Dimensions of Islam*, Chapel Hill: The University of North Carolina Press.

Shahrastānī, Muḥammad b. 'Abd al-Karīm al- (1984) *Muslim Sects and Divisions: The Section on Muslim Sects in Kitāb al-Milal wa 'l-Niḥal*, trans. A.K. Kazi and J.G. Flynn, London, Boston, Melbourne and Henley: Kegan Paul International.

Sha'rawi, Mohammad M. al- (1995) *Good and Evil*, London: Dar al-Taqwa.

—— (1998) *Fate and Predestination*, trans. Aisha Bewely, ed. Abdalhaq Bewely, London: Dar al-Taqwa.

Shihadeh, Ayman (2006) 'Suffering', in: Josef W. Meri *Medieval Islamic Civilization: An Encyclopedia*, vol. 2, pp. 771–773.

—— (2006a) *The Theological Ethics of Fakhr al-Dīn al-Rāzī*, Leiden: Brill.

Siddiqi, Mazheruddin (1953) 'Islamic Concept of Destiny', *Iqbal*, vol. II, no. 1, pp. 46–59.

Smalley, Kathy J. (2001) 'Open Wide the Doors to Christ: Persons with Disabilities and the Roman Catholic Church', in: William C. Gaventa and David L. Coulter (eds) *Spirituality and Intellectual Disability: International Perspectives on the Effect of Culture and Religion on Healing Body, Mind and Soul*, New York: The Haworth Pastoral Press. Co-published simultaneously as *JRDH*, vol. 5, no. 2/3, pp. 99–112.

Smith, Margaret (1935) *An Early Mystic of Baghdad: A Study of the Life and Teachings of Harith b. Asad al-Muhasibi*, London: The Sheldon Press.

Snir, Reuven (1999) '*Bāb al-Maḥabba* (The Chapter on Love) in *Al-Risāla al-Qushayriyya:* Rhetorical and Thematic Structure', *Israel Oriental Studies*, vol. XIX, pp. 131–159.

Snouck Hurgonje, C. (1888) *Mekka: Die Stadt und ihre Herren*, The Hague: Maritnus Nijnhoff.

Sobieroj, F. (2003) 'Al-Shiblī', *EI*, vol. IX, pp. 431–433.

Somogyi, J. de (2003) 'Al-Dhahabī', *EI*, vol. II, pp. 215–216.

Standard Rules on the Equalisation of Opportunities for Persons with Disabilities (1993) available at http://www.unhchr.ch (accessed 3 August 2007).

Steele, Robert (1920) *Secretum Secretorum*, Oxford: Clarendon.

Stegemann, Willy (1952) 'Polemon', *Pauly-Wissowa*, xxi, 2, col. 1320–1357.

Stern, Alexandra Minna and Howard Markel (2005) 'The History of Vaccines and Immunization: Familiar Patterns, New Challenges', *Health Affairs*, vol. 24, no. 3, pp. 611–621.

Stern, S.M. (2003) 'Abū 'Īsā Muḥammad B. Hārūn al-Warrāq', *EI*, vol. I, p. 130.

Stillman, Y.K. *et al.* (2003) 'Libās', *EI*, vol. V, pp. 732–750.
Stroumsa, Sarah (1987) 'From Muslim Heresy to Jewish–Muslim Polemics: Ibn al-Rāwandī's *Kitāb al-Dāmigh*', *JAOS*, vol. 107, no. 4, pp. 767–772.
Summers, Della (1992) *Longman Dictionary of English Language and Culture*, London: Longman.
Swain, Simon (ed.) (2007) *Seeing the Face, Seeing the Soul: Polemon's Physiognomy from Classical Antiquity to Medieval Islam*, Oxford: Oxford University Press.
Swartz, Merlin (2002) *A Medieval Critique of Anthropomorphism: Ibn al-Jazwī's Kitāb Akhbār al-Ṣifāt*, Leiden: Brill.
Teebi, A.S. and Farag, T.I. (1997) 'Genetic Disorders among Arab Populations', in: *Oxford Monographs on Medical Genetics*, vol. 30, New York: Oxford University Press.
Tha'ālibī, Abū Manṣūr 'Abd al-Malik b. Muḥammad al- (1968) *The Book of Curious and Entertaining Information: The Laṭā'if al-Ma'ārif of Tha'ālibī*, trans. C.E. Bosworth, Edinburgh: The University Press.
Townsend, Peter and Dorothy Wedderburn (1965) *The Aged and the Welfare State*, London: G. Bell.
Turki, Abdel-Magid (2003) 'Al-Ẓāhiriyya', *EI*, vol. 11, pp. 394–397.
Turmusani, Majid (2001) 'Disabled Women in Islam: Middle Eastern Perspective', in: William C. Gaventa and David L. Coulter (eds) (2001) *Spirituality and Intellectual Disability: International Perspectives on the Effect of Culture and Religion on Healing Body, Mind and Soul*, New York: The Haworth Pastoral Press, pp. 73–85.
Tyan, E. (2003) 'Īdjār, Īdjāra', *EI*, vol. III, p. 1107.
Tyan, E. and Káldy Nagy, Gy (2003) 'Ḳādī', *EI*, vol. IV, pp. 373–375.
United Nations (1983) *International Year of Disabled Persons: A Document of the UN General Assembly no. A/RES/36/77*, available on http://www.un.org (accessed 3 August 2007).
—— (1994) *Standard Rules on the Equalization of Opportunities for Persons with Disabilities*, New York: United Nations, available at http://www.unhchr.ch (accessed 3 August 2007).
—— (2006) *Draft Resolution: Convention on the Rights of Persons with Disabilities*, United Nations, General Assembly, 6 December 2006, available at http://www.un.org (accessed 3 August 2007).
—— (2007) *Convention on the Rights of Persons with Disabilities and Optional Protocol*, available at http://www.un.org/disabilities/default.asp?id=150 (accessed 18 April 2009).
Vahiduddin, S. (1968) 'The Qur'anic Visions of God, Man and his Destiny', *IC*, vol. LX, no. 1, pp. 1–18.
Walī Allāh, Shāh (1996) *Ḥujjat Allāh al-Bāligha: The Conclusive Argument from God*, trans. Marcia K. Hermansen, Leiden: Brill.
Watt, W. Montgomery (1948) *Free Will and Predestination in Early Islam*, London: Luzac.
—— (1973) *The Formative Period of Islamic Thought*, Edinburgh: Edinburgh University Press.
—— (1979) 'Suffering in Sunnite Islam', *SI*, vol. 50, pp. 5–19.
—— (2003a) 'Al-Ghazālī', *EI*, vol. II, pp. 1038–1041.
—— (2003c) 'Djahmiyya', *EI*, vol. II, p. 388.
—— (2003d) 'Djahm B. Ṣafwān', *EI*, vol. II, p. 388.
—— (2003e) 'Al-Ash'arī', *EI*, vol. 1, pp. 694–695.
Weismann, Itzchak (1997) 'Sa'id Hawwa and Islamic Revivalism in Ba'thist Syria', *SI*, vol. 85, no. 1, pp. 131–154.

Weisner, T.S., Beizer, L. and Stolze, L. (1991) 'Religion and Families of Children with Developmental Delays', *American Journal on Mental Retardation*, vol. 95, pp. 647–662.

Wensinck, A.J. (2003) 'Ṣabr', *EI*, vol. VIII, pp. 685–687.

Wensinck, A.J. and D.A. King (2003) 'Mīḳāt', *EI*, vol. VII, pp. 26–32.

Wiegers, Gerard (2002) 'Muslim Discussions on Organ Donations to Adherents of other Religions', in: W.A.R. Shadid and P.S. van Koningsveld (eds) *Intercultural Relations and Religious Authorities: Muslims in the European Union*, Leuven: Peeters, pp. 215–225.

Willems, P.J. (2000) 'Genetic Causes of Hearing Loss', *The New England Journal of Medicine*, vol. 342, pp. 1101–1109.

Williams, John Rodman (1996) *Renewal Theology: Systematic Theology from a Charismatic Perspective*, Michigan: Zondervan Publishing House.

Witkam, J.J. (1980) 'Aflimūn', *EI*, Supplement Fascicules 1–2, pp. 44–45.

Wolfson, Harry Austryn (1976) *The Philosophy of the Kalam*, Cambridge, Mass., and London: Harvard University Press.

World Health Organization (2001) *International Classification of Functioning, Disability and Health (ICF)*, Geneva: World Health Organization.

—— (2001a) *The UN Standard Rules on the Equalization of Opportunities for Persons with Disability: Main Report*, Geneva: World Health Organization.

Yin, Hongzhang (2006) 'Regulations and Procedures for New Drug Evaluation and Approval in China', *Human Gene Therapy*, vol. 17, pp. 970–974.

Zaman, Muhammad Qasim (2003) 'Al-Ya'qūbī', *EI*, vol. XI, pp. 257–258.

Arabic terms index

Name index

Subject index